The Medieval Mystical
Tradition in England

The Exeter Symposia on the Medieval Mystical Tradition in England seek a wider understanding of the subject by bringing together lines of enquiry being pursued by scholars in the field from various disciplines.

The proceedings of the fifth meeting include: studies of medieval mystics in continental Europe; clarification of the nature of Bridgettine spirituality through examination of the thinking that governed the practical details of their daily routine and their religious instruction; analyses of the distinctively creative quality of the writings of Julian of Norwich and of the status of visionary autobiography as a literary genre; comparison between modern philosophical understanding and that of a medieval mystic; enquiry as to what books were available and to whom in fourteenth-century Cambridge; radical questioning of the identity of the translator of the text known as *Benjamin Minor* traditionally ascribed to the author of the *Cloud of Unknowing*. All these papers, divergent in their scholarly particularity, enable a surer purchase on ways in which the witness of the medieval mystics in England my be understood.

THE MEDIEVAL MYSTICAL TRADITION IN ENGLAND

EXETER SYMPOSIUM V

Papers read at
The Devon Centre
Dartington Hall, July 1992

Edited by Marion Glasscoe

D. S. BREWER

First published 1992 by D. S. Brewer, Cambridge

D. S. Brewer is an imprint of Boydell & Brewer Ltd
PO Box 9, Woodbridge, Suffolk IP12 3DF, UK
and of Boydell & Brewer Inc.
PO Box 41026, Rochester, NY 14604, USA

ISBN 0 85991 346 5

ISSN 0950-7299

The paper used in this publication meets the minimum requirements
of American National Standard for Information Sciences –
Permanence of Paper for Printed Library Materials, ANSI Z39.48-1984

Printed in Great Britain by
St Edmundsbury Press Ltd, Bury St Edmunds, Suffolk

CONTENTS

FOREWORD

The last decade has seen a significant growth of interest in, and publications about, mysticism, not just in medieval Europe, but in a far wider historical and cultural context. Understanding of an experience that manifests itself in different cultures but transcends their differences in a shared agreement about ways of being that are fundamental to human fulfilment is all the time being complemented by more specific studies of individual mystics conditioned by particular contexts. The business of the Exeter Symposia is with such particularities, but the aim, as always, is that the details of scholarship should open up new possibilities for an enriched understanding of the wider field.

It is sometimes objected that a collection of such conference papers may lack coherence. Yet it is also arguable that the considerable limitations of the overall theme – the medieval mystical tradition in England – are sufficient to render the variety of approaches to subjects within, and contingent on, it valuable to the interested reader. Indeed, the very absence of any further obvious master-plan imposing a pattern on the contributors would seem to have a good theological precedent, inasmuch as the over-all pattern is not known but continually evolved in a process of individual discovery. These published symposium papers purport to be no more than a means of speedy dissemination to a wider audience of the kinds of lines of enquiry currently being pursued by scholars in the field, in the hope they may stimulate further enquiry and thus understanding of the total picture. Studies of medieval mystics in continental Europe, comparisons between modern philosophical understanding and that of a medieval mystic, enquiries into what books were available and to whom at a particular time and place, or as to the thinking that governed the daily routine of contemplatives, all give us a surer purchase on the ways in which medieval English mystics may be understood.

Thanks are due to Dr David Braund of this University for generous assistance with some Latin translations. And of course, as usual, I owe thanks to the contributors for their generous cooperation in submitting copy early enough to enable publication at the time of the symposium and for entrusting so much of the editing and proof-reading to me; it is at my door that all short-comings in these matters should be laid.

Marion Glasscoe   University of Exeter 1992

LATE FOURTEENTH-CENTURY
CAMBRIDGE THEOLOGY AND THE
ENGLISH CONTEMPLATIVE TRADITION

J. P. H. CLARK

WHILE MUCH IS KNOWN about the theological cross-currents in fourteenth-century Oxford, the same can hardly be said of the theology taught in her sister-university Cambridge. No doubt this is in part due to the fact that Oxford nurtured some of the greatest names in fourteenth-century scholasticism, including Duns Scotus, William of Ockham, Thomas Bradwardine, and John Wyclif – men who struck out in fresh directions, and who have a significance for the development of European as well as simply of English thought. In making any comparison between Oxford and Cambridge, we must bear in mind that a number of scholars lectured at different times in both universities, as well as at other centres of learning.

Cambridge in the fourteenth century, as Professor W. J. Courteney points out, was not only small in comparison with Oxford – about one third of its size – but it was regional, drawing its students largely from East Anglia and the north-eastern counties.[1]

The commonplace and traditional character of Cambridge theology appears to have contributed to its oblivion.[2] Where so few texts have been identified and studied, it is precarious to draw too hard and fast conclusions, but it is suggestive that the *Questions* of John of Walsham, O.F.M., a Cambridge Doctor of Theology who taught also at Norwich just after the middle of the fourteenth century, stands close to the old-fashioned positions of the *Summa Alexandri*, of Bonaventure, and of Henry of Ghent, while remaining apart from Scotus and Ockham; he explicitly rejects what he takes to be the determinism of Bradwardine.[3] The evaluation of Cambridge theology in the last three decades of

[1] W. J. Courtenay, *Schools and Scholars in Fourteenth-century England*, Princeton, 1987, pp.51–52.
[2] The frequent silences with reference to Cambridge in Professor Courtenay's magisterial book reflect the problem. *A History of the University of Cambrige*: Vol. 1, *The University to 1546*, by D. R. Leader, Cambridge, 1988, is a much more restricted book than the equivalent volume on Oxford, *The History of the University of Oxford*: Vol. 1, *The Oxford Schools*, ed. J. I. Catto, Oxford, 1984. Not only is the available material for Cambridge much less, but the book on Cambridge is the work of a single hand rather than of a team of scholars. Dr Leader indicates some but not all of the material available for the study of Cambridge theology.
[3] F. Pelster, 'Die Quästionen des Johannes von Walsham, O.F.M.', *Franziskanische Studien*, 34 (1952), 129–146.

the fourteenth century is a *desideratum* with reference to at least three, and possibly even four, significant figures in the English contemplative tradition.

Of those regions of England from which Cambridge especially drew its students, East Anglia had extensive trading and cultural links with the mainland of Europe, and so at any rate had the possibility of contact with the contemplative tradition found in the Low Countries and Germany, while the north-east of England had a long eremitical and monastic tradition going back to Ailred and indeed to such as Cuthbert. The north-eastern religious tradition of the fourteenth century includes not only Richard Rolle – a runaway Oxford man! – but such notable figures as the Augustinian friar John Waldeby – another Oxford man![4] – and the Augustinian canon St John of Bridlington.[5] Archbishop Thomas Arundel's campaign for spiritual and pastoral orthodoxy during his tenure of the see of York (1388–1396), in which he drew on the services of a number of men whom he must have known at Cambridge when Bishop of Ely – among them Walter Hilton – is one phase of a continuing process of clerical education in the northern Province of the Church, already clearly discernible during the archiepiscopate of John Thoresby.[6]

Walter Hilton is stated to have been an Inceptor in Canon Law[7] – that is, one who had fulfilled all the requirements to obtain the magisterium, but did not actually become a Master or Doctor. A letter of his refers to his having abandoned a promising legal career.[8] While we lack actual records of his academic progress at Cambridge, his associations and activities leave no room for doubt that he was a Cambridge man.[9] It has been observed that by the end of the fourteenth century law had replaced theology as the most prominent and popular of the higher faculties, first at Cambridge and then at Oxford.[10] Hilton's concern with moral and pastoral rather than with speculative theology is evident in his writings, though he is well able to absorb the common-places of scholastic theology and even to make fresh and creative use of material that is ostensibly

---

[4] Margaret J. Morrin, *John Waldeby, O.S.A., c.1315–c.1372, English Augustinian Preacher and Writer*, Studia Augustiniana Historica, Rome, 1975. For the location of Waldeby at Oxford, see p. 28. Cf. F. Roth, *The English Austin Friars, 1249–1538*: Vol. 1, New York, 1966, pp.400–404.

[5] For St John of Bridlington, bibliographical orientation may be found in D. Knowles, *The Religious Orders in England*, Vol. 2, Cambridge, 1955, p.117, n.2.

[6] Attention has been focussed on this by J. Hughes, *Pastors and Visionaries: Religion and Secular Life in Late Medieval Yorkshire*, Woodbridge, Suffolk, 1988.

[7] J. Russell Smith, 'Walter Hilton and a Tract in Defence of the Veneration of Images', *Dominican Studies* 7 (1954), 180–214, pp.184–185.

[8] *Walter Hilton's Latin Writings*, ed. J. P. H. Clark and C. Taylor, *Analecta Cartusiana* 124: 2, Salzburg, 1987, p.262.

[9] A. B. Emden, *A Biographical Dictionary of the University of Cambridge to A.D. 1500*, Cambridge, 1963, s.v. Hilton, Walter de. See further J. P. H. Clark, 'Walter Hilton in Defence of the Religious Life and of the Veneration of Images', *Downside Review* 103 (1985), 1–25, pp.1–2, with notes.

[10] Courtenay, *op. cit.*, pp. 365–366, with references; cf. Leader, *op. cit.*, pp.192–201.

very traditional.[11] It would be interesting to be able to relate Hilton's nuances of moral theology, and his occasional use of Canon Law in argument, to the varying strands of interpretation in these areas available in his day.[12]

In his renunciation of an academic career when a *baccalarius formatus* in order to follow a more distinctly religious vocation, Hilton stands close to an earlier Cambridge personality, the Augustinian Friar and Bachelor of Theology, William Flete, who in 1358 left Cambridge behind to become a hermit in Italy; he was to become a close associate of St Catherine of Siena. Flete's *De Remediis contra Temptaciones* is powerfully echoed at a number of points in both books of Hilton's *Scale of Perfection*.[13] We cannot tell whether Hilton knew who was the author of what was to become a very popular treatise, or the circumstances of his life; only one extant manuscript of *De Remediis* has the ascription to Flete,[14] who clearly sought the hidden life. On the other hand Flete did in 1380, shortly after the death of St Catherine, write three letters to the English Province of his Order, calling for a stricter observance of the rule and eremitical tradition of the Order, and this letter will have revived memories of him in this country. These letters will moreover have reached England at the point when Hilton was himself seriously considering his own vocation and future.

There is a reference to a Walter de Hilton, Bachelor of Civil Law, clerk of Lincoln diocese, included in a list of papal graces and granted the reservation of a canonry and prebend of Abergwili, Carmarthen, 28th January 1371,[15] and again a reference to a Magister Walter Hilton, B.C.L., who was present at the Ely Consistory Court in 1375[16] – no doubt our author. Hilton must meanwhile have progressed from the study of Civil Law to that of Canon Law; he could have been Bachelor of Canon Law by 1376, and ready to incept as Doctor of Canon Law in 1381–1382.[17] We do not know precisely how long Hilton remained at Cambridge, or whether he continued for a while to practise Canon Law after abandoning the prospect of an academic career. His friend Adam

---

[11] E.g. S. S. Hussey, 'Walter Hilton: Traditionalist?', in *The Medieval Mystical Tradition in England: Exeter 1980*, ed. M. Glasscoe, Exeter, 1980, pp. 1–16.

[12] As a point of departure, as well as the indications given by Leader, *op. cit.*, pp.192–201, there is D. M. Owen, *The Mediaeval Canon Law*, Cambridge, 1990, which examines the provision for students (especially in Cambridge) in the Middle Ages, and the choice of available textbooks.

[13] Hilton's debt to William Flete is indicated in the notes to *Walter Hilton: The Scale of Perfection*, ed. J. P. H. Clark and R. Dorward, Paulist Press, New York, 1991. Cf. also J. P. H. Clark, 'The *Cloud of Unknowing*, Walter Hilton and St John of the Cross', *Downside Review*, 96 (1978), 281–98, pp.289–290.

[14] B. Hackett, 'William Flete and the *De Remediis contra Temptaciones*', in *Mediaeval Studies presented to Aubrey Gwynn, S.J.*, ed. F. X. Martin, Dublin, 1961, pp. 330–348.

[15] Emden, *loc. cit.*

[16] Emden, *loc. cit.*

[17] Clark, 'Walter Hilton in Defence of the Religious Life', *op. cit.*, p.20, n.9.

Horsley entered the Charterhouse of Beauvale in 1386;[18] previous to this Hilton had written him a notable letter on the religious life in which he remarks in passing that he is not yet himself ready to take the step of entering a religious community,[19] so we may assume that Hilton himself is likely to have entered the community of Austin Canons at Thurgarton, his final home, not long after that date.

Hilton's reservation of the Abergwili prebend suggests the possibility that he may have been a member of Pembroke Hall; another Pembroke man held it before him.[20] On the other hand, he may have studied Canon Law at Peterhouse, a college with a strong bias towards Canon Law, where the Bishop of Ely retained the right of admission to fellowship.[21] Be that as it may, his activity at the Ely Consistory Court – in the company of Thomas Gloucester, Arundel's deputy official – indicated already a link between Hilton and the Bishop of Ely, before the latter's translation to York in 1388. Dr Hughes has indicated that Hilton was one of a number of northern clerks in Arundel's administration whose links with Arundel remained after Arundel's move to York, and who, especially after his translation, would be instrumental in a campaign of pastoral education, not least in attempting to regulate the 'enthusiasm' engendered in the popular eremitical movement in the aftermath of Richard Rolle,[22] at a time when the Lollard movement, in conjunction with the aspirations of a more subtle subversive character towards 'Liberty of Spirit', was to pose a threat to church polity and to the formation of a spirituality grounded in the traditional disciplines and sacramental practices. Among the many links which may be adduced, Thomas Dalby, an official of Ely Consistory Court while Arundel was Bishop there, and who was later Archdeacon of Richmond in Yorkshire, made a bequest to the Prior of Thurgarton in 1400, four years after Hilton's death.[23]

In 1387 the Austin Priory of Thurgarton was actively engaged in the ecclesiastical campaign against the Lollards.[24] It has been suggested that Hilton's *Conclusiones de Ymaginibus*, directed against the Lollards on this point, is an early work of his, and even that it may have been part of his academic exercises to incept in Canon Law; that status of images was a matter of academic debate before it became a matter of ecclesiastical controversy.[25] It would indeed be gratifying to possess a work issuing directly from the Cambridge Canon Law faculty at this time, but on internal evidence I am inclined to think that, at any

---

[18] M. G. Sargent, *James Grenehalgh as Textual Critic*, Analecta Cartusiana, 85:2, Salzburg, 1984, pp.580–581, note for p.44.

[19] *Walter Hilton's Latin Writings*, *op. cit.*, p.148.

[20] Clark, 'Walter Hilton in Defence of the Religious Life', *op. cit.*, p.19, n.8.

[21] Leader, *op. cit.*, p.62.

[22] Hughes, *op. cit.*, pp.177–187; 208–245.

[23] Notes by Hughes, *op. cit.*, p.214.

[24] Russell Smith, 'In Defence of the Veneration of Images', *op. cit.*, p.203.

[25] Clark, 'Walter Hilton in Defence of the Religious Life', *op. cit.*, p.16, with references.

rate in its present form, this tract of Hilton's – his only extant work which is actually constructed in the form of a scholastic treatise – is later than his letter to Adam Horsley, and that it was commissioned as an 'expert opinion' after he had joined the priory of Thurgarton, to assist the Community in their campaign against Lollardy.[26] Hilton shows his expertise in Canon Law in his letter *Ad Quemdam Seculo Renunciare Volentem*, and specially in *Scale 1*, he shows his competence in moral theology.[27]

If Hilton's professional interests lay at any rate in the first instance in Canon Law, he shows himself, as already indicated, well able to use and even to develop traditional theological teaching, with particular emphasis on material traceable to, or inspired by, Augustine, as well as a monastic theology that owes much to the Cistercian tradition.[28] How far this is specifically bound up with anything characteristic of the Cambridge milieu it is hard to determine in the absence of much comparative material, though again there are one or two suggestive straws in the wind which will be mentioned later.

There is evidence that while he was at Thurgarton Hilton was in touch with some people in academic circles at Cambridge, as well as with friends who had previously been at Cambridge. The implication is that such associates were bound up with him in the work for theological orthodoxy in the face of 'enthusiasm', Lollardy and the movement of the 'Free Spirit', and again, in a context which did not need to be controversial, with the spiritual formation of those who sought Christian perfection, whether in the vowed religious life or living in the world.

Hilton translated into English the *Eight Chapters on Perfection* which were 'founden in Maister Lowis de Fontibus booke at Cantebrigge'.[29] Luis de Fontibus, O.F.M., from Aragon, was assigned to read the *Sentences* of Peter Lombard at Cambridge in 1383[30] as part of the continuing practice of sending a Franciscan from the mainland of Europe to read the *Sentences* at Cambridge, in principle at three-yearly intervals in line with the Constitutions issued for the

---

[26] *Walter Hilton's Latin Writings, op. cit.*, p.175, with references.

[27] See the notes for *Ad Quemdam Seculo Renunciare Volentem* in *Walter Hilton's Latin Writings, op. cit.*, and for *Scale of Perfection*, ed. Clark & Dorward, *op. cit.*, Book One.

[28] This again is indicated in the notes for *The Scale of Perfection*, Clark & Dorward, *op. cit.* See also J. P. H. Clark, 'The Trinitarian Theology of Walter Hilton's *Scale of Perfection, Book Two*', in *Langland, the Mystics and the Medieval English Religious Tradition: Essays in Honour of S. S. Hussey*, ed. H. Phillips, Woodbridge, Suffolk, 1990, pp.125–140.

[29] *The Inner Temple Ms. of Walter Hilton's 'Eight Chapters on Perfection'*, ed. F. Kuriyagawa, *Studies in English Literature*, English Number, (1971), Tokyo, 1971, reprinted 1980, p.14.

[30] P. Michael, 'Bibliographia', *Archivum Franciscanum Historicum*, 17 (1924), 145–168, p.165.

Order by Benedict XII in 1336.[31] Luis is referred to here as 'Master' and not as Bachelor, so implying that he had completed his course of study and become a doctor of Theology. Depending on whether he had to reside for a year at the University in preparation for his year of opponency in the faculty of Theology, his regency may be dated 1391–3 or 1392–4, long after Hilton's departure from Cambridge.[32] (It is possible that Luis might have been dispensed from the second year of regency, though this should not be too readily assumed.) In keeping with this chronology, Hilton's version of *Eight Chapters* has a number of affinities with *Scale of Perfection, Book Two*, which must have been completed shortly before his death in 1396.[33]

The English version of *Eight Chapters* deals, amongst other things, with the distinction between true and false 'liberty of spirit'.[34] Since we do not have the original text from which the translation was made, we cannot tell how much of this is due to Hilton and how much to Luis. But it is reasonable to suppose that Hilton's version is at any rate closely based on what Luis wrote; so this controversial topic – already long familiar on the mainland of Europe – was in the air at Cambridge in the last decade of the fourteenth century.[35]

Hilton is credited – with some plausibility, though not with absolute certainty – with the English version of another book which is of Franciscan inspiration, though in its present form the work of various hands – the *Prickynge of Love*, a free translation of the *Stimulus Amoris*, itself a much expanded book built around the treatise of that name by the thirteenth-century Franciscan, James of Milan, and in Hilton's day commonly attributed to St Bonaventure.[36] The English version has a number of additions which are clearly intended to correct the kind of heresies against which Hilton and others were engaged.[37] But the *Stimulus* was

---

[31] Sbaralea, *Bullarium Franciscanum* 6, p.30; cited by A. G. Little, *Studies in English Franciscan History*, Manchester, 1917, pp.166–167.

[32] Clark, 'Walter Hilton in Defence of the Religious Life', *op. cit.*, p.2.

[33] *Ibid.*, with n.15.

[34] *Eight Chapters on Perfection*, *op. cit.*, c.3, pp.21–22.

[35] Cf. J. P. H. Clark, 'Walter Hilton and "Liberty of Spirit" ', *Downside Review*, 96 (1978), 61–78.

[36] There is an edition of the Middle English by H. J. Kane, *The Prickynge of Love*, Salzburg Studies in English Literature: Elizabethan and Renaissance Studies 92:10, 2 vols., Salzburg, 1983. Professor Kane was doubtful of Hilton's authorship of the English version. For a critical defence of the likelihood of Hilton's authorship, see J. P. H. Clark, 'Walter Hilton and the *Stimulus Amoris*', *Downside Review*, 102 (1984), 79–118. There are some corrections which I would want to make on points of detail, and some modifications. Thus it should be noted, with reference to p.81 of the article, that 'For why' is also used in the *Cloud of Unknowing* (ed. P. Hodgson, Early English Text Society, O.S. 218, London, 1958, pp.24/17, 116/21), and the scholastic technique of question and answer is used in the *Book of Privy Counselling* (edited with the *Cloud*, as above pp.152/23ff; 160/26–161/1) – though the formula is less close to Hilton's than is the formula in the *Prickynge*. But I still think that the cumulative effect of the arguments supports Hilton's authorship.

[37] Clark, 'Walter Hilton and the Stimulus Amoris', *op. cit.*, pp.96–97.

an extremely popular book, and even if Hilton did make the English version, the incentive to make it need not have come from specifically academic circles, nor from the Franciscan Order. A further significant link between Hilton and those who had been trained in academic theology at Cambridge is found with the Carmelites. As is well known, both books of Hilton's *Scale* were translated into Latin by Thomas Fyslake, O.Carm., who is described in the York Minster copy of the Latin version as 'Magister'.[38] Bale indicates that Fyslake was Bachelor of Theology at Cambridge c.1375.[39] Fyslake preached at the Ely Diocesan Synod in 1377.[40] The York manuscript – an excellent text – was made for John Pole, O.Carm., who is stated to have been Master of Theology at Cambridge and Prior of the Carmelite house there in 1381.[41] He was buried at the Coventry Carmelite house.[42] Fyslake's Latin version is likely to have been made by 1400, and may even have been made in Hilton's lifetime, though if so there is reason to suppose that Hilton did not check the whole of it.[43]

Fyslake was a northerner; he was ordained acolyte from the Doncaster Carmelite convent in 1358 by Archbishop Thoresby;[44] he is again one of the 'northern clerks' associated with Arundel at Cambridge and Ely and subsequently at York in the campaign for orthodox pastoral instruction. His link with Coventry in the person of John Pole is not the only sign of interest in Hilton's work in this city; the earliest extant copy of Hilton's letter to Adam Horsley – which may even be as early as the late fourteenth-century – is found in a manuscript which belonged to Coventry Cathedral Church; the Charterhouse at Coventry was presumably a means of propagating this letter.[45]

In the same diocese of Lichfield, there is another early link with Hilton, which points in turn to support from ecclesiastical interests in the north. The early copies of Hilton's *Mixed Life* and *Scale of Perfection, Book One*, found in the Vernon and Simeon manuscripts (and, indeed, the copy of the Psalm commentary *Qui Habitat*, of which Hilton may very well be the author, in MS Vernon) are explained if we suppose that these manuscripts may very well have been produced in the scriptorium of Lichfield Cathedral under the direction of

---

[38] MS York Minster XVI K 5, f.95v.

[39] MS Bodleian Library, Oxford, Bodley 73, f.79r.

[40] Ely Diocesan Record Office, Reg. Consist. 1373–1381, f.72r.

[41] MS York Minster XVI K 5, f.95v. On Pole at Cambridge, see MS Bodleian Library, Oxford, Bodley 73, f.79r.

[42] MS Bodleian Library, Oxford, Bodley 73, f.52r (not 32r as stated by Emden).

[43] J. P. H. Clark, 'English and Latin in the *Scale of Perfection* – Theological Considerations', in *Spiritualität Heute und Gestern*, Vol. 1, *Analecta Cartusiana*, 35:1, Salzburg, 1982, 167–212, pp.170–171.

[44] Borthwick Institute of Historical Research, York, Register of John Thoresby, 1358, noted by Russell-Smith, 'In Defence of the Veneration of Images', *op. cit.*, p.206, n.6.

[45] MS Bodleian Library, Oxford, Digby 33. *Walter Hilton's Latin Writings*, *op. cit.*, pp. 20–22.

Richard Scrope, a member of the great Yorkshire family, who would eventually in 1398 follow Arundel as Archbishop of York.[46]

On the Carmelites themselves, we have considerable information through the records of Bale;[47] indeed the information available on them must be disproportionate to that available on the other learned mendicant Orders, all of whom had a house at Cambridge. Bale gives us a list of the Priors of the Cambridge Carmelite house, together with lists of works by Carmelite authors, mostly with incipits, which may lead eventually to the identification of some lost works; on the other hand, many of the scholastic works which he lists probably existed in single copies in Carmelite houses in this country and did not travel abroad, so that with the heavy loss of manuscripts following the destruction of the religious houses in the sixteenth century, they are gone for ever.

We are fortunate in having the *lectura* on part of Psalm 118 by Thomas Maldon, Prior of the Cambridge Carmelite house in the years following 1369, and subsequently Doctor of Theology. Numerous other works by Maldon listed by Bale are lost.[48] This *lectura* discloses Maldon's theological positions on a number of points, including the status of theology as a science; the doctrine of the Holy Trinity and of the *imago Dei* in man; Creation and the Fall; the status of the Old Law beside the New Law of Christ; Justification and Grace (in which grace is taken to be an intrinsic principle of supernatural life within the soul, in line with St Augustine and St Thomas, and contrary to the positions taken by some 'Nominalist' theologians); conscious and unconscious intention; sacramental confession and lives of Action and Contemplation in relation to the pastoral office. Although his period of teaching must be a little earlier than Thomas Fyslake's baccalaureate in Theology, or Hilton's activity in Canon Law at Cambridge, and there is no hint of Wyclif or of the Lollard controversy, the *lectura* does give a previous clue as to something of the Carmelite milieu at Cambridge. Among the indications of a common milieu with Hilton are Maldon's use of Anselm's *Proslogion* on faith and understanding, and of Gilbert of Holland on the same topic.[49] His doctrine of grace deserves study by comparison with Hilton's.[50]

A sidelight on Carmelite history is provided by the defence of Carmelite claims at Cambridge in 1374 by John Hornby, regent Doctor of Theology of the Order. Interest in monastic origins and in the claims to antiquity of the different

[46] Hughes, *op. cit.*, pp.213–214.
[47] His *Scriptorum Illustrium Maioris Brytannie Catalogus* was printed at Basle in 1557. But there is also his *Index Britanniae Scriptorum*, ed. R. L. Poole and M. Bateson, Oxford, 1902. More authoritative than his *Catalogus* are his manuscript notes on Carmelite matters, found in MSS British Library Harley 1819, Harley 3838, and in Bodleian Library, Oxford, MSS Bodley 73, Selden supra 41, Selden supra 72.
[48] J. P. H. Clark, 'Thomas Maldon, O.Carm., a Cambridge Theologian of the Fourteenth Century', *Carmelus*, 29 (1982), 193–235.
[49] Clark, 'Thomas Maldon', *op. cit.*, pp.206–207.
[50] *Ibid.*, pp.225–228.

Orders was a feature of the fourteenth century.[51] The debate between Hornby and the rival Dominican doctor, John Stokes, covered ground which had already been trodden in debates on the mainland of Europe on Carmelite claims. Not only did the Dominican deny that the Carmelites could trace their spiritual descent from the prophet Elijah, but amongst other matters he alleged that the Carmelite Order, dedicated to Mary, took the name of Mary not from the Mother of God but from a Mary who was a converted heretic and became a preacher; the Dominicans are of course the Friars Preachers. Hornby won the day for the Carmelites, and the Order's claims were solemnly vindicated at a University ceremony; the occasion was marked by a splendid Marian sermon.[52]

A significant Carmelite figure at Cambridge between Maldon and the emergence of Fyslake and Pole must have been Robert Ivory who succeeded Maldon as Prior in 1372 and left this office by 1375. He is reputed to have been of Norman merchant stock; he entered the London Carmelite convent and became lector of theology there before moving to Cambridge. He was evidently marked out as one of exceptional gifts; among the papal letters of Gregory XI is one dated 17 July 1374 following Ivory's examination in theology at Avignon, providing a mandate for him to be promoted to the *magisterium* in theology and to lecture and be regent anywhere. It is stated that Robert 'Imon' has very often preached, has studied philosophy for ten, and theology for twelve, years at the Universities of both Oxford and Cambridge – an instance of cross-fertilization of the two universities among the mendicants. Bale lists various Scriptural commentaries and other works by Ivory, with varying degrees of information and precision.[53] Recently the British Academy catalogue of the medieval Friars' libraries has drawn attention to a commentary on the Apocalypse with the same incipit as that given by Bale for Ivory's, in MS Lambeth Palace Library 127. This requires investigation; other commentaries on the Apocalypse with closely similar incipits by other authors are known.[54] The study of a work which could be positively identified as Ivory's would be highly rewarding.

---

[51] D. Knowles, *The Religious Orders in England*: Vol. 2, *op. cit.*, pp.52–53; W. A. Pantin, 'Some Mediaeval English Treatises on the Origins of Monasticism', in *Mediaeval Studies presented to Rose Graham*, Oxford, 1950, pp.189–215.

[52] J. P. H. Clark, 'A Defence of the Carmelite Order by John Hornby, O.Carm., A.D. 1374', *Carmelus*, 32 (1985), 73–106. On the background to the debate, see Ioannes de Hildesheim, *Dialogus inter Directorem et Detractorem*, in *Mediaeval Carmelite Heritage*, ed. A. Staring, Rome, 1989, pp.326–388, and cf. the same author's *Opusculum Metricum, ibid.*, pp. 389–392. Hornby's Marian sermon draws heavily on John Baconthorpe, *Laus Religionis Carmelitarum, ibid.*, pp. 218–253.

[53] MS Bodleian Library, Oxford, Bodley 73, f.40v; MS British Library, Harley 3838, f.83r; *Catalogus*, I, p.504.

[54] See *Corpus of British Mediaeval Library Catalogues: The Friars' Libraries*, ed. K. W. Humphreys, British Library with British Academy, 1990, p.183; *Repartorium Biblicum Medii Aevi*, ed. Stegmüller, Madrid, 1940; 3122 (Pseudo-Haimo de Halberstadt); 6443 (Petrus de Caudia); 7247 (Ps-Remigius); 11002 (Anon. St Omer 233, s.xiii). (This reference kindly supplied by A. I. Doyle.)

Ivory may have followed Maldon as regent master at Cambridge, though this is not clear; Leland says that after completing his academic course he was appointed Provincial of the English Province of his Order at a chapter held at Oxford in 1379, and remained so until his death in 1392. Bale refers to his theological eminence, to the leadership which he gave to the spiritual life of his Order by the force of his example, being severe on himself and liberal towards others, and to his notable gifts to the library of the London convent. It is pleasing that some of the books which he gave to his Order survive – all on historical subjects.[55]

Ivory was the leader of the English Carmelites at just the point when they were becoming engaged, together with the other mendicant Orders, in the struggle against Wyclif and the Lollard movement. Ivory himself was present at the fifth session of the Blackfriars Synod in 1382 when Wyclif's errors were condemned.[56] The Carmelites have an important place in the defence of orthodoxy; the hidden work of Thomas Fyslake is matched by the more public writing of Richard Maidstone, Carmelite and Oxford Doctor of Theology.[57] In the following century the work of Thomas Netter would be renowned.

The identity of the author of *The Cloud of Unknowing* and its corpus remains a mystery. There is evidence of a close interchange of ideas between this author and Walter Hilton – evidence that each was capable of bringing to bear constructive criticism upon the other's theological expression.[58] Like Hilton, the author of the *Cloud* was concerned not simply to expound spiritual disciplines for their own sake, but also to uphold the way of the Church in the face of heresy, as well as counter-acting the 'enthusiastic' attachment to sensible religious phenomena associated with Rolle.[59] Dr Hughes has suggested that he

---

[55] For fuller documentation on Ivory, see J. P. H. Clark, 'A Note on Robert Ivory, O.Carm. (d. 1392)', *Carmelus*, 33 (1986), 35–39.

[56] MS Bodleian Library, Bodley 73, f.56v. Similarly *Fasciculi Zizaniorum*, ed. W. Shirley, Rolls Series, London, 1858, p.290. J. Crompton, 'Fasciculi Zizaniorum II', *Journal of Ecclesiastical History*, 12 (1961), 35–45, 155–166, pp.162–163, prefers to take the title *Fasciculi Zizaniorum* as including *all* the contents of the manuscript (MS Bodleian Library, Oxford, e Musaeo 86) – not only answers to Wycliffite views, but also the defence of the mendicants and especially of the Carmelites. The manuscript contains the work of John Hornby mentioned above. Although the manuscript itself is much later, Crompton argues that it was probably during Ivory's time as Provincial that the serious collection of this material began.

[57] For Richard Maidstone, see V. Edden, 'The Debate between Richard Maidstone and the Lollard Ashwardby', *Carmelus*, 34 (1987), 113–134. Dr Edden has produced an edition of *Richard Maidstone's Penitential Psalms*, Middle English Texts 22, Heidelberg 1990.

[58] J. P. H. Clark, 'Sources and Theology in *The Cloud of Unknowing*', *Downside Review*, 98 (1980), 83–109, pp.108–109. This is developed further in the Paulist Press edition of Hilton's *Scale*, and in the commentary on the English text of the *Cloud* in preparation by the present writer for *Analecta Cartusiana*.

[59] *The Cloud of Unknowing*, ed. P. Hodgson, Early English Text Society, O.S. 218, *op.*

may have been a Cambridge Dominican.[60] In this, he seems to be influenced by Dom David Knowles' assumption that the orthodox Thomist theology of grace which we find in *The Cloud* (and also in Hilton) has to be explained by the influence of the Rhineland, and specifically of Rhineland Thomists, in the face of a predominantly Nominalist theology of grace in the English universities, according to which grace is no longer necessarily seen as an intrinsic principle of supernatural life in the soul.[61] But as already indicated with reference to Thomas Maldon, the traditional understanding of grace was in any case held in at least some academic circles in this country, including circles close to that in which Hilton was to move. Nor do we need to posit Rhineland influence in order to explain *The Cloud*'s distinctive use of Pseudo-Dionysius; *The Cloud*'s author himself appeals to the familiar authority of Thomas Gallus.[62] The possibility of influence from some continental writers – more specifically Hugh of Balma – remains; but at the moment I believe that this is an open question to be treated by careful comparison of texts.[63]

It is true that there are indications of contact between the Cambridge Dominicans and Germany. There are records of Dominicans sent to study at Cambridge during the years 1378–1388.[64] Conversely, some Cambridge Dominicans went to Germany. Geoffrey Launde was ordained priest in 1382 from the Lynn Dominican convent; he was assigned to read the *Sentences* at Cambridge in 1393; he was at the Cologne Dominican house in 1396, in which year his assignment to the Cambridge house was renewed. This versatile friar, who was Doctor of Theology by 1398 was in that year allowed by the Master General of his Order to be confessor to Edward, Duke of York, and to practise medicine in the ducal household and elsewhere.[65]

Another Dominican who was something of a commuter between Cambridge and Cologne at about this time was John Edmonton. He was at the London convent in 1395–6, from where he was assigned in 1396 to read the *Sentences* at Cambridge. In the course of dispute between the Dominican Master General and the English crown, Edmonton's arrest was ordered in that year by Richard II; he was released soon after and transferred to Cologne; from there he was re-assigned to Cambridge in 1397. He was transferred again in January 1398 to

---

cit., chs.45–46, pp.85–87; cf. Hilton, *Scale, Book One*, 10–11, MS Cambridge U.L. Add. 6686, pp.284a–286a.

[60] Hughes, *op. cit.*, pp.349–350.

[61] Knowles, *op. cit.*, pp.121–122; cf. his *The English Mystical Tradition*, London, 1961, pp.71, n.11; 76; 95–96.

[62] *Deonise Hid Diuinite*, ed. P. Hodgson, Early English Text Society, O.S. 231, London, 1958, p.2.

[63] This is being worked out in the commentary for *Analecta Cartusiana* referred to above.

[64] References given in Hughes, *op. cit.*, p.350.

[65] Emden, *op. cit.*, s.v. Launde, Geoffrey; same author, *A Survey of Dominicans in England. . .* (1268–1538), Istituto Storico Domenicano, Santa Sabina–Rome, 1967, s.v. Launde, Geoffrey de.

Cologne in order to qualify for the degree of Doctor of Theology – a degree which he finally received by papal faculty in September of that year![66] There is also John Sygar, who was ordained deacon from the Cambridge Dominican convent in 1384, and who was lector at Ipswich in 1397. He was appointed *magister studentium* at the Cologne Dominican convent in November 1397 and given leave to proceed to the degree of Doctor of Theology at Cologne in March 1398 if he wished.[67]

However, I still find no compelling reason to believe that *The Cloud*'s author was a Dominican. The distinct possibility remains that he was a Carthusian of Beauvale, a house within striking distance of Hilton's final home at Thurgarton, and with which, as said, Hilton had contacts. As we do not know his identity, we cannot know precisely what his intellectual formation may have been before his putative entry into the Order.

The theology of Julian of Norwich raises important questions, not simply in its own right but because it clearly indicates that she had capable theological advisers at Norwich who helped her to articulate her understanding of her Revelations. Julian's statement that she is a simple unlettered woman[68] does not dispense us from trying to relate her teaching to the theological tradition which must have been readily accessible to her – a tradition which is that of the Latin Church and especially of Augustine. In their edition of the *Revelations*, Colledge and Walsh have tended to urge that Julian was a distinctly learned woman.[69] One may have reservations about some of the sources which they ascribe to her, but they have done a great service in relating her to theology, and also to the liturgy with which she would have been familiar.[70] A series of articles has indicated how Julian is capable of building on the commonplaces of theology and sometimes finds surprising implications in it.[71] As well as the Cathedral Priory, Norwich had houses of the four learned mendicant Orders; the house of the Austin Friars

---

[66] Emden, *Cambridge*, *op. cit.*, s.v. Edmonton, John.

[67] Emden, *Cambridge*; *Dominicans*; *op. cit.*, s.v. Sygar, John.

[68] *A Book of Showings to the Anchoress Julian of Norwich*, ed. E. Colledge and J. Walsh, Toronto, 1978. Short Text, c.6, p.222; Long Text, c.2, p.285; *A Revelation of Love*, ed. M. Glasscoe, Exeter, 1976, c.2, p.2.

[69] Colledge and Walsh, *op. cit.*, Introduction, pp.43–196; and notes to text passim.

[70] Marion Glasscoe explores some further aspects of liturgical influences on Julian in 'Time of Passion: Latent Relationships between Liturgy and Meditation in Two Middle English Mystics', in *Langland, the Mystics, and the Medieval English Mystical Tradition*, *op. cit.*, pp.141–160.

[71] J. P. H. Clark. '*Fiducia* in Julian of Norwich', *Downside Review* 99 (1981), 97–108; 214–299; 'Nature, Grace and the Trinity in Julian of Norwich', *Downside Review*, 100 (1982), 203–220. Two further articles, 'Predestination in Christ according to Julian of Norwich', *Downside Review* 100 (1982), 79–91, and 'Die Vorstellung der Mutterschaft Gottes im Trinitätsglauben der Juliane von Norwich', in *'Eine Höhe, über die nichts geht' – Spezielle Glaubenserfahrung in der Frauenmystik?*, ed. Margot Schmidt and Dieter Bauer, Stuttgart–Bad Canstatt, 1986, pp.217–243, need some reassessment; see further J. P. H. Clark, 'Time and Eternity in Julian of Norwich', *Downside Review* 109 (1991), 259–276.

was closest to her church. Norwich acted in the fourteenth century as a 'feeder' institution with ties to Oxford and London – Adam Wodeham in the earlier part of the century was lecturing at Norwich Greyfriars before going to Oxford – and more especially with Cambridge, sending there its more able minds and receiving them back.[72] It would be fascinating if we could learn more of the interplay between Norwich and Cambridge in the latter part of the fourteenth century.

A Cambridge Doctor of Theology with roots in East Anglia who returned home after studying at Cambridge is the Carmelite Alan of Lynn, who is familiar through the *Book of Margery Kempe*. Alan was born presumably at Lynn c.1348, and joined the Carmelite convent there. After his studies and teaching at Cambridge, he returned to the Lynn convent, where he is said to have been lector in 1407; he died there after 1423. Bale indicates that Alan was learned in the Greek Fathers (in translation, presumably), as well as in the Latin Fathers; Bale refers to sermons and Biblical works by Alan, together with *Elucudationes Aristotelis*, all lost. Of particular interest is Alan's work as a compiler of indexes; Bale describes his labours in this respect as 'Herculean', and lists indexes to fifty works compiled by Alan, which he saw in the library of the Norwich Carmelites.[73] Among the great monastic writers, Alan compiled indexes of Gregory the Great's *Moralia*, *Homiliae* and *In Ezechielem*; St Bernard's *Super Missus Est*, and 'tria opuscula'; various works of Hugh and Richard of St Victor; '*In sermonibus Gilberti*' (presumably Gilbert of Holland). Among the great scholastics, he compiled indexes of St Thomas Aquinas, *De Perfectione* and *In Sententias* – the *Summa Theologica* is not mentioned; Giles of Rome, *De Regimine Principum* – Giles' work on the *Sentences* is not mentioned; and Duns Scotus and his own confrére John Baconthorpe, both *In Sententias*. Among biblical commentators near to his own day he indexed John Lathbury, *In Threnos*; Nicholas Gorran, *Super Mattheum* and *Super Lucam*; and Henry Costessy, *Super Apocalypsim*. He indexed three works relating directly to the blessed Virgin. Among works which in one sense or another might be called 'mystical', he indexed the prophecies of St Bridget – one of two of his indexes of which a copy is known to survive[74] – and also the *Stimulus Amoris*, the

---

72 Courtenay, *op. cit.*, pp.106–111.
73 Emden, *Cambridge, op. cit.*, s.v. Lynn, Alan de. Among the references given by Emden, MS Bodley 73, f.119 should be corrected to f.119v, and f.204 to f.204v. MSS Bodley 73, ff.204v–205r, and British Library Harley 3838, ff.201v–202v, provide a full list of Alan's indexes, with incipits.
74 Alan's index to P. Bersuire, *Reductorium Morale Biblicum*, is extant in MS British Library, Royal 3 D iii. The index to St Bridget's prophecies is MS Lincoln College, Oxford, 69, ff.197r–233v, is presumably Alan's. Coxe gives the incipit as: *Ad laudem Dei et Marie Matris ejus, de cujus Ordine sum*; and of the Tabula as: *Abscondita erat nativitas*. MS Harley 3838, f.202r gives Alan's incipit for St Bridget as: *Afflictio est utilis*. But MS Bodley 73, f.200v, gives it as: *Ad laudem Dei et matris eius, de cuius ordine sum*, &c. Alan uses a similar Carmelite dedication to God and to Mary in a number of his indexes – see further MS Bodley 73, ff.204v–205r. MS Lincoln College

composite devotional work developed on the basis of James of Milan's book. These last two items are of interest when we recall that Margery Kempe – to whom Alan was a good friend – had a great affection for the hearing of 'Hyltons boke' (presumably the *Scale*), 'Seynt Brydys boke', the *Stimulus Amoris*, and the *Incendium Amoris* (of Richard Rolle).[75] There are various renderings into English of parts of the *Stimulus*,[76] and Hilton himself, as said, may be responsible for a more or less complete English version. It is true that Margery refers to these works in the context of her consultations with Richard Caister, Vicar of St Stephen's Church, Norwich, and with another unnamed priest who came to Norwich about 1413, and does not associate them specifically with Alan; but clearly both St Bridget and the *Stimulus* were popular reading with the devout, and Alan participated in this movement.

The mention of Norwich, and of Lynn, with the possibility of contacts with mainland Europe, brings us back to the question of contemporary theological influences from the Continent. Margery Kempe's *Book* shows how this English church-woman saw herself as very much a member of an international Church; amongst her other activities she met St Bridget of Sweden's servant in Rome.[77] As early as 1427 there is a record of a group of women living together after the style of a béguinage in Norwich; a second such group is known to have existed in the same city by 1443, living in a tenement which probably belonged to a merchant of Bruges domiciled in Norwich.[78]

But we are moving well into the fifteenth century, and away from Cambridge itself. For the period before Margery's particular devotional activity, Dr Roger Lovatt has shown that there is no evidence that the work of Eckhart or even of Tauler was known in fourteenth-century England, and that when in the last quarter of that century some of the work of Ruysbroeck and of Suso did begin to circulate in this country, it was valued for those anodyne elements in it which

consists of a collection of indexes of works by various writers, including (ff.132v–137v) one of Giles of Rome, *De Regimine Principum*. The incipit for the Preface is: *Sed sciat lector quod quamvis liber iste in tres libris. . .*; that of the Tabula: *Abstinencia, quam necessaria est*. MS Harley 3838, f.202r gives the incipit of the index which Alan wrote of this work as: *Ad laudem Christi Jesu* – a form which Alan used in introducing his index of Peter of Aurora, according to MS Bodley 73, f.204v. So we cannot ascribe this further index to Alan on the present evidence.

75 *The Book of Margery Kempe*, ed. S. B. Meech and H. E. Allen, Early English Text Society O.S. 212, London, 1940, repr. 1961, p.143; cf. *ibid*. pp.39, 47; with notes.

76 Cf. Clark, 'Walter Hilton and the *Stimulus Amoris*', *op. cit.*, p. 105. To the texts noted above there should be added the independent English version of *Stimulus* 3.13, in the Carthusian manuscript, British Library MS Add. 37049, f.94; cf. M. G. Sargent, 'Bonaventura English: A Survey of the Middle English Prose Translations of Early Franciscan Literature', in *Spätmittelalterliche Geistliche Literatur in der Nationalsprache*, Vol. 2, *Analecta Cartusiana* 106:2, Salzburg 1984, 145–176, p.162.

77 *The Book of Margery Kempe*, *op. cit.*, p. 95.

78 N. P. Tanner, *The Church in Late Mediaeval Norwich, 1370–1532*, Toronto, 1984, pp.64–66.

accorded with patterns of devotion long established here, rather than for its distinctive mystical doctrine.[79] There are instances where men educated at Cambridge can be shown subsequently to have known Suso's *Horologium Sapientiae*,[80] but no firm evidence has yet been found of an interest in the Rhineland writers specifically at Cambridge in the late fourteenth century, though in 1425 a distinguished Cambridge Austin Friar, a former Vice-Chancellor of the University, owned a manuscript containing the *Horologium* which is now in the Vatican Library and which has been dated to the fourteenth century.[81] A fair number of books from the Cambridge Austin, Dominican and Franciscan friaries have been identified, more especially those that came to the Vatican Library following the dissolution of the English religious houses,[82] and it may be that a close examination of these manuscripts, and of any annotations to them, would shed light on the outlook of the Cambridge friars.

We should avoid any facile antithesis between Cambridge and Oxford theology at the end of the fourteenth century, and should not be too ready to see a conscious reaction in Cambridge against the presence of heterodoxy in at least some circles in Oxford. But, as Professor Anne Hudson justly says, during the last fifteen years of that century, where there is academic discussion of matters reflecting Lollard points of view, Cambridge men are regularly to be found on the side of orthodoxy, while Oxford men appear on both sides.[83] Cambridge theology must have been content with the received wisdom, and not have sought

[79] R. Lovatt, 'The Influence of Religious Literature of Germany and the Low Countries on English Spirituality', Oxford Unversity D.Phil. thesis, 1965; 'Henry Suso and the Medieval Mystical Tradition in England', in *The Medieval Mystical Tradition in England: Dartington 1982*, ed. M. Glasscoe, Exeter 1982, pp.47–62.

[80] Cf. Lovatt, 'Henry Suso. . .', *op. cit.*, p.51, with notes 15–16. Robert Alne, whose bequest of a copy of the *Horologium* is recorded in *Testamenta Eboracensia* 2, pp.78–79, was admitted fellow of Peterhouse in 1400 and was still there in 1421; subsequently he was at York Minster; he died in 1440. See Emden, *Cambridge, op. cit.*, s.v. Alne.

[81] MS Vatican Library, Ottobon. Lat. 73. See N. R. Ker, 'Cardinal Cervini's Manuscripts from the Cambridge Friars', in N. R. Ker, *Book Collectors and Libraries: Studies in the Mediaeval Heritage*, ed. A. G. Watson, London, 1985, pp.437–458. The MS is described on p.452. It was given by Henry Stokton, O.E.S.A., to Walter Crome in 1425. Stokton was at the Cambridge O.E.S.A. convent in 1417. On Crome and Stokton, see Edmen, *Cambridge, op. cit.*, and further, Roth, *English Austin Friars, op. cit.*, Vol. 1, pp.574–575.

[82] See further N. R. Kerr, *Mediaeval Libraries of Great Britain: A List of Surviving Books*, 2nd ed., Royal Historical Society, London, 1964, pp.23–24; *Supplement* to the same, ed. A. G. Watson, Royal Historical Society, London, 1987, pp.7–9; J. P. Carley, 'John Leland and the Contents of English pre-Dissolution Libraries: the Cambridge Friars', *Transactions of the Cambridge Bibliographical Society*, 9, Pt 1 (1986), 90–100. There is now also the British Academy catalogue of the mediaeval English Friars' libraries – see note 54 above.

[83] A. M. Hudson, *The Premature Reformation: Wycliffite Texts and Lollard History*, Oxford, 1988, p.92.

to go beyond the 'mind of the Church'. Yet even the received wisdom must have contained within itself the germs of remarkable possibilities. If more of the academic theology of late fourteenth-century Cambridge could be identified and studied, this would be of great service to our understanding of the English contemplative tradition at a crucial phase in its development.

REFLECTING CHRIST:
THE ROLE OF THE FLESH IN
WALTER HILTON AND JULIAN OF NORWICH

TARJEI PARK

IN THIS STUDY I shall look at the presentation of self as outlined in Walter Hilton's *Scale of Perfection* and how it relates to operative christologies. I shall then analyse the first of Julian of Norwich's visionary sequences within her *Revelations of Divine Love* and in so doing show a significant difference between the two writers.

From the point of view of the philosophy of mysticism there might be here an initial problem. Hilton is writing primarily as a spiritual director, or mystagogue. The text is essentially a didactic missive concerned with the process of contemplation. Julian is, of course, more properly described as a visionary. The (admittedly problematic) distinctions between these two starting points[1] could lead to a questioning of the legitimacy of textual comparison. Having said this, Hilton is very much concerned with the 'siȝt of Ihesu' and a comparison of these two writers uncovers some interesting distinctions over the role of the physical body in the intimate relationship between self and God in Christ.

1

In Hilton's *Scale* the image of God as the 'kyndeli schap' is deformed, 'forschapen'. That which is to be regained is 'þe ful schap & þe liknes of His Sone Iesu' (2.28,f.99ʳ).[2] The soul acts as a mirror: 'for þe soule is bot a mirrour in þe whilk þu schalt see God gostly' (2.30,f.102ᵛ). This emphasis on the soul as visually receptive and perceptive is a major feature of Hilton's epistemology; blindness and sight being often played off each other: the 'blyndnes . . . in þis merknes' must be endured if one is to find Jesus (1.54,p.325ᵇ). At finding Jesus

---

[1] See Alisdair MacIntyre, 'Visions', in *New Essays in Philosophical Theology*, ed. A. Flew and A. MacIntyre, London, 1955, and Nelson Pike, 'On Mystic Visions as Sources of Knowledge' in *Mysticism and Philosophical Analysis*, ed. Steven T. Katz, London, 1978, for good discussion of visionary experience.

[2] Quotation from *The Scale of Perfection* is from MS CUL/Camb.Add.6686 for Book 1 and from MS BL/Harley 6579 for Book 2. My thanks go to Professors Stanley Hussey, Michael Sargent, and Toshiyuki Takamiya for their kindness and generosity in making texts available to me.

'þou schuldest fynde lyȝt of vnderstondyng, & no merknes of vnconyng' (1.53,p.325ᵇ). Specifically fused are notions of visual and cognitive perception, knowledge and its acquisition are as light to darkness. By grace the image of sin which distorts, shadows, and wraps the true image of Jesus is broken down and destroyed (1.91,p.360ᵃ⁻ᵇ). Here sin is presented as that which affects that which is *seen*.

Hilton is clear as to what must be abandoned for true vision/knowledge of the image of Jesus to be attained; it is the mind's fixation to embodiment:

> . . . drawȝe into þiself þi thoȝt fro þi bodily wittes . . . drawȝe innere þi thoȝt fro all ymaginyng (if þou may) of any bodily thyng, & out fro all thoȝtes of þi bodily dedes. (1.52,p.324ᵃ)

In 1,82 sin is itself embodied, parts of the body representing the different seven deadly sins. The body is emphatically to be subordinate to the spirit:

> Chastise þe flesch with discrecion for trespaces bifor don, and by swilk penaunce forto refreyn lustes and likynges of it, and make it buxum and redye to þe will of the spirite. (1.2,p.279ᵃ⁻ᵇ)

It is important to note that Hilton does not advocate bodily negation, the body is to be correctly ordered: 'be ryȝt bisye nyȝt and day with trauaile of bodie and of sprite' (1.3,p.279ᵇ).

The third and highest degree of contemplation detailed by Hilton involves the soul being 'reformed by fulhede of vertus to þe ymage of Iesu' upon its being

> taken up fro all erthly & fleschly affeccions, fro vein thoȝtes & vein ymaginynges of all bodily creatures, and as it were mykel rauisched out of þe bodily wittes; and þen by þe grace of þe Holy Gost is illumined forto se by vnderstondyng sothfastnes (whilk is God) and also gostly thynges, with a soft swete brennand loue in hym. (1.8,p.282ᵇ)

It is crucial to note here the belief that truth is God. This truth is perceived by spiritual vision, a 'vision' autonomous of the physical senses. Reformation and unity within the image of 'Oure Lord' is non-physically cognitive and affective. Again, the symbolism of mirrored light and darkness is central. A typical example is this expansion of 2 Corinthians 3:18:

> we, first reformed by vertus to lyknes of God, þe face of oure soule vnhiled by openyng of þe gostly eȝe, behalden as in a mirrour hevenly ioye, fulschapen and oned to þe ymage of Oure Lord, fro bryȝtnes of feith into bryȝtnes of vnderstondyng, or elles fro clertie of desire into clertie of blissid loue. (1.9,pp.283ᵇ–284ᵃ)

The operations of the 'gostly eȝe' are expressly non-physical. More traditional experiences of a visionary kind, although not necessarily dangerous, are not what Hilton intends:

> visions or reuelacions of any maner spirite, in bodily apperyng or in ymaginyng slepand or wakand, or elles any oþer felyng in þe bodily wittes, made as it were gostly, eiþer in sownyng of þe ere, or saueryng in þe mouth, or smellyng at þe nese, or elles any felable hete as it were fyre glouand and warmand þe brest, or any

oþer partie of þe bodie, or anythyng þat may be feled by bodily witt, þoȝ it be
neuer so comfortable & lykand, arn noȝt verrely contemplacion.   (1.10,p.284ª)

Hilton's determination to present bodily sensation as being of a lower, outer
order (a probable anti-Rolle polemic) stems largely from his belief in the chaotic
'vnskilful' and 'bestly' nature of the bodily; its insubordinate tendency when not
tempered by reason and *spiritual* love. Although by the death of the physical,
Hilton affirms that the bodily suffering and sacrifice of Jesus is the foundation
and means by which the soul might be reformed. It is interesting to note,
however, that Hilton regards Jesus' sacrifice as being made for 'veridical' or
'epistemological' concern: '. . . þat was for to gif his precious lif be wilful
takynge of ded for luf of soþfastnes' (2.2,f.64ᵛ).

The major theme of *Scale 2* is the dual reformation in faith and feeling
(experience). The higher reformation (in feeling) seems to be one that extends
beyond the confines of propositional faith. It is a full experiential reformation.
We might be tempted to assume that, in some way, Hilton is delimiting the
cognicentric in favour of the sentient. Yet Hilton then locates experiential
reformation and thus dissuades any such assumption; 'reformyng in felyng'
takes place in the higher part of reason, that unsoiled by the flesh. He states:

> For þou shalt vndirstond þat þe soule haþ two maner of felinges: one withouten of
> the fyue bodili wittes, anoþer wiþinne of þe gostly wittes, þe which arne properly
> þe miȝtes of þe soule, mynde, resoun, and wille.   (2.31,f.106ᵛ)

Then citing Ephesians 4:23 he continues:

> Be ȝe renewed in þe spirit of ȝoure soule; þat is, ȝe schul be reformed not in bodily
> felynge ne in ymaginacioun, bot in þe ouer party of ȝour resoun. And cloþe ȝow in
> a new man þat is schapen aftir God in riȝtwisnes, holynesse and soþfastnes. þat is,
> ȝour resoun . . . For whan þe soule haþe perfit knowynge of God, þan is it
> reformed.   (ibid.)

We should make distinctions between *Scale 1* and *Scale 2*. The later
recensions of *Scale 1* regularly substitute the name 'Jesus' for the earlier 'God'.
In many passages we thus find that what is meant by 'Jesus' ramifies predicates
of God the Father, the supra-incarnate Second Person, or perhaps a Pauline post-
Resurrection *soma pneumatikon* Christ. David Kennedy has written:

> . . . if the use of the name 'Jesus' in place of the word 'God' was an attempt to
> bring the incarnational element of spiritual theology to *Scale I*, then the author
> failed most miserably. . . . This 'Jesus' does not seem to be a man.[3]

A typical example of this de-anthropomorphizing tendency might be the
assertion that to encounter Jesus inwardly 'þe poynt of þi thoȝt' must be 'sett
upon nothyng þat is made' (1.46,p.319ᵇ). By the time of *Scale 2* Hilton presents

---

[3] David G. Kennedy, *Incarnational Element in Hilton's Spirituality*, Salzburg, 1982,
pp.178–9.

a far more cogent Chalcedonian christology. Having said this, the non-physical emphasis is still present:

> Biholde him wel, for he goþ beforn þe, not in bodily liknes bot vnseabley, bi priue presence of his miȝte. (2.24,f.89ʳ)

Jesus is uncreated nature:

> he þat wil seke God within, he schal forget first alle bodily þinge, for al þat is withouten, & his owne body; & he schal forgete þenkynge of his owne soule, & þenken on þat vnmade kynde, þat is Ihesu, þat made him, qwikneþ him, holdiþ him, & gifiþ him resoun & mende & lufe; þe whilk is within him þurgh his miȝt & souereyn sotilte. (2.33,f.109ᵛ)

Hilton is clear as to the comparative value of Jesus' humanity:

> þan riȝt as þe Godhed is more souereyn & more wurþi þan is þe manhede, riȝt so þe gostly biholdynge of þe Godhed in Ihesu man is more wurþi, more gostly & more medful þan the beholdynge of þe manhede alone, wheþer he behold þe manhed as dedly or *as glorified*. (2.30,f.103ᵛ. Italics mine.)

The incarnate Christ acts as a means of allowing our perception of the otherwise blinding divinity: 'oure Lorde Ihesu trempeþ his vnseable liȝt of his Godhed, & cloþiþ it vndir bodily liknes of his manhed'. Hilton explains potential problems here thus:

> I sey not þat we sul departe God fro man, but we schul loue Ihesu boþe God & man, God in man & man in God, gostly not fleschly. (2.30,f.104ᵛ)

In both 1.35 and 2.30 Hilton ruminates on the Passion or manhood of Christ. The meditating on Jesus in this way forms a less perfect devotion than on his divinity. We might at this point recall the hierarchical divisions outlined in 2.13. Concerning the God-man Jesus it would follow that in the Word taking flesh the mystery was not that God became enfleshed, but that God became revealed.

In 2.11 Hilton discusses the 'resoun of þe soule' which corresponds to the image of God, and the 'laghe of the þe flesch' which corresponds to the image of sin. Ungodly bodily impulses stem from the image of sin, yet the internal war is not between body (as flesh) and soul, but between soul and its powers and the *activity* of fallenness:

> a soule reformed to the liknes of God feȝtes ageyn þe fleschly styrynges of þis ymage of syn, & also þis ymage of syn stryfeþ agayn þe wil of þe spirit. (2.11,f.72ʳ)

The law of the flesh is operative when the soul avoids spiritual reason. Hilton connects the image of sin with irrationality:

> Loo here Seynt Poul in his own person conforteþ alle soules þat þurwȝ grace arun reformed in faiþ, þat þey suld not to mikel drede þe birþen of þis ymage with þe vnskilful stirynges þerof, if it so be þat þei sent not wilfully þerto. (2.11,f.72ᵛ)[4]

---

4 The same idea is found in 2.12:
> mannus soule . . . is foule in als mykel as it is ȝit medlid with fleschly felynges & vnskilful stirynges of þis foul ymage of synne. (2.12,f.73ᵛ)

Those who doubt the afterlife and believe the soul not to differ from that of an animal are called 'blinde & so bestly' (2.15,f.77ᵛ), governed, that is, by the animal soul devoid of reason. Physical location is not of itself sinful, nor are all fleschly stirings extremely so:

> a remedie þer is þat is sikir to swilk a simple soule þat is marred in itself & kan not helpen itself: þat he is not to bold in hymself, vtterly wenend þat swilk fleschly stirynges wiþ likyng arne no synnes . . . Ne also þat he be not to dredful ne to simple in witte for to demen hem alle as dedliche synnes nor as grete venials, for neiþer is soþ. (2.11,f.73ʳ)

Affection is sweeter in bodily feeling, contemplation in ghostly; contemplation is 'more inward' (1.9,p.283ᵃ). Physical sensations may be good or evil (1.10,p.284ᵃ), indeed, they may be a forshadow of the glorification of the body which shall be enjoyed in heaven (1.11,p.286ᵃ).

The 'knittyng' and 'festnyng' of Jesus to one's soul is dependent upon the degree of desire in the person:

> þe more þat þis desire is, þe faster is Iesu knitt to þe soule; þe lesse þat þe desire is, þe losier is he knitt. (1.12,p.286ᵇ)

From Philippians 3:13-14 Hilton states that hindward things are bodily, those forward are ghostly, Paul says that he must forget all bodily things, his own body included, if he is to see ghostly things (1.13,p.287ᵇ). The desire to be 'out of the flesh' is to be seen in the light of the need for bodily exercise that is harmonized with the spiritual:

> bot when by grace of Iesu & by gostly and bodily exercise þe reson is turned into lyʒt, & will into loue, þen has he vertus in affeccion. (1.14,p.288ᵃ)

Again, the emphasis on the sin in 'bodily lykyng' as against the functional bodily must be noted. In an image that is to be developed Hilton states that sins pour from the heart like water from a stinking well '& letten þe siʒt of þe soule' (1.15,p.288ᵇ). Although attempting balance, the scale is emphatically tipped in favour of the non-physical. This extends to Hilton's understanding of the Trinity. The emphasis on Trinitarian *perichoresis* or circumincession maintains a certain confusion of identities. Hilton states that 'oure Lord is a spirit. "Byfor oure face a gost is Oure Lord Crist" ' (1.16,p.289ᵃ⁻ᵇ). This he fuses with the worship of the Father in spirit and truth (1.16,p.289ᵇ from John 4:23-24) forming a particularly Johannine devotion; yet it entails a certain abstraction of the Son from anthropomorphous particularity.

In order to attain contemplation the priority must be to leave behind the fleshly. The anchoress is

> so bustues, so lewd, so fleschly, so blynde in gostly thynges, and namely of þin oun soule, whilk þe behouez first know if þou schuldest come to þe knowyng of God' (1.16,p.289ᵇ)[5]

---

[5] This is almost identical to the formula in Hilton's *Mixed Life*, ed. S. J. Ogilvie-Thomson, Salzburg, 1986, p.12.

Hilton says of himself 'I fele me so wrecced, & so frele, & so fleschly, and so ferre in trew felyng fro þat þat I speke and haue spoken' (1.16,p.290ᵃ). This linking of frailty and fleshliness (with its exemplar in the Passion) resonates in the advice that the anchoress not judge active people as they 'suffren mony tribulacions & grete temptacions, whilk þou sittand in þi house felez noȝt of' (1.17,p.291ᵇ).

For her own part the anchoress 'schalt hate synne & all fleschly loues & dredes in þi hert withouten cesyng' (1.22,p.296ᵇ), she is 'gode by grace, or bade by þin oun freltie' (1.23,p.297ᵇ).

Hilton then goes on to present a somewhat aggressive image:

> What þat þou felez, seez or herez, smellez or sauorez, withouten in þi bodily wittes, or withinne in ymaginyng or knowyng or felyng in þi reson – bryng it all withinne þe trowth & þe rewles of Holy Kyrk, and kast it al in þe mortere of mekenes, and breke it smal with þe pestel of drede of God, and throwe þe poudere of all þise in þe fire of desire, and offere it so to God, and I tell þe forsoþe, wel schal þat offryng like in þe siȝt of Oure Lord Iesu, and swete schal þe smoke of þat ilk fire smell to þe face of þi Lord Iesu. (1.23,p.297ᵃ)

This is not purely an example of Hilton's Pauline desire to be rid of the sin prone flesh, but involves a faculty and subfaculties of the soul. It's aggression is clear, these elements of self are to be 'kast(en)', 'breke(n)' and 'throwe(n) . . . in þe fire of desire'. The clue, I think, lies in this latter clause. What is omitted from this offering is the affective faculty of will. Rather than seeing this passage nihilistically, one must understand it as an emphatic injunction to conform these faculties to a christocentric affectivity. In this way the 'grace of oure Lord' may be received in a 'clene vescal' (1.24,p.297ᵇ), note that there is still some kind of vessel. The 'þat' of the opening sentence is the tendency to self of individual creatureliness. The movement is to be away from self as flesh (sinful and limited) to self in relation to God in Christ. This is borne out by the statement about prayer on waking, where the initial fleshly state must be quickly left by some devotion (1.24,p.298ᵃ).[6] Prayer is the movement away from all bodily things, desire must be 'bare and naked fro all erthly thynges' (1.25,p.298ᵃ).

In this plurivocal matrix, unsurprisingly, the Incarnational voice disrupts any neat dualisms, yet often produces a certain confusion. When 'Oure Lord ȝyuez a meditacion of his manhed, as of his birth, or of his passion, & of þe compassion of Oure Ladie Seint Marie' (1.34,p.306ᵃ) a rather disjunct consequence ensues. By such meditation 'þi thoȝt is drawen out fro all worldly and fleschly thynges, and þe thynkez as þou seez in þi soule þi Lord Iesu in a bodily liknes as he was in erth' (1.35,p.306ᵃ). Note that the apprehension of Jesus in bodily likeness is consequential on thought free from worldly and fleshly things. The 'gostly siȝt' of such a meditation is 'an openyng of þe gostly eȝe into Cristes manhed, and it may be called þe fleschly loue of God (as Seint Bernard callez it), in als mykel as it is sett in þe fleschly kynde of Crist' (1.35,p.306ᵇ). Here then is an answer.

---

6 Cf. *Mixed Life, op. cit.*, p.50.

Such meditation is acceptable in that it does not involve *our* flesh but is located in the fleshly nature of Christ, the distinction being the lack of sin active in Christ's flesh (cf.2.30). It is important to stress the non-physicality of this sight. In order that the ground of sin, misruled self-love, might be 'dried up' fleshly and worldly loves must be cast out:

> sothly, vntil þis ground be wel ransaked and depe duluen, and as it were nere dryed up by outkestyng of all fleschly and worldly loues, a soule may neuere fele gostly þe brennand loue of God, ne haue clere syȝt of gostly thynges by liȝt of vnderstondyng. (1.42,p.313ª)

This chapter contains some of Hilton's most potentially flesh-hating statements. Yet Hilton is no Manichaean. The flesh as flesh is not at issue, but, rather, the faculties of the soul directed towards created and fallen things opposed to God, and thus towards sin:

> þis is þe trauaile, þat a man behouez to drawȝe up his hert fro fleschly loue and þe likyng of all bodily creatures, and out fro þe loue and þe felyng of hymself, þat þe soule schuld mo no rest fynde in no fleschly thoȝt ne erthly affeccion. (*ibid.*)

That which must be redirected is the inner self. Thought and affection (from reason and will) are made blind when captivated by love and 'likyng' of the flesh. The connoted concept here is that of flesh as mantle or blind. This is borne out in Hilton's preceding discussion of meditation on Christ's manhood. The veil of flesh covers the godhead of Jesus, the exterior the interior. Yet, as stated above, Hilton goes further than a neat anti-flesh, pro-spirit dualism. It reaches a point in this chapter where, in a substantial expansion of Matthew 16:24, John 12:25, he states:

> 'Whoso wil come aftere me, forsake hymself & hate his own soule'; þat is forto sey, 'forsake all fleschly loue, and hate all his oun fleschly life and his bodily felyng of all his wittes for loue of me, and take þe cros'. (1.42,p.313ᵇ)

The clue to the explanation of this process then follows:

> þis is a streit way and a naroe, þat no bodily thynge may passe thoroȝ it, for it is a sleyng of all synne. (*ibid.*)

Sin functions through the body, when the soul is fixed upon the body it is blinded by sin. Again, Hilton is not against flesh as flesh, but flesh as sin-laden. This explains the (for Hilton) inverted approach to body and soul in the following expansion of Colossians 3:5:

> 'Slee ȝoure membres upon erth; noȝt þe membres of þe bodie, bot of þe soule, as vnclennes, lust and vnskilfull loue to oureself and to erthly thynges'. (*ibid.*)

The soul is affected not by the physical, but by the fallenness of the physical.

Following 1.43 which presents his operative Augustinian psychology, Hilton becomes more programmatic in his christocentricity. He establishes what must be left and what must be sought:

> he schuld loþe and despise in his hert al þe blis, þe likyng and þe fairnes of al þis world as stynk of carion . . .

> þe poynt of þi thoʒt is sett upon nothyng þat is made, ne felez no stiryng of
> veinglorie ne non oþere yuell affeccion.   (1.46,p.319ᵃ)

By this emphasis on concentration on the uncreated, Hilton's Christ remains
overtly abstracted. The overall structure of the rest of *Scale 1* is concerned with
the process of restraining or removing the image of sin that subjectively
displaces the image of Jesus within the soul. The normative function of the
immanent Jesus corresponds to the second part of the Augustinian triads
presented in 1.43, that is, 'wisdom' and 'siʒt'. Jesus has been hidden by the
blindness brought about by sin and is to be sought: 'seke þen Iesu whilk þou has
lost' (1.47,p.320ᵇ). The search for Jesus is the search for wisdom, 'seke wisdom
(whilk is Iesu)', it is a Jesus of a non-incarnational presence and, as stated,
overtly abstracted:

> delf depe in þi hert, for þerinne he is hid, and kast out ful clenely all loues and
> likynges, soroes & dredes of all erthly thynges; and so schalt þou fynde wisdom –
> Iesu.   (1.47,p.321ᵃ)

This process is achieved by reason, the corresponding second part of the human
triad:

> þe lantern of þi soule is reson, by þe whilk þe soule may se all gostly thynges. By
> þis lantern may þou fynde Iesu.   (1.48,p.321ᵇ)

What is interesting here is how Hilton's sensory terminological constructs
cohere with his christology. The manhood of Jesus (in one's meditation) serves
no more purpose than as a gateway to the essential godhead. Textually, physical
images and constructs serve no other purpose than pointing towards spiritual
development. In each case of the physical there is a certain vacuum of
meaning.[7] In each case the emptying of *meaning* is the emptying of the physical.
This vacuity is the locus for the spiritual apprehension of the immanent Jesus.

On introspective examination one does not apprehend Jesus immediately but a
'merk ymage & a peynfull of þin oun soule'. This image is 'al vmbilapped with
blak stynkand cloþes of synne' (1.52,p.324ᵇ).

Central here is the reflectivity or reciprocity of this immanence. It is itself an
image or shadow about which are wrapped the clothes of sin and from which
streams of sin run:

> it is an ymage of synne – as Seint Paule callez it, a bodie of synne and a bodie of
> deth; þis ymage & blak schadue þou berez about with þe where þou gos. Out fro

---

[7] To be more precise semiologically, on the plane of denotation the *sign* is the term's
meaning, on the connoted plane the *sign* now acting as the second order *signifier* is
emptied of *meaning* and refilled as *form* to redenote the *concept*. Thus the *form-
concept* relation as *signification* stems from the initially vacated *signifier* (first order
sign). The parallelism here, then, between spirituality and christology is that Hilton's
words (*sign-meanings/signifier-forms*) are gates to spiritual constructs of perceiving
selves (*signified-concepts*), and the Incarnate Word (*sign-meaning/signifier-form*) is
the gate to God (*signified-concept*).

þis spryngen mony grete stremes of synne & smale also: riȝt as out of þe ymage of Iesu, if it were reformed in þe, bemes of gostly liȝt schulden stiȝe up into Heuen (as brennand desires, clene affeccions, wise thoȝtes and all honestie of vertus), riȝt so out of þis ymage spryngen stirynges of pride, of enuye & swilk oþere, þe whilk kasten þe doun fro þe honestie of man into a bestes liknes. (1.53,p.324ᵇ–325ᵃ)

The image of Jesus requires reformation (1.69), it is not only occluded but mishapen or deformed. A further thing to be noted here is the secondary or non-primary nature of all this activity. Sin is from an image or shadow, it takes the form of streams – note that this emphasis on reflectivity and movement supports a neutral or vacuous foundation. There seems no active constitutional or foundational negativity. In 1.77 Hilton returns to the image of sin as a form of emptiness. Following Luke 16:26 he brings in the notion of the image as chasm: 'þis merk ymage in þi soule (& in myn also) may be called a "grete chaos", a grete merknes' (1.77,p.350a). The image of sin is 'like to no bodily thynge. . . . Sothly, it is Noȝt'. This 'Noȝt' is 'nothyng elles bot a lackyng of loue & of lyȝt, as synne is noȝt bot a wantyng of gode' (1.53,p.325ᵃ).

Although the image of sin is 'Noȝt', it also signifies Pauline constructs. It is the first Adam (1.54,p.325ᵇ–326ᵃ cf.1.Corinthians 15:49), it is also the body of death, 'þis bodie and þis ymage of deth' (1.54,p.326ᵃ cf.Romans 7:24). As an *activity* it is also the Augustinian *cupiditas*, a 'fals misrewled loue vnto þiself' (1.55,p.326ᵃ) from which come 'seuen ryuers', the seven deadly sins. Hilton even explicitly qualifies his earlier statement thus: 'þis ymage is not noȝt, bot it is mykel of badd' (*ibid.*).

Much of Hilton's theology of the image is along the lines of a single image of God that becomes distorted as a consequence of the Fall to the image of sin. The earlier *version* of the image is restored by reformation of the soul by the sacraments. Yet we also find the system whereby there exists two images and Hilton develops this theology within a Pauline framework. By glossing Galatians 5:17 and Romans 7:23 Hilton developes these images along the lines of spirit and flesh which become two *laws*. From Romans 7:23 he states:

I haue founden two lawes in myself, on laghe in my soule wiþinne, & anoþer in my fleschly lymes wiþouten feȝtand wiþ it, þat oft lediþ me as a wrecced prisoner to þe laghe of syn.

Be þese two laghes in a soule I vndirstonde þis double ymage. Be þe lagh of þe spirit I vndirstonde þe resoun of þe soule whan it is reformed to þe ymage of God; be þe laghe of þe flesch I vndirstonde þe sensualite whilk I calle þe ymage of sin. (2.11,f.72ʳ)

Here the image of sin is explicitly located within sensuality. By now we can see that the image of sin represents a dynamic fallenness.

In my soule, þat is in my wil & in my resoun, I serue to þe laghe of God. Bot in my flesch, þat is in my fleschly appetite, I serue to þe laghe of syn. (2.11,f.72ᵛ)

Note the emphatic explanation of flesh as fleshly appetite. As in *Scale 1* Hilton does not here mean flesh as flesh (matter). Yet as the post-lapsarian self has undergone 'corrupcioun of þe bodily kynde' it serves the law of sin against the

will of the spirit 'be felyng of þe vicious sensualite' (ibid.). What happens in the
flesh affects (the locus of) the image of God: 'þe likyng is so grete in his fleschly
felyng þat it troubleþ his resoun' (2.11,f.73ʳ).

Hilton's psychology is essentially dual. This is strikingly presented in the
opening paragraph of 2.12:

> Faier is þan a mannus soule, & foule is a mannus soule. Faire in als mikel as it is
> reformed in faiþ to þe liknes of God. Bot it is foule in als mikel as it is ʒit medlid
> with fleschly felynges & vnskilful stirynges of þis foule ymage of synne. Foul
> withouten as it were a beste, faire withinne like to an aungel. Foul in felyng of þe
> sensualite, faire in trouþ of þe resoun. Foul for the fleschly appetite, faire for þe
> good wil.   (2.12,f.73ᵛ–74ʳ)

The confused compositum is here emphasized in Hilton's reversing the order of
natures half way through the passage. It is simultaneously perceived as fair and
foul. The immediately preceeding chapter heading states that 'þis image is boþ
faire & foule'. As the chapter then substitutes the term 'soule' we are again left
unclear as to the exact relation between image and soul. The title implies an
equivalance of terms, the passage that the image is co-existent with or in the
soul. Just after this passage in a gloss of Canticles 1:4 he again refers to the
image of sin as 'my blake shadwe', indicating co-existence of the image with the
'I' of the sentence.

In the same gloss he presents the externality of the foule image:

> I be blak withouten because of my fleschly kynde, as is a tabernacle of cedar,
> nerþeles I am ful faire withinne as þe synne of Salamon for I am reformed to þe
> liknes of God.   (2.12,f.74ʳ)

The black shadow is then termed the 'body of syn', recalling the 'mahmet' of
1.84. For a soule reformed in faith this 'blackness' is external only:

> Reproue me not for I am swart, for þe swartnes þat I haue is al withouten, of
> touchyng & of beryng of þis ymage of synne. Bot it is noþing withinne.   (ibid.)[8]

This is so even though such a 'chosen soule' dwells in the 'body of syn' and
experiences the same fleshly stirrings as an unreformed person. Thus externally
there exists no perceivable distinction between those unreformed and those
reformed in faith, 'nerþeles withinne in þaire soules þer is ful grete diuersite &
in siʒt of God þer is ful mikil twynnyng'(2.12,f.74ᵛ). The distinction between
the two is that the reformed person loathes his/her fleshly 'wittes' and
'stiryngges' 'for he wulde for noþing fully reste in hem' (ibid.).

In 2.13 Hilton maintains that the soul is composed of two faculties,
'sensuality' and 'resoun'. The higher part of these two, reason, is further divided
into higher and lower parts. The higher is the centre of control in which God's
likeness exists. It is in this part that the soul knows and loves God. The lower
part understands and controls mundane things; restraining the self from being

---

[8] This is, of course, at variance to much that has gone before regarding the image of sin
as interior and equivalent, fastened, etc. to the soul.

controlled by 'þe lustes of his flesch, as it were an vnskilful beste'.[9] This is the anthropology taken over by Hilton. The lower part of reason keeps the image of God unsoiled by the physical. The sentient reasoning self is, then, no more than a protective boundary between the cognicentric (sacred) and the flesh (profane).[10] Hilton's presented sequence of spiritual transformation is governed by this anthropology. The process is a movement through a series of boundaries that blind one from perceiving God, one is covered in ghostly light yet one is blind (2.16,f.78ᵛ). The movement from flesh to higher reason, a movement from the lowest, most sin orientated part of self to the image of God and thus God, the soul functioning here as mirror, involves a putting right or calming of the

[9] The higher being 'likned to a man', the lower 'likned to a woman'. This chapter comes, of course, directly from Augustine. Hilton legitimates the subordination of the lower part to the higher by the example of an affirmed relationship of subordinate wife to husband. This chapter is very little more than a rewriting of the passage from Augustine's *De Genesi ad litteram* (Gen.ad litt.II,22.VI.7.X,2). What Hilton does not take up at this point is *Augustine's* distinction between the internal and external self. Augustine is clear that there exists no difference between male and female *faculties*. There exists sexual differentiation only in the realm of material substance. It is within the realm of the *homo exterior* that, according to Augustine, woman remains inferior as man's helpmate:

> Sex is linked exclusively to the material substance of the human body, and consequently sexual difference is found only on the bodily level. In so far as it is incorporeal the rational soul has no sex. As a result there exists in in every human being a duality, the asexual soul which makes it *homo*, and the sexual body, which makes it either *vir* (man) or *femina* (woman). . . . the inferiority of *femina* is closely bound up with bodily inferiority. It is her quality as helpmate, representing that part of the soul which deals with mundane needs, which justifies the analogy employed by Augustine. The whole of his argument emphasizes that woman's *imago Dei* dwells in her rational soul, which is identical with that of man. The duality between her *homo interior*, which shares the superiority of man's soul, and her *homo exterior*, which remains inferior because of her position as man's helpmate, is sharply defined. (Kari Børresen, *Subordination and Equivalence. The Nature and Role of Women in Augustine and Aquinas*, Univ. Press of America, 1981, pp.26-9)

It is fair to say, however, that in the Augustinian Medieval West (and beyond) woman is primarily identified with corporeality, being seen as *intrinsically* carnal. See Sarah Coakley, 'Creaturehood before God', and Grace Jantzen, 'Who Needs Feminism?' in *Theology*, 93 (1990), 339-354. Hilton's (and general) shying away from the more physicalist ramifications of the Incarnation might be seen in the light of this. Was the Word becoming flesh in some sense the masculine becoming feminine?

[10] Hilton's anti-physicalist anthropology is consonant with his adoption of the Thomist understanding of how and where Christ's two natures were unified, here illustrated by a passage from *Mixed Life*, *op. cit.*, pp.55-56.

> þe soule of oure lord Ihesu . . . was fulli ooned to þe Godhede. . . . For in þe persone of Ihesu aren two kyndes, þat is God and man, fulli ooned togidere. Bi þe vertu of þis blissid oonynge . . . þe soule of Ihesu receyued þe fulheed of wisdoom and loue and al goodnesse. . . . þe godhede was ooned fulli to þe manhede in the soule of Ihesu, and so bi þe soule dwellide in þe bodi. (Cf. Aquinas, *Summa Theologica* 3a.2-5.)

various strata of self. Bodily work and customs are preliminary and but co-operant means by which a soul is led to perfection (2.19,f.81ʳ⁻ᵛ). The contemplative conscious self must move from flesh to spirit. In this the soul's subfaculties are discarded:

> I hope þat a soule þat is reformed in felyng bi rauischyng of luf into contemplacioun of God, may be so ferre fro þe sensualite & fro vayn ymaginacioun, & so ferre drawen out & departid fro þe fleschly felyng for a tyme, þat it schal not felen bot gode; bot þat lasteþ not ay. (2.11,f.72ʳ)

When one takes from a person their past actions, their sensuality and imagination (plus their family; forsaking one's family is the 'gate of contemplacioun' 2.27,f.97ʳ from Matthew 19:29), one is close to finding that which Hilton means by a person ready for contemplation, a consciousness of a rather disembodied and temporally dislocated sort. The reason for this strand in Hilton's missive is his notion that humanness is essentially of limitation. Human action, sensation and imagination are signifiers for limitation. This is one reason why Hilton favours vacuity as a means for expressing the relationship between human beings and God. Emptiness signified by the signs of the image and mirror evades the particularity of the individual most forceably demonstrated by self as matter. The *size* of the soul is determined by the moral effects of one's mortal, limited self (2.29,f.100ᵛ). The soul is a vessel (2.21), a vacuity, filled with liquor, God, the limitless.

Barriers in the form of blindness characterize ungodly love. *Cupiditas* between man and woman is 'blind luf' (2.27,f.96ʳ). Reason acts as the medium between limited human particularity and the unlimited: 'þou art not elles bot a resonable instrument wherin þat he wirkiþ' (2.24,f.89ʳ). Self emptying in the form of meekness and love becomes functionate when activated by reason. An untranquil and unstable body is no foundation for contemplation, as in a chaotic state it draws attention to itself as fallen and thus away from God. Having said this, Hilton argues that bodily pain is preferable to love of the world outside of God. Bodily pain, furthermore, separates the soul from love of sensuality. The soul when externalized suffers pain: 'withouten itself it schal be mortified & pyned in þe sensualite' (2.28,f.99ᵛ). The soul does not know the reason for its location:

> þe sely soule bi felynge & berynge of þe wrecced body sal be so pyned, & it schal not witen where ne how þat it schuld not mown suffren for to ben in þe body, ne were þat oure Lord Ihesu kepiþ it þerin. (2.28,f.99ᵛ)[11]

---

[11] What is interesting is Hilton's use of the word 'sely' of the soul. The Middle English 'sely' has the meanings 'happy', 'lucky', 'good', or 'innocent' (in a possibly contemptuous sense). The meaning here, I think, is, indeed, 'innocent'. Thus we get the sense of the innocent soul put in pain by its bearing the wretched body. 'Sely' has in this sentence been translated 'silly', 'unfortunate', 'poor', and 'hapless'. Bodily pain is purgatory and should be suffered gladly, though the soul's being blinded by a 'fals luf of þe werld' is hell.

Because some souls are 'as it were fleschly, festned to þe flesch', as a result of the 'litelnes & weiknes of here soule' grace is manifest in outward experiences (2.29,f.100ᵛ). Love bursts out in tears and speech, yet this is due to 'weiknes & feblenes of þe soule þan for mikelnes of luf' (2.29,f.101ʳ).

Bodily tranquillity has a negative worth, in that it is valuable in not disturbing the progress of the soul. Ultimately, however, contemplation has little to do with embodiment other than that its form is largely such as a consequence of embodiment. The soul must have knowledge of itself before it can have knowledge of a nature above itself. This is done through introversion until 'it feliþ itself as it is in þe owne kynde withouten a body' (2.30,f.102ʳ). When detailing dependence and distinction between soul and body, Hilton again brings in notions of the visual:

> For þi soule is no body, but a lif vnseable; not hid & holden within þi body as a lesse þinge is hid & holden within a more, bot it is holdend & qwiknende þi body, mikel more þen þi body is in miȝt & in vertue. (2.30,f.102ʳ)

(There should possibly be a comma after 'bot it is' for the second half of the sentence to carry the intended sense.)

The soul wrongly imagines a bodily form for itself or God, 'And þat may not ben; for alle gostly þinges ere seen & knowen by vndirstondynge of þe soule, not bi ymaginacioun.' (2.30,f.102ᵛ) Hilton emphatically points to the formlessness and the soul's reflectivity of the unlimited: 'For þi soule is bot a mirrour in þe whilk þu schalt see God gostly' (*ibid.*). Here there is ambiguity over the action of seeing. Is the seer looking into the mirror, or does the seer see as the mirror?[12]

---

[12] In this same chapter Hilton seems to argue that perception is dependent upon how flesh-governed a person is; we might say that one sees what one is. He details three types of understanding of the love of God. Firstly, 'faiþ withouten gracious ymaginacioun or gostly knowynge of God'. Secondly, 'faiþ & ymaginacioun of Ihesu in his manhede'. Here the 'gostly eiȝe is opened in beholdynge of oure Lordes manhede'. Thirdly, the soul 'feliþ þurgh gostly siȝt of þe Godhed in þe manhede, . . . þat is perfit luf' (2.30,f.103ʳ). The personal journey from the flesh is reenacted in the perception of the godhead in Jesus:

> þe gostly beholdynge of þe Godhed in Ihesu is more worþi, more gostly & more medful þan þe beholdynge of þe manhode alone, wheþer he behold þe manhed as dedly or as glorified. And riȝt so bi þe same skil, þe luf þat a soule feliþ in þinkynge & beholdynge of þe Godhede in man, when it is graciously schewed, is worþier, gostlier, & more medful þen þe feruour of deuocioun þat þe soule feliþ bi ymaginacioun only of þe manhede, schew it neuer so mikel outward. (2.30,ff.103ᵛ–104ʳ)

Hilton rarely retains a unitive voice. Following the above passage he presents a mixture of images with both ascetic and eucharistic encoding: Jesus shows himself in bodily likeness to 'þe inner eiȝe of a soule & fediþ it with þe luf of his precious flesche gostly' (2.30,f.104ʳ). The eating metaphor returns later (the soul as mouth needs 'white teþe & scharpe & wel piked') with the juxtaposition of good nourishment and filthied taste:

> To a clene soule þat haþe palet purified fro þe filþe of fleschly lufe, Holy Wryt

Aware that anti-physicalism has possibly damaging implications for the doctrine of the Incarnation, Hilton states that the Incarnation must not be split, but should be loved ghostly rather than fleshly (2.30,f.104ᵛ). Yet over all this there resonates a voice that feels uneasy with a relational exchange between Jesus and the flesh. The tone of this voice is heard in such statements as that Jesus casts a 'gostly schadwe' over the soul (2.30,f.104ʳ). Here we are back to the intangible realm of mirrors and images. The shadow exists as something seen and felt only by an absence of radiation. Such a notion is commensurate with the pervasive notion that 'Crist lifiþ & is hid in His Godhed fro þe luf & þe siȝt of fleschly lufers' (2.27,f.97ʳ). Jesus is perceived not as he is, but clothed under the likeness of works and words, he is known 'by a mirour & by a liknes' (2.43,f.135ʳ cf.1.Corinthians 13:12). Spirituality is confined to the principal powers of the soul, the intermediary subfaculties by location are unspiritual in this sense. Physical fervours

> are not gostly felynges, for gostly felynges are felt in þe miȝtes of þe soule, principally in vndirstandynge & lufe & litel in ymaginacioun. Bot þese felynges are in ymaginacioun, & þerfore þei are not gostly felynges, bot whan þei are best & most trewe ȝit are þei bot outward toknes of þe inly grace þat is felt in þe miȝtes of þe soule. (2.30,f.105ʳ⁻ᵛ)

Such a spiritual theology of self entails a dephysicalizing rereading of Scriptural narratives such as that of Pentecost. The Holy Spirit 'enflammed her hertes & sat vpon ilke of hem', that is:

> þe Holy Gost, þat is God in himself vnseable, . . . was vnseably felt in þe miȝtes of her soules; for he liȝtend here resoun & kyndeled here affeccioun . . . so clerly & so brennandely þat þei haden sodenly gostly knowynge of soþfastnes & þe perfeccioun of luf. (2.30,f.105ᵛ)

The soul receives new powers of experience, there are two types of sense:

> þe soule haþ two maner of felinges: on withouten of þe fyue bodili wittes, anoþer wiþinne of þe gostly wittes, þe which arne properly þe miȝtes of þe soule, mynde, resoun, and wille. Whan þese myȝtes arne þurȝ grace fulfilled in al vndirstondyng of þe wille of God and gostly wisdam, þan haþ þe soule new graciouse felynges. (2.31,f.106ᵛ)

Principal amongst the senses associated with the soul's powers is the 'gostly eiȝe':

> Jesus 'openeþ þe innere iȝe of þe soule when he liȝtneþ þe resoun þurgh touchyng & schynynge of his blissed liȝt'. (2.32,f.107ʳ)

Bodily nature corresponds to the closing of eyes. We are now close to the heart of Hilton's spiritual theology. It is interesting to note that he still employs sensory metaphor, specifically that of vision. We still see God. Although occasionally using other verbs indicating sense perception in this way, this

> is lifly fode & sustenance delectable; it sauoriþ wondir swete whan it is wel chewed by gostly vndirstondynge. (2.42,f.134ʳ)

analogous verb is the one preferred by Hilton. This notion of seeing is preferable to tangible first order sensation in that it retains a tension between the physical and the transcendent, particularly when carrying the dream-like undertone of 'vision'. The notion of 'seeing' acts as a signifying bridge over the epistemological collapse entailed by limited self apprehending the ineffable uncreated.[13]

The term 'gostly eiʒe' is the one most frequently used by Hilton of spiritual apprehension. Syntagmatically the reader follows a movement where they assume a 'transcendent', non-physical sense but then are disrupted by the subversion to the physical 'eiʒe'. The spiritual is resignified to denote physical sight. Then recollectively the injunction against physical interpretation is recalled and the sense floats as an analogy, this movement being away from fleshliness. 'Sauour of God' works syntagmatically toward the same end, flesh to unflesh, created to uncreated, though omitting the initial spiritual paradigm.[14] Hilton's use of sensory metaphor is also a movement towards the reader. The reader is made to think of their own senses. The signifying of 'sight' makes one think of or through one's own sight. With this Hilton encourages transference of the reader-self into the narrative paradigm person.

Occasionally vocative/aural metaphor is used of God and self, though this can obviously carry the signified disjunctive relationship between created and uncreated. Indeed, non-tangibility in the first order sign, also emptied, is more in harmony with its connoted sense. It is noticeable that when Hilton at one point details bodily sensations that must be avoided/ignored in prayer, he deals only with 'smellynge & sauorynge & touchynge' (2.39,f.123ʳ). Ultimately the oxymoronic alone (containing a tension of defered meaning) suffices. Note in this passage how the unmade is to be seen and loved:

> . . . not ageynstondende þe bodily kynde; & þe more clene & sotil þat þe soul is made, & þe more it is departid fro fleschlied, þe scharpere siʒt it haþ & þe miʒtier lufe of þe Godhed of Iesu.   (2.32,f.108ʳ)

The notion of non-physical sight welds the two parts of this 'category mistake' (finite seeing infinite) together. When Hilton uses 'siʒt' in this way it signifies both sensuality and the transcendent. Now on closer inspection there is no reason why this should not be so. In this passage 'siʒt' and 'lufe' are, of course, analogous to the Son and Spirit of the Augustinian triad. 'Siʒt' functions as the inverse of 'the Word become flesh'; connoted is the Athanasian 'God became a human being so that human beings might become God'. The process of

---

[13] A similar dialectical clash is manifest in the lengthy discussion of the dark night perceived as the 'liʒtsom derknes'.

[14] The 'gostly eiʒe' is a good example of a Barthesian 'symbolic' coding, an antithetical structure. As an 'opposition' having no tangible referent it becomes special or *other*. Like 'daydream', where the signifying process of opposites at work creates a sense of *ekstasis*, Hilton's phrase moves to the *other*. See Roland Barthes, *S/Z*, Oxford, 1974, pp.17–18.

contemplation is a reflection of the Incarnation. The reflection is a reversal, within the signifying chain is the 'image of Ihesu'. 'Gostly siʒt of Ihesu' is achieved in the soul as mirror. The contemplative self has moved from sinful fleshliness to disembodied wisdom, as spirit became flesh, so the human self must move its centre from flesh to spirit.

2

Before specific analysis of Julian's first revelation I would like to draw attention to some images and statements made by her to illustrate a significant difference to Hilton.

What Julian intends by 'substance' and 'sensuality' is different from Hilton's delineation of 'reason' and 'sensuality' in *Scale* 2,13. What can be argued for is an identity between the lower part of reason in Hilton's system, and Julian's understanding of 'sensuality'. Both are penetrating boundaries between the flesh and that part of the self in which God is reflected or grounded.

Julian regularly uses the expression 'our foule dedly flesh'. She does not present a neat antithetical voice to Hilton. In ch.64 she explains the used image of the young child in the pit thus:

> . . . the bolnehede of the body betokenith gret wretchidnes of our dedly flesh, and the littlehede of the child betokenith the clenes of purity in the soule. (64/79:9–11)[15]

As opposed to Hilton's emphasis on reason, Julian concentrates on our 'substance'. Whereas Hilton's 'reason' acts as a foundational power of spiritual perception, 'substance' is more organically constitutional. For Julian the miracle is that Jesus reintegrated substance and sensuality and thus brought a wholeness to the fallen self. Sensuality acts as the bridge between flesh and spirit, it is inhabited by God:

> . . . I saw that in our sensualite God is; for the selfe poynte that our soule is mad sensual, in the selfe poynt is the cite of God, ordeynid to him from withouten begynnyng. (55/66:28–30)

Roland Maisonneuve has written:

> The words 'ground, substance, sensuality' cannot be understood except in the conceptual unity which links them. They encompass total man, trinitarian man: *soma, psyche, pneuma.*[16]

Furthermore, our apprehension of God is not restricted to a non-physicalist analogy. Again Maisonneuve:

---

[15] All quotation from Julian is taken from *Julian of Norwich: A Revelation of Love*, ed. Marion Glasscoe, Exeter, 1976 and takes the form ch./page:line.

[16] In 'The Visionary Universe of Julian of Norwich', *The Medieval Mystical Tradition in England*, ed. Marion Glasscoe, Exeter, 1980, p.90.

[For Julian] the organ of sight seems to be a synthesis of all the other senses.[17]

Her interphysicality is well illustrated by this passage from ch.43 where she writes of our seeing, feeling, hearing, smelling, and swallowing God:

> And than shal we all come into our lord . . . hym verily seand and fulsumly feland, hym gostly heryng, and hym delectably smellyng and hym swetely swelow-yng. (43/46:31-35)

In ch.6, although acknowledging that the images by which one prays, Jesus' 'holiy flesh . . . prectious blode . . . holiy passion . . . deare-worthy death and wounds', are intermediary, Julian maintains that our embodiment is intimately enclosed in the goodnesse of God.

Although defining Jesus as Wisdom, Julian presents an incarnate Christ whose humanity extends to blindness and ignorance: '. . . he was blinded in his reason and stonyed in his mend so ferforth that almost he had forgotten his owne luf' (51/54:43). The complete identification of Christ with each human is further demonstrated in the Servant representing the three Adams: the first, humanity, and Jesus. We are part of the incarnate Christ: 'for in al this our good lord shewid his owne Son and Adam but one man' (51/59:5-6). Julian maintains that Jesus is not yet fully glorified in that he still thirsts and shall until the last person is saved and is raised to heaven (31/32). Of paramount importance for Julian is the potential we enjoy as humans. The hidden treasure is sinful human personhood (51/58f).

I would like to demonstrate Julian's integrationist physicalism by an analysis of her first revelation which appears between chs.3-9. The degree to which metaphor is operative in her revelations very much distinguishes Julian from Hilton. What is of interest is the polysemic matrix within which Julian attempts to articulate the 'meneing' of her visions. The first revelation is layered upon a connoted subtext that acts as the sequence with which Julian experiences and articulates her vision. The subtext here, I believe can be argued, is of the sequence of childbirth.[18]

In ch.3 Julian experiences fluctuating pain and numbness between her upper and lower body. Furthermore, she experiences shortness of breath:

> After this the other party of my body began to dyen so ferforth that onethys I had ony feleing, with shortness of onde. (3/3:43-4:2)

Notice that it is only her upper body that seems to revive:

> sodenly all my peyne was taken fro me and I was as hele, and namely in the other party of my body, as ever I was aforn. (3/4:3-5)

She then states that this ease was not such that she felt she might live. Note how she represents dying in the last line here:

[17] *Ibid.*, p.96, n.25.
[18] For a stimulating and convincing historical argument that Julian may well have been a young widow see Sr Benedicta SLG, 'Julian the Solitary' in *Julian Reconsidered*, Oxford, 1988.

> And yet by the feleing of this ease I trusted never the more to levyn; ne the feleing
> of this ease was no full ease to me, for methought I had lever a be deliveryd of this
> world. (3/4:6-9)

In ch.60 Julian states that Christ's pains on the cross were the pains of childbirth.
With this in mind one might tentatively argue that 'than came suddenly to my
minde . . . that my body might be fullfilled with minde and felyng of his blissid
passion' (3/4:9-12) resonates 'may my body be fulfilled by the experience of
childbirth'. Even the base sense itself contains the pregnancy image of her body
being *filled full* of the Passion. Christ's bleeding head then appears; a parallel
with that of a child from the womb is striking, as is Julian's response:

> And in the same sheweing sodenly the Trinite fullfilled the herte most of ioy. (4/
> 4:28-29)

When aware of the possible birthing subtext one cannot help but think of the
pain-joy switch at childbirth.

Two further occasions from which this argument might be substantiated both
suggest Julian in the place of the Virgin Mary.[19] The first is her statement that
she 'conceived treuly and mightily that it was himselfe shewed it me without ony
mene.'[20] 'Without ony mene' – a conception without intermediary – strongly
resonates the Virginal Conception. The second point is that when the chapter
ends with a vision of Mary declaring 'Lo me Gods handmayd', Mary's
receptivity images, or even grounds Julian's receptivity to the visions. The
ramifications of this substitutionary role-play are striking in their signification.
See how the following chapter opens:

> In this same time our lord shewed to me a ghostly sight of his homely loveing. I
> saw that he is to us everything that is good and comeofortable for us. He is our
> clotheing that for love wrappith us, halseth us and all beclosyth us for tender love,
> that hee may never leave us, being to us althing that is gode, as to myne
> understondyng. (5/5:20-25)

What is in fact happening is that Julian is presenting a surface narrative of the
Passion whilst simultaneously signifying the Incarnation. With her typical
integration we become the infant Jesus wrapped in swaddling bands, our

---

[19] I am indebted to Dr Vincent Gillespie for these two starting points.
[20] In *Scale* 1,91 Hilton, following Galatians 4:19, uses this image of mutual pregnancy
    and uses the paradigm along with Julian of our 'conceiving' Christ:
    > 'My dere childre, whilk I bere as a woman berez a barn vntil Crist be aȝeyn
    > schapen in ȝow.' þou has conceyued Crist by trouth, and he has life in þe in als
    > mykel as þou has a gode will and a desire forto serue hym and plese hym, bot he
    > is noȝt ȝit full schapen in þe, ne þou in hym by fulhede of charite; and þerfore
    > Seint Paule bare þe and me and oþere also with trauaile, as a woman berez a
    > childe, vnto þe tyme þat Crist haue his full scappe in vs and we in
    > hym. (I.91,p.360[b])
    Although it is a borrowed image, it is noteworthy that following the pregnancy image
    the diachronic is subverted in a way very reminiscent of Julian.

receiving of his love is as that of a mother to her child (ch.60). *Jesus is as Mary to us*. We enter his side and dwell in him (ch.24) and he gives birth to us on the cross feeding us with his blood (ch.60).

This connoted sequence is harmonized with the denoted image of the Passion. Between the two resonate various 'meneings'. Primarily, that in Christ's death one is born. The, for Julian, *natural* fusion of humanity with Christ serves to present the closeness of God. In Christ's enfleshment God showed his nearness, God became 'homely'. The clothing metaphor returns later when Julian speaks of Christ wearing 'Adam's tunic' – 'clothing' that becomes 'fairer and richer than was than the clothyng which I saw on the Fadir . . . for it is al of very worshipps' (51/60:36–39).

This identity between Christ and one's humanness extends to a point where the language used by Julian resonates traditional incarnational language:

> til I am substantially onyd to him, I may never have full rest ne very blisse; that is to sey, that I be so festined to him that there is right nowte that is made betwix my God and me. (5/5:16–19)

One's end is, then, a unity of substance. Not that one *becomes* God, but one's *fallen* createdness is no longer a barrier and one becomes free to live in God. There is still distinction between humanness and Godhood, a distinction made by our dependence on God; he is our 'grounde' and our 'beyng' (ch.41). By taking flesh the Word dwelt among us, by our losing ours we are 'substantially onyd' to God. The centre point in all this is the fallen created. Julian's first vision is of Christ suffering. Yet specifically from the blood of the crown of thorns she sees that Christ was God and man:

> In this sodenly I saw the rede blode treklyn downe fro under the garlande, hote and freisly and ryth plenteously, as it were in the time of his passion that the garlande of thornys was pressid on his blissid hede, ryte so both God and man, the same that sufferd thus for me. 4/4:23–27)

God suffered for humanity as a human, in the limitation of God she sees God. This limitation or emptying becomes the process by which we are 'onyd' to God. The pattern of kenosis in *our* dwelling *with God* is strikingly connoted:

> . . . and this is the cause why that no soule is restid till it is nowted of all things that is made. Whan he is willfully nowtid, for love to have him that is all, then is he abyl to receive ghostly rest. (5/6:3–6)

As Julian's openness to the revelation correlates to Mary's receptivity in that one sequence is located within the other, Julian's revelation is presented in the same form as the language used of the Trinity; sequences in which a mid-part (the Son) corresponds to pain:

> And he hath made us only to himselfe and restorid us be his blissid passion and kepith us in his blissid love. (5/6:17–19)

God is the maker who restores us through suffering and death and sustains us through love. Now note the structure in which she describes her vision:

> This shewing was quick and lively, and hidouse and dredfull, swete and lovely.   (7/8:27–28)

This reciprocity is also found in Julian's forming a matrix within which exists a fusion of a dynamic of wills:

> for our kindly will is to have God and the gode will of God is to have us.   (6/7:31–33)

This seemingly straightforward statement needs a little unpacking. What is interesting here is that Julian refers to our having a 'kindly will' and God a 'gode will'. Later Julian discusses the source of our 'kind' and what it is. Our nature is God, 'kind is God' (67/77:16), and sin is unnatural because not of God:

> . . . for as sothly as synne is onclene, as sothly is it onkinde.   (67/77:22–23)

Here therefore Julian presents our will as being of God's nature. Yet the second half of the statement maintains a similar fusion, the 'gode will' of God preludes the 'godly wille' within us later discussed (ch.37). Indeed, the short text of Julian's revelations carries the reading 'goodly wille'.[21] Either way the relationship is clear; there is a reciprocity of will.

Much of what has been discussed so far should not be surprizing when one takes account of the three 'gifts' desired of God by Julian:

> the first was mende of his passion, the ii was bodily sekenesse in youth at xxx yeers of age, the iii was to have of Gods gift iii wounds.   (2/2:19–21)

Julian wishes to know the pains Christ suffered:

> I desired a bodily sight wherein I might have more knowledge of the bodily peynes of our saviour.   (2/2:25–26)

The sequence of time before Julian's revelations is telling. She details that she 'langorid forth ii days and ii nights' (3/3:14) and on the third day her visions began. The descent into hell is even resonated around the crucifix on which she has fixed her eyes:

> All that was beside the cross was uggely to me as if it had be mekil occupyed with the fends.   (3/3:42–43)

It is thus tempting to see what was happening physically to Julian as corresponding to details of the Passion; the darkening of her room, for example, as a correlate of Mark 15:33 and parallels. What can be said is that such occurances, whether natural symptoms of her illness or not, create a background or foundation in which the sequence of the Passion interplays. The Passion does not become a momentous act retrospectively responded to, but exists as a dynamic. It involves a synchronicity that demands the response of encounter, its nearness spills into the visionary becoming the *first order sense experience* of the

---

[21] See *Julian of Norwich's Revelation of Divine Love*, ed. F. Beer, Heidelberg, 1978, C.XVII, p.65, l.14. See further Wolfgang Riehle, *The Middle English Mystics*, London, 1981, p.158.

visionary rather than that seen. What is signified therefore is the Incarnation. In Julian's bodily response is found Christ's agony. This divine action finds location in our physical humanness. That it is *our* humanness emphasizes God's identity with us in Christ and thus our own reintegration; to use Julian's language, our sensuality is brought back for our substance. In this, though using different terminology, Julian's visionary process is the inverse of Hilton's contemplative movement from the flesh.

The layers of signification in the matrix within which Julian presents her vision are complex. They involve a cyclical interaction subverting the linear and diachronic. In the Passion we encounter a birthing sequence that connotes Christ, Mary, and Julian giving birth. Julian's body acts as signifier. Our being wrapped in clothes creates a dynamic that shifts from ourselves to the Nativity and thus back through the 'medium' of the Incarnation; God coming to us as *ourselves*. As we have seen, this interactive movement is presented syntactically, the Trinitarian sequence and patterns of kenosis being present within her language when applied to herself or humans generally. Finally, Julian's physical situation resonates that of the Passion, Christ's action becoming her experience. Sequentially hers is a theology of interaction: she desires experience of the Passion, she becomes ill, in the animated crucifix Christ as Trinity appears, there is a discourse of pain and exultation between Christ and herself; divine action and will being transposed from Christ to her.[22] Where in Hilton the signs of 'siʒt' and 'Ihesu' are emptied of physicality, Julian's expand in celebration of the Incarnation and Passion, of birth in death, of our organic humanness in Christ.[23]

[22] Julian's identity of will has caused critical responses (see *Revelations of Divine Love*, trans. Clifton Wolters, Harmondsworth, 1966, p.37f.), yet I think it fair to argue on the basis of the analysis of the first revelation such fusion finds location at a greater depth than her 'surface' theology.

[23] I am most grateful to Dr Vincent Gillespie, Pamela Hill, Dr Trevor Park and Professor Rowan Williams for their helpful critical comments on an earlier draft of this paper.

TRANSFORMATIONAL PROCESSES IN THE WORK OF JULIAN OF NORWICH AND MECHTHILD OF MAGDEBURG

OLIVER DAVIES

THERE ARE A NUMBER OF REASONS why the principle of transformation is of critical importance to our understanding of the writings of Mechthild of Magdeburg (c.1208–1282/97) and Julian of Norwich (c.1343–post 1416).[1] First and foremost, the origin of their writings lies in an *excessus*,[2] which is to say a transformational state located between ordinary and extraordinary perception. Secondly, the impact upon their respective persons and lives of this experience was itself transformational in so far as it led to a changed sensibility and a new condition of being. Thirdly, both women chose to articulate their experience in the form of the written word for didactic reasons. In so doing they implicitly had recourse to the resources of language in order to effect a conditioned transformation within their readers, one moreover which accords with their own changed state of being. The principle of transformation emerges therefore as a key element surrounding the texts, their genesis, their private reception in the context of the mystics' individual lives, and their public reception by a wider audience.

The genesis of Julian *Showings* in vision is more easily established than is the case with Mechthild. She herself tells us of the occurrence of the visions in the early morning when she lay seriously ill.[3] The timing of the visions is therefore itself liminal: night is passing into day and Julian is herself poised between life and death. But the visions also represent a transformational stage, for they represent an *excessus*, that is a dislocation between the site of Julian's physical being and that of her cognitive awareness.[4] She 'sees' things which for others are

---

[1] For the theme of mystical transformation in the context of modern scientific and psychological theory, see John. E. Collins, *Mysticism and New Paradigm Psychology*, Maryland, 1991.

[2] In Classical Latin this term has the meaning of 'departure' or 'death'; only in Christian literature does it take on the sense of the *excessus mentis*, which closely approximates to that of ecstasy. See Peter Dinzelbacher, *Vision und Visionsliteratur im Mittelalter*, Stuttgart, 1981, p.47.

[3] C.3, pp.289–93. All references to the *Showings* are to the edition by E. Colledge and J. Walsh, Toronto, 1978, unless otherwise stated.

[4] According to Peter Dinzelbacher's definition, visions involve 'translocation', the working of a 'suprahuman power', 'ecstasy' (in the sense of the soul's departure from the body), and 'revelation', and they must lend themselves to visual description. *Op. cit.*, p.29.

not there. In so far therefore as her writings either seek to record the visions or are a studied reflection upon them, it is fair to say that their origin lies in the visionary state itself. But it is not the case that Julian believes her own words to be divinely inspired, even if she occasionally repeats, in the form of direct speech, the utterances of her visionary Christ.

In the case of Mechthild, however, we cannot trace the origin of her book back to a point of vision, although there are evidently passages in her work, *The Flowing Light of the Godhead*, which narrate visionary experience.[5] And yet the origin of her work can also clearly be shown to lie in an *excessus*, if we understand this term to straddle both vision and ecstasy, for Mechthild speaks repeatedly of the divine origin of her inspiration. In the opening chapter we find a dialogue between the soul and God in which God claims authorship of the book: ' "Lord God, who made this book?" "I made it through my own helplessness, for I was not able to refrain from bestowing my gift" '[6]. In two other passages however Mechthild denotes the divine authorship of the book by introducing the notion that it specifically 'flowed' from God. In one passage from Book Two God tells Mechthild that 'the words flow from one hour to the next into your soul from my divine mouth',[7] and in another the soul declares:

> Lord, then I wait with hunger and thirst, with seeking and desire, until the playful hour comes when from your divine mouth the chosen words flow forth, which no one can hear but the soul alone which sheds the earth and places its ear to your mouth. Yes, she understands love's font.[8]

The use here of the term 'flowing' with respect to the book's genesis, is not without significance for it is this same term which Mechthild uses in various contexts to denote either the *perichoresis* of inner-Trinitarian life, grace and the gifts of God, or the processes of the Creation itself. Although these associations will require further and more exact scrutiny, their existence confirms that

---

[5] E.g. Book II, ch.20, 1.21 and III, ch.21. All references to Mechthild's work are to *Mechthild von Magdeburg 'Das fliessende Licht der Gottheit'*, ed. Hans Neumann, Munich, 1990. Such passages contain a form of the verb 'to see', although Mechthild nowhere shows the intense interest in the unfolding of vision which we find in Julian. Certain of the visionary passages are extended however and full of detail. The Romanesque description of hell in III, 21, is powerfully reminiscent of Hildegard's figural representation of human vices in her *Liber vitae meritorum*, as it is of Dante's *Inferno*. It seems likely on balance that Mechthild had some acquaintance with Hildegard's work. See my comments on this in 'Hildegard of Bingen, Mechthild of Magdeburg and the young Meister Eckhart' in *Mediävistik* IV, (1991) (forthcoming).

[6] '*Eya herre got, wer hat dis bůch gemachet?*' '*Ich han es gemachet an miner unmaht, wan ich mich an miner gabe nút enthalten mag.*' (I, prol., 1.8-9).

[7] *du vliessent von stunde ze stunde in dine sele us von minem goetlichen munde* (II, ch.26, ll.13-14).

[8] *Herre, so beite ich denne mit hunger und mit durste,/ mit jagen und mit luste/ unz an die spilenden stunde,/ das us dinem goetlichen munde/ vliessen die erwelten wort,/ die von nieman sint gehort/ mer von der sele alleine,/ die sich von der erden enkleidet/ und leit ir ore fúr dinen munt./ Ja die begriffet der minne funt!* (II, 6, 12-21).

Mechthild understands her book to participate in the self-communication of God which underlies the scholastic theory of grace and of the Creation.[9]

This therefore is an important distinction between Julian and Mechthild's work. For the former, it is the series of visions which constitute the divine revelations she has received, and her book is an attempt on the one hand to describe the visions for others and, on the other, to reflect in depth upon their meaning. For the latter however the book itself constitutes a self-communication of God, and it is itself visionary in so far as it is a creative out-flowing from the heart of the Godhead.[10]

But if what constitutes revelation in Julian and Mechthild's work can be said to differ, the two women are united in the common experience of change and transformation within themselves which the divine intervention brings about. This, again, can be more clearly shown in Julian since, quite apart from other considerations, we possess from her hand two texts which date from different periods in her life. Julian is likely to have written the Short Text shortly after receiving the visions in 1373, and the second text, which she says was written 'fifteen years or more' after the first,[11] is included within the Long Text, which was completed only in 1393. Some of the differences between the Short and the Long version seem to have little significance, such as the dislocations in chapters 4, 8, 9, 20, 40, 47 and 64,[12] but Simon Tugwell has correctly identified a decided shift in sensibility between the two versions which can be summed up as the evolution from a neoplatonic spirituality of ascent to an incarnational spirituality whereby 'redemption is a redemption *of* this life, not a redemption *from* it'.[13] This change can be generally felt throughout the Long Text, but is well exemplified by the passage on other-worldly contemplatives from chapter four of the Short Text which the Long Text omits and the addition in the Long Text of the passage which concerns God's agency in lowly bodily functions, to which Tugwell refers.[14] The many extended meditations of the Long Text, such as the master and servant theme, the meditation on the threefold motherhood of Christ, the reflections on freedom and redemption and the passages on prayer, show greater assuredness, doctrinal perception and subtlety on Julian's part and testify to the process of intellectual and spiritual maturation which she underwent in the period between the completion of the two texts.

---

[9] See also J. C. Franklin, *Mystical Transformations: the Imagery of Liquids in the Work of Mechthild of Magdeburg*, New Jersey, 1978, for comment on the 'flowing' imagery in Mechthild in the light of alchemical transformations.

[10] Nigel Palmer has shown the way in which the Latin prologue to Mechthild's text employs formulae borrowed from contemporary prologues to works of biblical exegesis in order to stress its divine provenance. See his 'Das Buch als Bedeutungsträger bei Mechthild von Magdeburg' in *Festschrift for Friedrich Ohly*, ed. K. Speckenbach and W. Harms, forthcoming.

[11] ch.86, p.732, l.14.

[12] Here I am following Colledge and Walsh, pp.21–3.

[13] Simon Tugwell, *Ways of Imperfection*, London, 1984, p.201.

[14] Short Text, ch.iv, p.215, ll.42–6 and Long Text, c.6, p.306, l.35–p.307, l.41.

This process of personal transformation can be shown to derive from the very nature of the visions themselves. They are, first and foremost, didactic visions which exemplify Christian truth.[15] Julian herself is in no doubt about this fact and, at the end of the ninth chapter, she describes the threefold character of the revelatory or didactic quality of her visions:

> All this was shewde by thre partes, that is to sey by bodyly syght, and by worde formyde in my vnderstondyng, and by goostely syght.[16]

The bodily sight here refers to the visionary data which take the place of Julian's normal visual perception, the words formed in her understanding signify the soundless voice which acts in her 'reason', thus aiding her judgement and her understanding, and the ghostly sight is spiritual insight, which differs from the second in that it is not communicated verbally but rather takes the form of directed spiritual understanding.[17] To these, of course, we should add those occasions when Julian speaks for herself and employs her natural reason. Julian's own triadic scheme then maps out the distinct layers of her growth in understanding, the first of which is constituted by a divinely inspired physical vision of variations upon the Passion of Christ, while the second and third are no less divinely inspired elucidations upon the meaning of what she sees.

The dynamic character of Julian's visions are best exemplified by those occasions when the visionary Christ actually enters into conversation with Julian or himself directs her attention in order that she should better understand. A classic instance of both occurs in chapter twenty-four of the Long Text:

> Wyth a good chere oure good lorde lokyd in to hys syde and behelde with joy, and with hys swete lokyng he led forth the vnderstandyng of hys creature by the same wound in to hys syde with in; and ther he shewyd a feyer and delectable place, and large jnow for alle mankynde that shalle be savyd and rest in pees and in loue. And ther with he brought to mynde hys dere worthy blode and hys precious water whych he lett poure out for loue. And with the swete beholdying he shewyd hys blessyd hart clovyn on two, and with hys enjoyeng he shewyd to my vnderstandyng in part the blyssydfulle godhede as farforth as he wolde that tyme, strengthyng the pour soule for to vnderstande as it may be sayde, that is to mene the endlesse loue that was without begynnyng and is and shal be evyr.
> And with this oure good lorde seyde well blessydfully: Lo how I loue the . . .[18]

---

[15] In the continental traditions the didactic vision is more generally associated with a period earlier than the fourteenth century when, under the influence of the vernacular translations of the *Song of Songs* and the Courtly Love lyric, the unitive type is more prevalent. See for instance Margot Schmidt's important article 'Hildegard von Bingen als Lehrerin des Glaubens', *Hildegard von Bingen, 1179–1979, Festschrift zum 800sten Todestag der Heiligen*, ed. A. Brück, Mainz, 1979, pp.95–158.

[16] ch.9, p.323, ll.29–30.

[17] There is one instance in which Julian receives a pictorial image of Mary as a result of ghostly sight, but this need not be thought of as an image which replaces the bodily sight but rather as a process of recollection. See c.7, pp.310–11.

[18] c.24, pp.394–5, ll.1–16.

The fact that this intervention for the sake of explanation proceeds from the primary visionary level, which is to say that of 'bodily sight', reinforces the view that Julian's visions are noetic at their very source. Far from being static statements of truth, they are an exercise in the communication of truth which assumes Julian's own participant subjectivity. They are visions of a truth which explicates itself, which by its nature communicates itself to the observer who is thus caught up in the very processes of truth's self-communication. Transformation therefore is at the core of Julian's visionary experience, for this experience necessitates of itself her passsage into deeper understanding.

There is a further point that needs to be made about the structure of this transformation however, which is that the knowledge for which Julian strives is fundamentally a liberating knowledge. In the fifth chapter of the Long Text, after being shown the hazel nut, she writes:

> In this littil thing I saw iii properties: the first is that God made it, the second is that God loveth it, the iiid, that God kepith it. But what is to me sothly the maker, the keper, and the lover I canot tell; for, till I am substantially onyd to him, I may never have full rest ne very blisse; that is to sey, that I be so festined to him that there is right nowte that is made betwix my God and me. It needyth us to have knoweing of the littlehede of creatures and to nowtyn all thing that is made for to love and have God that is unmade.[19]

A growth in knowledge, or understanding, here is simultaneously growth towards God, for it is this which removes the obstacles of creatureliness. Indeed, it is this experience of knowledge as sanctification that places it on an eschatological plane. Julian is intensely aware that her questions will not be adequately answered until she is in Heaven and that the struggle in this life is precisely an orientation to an ultimate and eschatological fulfilment.[20] It is the case also, of course, that Julian initially desired the visions in order to 'haue the more trew mynd in the passion of Christ',[21] to 'be purgied' by sickness[22] and to have the three wounds of 'verie contricion', 'kynd compassion' and 'willfull longing to god',[23] all of which point to an increase in holiness of life through personal participation in the redemptive suffering of Christ.[24]

Within the context of medieval women's religious experience, Julian's emphatically noetic spirituality might seem a little extraordinary. Although capable of criticism of the church of her day, she does not have the prophetic

---

[19] *Julian of Norwich: a Revelation of Love*, ed. Marion Glasscoe, rev. ed. Exeter, 1986, ch.5, p.5, ll.14–22. The Sloane MS reading seems preferable here to that of P, which is something of a non sequitur (cf. Colledge and Walsh, ch.5, p. 300, ll.18–19).

[20] E.g. ch.6, p.309, ll.59–61.

[21] ch.2, p.286, ll.19–20.

[22] ch. 2, p.287, ll.29.

[23] ch.2, p.288, ll.42–43.

[24] See the discussion of this theme in Julian against the background of her age by Domenico Pezzini in his article 'The Theme of the Passion in Richard Rolle and Julian of Norwich' in *Religion in the Poetry and Drama of the Late Middle Ages in England*, ed. Piero Boitani and Anna Torti, Cambridge, 1990, pp.29–66.

aspect of Hildegard and, despite her talk of love, she is far from the Bernardine grades of love we find in Beatrice of Nazareth or the intense *Brautmystik* of the Beguine writers. But she does nevertheless stand squarely within a Christian spiritual tradition, which is that of the *lectio divina*.

The extent to which Julian belongs to this exegetical tradition can be seen from the preponderance in her work of words which express *interpretation*.[25] Phrases such as 'I conceived', 'I vnderstode', 'wonder', 'marvayle', 'thus I toke it', 'me thought', 'as to my vnderstanding'[26] sound throughout Julian's writings and express her ever present desire to understand her 'lesson of loue' aright.[27] Most importantly, this lesson is mediated to her chiefly in two ways, that is in 'bodily sight' and in 'ghostly sight', both of which are divinely inspired and represent the self-communication of God's truth. These two phrases parallel the two most fundamental terms of medieval scriptural exegesis, which is to say the 'literal meaning' (sometimes known as the *sensus corporalis*) and the 'figurative meaning' (often known as the *sensus spiritualis*). Despite the frequent subdivision of the latter into further categories (e.g. allegorical, moral and anagogical meanings), this dual system which is in particular linked with the name of St Augustine set the parameters for understanding Scripture throughout the Middle Ages.[28] The medieval exegete would firstly attempt to understand God's word *proprie*, that is according to the literal meaning of the words, and then *analogiter*, which means in terms of its figurative and spiritual meanings, which are mediated to his mind by the light of the Holy Spirit. The Holy Spirit is thus often thought of as being the author of both the word of Scripture and its rightful understanding.[29]

---

[25] Julian's proximity to the *lectio divina* is noted in Colledge and Walsh, p.132. Vincent Gillespie has also drawn attention to the emergence of the crucified body of Christ as *text* in late medieval English piety, which constitutes a movement away from the *lectio divina* of tradition to a *lectio domini* in which imagery replaces literary text. See his fascinating 'Strange Images of Death: the Passion in Later Medieval English Devotional and Mystical Writing' in *Zeit, Tod und Ewigkeit in der Renaissance Literatur*, ed. James Hogg, Salzburg, 1987, pp.111–59. While standing within this tradition, it seems that Julian's engagement with her 'text' goes beyond the contours of a devotional one and becomes positively exegetical. See also Gillespie's remarks on the role of devotional artifacts as a stimulus to meditation on the Passion (pp.113–14) and Dinzelbacher's description of a Silesian *crucifixus dolorosus* which closely conforms to Julian's vision (*op. cit.*, p.264). Expressive crucifixes of this type are also particularly characteristic of the fourteenth-century Tirol.

[26] E.g. ch.4 & ch.5, pp.294–299.

[27] ch.6, p.309, l.62.

[28] At the height of the scholastic period, Bonaventure uses this same twofold system in his *Breviloquium*, Prologue, 6, 3 (*Obras de San Buenaventura*, Vol. 1, Biblioteca de Autores Cristianos, Madrid, 1945, p.192), as does Meister Eckhart in the first part of the fourteenth century (see my *Meister Eckhart: Mystical Theologian*, London, 1991, Appendix 2).

[29] This idea, and that of the body/spirit distinction, are traceable to the influence of Origen who conceived of Scripture as being a second form of divine Incarnation.

This spiritual dimension is no adjunct to the medieval process of exegesis but is rather its essence and its goal,[30] and it is the spirituality of exegesis which led to the centrality of *lectio divina* as a devotional practice in the monasteries and cloisters of medieval Europe. Furthermore, the experiential dimension of this practice is often described in terms of *contemplatio*.[31] According to Thomas Aquinas' classic definition, the latter possesses three constituent elements, namely 'lectio, meditatio et oratio'.[32] While the middle element represents the necessary personal effort, the first and the third provide for the influx of wisdom required for the perception of that divine truth (or indeed God himself) which is the sublime object of contemplative knowing. Indeed, it is this infused element, deriving on the one hand from Scripture and on the other from prayer, which sets the medieval concept of contemplation apart from other forms of knowing. According to Richard of St Victor, if 'the work of meditation is to seek out hidden things' then that of contemplation is 'to wonder at clear truths'.[33] For Hugh of St Victor, meditation is 'a certain inquisitive power of the soul, that shrewdly tries to find out things that are obscure and to disentangle those that are involved', whereas contemplation is 'the alertness of the understanding which, finding everything plain, grasps it clearly with entire comprehension'.[34] Again according to Hugh, contemplation is that which frees us from the shackles of the world and allows us to understand that all is vanity.[35] Contemplation also differs from other forms of cognition in that it is affective and mediates a sense of 'sweetness' or 'delight' to the soul, leading even to an ecstasy of love.[36]

Julian quite clearly lays aside a narrow and elitest view of contemplation when she omits in the Long Text her brusque opposition between that man or woman

According to the Alexandrian, Scripture could only be understood correctly if the mind of the exegete was itself united with its divine author. See in particular his prologue to the Song of Songs. For the predominance of these ideas in the middle ages, see Beryl Smalley, *The Study of the Bible in the Middle Ages*, Oxford, 1983 (3rd ed.), pp.1 f. and 12.

30 See Beryl Smalley, *op. cit.*, viii.

31 Under the influence of Spanish and French spirituality of the sixteenth and seventeenth centuries, 'contemplation' has tended increasingly to take on the meaning of an interior state of imageless union with God. This masks its original patristic and medieval usage which, though not exclusively so, generally linked *contemplatio* with *lectio divina*.

32 *Summa Theologica* 2-2 q. 180 3 ad 4.

33 Richard of St Victor, *De exterminatione mali* II, xv (Migne, Patrologia Latina (PL), 196, col. 1102).

34 *In Salomaris Ecclesiasten*, Homilia Prima, PL, 175, col. 117.

35 This is the thrust of Hugh's discussion of contemplation in his unfinished commentary on Ecclesiastes: PL 175, cols. 116–18. Hugh is saying something very similar to Julian here in that the understanding which comes from contemplation liberates the soul from the world.

36 This is very much the Victorine position which Hugh of St Victor presents, for instance, in PL 175, col. 118 and which appears in Thomas Aquinas (cf. *Summa Theologica* 2-2, q.180 7 ad 1).

who 'desyres to lyeve contemplatyfelye' and those who 'er occupyede wylfullye in erthelye besynes'.[37] And she insistently repeats in the Long Text that she is writing for her fellow-Christians, which contrasts starkly with the celebration of an elitest contemplative vocation such as we find, for instance, in the author of the *Cloud*. But Julian remains nevertheless a thoroughly contemplative writer, in the sense which this term possesses in the medieval tradition of *lectio divina*. Even the fact that her attempt to understand the mysteries she is shown culminates in the perception that 'love is his meaning', sits well with Augustine's principle that all exegesis should serve to 'establish the reign of charity'.[38] The fact that her 'text' is not Scripture but is vision, should not mislead us into failing to see the textual character of her spirituality. Indeed, in view of the fact that Julian was denied access to the formal study of Scripture in the schools by virtue of her gender, it is perhaps possible to see her visions and her work as forms of textuality gathered around a point of absence.[39] In the context of medieval devotional exegesis, the successive layers of interpreted and self-interpreting meaning which constitute Julian's 'revelation' cannot but seem to take place within a space in which the Word of God is everywhere present by virtue of its absence.

2

Unlike Julian, who received her 'revelation' on one occasion and meditated upon it for the rest of her life, Mechthild received her 'visionary' inspiration over a considerable number of years. But in a way that parallels Julian, there is evidence of a deepening in the incarnational dimension of her spirituality. Although Mechthild is never harsh in her attitude to the body (even if she can call it the 'enemy') and is strongly opposed to extreme forms of asceticism,[40] virtually the whole of the *Flowing Light* is permeated with a sense that it is the body which prevents the ultimate union of her soul with God. And yet, particularly in the final book of the *Flowing Light*, which was written towards the end of her life, we find a noticeable softening in her attitude to her own physicality. There she speaks repeatedly of the place of the five senses in her

---

[37] Short Text, ch.4, p.215, ll.42,44–5.

[38] *De Doctrina Christiana*, III, ch.15 (PL 34, col. 74).

[39] It is also by no means clear that her protestation that she is 'vnlettyrde' (ch.2, p.285, 1.2) is a wholly strategic one. Julian may well have lacked an adequate knowledge of Latin for exegetical purposes. Compare Hildegard who, though she writes in Latin, states that she lacks the formal knowledge of grammar necessary for textual analysis (*Letter to Bernard of Clairvaux*, PL, 197, col. 190).

[40] IV, ch.2, 1.106; ch.V, 1.5. Hans Urs von Balthasar writes interestingly on this, and other aspects of Mechthild's spirituality, in his important introduction to Margot Schmidt's modern German translation of the *Flowing Light*. See M. Schmidt, *Mechthild von Magdeburg. Das fliessende Licht der Gottheit*, Einsiedeln, 1955, pp.19–47.

dialogue with God, and recognizes that they are the site of eschatological decision. She writes a dialogue set on the Day of Judgement in which the soul gladly and gently reassumes its body and she praises the body's worth since Christ himself took on human flesh.[41]

Mechthild's 'visions' began, she tells us, in her twelfth year and continued for thirty-one years.[42] They were also unexpected, to the extent that she had not prayed for them.[43] Prior to this experience, Mechthild tells us, she was the 'most naive of people there had ever been in the religious life'. She knew 'nothing of the Devil's malice' or of the 'wretchedness of the world' and 'the falsity of religious people' was 'alien' to her.[44] The reference to her discovery of 'the Devil's malice' and to the 'falsity of religious people' can be taken in two ways, and both have considerable significance with respect to the transformational aspect of Mechthild's experience. The first is that Mechthild, like Julian and many other of the women mystics of this period, believed herself to be called, through her visions, to exercise a healthy *Kirchenkritik* and thus precisely to expose abuses in the Church.[45] Alternatively or additionally, Mechthild may also be referring here to the assaults which she endured as a result of having written her book.[46] This latter point is reinforced by her confession that, although she did not pray for the visions, she had long since prayed that she might suffer 'without guilt'.[47] This same theme reoccurs later in a passage in which Mechthild states that God gave her the book in three ways, firstly in 'tenderness', then with 'great intimacy' and finally 'with grievous pain'. She says that she wishes to remain in the third more than in the two, and accepts the suffering which befalls her on account of the book as being an inevitable part of her high calling. She speaks of the pain that Christ himself had to endure and concludes: 'it is the nature of love firstly to flow in sweetness, then to become rich in knowledge and thirdly to become desirous and hungry for disdain'.[48] And it is precisely this

---

[41] E.g. VII, ch.52; VII, ch.46, ll.16–18; VI, ch.35; VI, ch.31, ll.16–17.

[42] See IV, ch.2, ll.11–13. Since Mechthild continued to write until well into her seventies, it is reasonable to suppose that the age she is referring to here (forty-three years) is the point at which she began to write the fourth of her seven-volume work.

[43] IV, ch.2, ll.15–17, although she does state in this same passage that she 'had long desired to suffer innocently'. It is clear from passages such as II, ch.26 that Mechthild's book did indeed attract some criticism.

[44] IV, ch.2, ll.5–7.

[45] E.g. V, ch.14 where she graphically describes, in a manner strongly reminiscent of Dante, the horrors which await wicked priests in Purgatory.

[46] Some of Mechthild's problems seem to have come from her vision of John the Baptist (a layman) officiating at the Eucharist (II, ch.4). Caroline Walker Bynum discusses Mechthild's troubles against the background of the Helfta writers as a whole. See her *Jesus as Mother*, California, 1982, pp.237–242.

[47] *Do hatte ich lange vor gegert, das ich ane mine schulde wúrde versmahet* (IV, ch.2, ll.19–20).

[48] *Aber der minne nature ist, das si allererst vlússet von suessekeit, dar nach wirt si riche in der bekantnisse, zem dritten male wirt si girig in der verworfenheit* (VI, ch.20, ll.11–13).

'innocent suffering' which unites us with the suffering of the Saviour.[49]

If Mechthild is willing to embrace the purgative suffering which comes as a result of her work, seeing in it an unavoidable part of love's nature and thus of her own calling, then it is significant also that she can speak of her work as love or in terms of love. In Book Four she tells us that it was given to her by God 'lovingly' and thus was not the product of any human thinking.[50] She tells us too that the source of her work is 'violent love' which bestows these 'wonders' upon her so that she 'dare not be silent',[51] and at the end of the same Book, she tells us that her work 'was begun in love and in love it shall end, for there is nothing as wise, holy, beautiful, strong or perfect as love'.[52] But there are other passages which invite us to think that Mechthild's book not only has its source in love but is even itself *constituted by love*. Something of this is conveyed in the striking line in which God asserts that his 'heart's blood', which shall 'flow again' at the end of time, 'is written in this book'.[53] It is the very image of 'flowing' and 'flood' however which above all sustains the parallel between the love which flows from God and Mechthild's own 'Flowing Light of the Godhead'. We have already noted the two occasions in Book Two when Mechthild speaks of the origin of her book, describing how it 'flowed' from God to herself, and she uses this same term when, in the autobiographical passage from the beginning of Book Four, she describes how she first felt the inspiration for the book in her twelfth year: 'I, unworthy sinner, was so flowingly greeted by the Holy Spirit'.[54] But 'flowing' and 'flood' are terms which Mechthild also specifically uses for God's self-communication which is the outflow of love. In Book Five she speaks of the 'flood' of love and of the 'flowing fire of God's love', while, in Book Seven, she writes of the 'great overflow of God's love, which never stands still and always flows effortlessly and without ceasing in so sweet a flood so that our small vessel is filled and brims over . . .'.[55] In Book Seven, the 'playful flood of love flows into the soul'[56] and, in Book Three, the 'hot fire of the Godhead' is juxtaposed with the 'flowing wax of the loving soul'.[57] This latter line parallels those passages in which the image of 'flowing' expresses the return of the soul into God, as in Book Five where God's love causes Mechthild's soul 'to flow'

---

[49] E.g. V, ch.3. For a study of the theme of the *compassio* in Mechthild, see Elisabeth Schwarz-Mehrens, *Zum Funktionieren und zur Funktion der Compassio im 'Fliessenden Licht der Gottheit' Mechthilds von Magdeburg*, Göppingen, 1985.

[50] IV, ch.2, ll.133–4.

[51] IV, ch.2, l.116.

[52] IV, ch.28, ll.3–5.

[53] V, ch.34, ll.43–4.

[54] The imagery of 'flowing' seems more comprehensive in Mechthild's work than that of the 'greeting' or *grus*, although the latter is also used to describe Mechthild's inspiration, the state of union with God, and is specifically linked to the inner-life of the Trinity (e.g. I, ch.2, ll.2–5; V, ch.18, l.2; VI, ch.39, ll.5–7).

[55] V, ch.31, l.6; V, ch.1, ll.30–1; VII, ch.55, ll.6–8.

[56] VII, ch.45, ll.14–15.

[57] III, ch.24, ll.10–11.

and, in Book Six, where Mary 'flows back' into God.[58] The soul is permeated with love (literally 'flowed-through'), as are the martyrs and saints, and 'all sweet and holy voices' have 'flowed forth' from God.[59] But the image of 'flowing' is used also of grace, the virtues and the 'gifts of God' as it is of the creation.[60] Creatures are said to have 'flowed forth' from God and the creation is founded upon love and is understood by Mechthild as being the expression of God's love.[61]

The bewildering fertility of Mechthild's conception of the theme of 'flowing', which we can only touch on here, finds its centre in her understanding of the Christian Trinity. It is this which is the conceptual basis which underlies the unifying image of 'flowing' and which serves to unite the disparate themes of cosmic creation, Mechthild's own literary creation, the outflow of grace and God's gifts, as well as the soul's ecstatic *redditus* to God into a single integral vision of the dynamic fecundity of the Godhead. In Book Three she describes the 'threefold, playful flood' which flows from God towards the saints in Heaven and it is the same 'playful flood' that 'flows in the Holy Trinity' which she beseeches the Son to release upon her.[62] In Book Five she speaks of the 'restless Godhead', of the Father who is an 'overflowing spring', and of the Son who is 'an ever returning treasure which no one can keep but only the mercy which always has flowed and ever shall flow from God and ever returns in His Son'.[63] In this passage in particular, Mechthild's interest in the rhythms of the inner-Trinitarian life, the *perichoresis*, becomes apparent as she dwells upon the loving communion of the Persons. The Trinitarian dimension can be seen also in the fact that she frequently links the language of flowing with the Third Person, and also uses this term in order to speak of the generation of the Son from the Father.[64]

If her book is the product of (divine) love and itself conforms to that love as an outflow from the inner life of the Godhead, then the experience of its reception is, for Mechthild, one in which the language of affective union combines with the language of knowledge:

> it is the nature of love firstly to flow in sweetness, then to become rich in knowledge and thirdly to become desirous and hungry for disdain.

The sweetness (of union) combines with knowledge (of herself and of the Church, of Heaven and Hell), and both are transmitted and contained in love. A few lines later in the same passage, and speaking of the same early period in her life, Mechthild reiterates this combination of ecstatic union and knowledge:

---

[58] V, ch.20, ll.7–8 and VI, ch.39, ll.16.
[59] *durchvlossen* V, ch.4, ll.18 and 64; III, ch.1, l.117 and ch.10, l.60; V, ch.26, l.6.
[60] V, ch.11, l.29; VI, ch.13, l.28; V, ch.22, ll.40 and 46.
[61] V, ch.35, ll.22–4 and IV, ch.21, l.16; VII, ch.25, l.3.
[62] III, ch.1, ll.108–10; IV, ch.12, ll.17–18.
[63] V, ch.26, ll.9 and 11; V, ch.26, ll.13–15.
[64] VII, ch.24; V, ch.6, l.2.

'God never left me on my own anywhere. He brought me into such blissful sweetness, such sacred knowledge and such incomprehensible wonders that I could make scant use of earthly things'.[65] But, as Mechthild knows, the price of such knowledge and the responsibilities it entails, is the suffering which comes from rejection and persecution.

In this all too brief summary of the complex unity of Mechthild's work, which is simultaneously union and calling to prophecy, *Leidensmystik* and ecstasy, illumination and creation, we can identify four levels of personal transformation. The first is that of a transformational ecstasy which is a union both of knowledge and love and which entails a process of sanctification, or infectious beauty. The sanctifying dimension of her unitive experience can be felt throughout the *Flowing Light* and is well summed up in Mechthild's memorable lines:

> Lord, love me greatly, love me often and long! For the more you love me, the purer I become, the more often you love me, the more beautiful I become and the longer you love me, the holier I become on earth.[66]

The second dimension derives from the first and can be described as a growing awareness of wrongs in the church and her own prophetic responsibility (and authority) to correct them. The third is purification through suffering, a suffering which seems itself to be the consequence of her writings. And fourthly, we find in Mechthild the same movement away from a neoplatonic dualism in the direction of an emphatically incarnational spirituality.

3

The two mystics we have considered are among the most skilled writers of their age, and both hold an honoured place in the history of their respective literatures. Their distinguished place in the history of Christian spirituality moreover is guaranteed as much by their capacity to communicate their experience through a textual medium as it is by the freshness and vitality of their vision. In so far as both women are drawn into a dynamic truth, their recourse to the objective medium of the text can be seen to be a reflex of the original ecstatic, self-communicating and transformative state. Having been touched and changed, then, in their deepest being, they give expression to this encounter through the medium of a text which itself becomes the means whereby other persons, the readers of the texts, are themselves drawn into their original experience. The self-communicating, self-propagating character of the truth

---

[65] IV, ch.2, ll.23–5.
[66] I, ch.23. The original is worth giving here: *Eya herre, minne mich sere und minne mich dike und minne mich lange! Wande ie du mich serer minnest ie ich reiner wirde, ie du mich dikker minnest ie ich schoner wirde, ie du mich langer minnest ie ich heliger wirde hie in ertrich.*

they have glimpsed engenders a transformative textuality which, being objectified, is open-ended and unlimited.[67]

When the reader enters the semiotically charged environs of Julian's text(s), he or she is invited to engage with the same primal theological problems as the mystic herself and to share in her struggle to achieve stillness by attaining understanding. Through compression and displacement, the different lines of description, interpretation and communication, Julian's exegesis is fractured and fragmented and is ultimately projected towards an eschatological fulfilment. Thus the reader is taken up into a world of shifting semiological contexts of vision, visionary communication and reflection whose ultimate ground is Julian's own consciousness as it strives for the comprehension in this life of what will be revealed fully only in the next.

But counter to this exploration of the transcendence of God there is an alternative lexical system which conveys his immanence. God thus displays 'homelynesse' and is 'curtayse' and his proximity to us is captured in the metaphor of a human mother. Indeed, in this paradoxical contiguity of a God who is both 'with us' and yet whose meaning constitutes a grammar which transcends any human decoding, we see the foundational mystery of the Christian religion whose point of departure is the crucified God. Julian's hard-won insight that 'love is his meaning' seems less a resolution of this paradox than its whole-hearted embrace.

The immanence and transcendence of God is a foundational theme in Mechthild's work too, and it is one which she chiefly explores through imagery which derives from the Courtly Love tradition.[68] From the German Minnesang Mechthild takes her emphasis upon unfulfilled longing, the absence of the lover, the messenger of love, the service of and suffering for the sake of love, the theme of the court and its music. Indeed, in one fine passage we even find a clear echo of the *alba* genre, which details the lovers' parting at dawn. The adaptation of secular eroticism for the purposes of a full-blooded *Brautmystik* aptly depicts the paradoxical relationship between the soul and her transcendental lover, who is both present to her and absent from her, who both fills her beyond her greatest expectation and leaves her empty. Mechthild is not, of course, the first Christian mystic to explore this theme in terms of a tactile love, but she is one of its

---

[67] This is not to say, of course, that the hermeneutical horizons of the modern reader are those of the contemporary one, or indeed that the modern reader, removed from the semiological contexts of Julian's world, can entirely reconstitute the experience of the audience of her own day.

[68] I, ch.44. For Mechthild's language, see Grete Lüers, *Die Sprache der deutschen Mystik des Mittelalters im Werke der Mechthild von Magdeburg*, Darmstadt, 1966 (2nd ed.), Horst Laubner, *Studien zum geistlichen Sinngehalt des Adjektivs im Werk Mechthilds von Magdeburg*, Göppingen, 1975 and, in particular, Alois Haas, 'Dichtung und Mystik' and 'Struktur der mystischen Erfahrung' in *Sermo mysticus*, Freiburg, Switzerland, 1979, pp.67–103 and 104–135. For Mechthild and the Courtly Love tradition, see Elizabeth Wainwright-deKadt, 'Courtly Literature and Mysticism: Some Aspects of their Interaction', *Acta Germanica* 12, (1980) 41–60.

greatest exponents. Above all, it is the Minnesang which allows her to develop an existential dimension to the *unio mystica* through combining with an affective union of wills the motif of a life lived out in service and self-dedication to her divine lover.

We should note moreover that it is a literary stratagem which conveys the full metaphysical dynamicism of Mechthild's work. It is through her careful use of the metaphor of 'flowing' in its diverse forms that she is able to build up the multi-dimensionality of her work as being simultaneously inspiration, union, grace, creation and an outflow from the superabundance of the Trinity.[69] Indeed, it is this same sense of flowing which is embodied in the effusive character of her style with its ecstatic dialogues and passages of rhyme as well as in her imagery of love-making, movement and dance. And it is precisely because the work is itself a literary embodiment of flowing and fusion that it receives its divinely ordained title: 'It shall be called a light of my Godhead which flows into all hearts which live without falsity'.[70] And so the transformation which began as an interior movement in the soul of the mystic is itself incarnated in literary form and becomes communicable to those of us who come after.

---

[69] This combination of divine inspiration, vatic authority and poetic sensibility suggests that Mechthild stands at the beginning of the distinguished German traditiwith the generative power of the poetic word and which include, amongst on of poet-prophets, which is to say those poets who are most concerned others, Angelus Silesius, Novalis, Friederich Hölderlin and Gottfried Benn.

[70] *Es sol heissen ein vliessende lieht miner gotheit in allú dú herzen, dú da lebent ane valscheit* (I, prol., ll.10–11).

THE APOPHATIC IMAGE: THE POETICS OF EFFACEMENT IN JULIAN OF NORWICH

VINCENT GILLESPIE AND MAGGIE ROSS

AT THE HEART OF SCRIPTURE stand two empty spaces. The Mercy Seat in the Temple at Jerusalem was a vacant space between the cherubim in the Holy of Holies. This 'great speaking absence between the images' signified both Israel's repudiation of earthly representations of the deity and the imageless space into which they sought to come by prayer and devotion.[1] In the New Testament, the empty tomb is similarly eloquent in its absence of presence. The angel's question in St Luke, 'Why seek you the living with the dead?' (24:5), signals the necessity of a passover into a new perception of the living Christ and a putting away of the old certainties. Christ's injunction to Mary Magdalene, *Noli me tangere* (John 20:17), reinforces the sense of his transfiguration beyond the realm of earthly signification.

The play of absence and presence characterizes the human experience of engagement with the ineffable.[2] The search for the Transcendental Signified which is God requires not only a struggle with the fallen will but also the necessity of wrestling with a fallen language which resolutely anchors itself in the world of signifiers. As Rowan Williams has written, 'any speech about God is a speech about an *absence*.' This absence, as Derrida has noted 'extends the domain and play of signification infinitely.'[3] The game of mystical hide and seek acted out over the centuries generates a longing for release from the play of language. In Derrida's view, this hermeneutic appetite 'seeks to decipher,

---

[1] The phrase comes from an unpublished sermon of Rowan Williams; cf. Exodus 25:17–20.

[2] Hugo Rahner, *Man at Play*, trans. B. Battershaw and E. Quinn, London, 1965; Robert Neale, *In Praise of Play: Towards a Psychology of Religion*, New York, 1969; Marion Glasscoe, 'Means of Showing: An Approach to Reading Julian of Norwich', in *Spatmittelalterliche Geistliche Literatur in der Nationalsprache*, 1, Analecta Cartusiana, 106 (1983), pp.155–77, esp. pp.159–60; Vincent Gillespie, 'Strange Images of Death: The Passion in Later Medieval English Devotional and Mystical Writing', in *Zeit, Tod und Ewigkeit in der Renaissance Literatur*, 3, Analecta Cartusiana, 117 (1987), pp.111–59, esp. pp.141–3; Rene Tixier, ' "Good gamesumli pley": le jeux de l'amour dans *The Cloud of Unknowing*', *Caliban*, 24 (1987), 5–25. An English version appears in *Downside Review*, 108 (1990), 235–53.

[3] Rowan Williams, *The Wound of Knowledge: Christian Spirituality from the New Testament to St John of the Cross*, London, 1979, p.146; Jacques Derrida, 'Structure, Sign and Play in the Discourse of the Human Sciences', in *Writing and Difference*, trans. A. Bass, London, 1978, pp.278–93, esp. pp.279 and 292.

dreams of deciphering a truth or an origin which escapes play and the order of the sign, and which lives the necessity of interpretation as an exile.' Centuries earlier, the same fundamental yearning was expressed by John the Solitary:

> How long shall I be in the world of the voice and not in the world of the word? For everything that is seen is voice and is spoken with the voice, but in the invisible world there is no voice, for not even voice can utter its mystery. How long shall I be voice and not silence, when shall I depart from the voice, no longer remaining in things which the voice proclaims? When shall I become word in an awareness of hidden things, when shall I be raised up to silence, to something which neither voice nor word can bring.[4]

The desire to escape from the prison-house of language, and from the flickering play of signification is fundamental to apophatic theology. Language becomes a hindrance to our understanding:

> For in-as-moche as we beholden to þinges þat ben moost hiȝe, in-so-moche þe wordes þat ben spokyn of hem to oure beholdynges maken streite oure vnderstondyng.[5]

When we enter into the darkness that is above mind, we shall find not only 'þe schortyng of wordes, bot as it were a madnes and a parfite vnresonabilitee of all þat we seyn' (*DHD*, p.8.13–15). This is an unequivocal truth in affirmative and negative theology. In both traditions, God is 'merked' by a language of gesture and denial, a recognition that language is ultimately self-referential and self-consuming. God escapes the play of meaning:

> His not-vnderstondable ouerpassyng is vnvnderstondabely abouen alle affermyng and deniinge.[6]

For us to affirm or deny God would be to seek to fetter him into the chains of human signification.

> In biblical faith, human beings discern that presence is a surging which soon vanishes and leaves in its disappearance an absence that has been overcome. It is neither absolute nor eternal, but elusive and fragile, even and especially when human beings seek to prolong it in the form of cultus . . . Presence dilutes itself into its own illusion whenever it is confused with a spatial or temporal location. When presence is 'guaranteed' to human senses or reason, it is no longer real presence. The proprietary sight of the glory destroys the vision, whether in the temple of Zion or in the eucharistic body. It is when presence escapes man's grasp that it surges, survives, or returns.[7]

---

[4] Sebastian Brock, 'John the Solitary, *On Prayer*', *Journal of Theological Studies*, New Series, 30 (1979), 84–101, p.87.

[5] From *Deonise hid Diuinite* (*DHD*), the *Cloud*-author's version of *The Mystical Theology* of Pseudo-Denys, in *Deonise hid Diuinite*, ed. Phyllis Hodgson, EETS, O.S. 231 (London, 1955 for 1949), pp.8, 9–12. For a recent account of Denys see Andrew Louth, *Denys the Areopagite*, London, 1989.

[6] *DHD*, p.10.22–3.

[7] Samuel Terrien, *The Elusive Presence*, New York, 1978, p.476, who also writes:
Presence perceived in an epiphanic visitation, a theophany, or the invaded solitude of a prophetic vision was 'swift-lived', yet the acceptance of the

To seek to capture God in language is to seek to enmesh him in the nets of fallen meaning and understanding. Whereof we cannot speak thereof we must be silent. As Hebrew tradition emphasised, God cannot be spoken or written.

But the word was made flesh. Christ's lapse into language in the incarnation is his own freely given sacrifice of his ineffable nature on the altar of human meaning.[8] The incarnation of the *logos* allows him to speak to us and through us and to redeem our language through his words. The Word becomes the bridge between voice and silence, the means of passing over from earthly signification to unmediated truth. The initiative rests exclusively with God. As John the Solitary puts it:

> God's silence spoke with our voice so that we might hear.

The aspiration of mystical longing is to become the word uttered by God, the prayer prayed by God through us. The necessity of interpretation, which we tolerate as exiles from unmediated wisdom, becomes a struggle to escape the play of signification.

Fundamental to this struggle is the rejection of the desire to control and the recognition that God cannot be comprehended either by the human mind or by human language. He can only be loved, not thought. The individual soul longing for the incarnation of meaning must take as its paradigm the humble obedience of Mary at the Annunciation in yielding control and self-will, in submitting to the imperatives of becoming God's meaning. In forgetting self, the soul must cast off the restrictions of language and cross the Jordan from discursive consciousness to apophatic consciousness in which will be found the promised land of truth. This is the passover experience of many mystical writers who struggle to record or recreate their encounters with the ineffable. Fundamental to their struggle is their attempt to articulate their sense of this key movement from the world of signs to the world of the apophatic.[9]

> promise it carried transformed those who received and obeyed the command. Faded presence became a memory and a hope, but it burnt into an ally of inward certitude, which was *emunah*, 'faith'. When God no longer overwhelmed the sense of perception and concealed himself behind the adversity of historical existence, those who accepted the promise were still aware of God's nearness in the very veil of his seeming absence. For them, the centre of life was a *Deus absconditus atque praesens* (p.470).

8 Textual meaning is at best a gesture towards what we may become by God's gift of the divine being, which is our deification. For Julian, for example, meaning is a process by which humanity comes to the fullness of the complex mystery of God's gift of being incarnated in human life.

9 It should be noted that these are not two different worlds: consciousness is a continuum usually dominated by the discursive mode of awarenesss. The world of signs belongs to self-consciousness and the apophatic to the progressive loss of self-consciousness, the noughting of the self so often described in mystical writing. These two aspects of the continuum are integrated, dependant on, and enriching to, each other. For modern accounts of noughting, see John Main, *Word into Silence*, London, 1980; Maggie Ross, *Mysticism: Assent to the Death of Self-Consciousness* (forthcoming).

To enter apophatic consciousness, the seeker must simultaneously desire it intensely and give up all desire.[10] This paradox is deliberately subversive. It threatens the logical, hierarchical command and control structures that motivate the human need to resolve, categorise and classify. It challenges our sense of the ordinary, threatens our usual interpretative patterns and displaces our dominant modes of perception. Like the self-emptying humility of Christ on the cross, it defies reconciliation to the logic of the world. It is a sign of contradiction, allowing the creative tension between its conflicting significations to generate a precious stillness, a chink in the defensive wall of reason that allows slippage into apophatic consciousness – a *jouissance* of unmediated wisdom, a new virginity of mind that is likened by many mystical writers to sexual fulfilment.

To achieve this loss of self-consciousness implies the abandonment of control. It is necessary to jettison the techniques of analysis which classify experiences, sights, words and sense impressions by defining them against and incorporating them into repertoires of signification. Discursive consciousness makes sense of its experiences by activating its mental archive which serves to delimit the play of any signifier by giving it contextual meaning, by fettering it into a system of likeness and difference. By contrast, the stilling and letting go characteristic of contemplative experience facilitates the liberation into and assumption of the different perspectives of the apophatic consciousness, by yielding the herme-neutic initiative. In allowing itself to be read by the Transcendental Signified, the soul learns a new way of reading – *lectio Domini* – that allows it to escape, albeit fleetingly, from the play of absence and presence.[11] The problem facing the mystical writer is how to generate in his own engagement with language a sense of such an experience. He must seek to create what Barthes has called an 'orgasmic text' which:

> dislocates the reader's historical, cultural and psychological assumptions, the consistency of his tastes, values and memories, and brings to a crisis his relation with language.[12]

Apophatic images and apophatic surfaces contribute to this process by the effects they have on the ratiocinative and interpretative processes of the discursive mind. Like language, imagery exists in syntactical and grammatical patterns and acquires meaning through its position in the iconic repertoire. It operates a lexis of likeness and difference within a system of conventional signs.

---

[10] On this paradox, see Marvin Shaw, *The Paradox of Intention*, American Academy of Religion Studies in Religion, 48, Atlanta, 1988.

[11] On *lectio Domini* see Vincent Gillespie, '*Lukynge in haly bukes*: *Lectio* in some Late Medieval Spiritual Miscellanies', in *Spatmittelalterliche Geistliche Literatur in der Nationalsprache*, 2, Analecta Cartusiana, 106 (1984), pp.1–27; Gillespie, 'Strange Images', *op. cit.*, *passim*, esp. pp.122–30.

[12] Roland Barthes, *The Pleasure of the Text*, trans. Richard Miller, New York, 1975, p.14.

By denying the imagination the raw material for the kind of imagistic chain reactions so effectively described by the *Cloud*-author, an apophatic image or surface can allow the eyes of the soul to be focussed without interference from the fallen powers of the mind. They gesture towards the apophatic like the angels gesturing towards the imageless heart of the Holy of Holies.

Such images and surfaces tend to the paradoxical. Water, wine, pearls, the moon, clouds, a flame, all partake of a play of light and darkness and offer neutral surfaces on which images can resolve and dissolve themselves. The co-inherence of meanings or layers of meaning in a single image is a hallmark of the liminal signifiers of the apophatic. They defy or defer the lapse into linearity and monovalency that characterises most conventional interpretation and allow for the generation of productive paradoxes within the same signifier. The Middle English *Pearl* becomes an apophatic image for a range of spiritual truths that resonate together with incrementally synergistic force even though their host image has no necessary figural relationship to them. The pearl of Ephrem the Syrian, with its translucent opacity, becomes the gateway to new perception:

> I saw in the pearl hidden places, that had no shadows,
> for it is the Luminary's daughter.
> in it types are eloquent,
> although they have no tongue;
> symbols are uttered,
> but without the help of lips
> the silent lyre
> though it has no sound, gives forth its song.[13]

Freed from earthly sytems and signs, symbols are uttered without the help of lips. This is a communication that is above the mediation of language.

Apophatic images and surfaces are themselves non-figural but allow projection from within the viewer or perception derived from ineffable knowing. Moses' encounter with the burning bush is a classic apophatic image which allows the focussing of the imagination on a single image but which eschews representation of what it communicates. Similarly a candle flame offers a non-figural, non-linear and non-representational surface over which the mind can play and by which it may come to stillness. But even representational images can become springboards into the apophatic. Intense, unwavering attention to an image can cause it to lose its primary figural significance and to dissolve into constituent shapes, colours, patterns or textures. This commonplace deconstruction of the figural illustrates the metamorphosis of the figuratively allusive into the figurally elusive when the usual interpretative strategies are temporarily suspended.

---

[13] Hymns on Faith no.81: 'On the Pearl and its Symbols', edited and translated by Sebastian Brock in *A Garland of Hymns from the Early Church*, McLean, Virginia, 1989, pp.80–4, p. 81. See the discussion by Sebastian Brock, *The Luminous Eye: The Spiritual World Vision of St Ephrem*, Rome, 1985.

Such strategies of imagistic effacement offer mystical writers a means of counteracting the pull of referentiality in their handling of language. But to succeed it requires a recognition of and openness to those strategies on the part of readers of mystical texts. In the case of Julian of Norwich, the Long Text account of her early showings is an attempt to map out with unusual fidelity the landscape and contours of her mystical newfoundland through leading us calmly into the jaws of apophatic paradox.[14]

Julian's presentation of the fruits of her long *ruminatio* on the showings has sometimes been likened to the exegetical techniques developed out of monastic and scholatic *lectio*.[15] Even if we recognise that she is meditating on pictures and words formed in her understanding rather than written texts, the danger remains that we will seek to assimilate her text to the layered schematics of academic analysis. To replace the traditional fourfold categories of scriptural exegesis with new categories reflecting apparently major strands in her text (for example: narrative, biblical, theological and apophatic) would be to reduce into strata a text that deliberately aspires towards the complexity of the molecular. Her text invites us to enter a relational universe. She wishes to present the showings globally, not locally.[16] Like modern chaos mathematicians, she refuses 'to accept any reality that could be frozen motionless.'[17] Her text seeks to enact a nonlinear dynamic that is the world suffused, enfolded and sustained by the God imaged in the crucifix of her early showings. For chaos mathematicians, 'nonlinearity means that the act of playing the game has a way of changing the rules.'[18] This is close to Julian's experience of her seeking into the beholding of

---

14 Our reading of the early showings of Julian tries to explore the textual dynamic that she creates. We have deliberately not referred to later developments of themes and ideas or to changes in her handling of issues and perceptions in the later revelations. Rather than plot detailed theological echoes or influences in the text, we have paid close attention to the texture and rhythm of the writing. By analysing her semantic and syntactical procedures, we have tried to illustrate some of the ways in which she seeks to involve her readers in the metaphorical landscape of her text. This preliminary paper forms part of a larger study of Julian and of other medieval texts that seem to us to exploit apophatic surfaces and images.

15 E.g. by Edmund Colledge and James Walsh, *A Book of Showings to the Anchoress Julian of Norwich*, Pontifical Institute of Mediaeval Studies, Studies and Texts, 35, Toronto, 1978, pp.131–2.

16 This point is well made by Brant Pelphrey, *Love Was His Meaning: The Theology and Mysticism of Julian of Norwich*, Salzburg Studies in English Literature, 92:4, Salzburg, 1982, pp.84–5; Roland Maisonneuve, 'The Visionary Universe of Julian of Norwich', in *The Medieval Mystical Tradition in England*, 1, ed. Marion Glasscoe, Exeter, 1980, pp.86–98; his *L'univers visionnaire de Julian of Norwich*, Paris, 1987 offers an important and valuable account of 'le langage visionnaire' and 'l'univers visionnaire un et multiple'.

17 James Gleick, *Chaos*, New York, 1987, p.196.

18 Gleick, *op. cit.*, p.24.

God, and the strategy of her text is to make it the experience of her readers as well.

The play of absence and presence so fundamental to mystical experience has its place in Julian's visionary universe. It has its own changing textures, creates its own tides of anxiety and security, offers a rhythmical contraction and dilatation of perception, and seeks to reflect and recreate the movement into and out of the apophatic that lies at the core of her early showings.

Fundamental to Julian's verbal and visual strategies is the emblem of the crown of thorns at the moment of its imposition on the head of Christ:

> and therewith was comprehended and specifyed the Trinite with the incarnation and unite betwix God and man soule, with many faire sheweings of endless wisedome and teacheing of love, in which all the sheweings that follow be grounded and onyd. (c.1, p.1)[19]

The description of this emblem, with its apophatic centre surrounded by the signs of human suffering, characterizes the synthetic writing of so much of the text in the way it holds in tension conflicting perpsectives. It is the ground on which all the showings are founded, but it encompasses them and unifies them. The Trinity is both comprehended and specified by it, suggesting a broad perspective and a minutely particular analysis. It exists in historical, linear time, but comprehends and circumscribes the whole of creation history.[20] Its paradoxical resonance signifies the experience of humiliation for the sake of truth and love that lies at the heart of the trinity and of the incarnation.[21] It places a model of self-emptying humility as the cornerstone of the textual edifice, invoking the kenosis of Christ in his incarnation and passion described by St Paul:

> For let this mind be in you which was also in Christ Jesus, who . . . emptied himself, taking the form of a servant, being made in the likeness of men and in

---

[19] All quotations from the Long Text are taken from London, British Library MS Sloane 2499 (S1); *Julian of Norwich: A Revelation of Love*, ed. Marion Glasscoe, Exeter, 1976. References are to chapter and page number of this edition. Our preference for Sloane over Paris (used by Colledge and Walsh) is based in our sense of its greater theological subtlety and complexity, and a feeling that Paris consistently avoids the theological *lectio difficilior*, preferring the orthodox to the audacious.Glasscoe's edition is alive to the ambiguities and resonances of the text, though on occasion we have modified or omitted her punctuation. For an assessment of the textual problems and a good account of some aspects of S1's superiority, see Marion Glasscoe, 'Visions and Revisions: A Further Look at the Manuscripts of Julian of Norwich', *Studies in Bibliography*, 42 (1989), 103–20.

[20] See 2 Esdras 5:42 and 6:20 (4 Ezra in the Vulgate of Julian's time): 'He said, "I shall compare my judgement to a circle: the latest will not be too late, nor the earliest too early" . . . and all will see my judgement at the same moment.' This resonates with one sense of her later showing of God in a point (see below note 46).

[21] It is only in St John's Gospel that the crowning with thorns acquires a similar ironic prominence through the revelation of Jesus as Truth (John 18:33–19:5).

habit found as a man. He humbled himself, becoming obedient unto death, even to the death of the cross. Therefore (for which cause) God hath exalted him.[22]

The paradox of the exalted kenosis of the cross becomes a paradigm for the procedures of the text, for Julian's approach to God and for her relationship to her audience.[23] To inhabit the text, the reader must be prepared to inhabit the paradigm. Both Julian and her readers must put on the mind of Christ. Enclosure in the text will paradoxically deliver the reader into a limitless landscape. But the necessary suspension of preconceptions, hermeneutical models and critical faculties is to undergo a displacement from the 'ordinary' and a loss of control that is a form of death. It is significant, therefore, that Julian's revelations and her passover into a profounder perception of them is played out against the background of her coming to terms with her own approaching death.

By the time her curate comes to assist her with the rites of passage, Julian's eyes are set upwards towards heaven, where she hoped to come by the mercy of God. Encouraged to look at a crucifix, she agrees with reluctance, as if regretting the interposition of the figural. In a significant paradox of intention, her delivery into the first showing comes not from a vague imageless gazing in the direction of heaven, but by an intense focussing of her waning powers on an earthly image of the suffering Christ.[24] This movement, which she will later be tempted to reverse at a key point in her spiritual development, allows her to concentrate her attention to the exclusion of other sights:

> After this my sight began to failen and it was all derke about me in the chamber as it had be night, save in the image of the cross wherein I beheld a comon light. (c.3, p.3)

Feeling herself to be on the point of death, Julian is *sodenly* relieved of her pain (the adverb is repeated three times in seven lines and is one of her most common descriptors, signalling the suspension of 'ordinary' time). Equally suddenly she decides to ask for 'minde and felyng of his blissid passion' (c.3, p.4). She specifies that she did not desire a 'bodily sight nor scheweing of God', but rather compassion 'and afterward longeing to God' (c.3, p.4). Traditionally,

---

[22] Philippians 2:5–7. We have used the Douay-Rheims translation. Julian alludes to this passage in the Short Text in one of her few direct citations of Scripture: 'Swilke paynes I sawe that alle es to litelle þat y can telle or saye, for itt maye nouȝt be tolde, botte ylke saule aftere the sayinge of saynte Pawle schulde feele in hym þat in Criste Jhesu', Colledge and Walsh, *op. cit.*, p.234.; Both Pelphrey (*Love Was His Meaning*, p.261) and Colledge and Walsh (p.97) discuss the influence of this passage on Julian, but in connection with later showings. Neither sees it as fundamental to Julian's strategy.

[23] On the importance of paradox, see Maisonneuve, *L'univers visionnaire, op. cit.*, pp.92–5.

[24] This point is well made by Simon Tugwell, *Ways of Imperfection: An Exploration of Christian Spirituality*, London, 1984, p.188: 'the "upward" movement towards God . . . is redirected towards the suffering humanity of Christ. *That* is where heaven must be sought'. See Gillespie, 'Strange Images', *op. cit.*, pp.130–1.

mind of the passion had been associated with strong emotional reactions and
affective identification with the sufferings of Christ, as the lyric suggests:

> The mynde of thy swet passion, Jesu –
> Teres it tolles,
> Eyene it bolles,
> My vesage it wetes,
> And my hert it swetes.[25]

But this form of compassion had become a debased commodity in the late
fourteenth century, often amounting in popular devotion to little more than the
production of an extreme kinaesthetic response of the sort castigated by the
Cloud-author for its undue agitation of the imagination.

The compassion Julian receives takes her far beyond this tinkering with
emotive pictures into something closer to the Pauline kenotic mind of Christ. She
has already said that she hoped to be 'deliveryd of this world' (c.3, p.4) and it is
soon apparent that in the labour pains of her illness she has also been delivered
from the weary conventions of contemporary passion poetry.[26]

'In this sodenly' (c.4, p.4), she perceives the blood trickling down from the
freshly imposed crown of thorns. The opening of the chapter typifies our
experience of Julian's syntactical virtuosity, for *sodenly* can be read here both as
having a simple adverbial function (In this vision, suddenly I saw) and as
functioning as the subject of the sentence (within this 'suddenly', I perceived the
trickling blood). She signals the conflated time scale of her vision and its
subsequent process of revelation by creating a multilayered sequence of showings
and perceptions all happening in the apophatic landscape of her sudden instant.
Through her use of insistent present participles she sustains us in a timeless
beholding of the mystical context in which the historical moment is suspended.[27]

Julian's focus on the immediate physical consequences of the crowning alludes
to conventional passion meditation, but only long enough to allow the reader to
register her departures from the usual catalogue of Christ's wounds. Having
been delivered of the world, she immediately *conceives* that Christ is showing
her this image without any 'mene' (c.4, p.4).[28] The spiritual pregnancy on which

---

[25] *Index of Middle English Verse*, ed. Carleton Borden and R. H. Robbins, New York,
1943, 3433, printed in *A Selection of Religious Lyrics*, ed. Douglas Gray, Oxford,
1975, p.31, and see note, p.117.

[26] See *Middle English Dictionary*, ed. Hans Kurath et al., Ann Arbor, 1954– (hereafter
MED), sv *deliveren*, v. The senses recorded include deliverance from bondage, prison
or captivity; giving up or relinquishing; and giving birth to.

[27] Indeed several features of her text, including her later statement 'It is today domysday
with me' (c.8, p.9) suggests that Julian's text may have some of the generic
characterisics of apocalyptic writing.

[28] Julian's lexical exploration of the word *mene*, as a noun, adjective and verb, is one of the
most dazzling illustrations of her verbal dexterity in creating semantic clusters or 'word-
knots'. Here she seems to imply that the showing was without speech and without
intermediary. The nominal senses of *mene* include: sexual intercourse; fellowship; a
companion; a course of action, method or way; an intermediary or negotiator; an agent or

she embarks involves learning a new way with the liminal imagery of her showings which consistently leads her into the timeless and imageless world of the apophatic.[29]

The stress on the lack of intermediaries between Christ and Julian emphasizes that Christ is not obeying the conventions of passion meditation, nor is he communicating through the codified decorums by which signification is usually controlled in human rhetoric. Her bleeding head image is uncoupled from its usual chains of signifiers and of significations, and she is forced to develop a new lexis to cope with the strands of meaning inherent in it and with the temporal and atemporal modes in which those strands are revealed:

> This shewing was quick and lively, and hidouse and dredfull, swete and lovely. (c.7, p.8)

Julian makes no attempt to resolve the paradoxes of this description. Instead she allows them to imply the different perspectives (visionary, historical and theological) which simultaneously coinhere in the showing. These dislocations are the beginning of Julian's 'orgasmic' text.

The initial description of the head is immediately followed by a substantial meditation on the Trinity signalling a shift of mood from sorrow and pain to joy: 'sodenly the Trinite fullfilled the herte most of ioy' (c.4, p.4). Again this is not a process but an instantaneous perception; in effect another moment of conception.[30] The lack of *means*, the suspension of the usual conventions of

---

instrument; an intermediate state; something uniting extremes; mediation or help; argument, reason or discussion. Adjectivally it can mean 'partaking of the qualities or characteristics of two extremes'. As a verb it has the senses of: to intend to convey something; to signify; to say or express something; to remember something; to advise, admonish or urge somebody to do something. It can also have the sense of: to complain; to cry out for help; to pity, sympathise with or condole with somebody. A further adjectival set of senses coheres around notions of lowness, inferiority and smallness which resonates with Julian's sense of humble self-emptying.(*MED*, sv *mene*, n.; *menen*, v.) Julian's exploitation of the polysemousness of this word means that it becomes the meeting place for many of her key ideas, perceptions, responses and expressions.

29 Cf. Paul's words in Galatians 4.19: 'My little children, of whom I am in labour again, until Christ be formed in you.' In view of her Pauline sense of responsibility towards her 'even-cristens', Julian may well see her spiritual pregnancy as part of her 'meaning' or intermediary function. This notion of spiritual childbirth fits well with the theme of the labour and motherhood of God extensively explored later in the *Showings*, offering another form of *compassio* with Christ. On the motherhood theme, see Caroline Walker Bynum, *Jesus as Mother: Studies in the Spirituality of the High Middle Ages*, London, 1982, with bibliography; J. P. H. Clark, 'Nature, Grace and the Trinity in Julian of Norwich', *Downside Review*, xxx (1982), 203–20, pp.211–4; Colledge and Walsh, pp.151–62; Pelphrey, *Love Was His Meaning*, pp.184–9, and his recent *Christ Our Mother*, London, 1989.

30 This apparently tangential excursion from the normal trajectory of affective response to passion meditation is not found in the Short Text, which is generally more conventional and cautious in its articulation of ideas, not least because in that version

interpretation, allows her to impact the joy of the Trinity onto the grief and humiliation of the crowning with thorns. This allows the physical paradox of the mocked kingship of Christ to resonate with its full theological force in a manner unusual in late medieval Passion narratives.

Julian's verbal reaction to the shewing – *Benedicite domine* – is said 'for reverence in my meneing' because her rational powers are astonished:

> for wonder and mervel . . . that he that is so reverend and dredfull will be so homely with a synfull creture liveing in wretched flesh. (c.4, p.4)

Again, the syntactical looseness (which so annoyed Colledge and Walsh) is revealed as a functional part of Julian's theology of immanence. Christ is *reverend* and *dredfull* (in both senses) but also *homely*: the nature of the paradox is manifest in the final clause 'liveing in wretched flesh' (c.4, p.4), the antecedent for which can be both Julian and Christ. His homeliness with his creatures extends to occupying the same syntactical space as them. Her *conceiving* of the significance of the shewing is acted out by the way the spirit of God fills her syntax and occupies her subclauses in a grammatical parody of the Incarnation. Her puzzlement is overcome by her reverence as she is led into the annunciation of truths whose enunciation defies language.

This conception of Christ's meaning without means, analogous to the Incarnation without physical intermediary, is only possible because she has moved to a position of true *compassion* with Christ: a genuine sharing with the will of God

> as a kinde soule might have with our lord Iesus, that for love would beene a dedely man; and therefore I desired to suffer with him. (c.3, p.4)

Christ's willingness for death becomes real for her at what she believes is the moment of her own death, the labour pains of which she reclaims as an act of willed self-emptying. Her commitment to Christ hinges on the *therefore* in the last clause of chapter 3, which echoes the paradoxical causality of St Paul's 'therefore God has exalted him.'[31] Julian's *therefore* is an act of kenosis, an imitation of Christ in her willingness to die to the world. She is delivered of the world and of the world's images and in the act conceives again and is 'fullfilled . . . most of joy', a moment of *jouissance*.

Although she has asked for mind of the Passion, what she has received is far removed from the usual images of torment and suffering. Julian's showing has made the bleeding head resonate as an image in new and unusual ways; it *means* both the exaltation of the Trinity and the humility of the incarnation, but it can

Julian has yet to arrive at a sense of the authority of her own text. In this respect, chapter 9 of the Long Text is significant, as she there articulates her almost Pauline sense of her role as a signifier or mean of God's message.

[31] Only S1 and S2 have *therefore* at this point; the Short Text and Paris agree in reading 'With him I desyred to suffer, liuyng in my deadly bodie, as god would giue me grace' (LT, Colledge and Walsh, *op. cit.*, p.293, cf ST, p.210.).

only do so because it is liberated from the *means* or hermeneutic repertoires which clogged the arteries of contemporary devotional writing.

The virtuosity of this first chapter of the showing is completed by the way she relates all that has happened back to another cliche of popular meditation – the image of Mary at the Annunciation. This allows her to focus the language and concepts of the bleeding head and its associated significations, but it is done with such panache that a tired visual reference is reconstituted into something much more theologically subtle. We see Mary 'wan she conceived with child', echoing and reverberating against Julian's own conceiving of her revelation. We see her wisdom and truth:

> wherein I understood the reverend beholding that she beheld hir God and maker, mervelyng with greate reverence that he would be borne of hir that was a simple creature of his makeyng. (c.4, p.5)

Julian's syntactical openness again allows theology to take place within the grammatical interstices of the sentence. When we ask who is 'mervelyng with greate reverence' at this scene, we realise that it must be *both* Mary and Julian. Their responses are twinned just as their vocabulary of reverent dread at God's homeliness with creatures has also been subliminally twinned. Mary's meekness in acquiescing (Lo me, God's handmayd) is a scriptural analogue (and a *post hoc* validation) of Julian's earlier *Benedicite domine*. Moreover Mary's *beholding* of God ushers in a major theme of later revelations; how God is to be perceived and how that perception is to be articulated. *Beholding* is a key term in Julian's apophatic vocabulary, signalling not an analytical, critical or interpretative seeing, but rather a still and mutual enjoyment of and exchange of being between God and the soul.[32]

Julian's use of the Annunciation could have been a crude claim for the orthodoxy and authority of her vision. Instead her exploration of a traditional image allows, and indeed requires, the reader to make the connections and parallels between the acts of obedience and humility that bind together Christ, Mary and Julian in a trinity of homely reverence and self-emptying humility.[33] The rejection of earthly means is already found in the description of Mary:

> for aboven hir is nothing that is made but the blissid [manhood] of Criste. (c.4, p.5)

In similar terms, Julian's delivery from the world brings her to the threshold of the apophatic:

> till I am substantially onyd to him I may never have full rest ne very blisse; that is to sey, that I be so festined to him that there is right nowte that is made betwix my God and me. (c.5, p.5)

---

[32] For a more systematized account of beholding, see Pelphrey, *Love Was His Meaning*, *op. cit.*, pp.229–47; Maisonneuve, *L'univers visionnaire*, *op. cit.*, pp.125–53.

[33] The link between Mary and Julian is brought out explicitly later on, when she is taught about 'her truth, her wisdam, hir charite; wherby I may leryn to know myselfe and

The soul's restlessness will continue until it is 'nowted of all things that is made.' Willful noughting (a typical paradox of intention) is a function of our love for God and God's will to be known. The subliminal connections between the key words in this discussion create a punning word-knot (knowing, noughting, nothing, no thing) of overlapping and interpenetrating notions offering a powerfully incremental substructure of resonance and allusion which uses connotation to overpower simple denotation. Like the crown of thorns, this semantic garland of near homonyms both comprehends and specifies ideas fundamental to Julian's seeking in to the beholding of God.

Julian creates in her text a dialogue with conventional images. But she is acutely aware of the dangers of those images fettering her showings into an earthly order of signifying. Later in the first revelation, she returns with a fixity of focus to the drops of blood on Christ's face. Like the disruption and deconstruction of a picture consequent on fixed attention to a small part, she dismantles the bleeding into a series of discrete images: pellets, rain and herringbones (c.7, p.8). The images suggest an urge to 'domesticate' the horror of the passion, to defuse the challenge of its physicality by invoking homely *means* to interpret it. But God showed it without means and the effect of her gesture to conventional analogy is paradoxically to imbue the domestic and mundane with the force of the original image and with the substance of its subsequent significations. By making immanence more openly manifest, Julian also reclaims these homely images as gateways into the apophatic.

Similarly, Julian also embarks on a conventional simile to describe the appearance of Christ's head: 'the fairhede and the livelyhede is like . . .' As if recognizing that the simile creates a centrifugal force in the text, drawing attention away from the core image and setting off a chain reaction of linked signifiers, in effect subordinating her showing to the very *means* from which Christ has liberated it and her – she overthrows the analogy with an enigmatic assertion of irreduceability: 'the fairehede and the livelyhede is like nothing but the same' (c.7, p.8).[34]

Like the experience of childbirth that seems to inform so much of Julian's imagery in these early showings, her text has a rhythm, a pattern of movement.[35] It has moments of great difficulty and density where meaning is intense and

---

reverently drede my God' (c.25, p.27); see Glasscoe, 'Means of showing', *op. cit.*, p.164.

[34] The apophatic force of this is entirely suppressed in the persistently puzzled Paris Manuscript, which reads 'Nevertheles the feyerhede and the lyuelyhede continued in the same bewty and lyuelynes' (Colledge and Walsh, *op. cit.*, p.312). *Pace* Colledge and Walsh, this looks like an attempt to make sense of something like Sloane's reading.

[35] For some provocative speculations about Julian's life, see Sister Benedicta (Ward), SLG, 'Julian the Solitary', in *Julian Reconsidered*, Oxford, 1988, pp.11–35.

contracted; and it has moments of easier comprehension, relaxation, reflection and consolidation. These textual and spiritual contractions are the means by which the spiritual perception of Julian and her audience is dilated, making us open to new understanding, moving us closer to the moment of spiritual delivery, which may be deferred beyond the confines of the written text.

The dramatized groping and uncertainties of these early chapters prepare us to welcome those passages of clarity and calm exposition that invariably follow. Her enfolding texture comforts us in the way that the enfolding love of God comforts her. The 'ghostly sight of his homely loveing' in chapter 5 (p.5) sees God as everything that is good and comfortable for us. The discomfort of our earlier textual labours is rewarded with images of nurturing reassurance that invoke the registers of maternal and sexual love

> He is our clotheing that for love wrappith us, [halseth] us and all beclosyth us for tender love.   (c.5, p.5)[36]

We cannot rest until we are 'beclosyd' in God, but this is only achieved by our approaching him 'nakidly and pleynly and homely' (c.5, p.6). We must divest ourselves of things that are made and avoid sophistication and arcane complexity if we are 'wisely to clevyn to the goodnes of God' (c.6, p.6). This passover, or death to the world liberates us from the enclosure of worldly thought and into the enclosing and clothing love of God. Her language here is finessing the liturgy of monastic clothing and of the enclosure of hermits and anchoresses to offer, in effect, a theology of enclosure for all Christians.[37]

But with her characteristic suspicion of analogy, she moves quickly to preempt crude schematization. Starting from the theological principal of our likeness to God, she exploits the enclosure imagery in a dazzling parabola of similitudes, only to efface them with a new assertion of the uniqueness of our transfigured relationship with God:

> for as the body is cladde in the cloth, and the flesh in the skyne, and the bonys in the flesh, and the herte in the bouke, so arn we, soule and body, cladde in the goodnes of God and inclosyd.   (c.6, p.7)

This sequence of physical analogies initiates a journey inward, pulling us from the external and visible into the internal and invisible: our very physiology becomes a pathway to the apophatic. But she immediately goes further:

> ya, and more homley, for all these may wasten and weren away; the godenes of God is ever hole and more nere to us withoute any likenes.   (c.6, p.7)

---

[36] The Short Text and Paris add after 'beclosyth', 'hangeth about vs' (Colledge and Walsh, p.299, cf. p.212.).

[37] On the change in intended audience from Short to Long Text, see Barry Windeatt, 'Julian of Norwich and her Audience', *Review of English Studies*, New Series, 28 (1977), 1–17; Windeatt, 'The Art of Mystical Loving: Julian of Norwich', in *Medieval Mystical Tradition*, 1(1980), *op. cit.*, 55–71; Glasscoe, 'Means of Showing', *op. cit.*, p.157.

Having used the analogy of concentric layers to emphasize the enfolding love of God, she inverts this initial perspective of enclosure, liberating us into the boundless wholeness of God by the peripeteia of our expectations and the denial of the similitude ('withoute any likenes').[38]

Apophatic effacement also governs the showing of 'a littil thing, the quantitye of an hesil nutt in the palme of my hand; and it was as round as a balle' (c.5, p.5). Our visual perspective is wrenched from the centre of God's envaginating love for the world to looking at all that is made, as if from the perspective of the creator. Simultaneously we are being offered an image which does not exist. What Julian sees is not a hazelnut but an unspecified thing, about the size of a hazelnut if it were in the palm of her hand (which it is not), and as round as a ball. The 'littil thing' is described by gesture towards material objects but its true properties, as perceived by Julian are *not* its materiality or referentiality but rather aspects of God's relationship to it:

> the first is that God made it, the second is that God loveth it, the iiid, that God kepith it.   (c.5, p.5)

It has being in our minds only as a function of God's creative and sustaining love. She even refuses to attribute these powers to the particular persons of the Trinity. So we are left with an effaced image of creation held in being by a power whose trinitarian functions are denied exact demarcation in terms of earthly activity or theological convention. Julian again balances her description on the brink of the apophatic.

By emphasising that the first showing teaches the soul 'wisely to clevyn to the goodnes of God' (c.6, p.6), Julian has also taught us that the conventionally sanctioned means to God are, for the most part, inadequate. By encouraging us to cross the threshold of the apophatic she has created in these early chapters an appetite for security and a yearning for certainty that has been counterpoised against the enfolding maternal care of the Almighty. Her critique of human *means* in devotion is hard hitting. Most are 'to litil and not full worshippe to God' (c.6, p.6).[39] She includes many of the common objects of affective devotion and prayer: his holy flesh, pretious blood, passion, death and wounds, his mother, the cross and the saints. These human and earthbound devotions are all aspects and functions of the divine goodness. They are too often seen as ends in themselves not as proper means to the apprehension of the deity, of cleaving to him with the love to which we must aspire. 'The chiefe and principal mene is

---

38 Cf. *MED* sv *liknes(se)*, n.: 2(a) similarity, resemblance, analogy; 3(a) parable, simile, analogy; 4(a) the visible appearance of something, (b) a mental image retained in the *Imaginatio*; 5(b) basic quality?; substantial form.

39 'Making means' is an idiom referring to making a complaint or a petition (*MED*, sv *mene* n.(2).) Thus Julian is criticizing the usually selfish and acquisitive nature of petitionary prayer, as well as the inadequacy (or meanness) of many of the intermediary and intercessory techniques commonly employed.

the blissid kinde that he toke of the mayd' (c.6, p.7).[40] To come to him nakedly, plainly and homely may require the shedding of artificial means and techniques. By passing over from earthly means we are enabled to apprehend something of the love of God, which 'overpassyth the knoweing of all creatures' (c.6, p.7). But her careful and circumspect criticism of 'the custome of our prayeing' (c.6, p.6) is not founded on a despairing silence. Her prayer at the end of chapter 5 is based on her psychology of human need expressed in chapter 6. Our words 'arn full lovesome to the soule' (c.5, p.6) and offer verbal formulae that allow us to enact a kenotic gesture towards the ineffable will of God. Indeed they 'full nere touchen the will of God and his goodness' (c.5, p.6). The groping into the unsayable, itself stimulated by the touching of the Holy Spirit, will be comprehended by the goodness of God. The gesture is of humility not of control. God's comprehension of us encloses us as well as understands us. God is able to read us, no matter how flawed the text, and we seek to read God by allowing God to read us: this is the essence of *lectio Domini*.

Absence and lack, the sense of figural emptiness that Julian generates in these early chapters produces the attentive silence of beholding necessary for transfigured perception:

> he will that we be occupyed in knoweing and loveing til the tyme that we shall be fulfilled in hevyn. (c.6, p.7)

By putting away the artificial means that inhibit this focussed longing, we come to the prayer of self offering and self-opening:

> for of all thing, the beholding and the lovyng of the maker makith the soule to seeme lest in his owne sight and most fillith it with reverend drede and trew mekenes. (c.6, p.7)

This formulation is saved from abstraction by the fact that it is grounded and specified in the responses of Mary in the Annunciation and of Julian to her first showing: she is becoming a signifier, a means for the transmission of God's message in the way she opens herself to be read by God and by her readers. Signs are not rejected or despised; they are exalted by being transfigured. The emptiness of the ineffable and the apophatic becomes occupied, filled and fulfilled 'in fullhede of joy' (c.6, p.7) (another word-knot) by the love of God. 'Beholding and lovyng of the maker' (c.6, p.7) is transactional: God and the soul behold and love each other.

It is this occupation and comprehension that allows Julian to expound the showing with confidence:

> I beheld the shewing with al my diligens; for in al this blissid shewing I beheld it as one in Godys meaning. (c.9, p.11)[41]

---

[40] Here she is punning on the role of Christ as intercessor, intermediary, and companion, as well as alluding to the humanity of Christ as a *mene* state, both in its lowness and its function as a link (I am the way . . . (or means)) between humanity and God.

[41] Paris reads 'I behelde it as in gods menyng' (Colledge and Walsh, p.323).

Her beholding allows her to see from God's perspective (as one who shared God's meaning); her beholding allows her to see the irreduceable unity of the showing (I beheld it all in one, by means of God's showing); and she beholds it as someone who has herself become a means of showing, a signifier for those who, she expects, will survive her:

> And that I say of me I sey in the person of al myn even cristen, for I am lernyd in the gostly shewing of our lord God that he menyth so. (c.8, p.10)

God means her to be the means of communicating to all Christians.
This is how God 'menyth' or speaks: she becomes the word spoken by God.

Julian's second revelation is even more dramatic and becomes even more abstract. Still *beholdyng* in the crucifix, she sees a part of the Passion narrative preceding the Crucifixion itself – the insults and tortures heaped on Christ at his scourging and on the *via dolorosa*. Momentarily she contextualizes the abstracted image of the defiled Christ by reanimating the traditional linear passion narrative from which it evolved. She puts the suffering back into its historical context. But having alluded to the familiar world of Bonaventuran meditation, she embarks on a tangential meditation on the changing colour of Christ's face, typically welding the static and the kinetic, the spatial and the linear. The blood closes over the face, veiling it from view behind an apophatic surface:

> And one time I saw how halfe the face, begyning at the ere, overrede with drie blode til it beclosid to the mid face, and after that, the tuther halfe beclosyd on the same wise. (c.10, p.11)

At this early stage of the showing her perception is unable to penetrate beyond the apparent denial of this bodily sight:

> This saw I bodily, swemely and derkely and I desired more bodily sight to have sene more clerely. (c.10, p.11)[42]

This is an important moment of *impasse* for Julian's perception of the imagery of her showings. She wishes to see more clearly with her bodily sight, but the image is 'derke' – both in the sense of lacking illumination and in the cognate sense of enigmatic. She is unwilling to relinquish control of the signification of her vision. Her reliance on bodily sight is answered in her reason –the seat of this controlling impulse:

> If God wil shew thee more, he shal be thy light. Thee nedith none but him. (c.10, p.11)

God will be the means of the showing and will provide the means by which she should receive and respond to it. God again has the initiative in the hermeneutics of the text. She sees him but seeks him, recognising that we are now blind and

---

[42] The Short Text and Paris both read 'bodely light' for S1's bodily sight; either way, she is seeking to use bodily means for something that can only be seen in a ghostly light.

unwise. She has him, but wants him; the play of absence and presence flickers between her bodily sight and her sense of something more beyond for which she longs, but which she is prevented from seeing by the veil of blood and by her own blindness and lack of wisdom (a wisdom associated with the self-emptying of Mary in the first showing).

We never seek God until he shows himself through Grace 'than arn we sterid by the same grace to sekyn with gret desire to se him more blisfully' (c.10, p.11). This desire, this thirst for blissful sight, is a function of the lack she feels in this second showing. She worries that it is so 'low and so litil and so simple' (c.10, p.11). Indeed she is 'mornand, dredfull and longand' (c.10, p.11). Picking up the birthing imagery, her spirits are in *travel*. This is clearly a crisis in interpretation for her.

Having conceived God in the first chapters, she now labours to give birth to a more profound articulation of her understanding, at the same time *mornand* the loss of old certainties and longing for new clarities and for illumination. She describes this state of labour, bereavement and quasi sexual longing as a 'comon werkeyng' (c.10, p.11). God's role in this process is more clearly explored here:

> he will be sene and he wil be sowte; he wil be abedyn and he wil be trosted.   (c.10, p.11)

Again her grammatical skills allow a density of reference. The future tenses imply an idealised future perfect; *will* as a modal auxiliary implies the determination of God to reveal himself to his creatures; and the mood allows a sense of God tolerating his creatures feeble attempts to conform themselves to his will.

Her *travel* in the showing is rewarded with more sight. Recognizing that the opening image gestures rhetorically towards something deeper and darker, she says that it is a 'figure and likenes' of the 'dede-hame' (c.10, p.12) born by Christ for our sins. The puzzling ' "garment" or "skin"'[43] of deeds' conceals, we learn later, our fair bright blessed lord. Her darkness at the sight of the original image is because the brightness of the Lord is hid and only he can be her light. It is a garment of deeds and a garment of death. The punning assonance on *dede* brings together the covering of the veil of blood and the clothing of sin which are a necessary consequence of the Fall and a function of the Incarnation and Passion. Julian is doing hard theology through the association of her images.

Things seem to get even harder when she introduces the vernicle, the *locus classicus* of meditation on the face of Christ and, like her other core images, locked into the conventions of affective devotion. Julian emphasizes the paradox of the vernicle. How could such a foul image, so discoloured, be deliberately *portrayed* (the verb is used twice) by so fair a face? At once the paradoxes line up: blood covers the face; the garment or skin of deeds covers the bright beauty of Christ; the vernicle has a foul image of a fair visage. Julian's explanation of

---

[43] *MED* sv *hame* n.(1): a skin, integument or membrane; n.(2): each of two pieces of wood or metal forming part of the collar of a draught horse. Paris omits the word.

this imagistic conundrum highlights her labouring into a different realm of perception, for she sees the answer as lying in the necessary assumption of man's fallen state by Christ to effect the redemption of the clouded image of God in man:

> like as we were like made to the Trinite in our first makyng, our maker would that we should be like Iesus Criste our saviour in hevyn without ende, be the vertue of our geynmaking. (c.10, p.12)

Our perception of the head of Christ as damaged, discoloured and emaciated is a function of our bodily sight, which is a function of the blindness and unwisdom of the fall. Only a ghostly or blissful way of seeing Christ can perceive the beauty that lies behind the veil, under the clothing or beyond the vernicle. Our *geynmaking* must be achieved by a renewal or uncovering of the image and likeness of God in our soul.

Christ is so determined that we should see him that in the Incarnation and Passion he uses our sins (linked to the blood by the collocations on *dede*) as the *means* of renewing that image. The vernicle, which has been deliberately portrayed by God for us, is thus an acutely imagistic formulation of Julian's understanding of the theology of the Incarnation. But it also simultaneously entices us to pass beyond it into the apophatic.

If the blood is sin besmirching the face of Christ and hiding it from our view, it also becomes the *means* by which Christ can portray his image. Sin is turned to our advantage by the emptying humility of the passion. Like the blood, sin clouds the true sight. In using it to impress his image on the vernicle, God redeems it and forces it to be a *means* of seeing God clearly. The blood is wiped from Christ's eyes and his true beauty shines out for us to contemplate in our ghostly sight. Christ has used the means of imagery to draw us into the apophatic.

Julian dramatizes the process of seeking into the beholding of Christ 'the principal mene' (c.6, p.7), which she asserts is God's will for us. Seeking into the beholding is the work of life – the 'travel' of spiritual childbirth.[44] Finding 'plesyth the soule and fulfillith it with joy' (c.10, p.12). Labouring to give birth to new understanding is also labouring to see God's image clearly in ourselves, unclouded by sin, unmediated by the 'means' of earthly imagery. Beyond the veil of paradox, we behold God just as God eternally beholds us. This mutual beholding restores the image that gives us clearness of sight, effecting blissful contemplation.

Faith seeking understanding manifests itself here by a seeking into images to find a way of beholding God; a new grammar of spiritual imagery. Only the Transcendental Signified can reveal that grammar: 'how a soule shall have him

---

[44] Paris reads 'It is gods will that we seke into the beholdyng of hym' (Colledge and Walsh, *op. cit.*, p.333); S1 has 'It is God wille that we seke him to the beholdyng of him' (p.12). The sense of process is common to both.

in his beholdyng he shall teche himselfe' (c.10, p.12). The yearning of the soul for blissful sight always invites God with the words of Mary: *Ecce ancilla domini*. Seeking is the *Ecce* of the soul, a self-emptying in readiness for the Holy Spirit's annunciation of new meaning:

> We knowen he shall appere sodenly and blisfully to al his lovers; for his werkyng is privy, and he wil be perceivid, and his appering shal be swith sodeyn, and he wil be trowid, for he is full hend and homley – blissid mot he ben!   (c.10, p.13)

Apophatic consciousness exists in a continuum with discursive consciousness, and there is constant exchange and interpenetration. Seeking into the beholding of God – the common working of this life – does not produce a once for all transition. Mystical tradition eloquently describes the ebb and flow of apophatic consciousness. Julian responds to this in her third revelation (chapter 11) with a fastidious transcription of her own responses to the new showing:

> And after this I saw God in a poynte, that is to sey, in myn vnderstondyng, be which sight I saw that he is in al things.   (p.13)

The sense of this highly elliptical passage has preoccupied commentators from the time of the Paris manuscript onwards. Syntactically and lexically she is going to considerable lengths to signal that the ground of this showing (I saw God in a point) defies simple categorisation. She gives no indication whether this is a bodily sight, word formed in her understanding or ghostly sight (indeed she may mean that all three modes are simultaneously present in all the showings when they are fully perceived and realized). God in a point may be deliberately enigmatic: it is certainly non-figural and non-referential. It is apophatic in that one can imagine what she means without being able to represent it in terms of imagery. Her qualification of the main clause – 'that is to sey' – purports to offer clarification but ushers in further complexity. 'In myn vnderstondyng' can relate adverbially to *saw* (I saw in my understanding). It can also stand in apposition to the object of the main clause: I saw God in a point, that is to say in my understanding. This would reinforce her developing awareness of God's indwelling and immanence. If *point* also means an instant of time (like the *sodenly* of her first showing), then she is further effacing the referential towards a moment of blissful sapiential *jouissance*. Certainly her attempt to capture her response to it reverberates with complexity and an unwillingness to affix simple psychological labels:

> I beheld with avisement, seing and knowing in sight with a soft drede, and thought: 'What is synne?'   (c.11, p.13)

There is a strategic overloading and juxtaposing of terms of perception here which signposts her difficulty with denotative psychological vocabulary. She deliberately combines intellectual processes with intuitive responses – 'knowing in sight with a soft drede' – in a manner reminiscent of other attempts to describe that sapiential knowing which is also a feeling and a tasting. By conflating affective and intellective modes of perception she tries to open up in the reader's experience some sense of her own experience. This use of apophatic paradox is a response to her avowed inability to represent the ghostly sight 'as hopinly ne as fully as I wolde' (c.9, p.11).

Her return to discursive processes is almost immediate: 'and thought: What is synne?' She has moved from apophatic beholding to intellectual analysis, exploring and exploiting the language and procedures of philosophical debate in a Boethian discussion of divine providence and foresight and human 'unwetyng' and 'onforesight' (c.11, p.13).[45] The logic of her analysis forces a swift *concessio*:

> Wherfore me behovith nedes to grant that althing that is done, it is wel done, for our lord God doth alle. (c.11, p.13)

But the pull of the apophatic begins to reassert itself, signalled by Julian's playfully strategic dalliance with the language of negative theology:

> [God] is in the mydde poynt of allthyng and all he doith, and I was sekir he doith no synne. And here I saw sothly that synne is no dede, for in al this was not synne shewid. (p.13)[46]

Although she is still seeing rationally or discursively here, sin is denied materiality or representation. She does not see sin and she sees no-sin: both her perceptions are, of course, perceptions of God, and profoundly apophatic answers to her discursive question 'What is synne?' (c.11, p.13)[47] The slippage of the prose away from referentiality invites her to yield up ratiocinative curiosity and the hermeneutical initiative, and return to a state of beholding:

> And I wold no lenger mervel in this, but beheld our lord, what he wold shewen. (c.11, p.13)

God's works are 'easye and swete' for the soul that is 'turnid truly into the beholdyng of him' (c.11, p.14). This turning requires a shift from the false beholding of 'the blind demyng of man' to the true beholding of 'the faire swete demyng of God' (c.11, p.14). The complacent beholding of her own logical processes is more difficult and less satisfying than the message of God's benevolent immanence: 'How should anything be amysse?' (c.11, p.14). Indeed Julian recognises the folly of her earlier *questio* on sin and the subsequent one-sided *disputatio* when she concludes the showing with an amused parody of the language of the schools:

> Thus migtily, wisely and lovinly was the soule examynyd in this vision. Then saw I sothly that me behovyd nedis to assenten with gret reverens, enioyand in God. (c.11, p.14)

[45] See Colledge and Walsh, p.226.7 note and 338.17 note.
[46] As well as echoing the idea of God as an intelligible sphere whose centre is everywhere, this image also calls to mind her foundational image of the crown of thorns with its apophatic centre.
[47] In her text Julian shows us two kinds of emptiness. There is the emptiness of sin, which is nullity and there is the emptiness of noughting which is the prerequisite for oneing, a blessed fulness. She is deeply concerned with spiritual counterfeits.

Recognizing that the ontological imperative of her need for God is stronger than her rational processes, she rests in a state of communion: her reverence here, reunited with her soft dread at the beginning of the revelation, brackets her excursion into the world of philosophy and systematic theology with the hallmarks of her more usual state of longing and love.

Julian's dialogue with the conventions and techniques of affective piety extends to a virtuosic manipulation of linguistic register. The opening of the fourth revelation (chapter 12) returns to the linear narrative of the Passion meditations, subjecting another episode to her intense and unwavering attention:

> And after this I saw, beholding, the body plentiously bleeding in seming of the scorgyng. (p.14)[48]

Still in the non-discursive mode of beholding, she sees the bleeding body not in the context of the historical or temporal narrative of the Passion. 'In seming' alludes to the context of the scourging, but its referentiality gestures elsewhere. Julian recognizes this in the way she grounds her description in the discourse of affective meditation, but she signals that this grounding is tactical rather than definitive by drawing attention to the consciously heightened language and the provisionality of the register:

> as thus: the faire skynne was brokyn ful depe into the tender flesh with sharpe smyting al about the sweete body. (c.12, p.14)

There is something artfully contrived here: the onomatopoeic rhythm; the alliteration on f and s; the mechanically regular alternation of adjectives and adverbs; the conventionalized epithets. Most significant is the way the introductory 'as thus' keeps the language at arms length. Julian is employing this emotionally coded discourse as a springboard, an affective trigger, and she moves almost immediately to begin the process of effacing the materiality of the description and of our response to it. Introducing the key concept of plenitude, she again uses the blood to create an apophatic surface:

> so plenteously the hote blode ran oute that there was neither sene skynne ne wound, but as it were al blode. (c.12, p.14)

Denying us the affective means of a conventional response, she provides us with a gathering image on which to still the imagination. Only the detail of the hot blood is allowed to continue to resonate, emphazising the immediacy of the encounter and the eternal present tense in which her beholding unfolds. In other respects the blood denies its materiality:

> And whan it come wher it should a fallen downe, than it vanyshid . . . And this was so plenteous to my sigt that methowte if it had be so in kind and in substance

---

[48] Colledge and Walsh, *op. cit.*, p.342, point out that the Short Text reading 'in semes' might refer to long incised wounds, such as might be caused at the scourging. The Long Text's 'in semyng', therefore, puns on the physicality of the suffering and its function here as a figure or likeness of something else.

for that tyme, it should have made the bed al on blode and a passid over
aboute. (c.12, pp.14–15)

This frustration of the linear and the temporal draws us deeper into the showing
by creating an appetite for the apophatic from her (and our) curiosity about its
fate. The bleeding continues until, seeing 'with avisement' [cf. chapter 11], she
is able to penetrate the surface 'seemings' of the image. Instead of the blood
passing over the bed, Julian's perception passes over into a meditation on the
precious plenty of God's love, transforming the image of physical excess into a
metaphor for overpassing generosity and self-emptying:

it is oure kinde and alblissfully beflowyth us be the vertue of his pretious love . . .
The pretious plenty of his dereworthy blode overflowith al erth and is redye to
wash al creaturs of synne. . . . (c.12, p.15)

In an inversion of human values, the abundance of the love/blood is the
guarantee of its value:

The dereworthy blode of our lord Iesus Criste, as verily as it is most pretious, as
verily it is most plentivous. (c.12, p.15)

The kenotic gesture of God's love links the hot blood of the Passion to the
moment of the showing and to the eternal generosity of Christ:

The pretious plenty of his dereworthy blode ascendid up into hevyn to the blissid
body of our lord Iesus Christe, and there is in him bleding and praying for us to the
Father . . . And evermore it flowith in all hevyns enioyng the salvation of al
mankynde. . . . (c.12, p.15)[49]

The theological force of this fluid word-knot (fill, fulfill, flow, overflow,
beflow, overpass, passover) derives from her earlier explorations of many of its
terms, but its pictorial and imagistic potential are held at arms length. The text
passes us over the Jordan into the apophatic.

As her contemplation of the Passion deepens and unfolds, Julian comes to
understand that the contrition and compassion of her beholding of Christ's 'herd
peyn' (c.21, p.23) is only one mode of beholding. In the ninth revelation she will
be shown two more perpsectives: that the love that made him suffer surpasses all
his pains; and the 'ioy and the blis that make hym to lekyn it' (c.23, p.25). In fact
all three perspectives are immanent in the earlier showings and gradually begin
to emerge with increasing clarity as her 'avisement' develops. But the eighth
showing is the last to be grounded on the suffering and death of Christ.
Labouring through his grief and pain, she reinforces and deepens her
understanding of the mutual self-emptying involved in true compassion:

Thus was our lord Iesus nawted for us, and we stond al in this manner nowtid with
hym; and shal done til we come to his blisse. . . . (c.18, p.21)

---

[49] Julian here emphasizes once again that the way (but not the means) to apophatic union
is *through* our bodies and created things, not by rejecting or destroying them.

In a further paradox, noughting is the route to oneing. This gives her the strength to resist the temptation to look away from the Cross which comes as a 'profir in my reason as it had be frendly . . .' (c.19, p.21). This temptation, masquerading as a reasonable development of her spiritual sight, seeks to lure her into a false apophatic. Its appearance in her reason is significant as it seeks to reintroduce the analysis, temporality and linearity that Julian has learned to suspend:

> Loke up to hevyn to his Fader.   (c.19, p.21)

Heaven is physically distant, materially visible and occupied by a Father who is hierarchically superior and distinct from the Son. This is contrary to the enfolding and unitary dynamic of her showings.

Julian recognizes, however, that the image of the crucified Christ, resonant as a new kind of signifier, offers no hindrance to her apophatic beholding and is, indeed, the guarantee of her spiritual well-being:

> And then saw I wele with the feyth that I felte that ther was nothyn betwix the crosse and hevyn that myght have desesyd me.   (c.19, p.21)

Scorning the premises of the offer, she reasserts her earlier desire 'that I be so festined to him that there is right nowte that is made betwix my God and me' (c.5, p.5).[50] She prefers to cleave to Christ, refusing to reclaim the initiative and happy to wait for him to unbind her into eternal bliss. Like Mary (as in chapter 18), she stands at the foot of the cross, manifesting her compassion.

In chapter 21, her expectations of the imminent death of Christ are overthrown:

> And I loked after the departing with al my myght and [wende] have seen the body al ded, but I saw him not so. And ryth in the same tyme that methowte, be semyng, the life myght ne lenger lesten and the shewyng of the end behovyd nedis to be, sodenly, I beholdyng in the same crosse, he chongyd his blissfull chere.   (p.23)

Physiological necessity and narrative logic have lead her to attempt to extrapolate the 'shewyng of the end'. But as so often before, the divine logic is unpredictable and unreadable. The *sudden* change of cheer changes hers, 'and I was as glad and as mery as it was possible' (c.21, p.23). The question that forms in her mind ('Where is now ony poynt of the peyne or thin agreefe?') triggers a passover experience of overpassing understanding:

> I understode that we be now in our lords menyng in his crosse with hym in our peynys and our passion, deyng, and we wilfully abydyng in the same cross with his helpe and his grace into the last poynte, sodenly he shall chonge his chere to us, and we shal be with hym in hevyn.   (c.21, p.23)

She inhabits the bliss of his meaning here in a new and profound sense. Our pains, passion and death (to ourselves, to the world, to the flesh and to the devil)

---

[50] This episode needs to be read in conjunction with chapter 13, when she sees God scorning the malice of the devil, and learns that this is the appropriate response.

help us to share in his cross and to see from the divine perspective. The undoing of the word-knot around *means* is just the unbinding that Julian has longed for. God's meaning possesses her, and she sees clearly her role as the means by which the kenotic paradigm can be displayed through the transfigured means of earthly language.

Julian draws together the accumulated resonances and overtones of the preceding revelations and discharges them in a blaze of apophatic glory:

> we wilfully abydyng in the same cross with his helpe and his grace into the last poynte, sodenly he shall chonge his chere to us, and we shal be with hym in hevyn.   (c.21, p.23)

The extraordinary power of this passover derives partly from the fact that almost every word has been explored, ruminated and potentiated in the preceding chapters. The 'desese' and 'travel' of our earthly labouring are a function of our 'frelete' (p.23) and our fettering into the 'blind demyng' (c.11, p.14) of the human perspective. But Christ's redemptive power ultimately transfigures us into a 'hey endles knowyng in God' (c.21, p.23) by working through the linear temporal world in showing us his 'time of passion' (c.21, p.23). His meaning (his self-humbling, his passion, his love, his intention, his intercession, his incarnation) opens the door to the bliss of heaven. His meaning is eternal; his means are temporal. Our wilful abiding, the paradox of intention and self-emptying, of noughting and knowing, will lead us finally to know and to become what he means:

> Betwix that one and that other shal be no tyme, and than shal al be browte to ioy.   (c.21, p.23)

THE TRINITARIAN HERMENEUTIC
IN JULIAN OF NORWICH'S
REVELATION OF LOVE

NICHOLAS WATSON

If we want to reach a more elevated understanding of the mind intelligently, a useful preliminary task is to take note of the ways in which we generally arrive at our knowledge of things. So: unless I am mistaken, we arrive at knowledge of things in three ways. For some things we discover by experience, others we acquire by reasoning, and a belief in yet others we hold by faith. Thus, for example, we come to know temporal things by experiencing them, but we rise to knowledge of the eternal by way of reasoning or by way of faith.[1]

(Richard of St Victor)

Be iii things man stondith in this life, be which iii God is worshipped and we be spedid, kept and savid. The ist is use of manys [kyndly reson]; the ii is commen teching of holy church; the thred is inward gracious werking of the Holy Gost. And these iii ben all of one God: God is the ground of our kyndly reason, and God the teaching of holy church, and God is the Holy Gost. And all ben sundry gifts, to which he will we have gret regard and attenden us therto. For these werkyn in us continualy all to God. And [thoo] ben grete thyngs, of which gret things he will we have knowing here as it were in one ABC: that is to seyn, that we have a litill knoweing whereof we shall have fullhede in hevyn, and that is for to spede us.[2]

(Julian of Norwich)

[1] *Si ad sublimium scientiam mentis sagacitate ascendere volumus, opere praetium est primo nosse quibus rerum modis notitiam apprehendere solemus. Rerum itaque notitiam, ni fallor, modo triplici apprehendimus. Nam alia experiendo probamus, alia ratiocinando colligimus, aliorum certitudinem credendo tenemus. Et temporalium quidem notitia per ipsam experientiam apprehendimus; ad aeternorum vero notitiam, modo ratiocinando, modo credendo assurgimus.* Richard of St Victor, *De Trinitate*, Book I, ch.1, in Migne, Patrologia Latina (PL) 196, col.1891; the translation is my own.

[2] *A Revelation of Love*, Long Text (LT), ch.80, from MS Bl Sloane 2499 (S1), edited by Marion Glasscoe, Exeter, 1976 (reprinted 1986), p.97, although punctuation in this and all other quotations from medieval sources is my own. Unless otherwise indicated, readings in square brackets are taken from MS Paris, BN fonds anglais 40 (P), edited by Edmund Colledge and James Walsh, *A Book of Showings to the Anchoress Julian of Norwich*, 2 vols, Toronto, 1978 (cited as Colledge and Walsh). (Citations from Julian's Short Text [ST] are from volume 1 of this edition.) Here, S1 reads 'reason naturall' for 'kyndly reson', and 'these' for 'thoo' (which seems wrong, since the 'common teching of holy church' *can* be understood in this life, for Julian). It is tempting to think that Julian originally wrote 'And *there* ben grete thyngs', pointing forward to the rest of the chapter, which lists some of them.

1

HOW DOES THE *REVELATION OF LOVE* describe and interpret the experience that forms its starting-point? In what ways does it claim to be a true account of that experience, and in what ways does it treat the experience itself as truth-bearing? What principles govern the relationships between Julian's memory of her revelation, her subsequent meditations on it, and the written accounts that attempt to articulate it? In spite of the fact that these hermeneutic questions, and the host of others which they bring to mind, are of obvious importance and difficulty, they have received oddly little by way of detailed attention.[3] Indeed, Julian scholarship – which, when it is not singing its subject's praises, is still often perceptibly apologetic in its tone – has, I think, been guilty of a kind of fundamentalism in its treatment of such questions. Perhaps this is because most scholarly work on Julian since the turn of the century has been motivated at least in part by the desire to confirm that her vision of an all-unifying cosmic love is in some final sense right;[4] under these circumstances, it may have seemed to be in everyone's interests to protect the *Revelation of Love* from the fissuring process that hermeneutic enquiry tends to initiate.

The present paper is written in the belief that any such protection, for two reasons, is inappropriate. The first reason is that a fundamentalist reading of the work – one which insists upon, for example, an absolutely literal meaning for phrases like 'I saw', or 'I understood', or 'these iii come to my [mynde] in the tyme'[5] – finally provides as partial and misleading an understanding of the work

---

3 A number of studies touch on hermeneutic issues. See especially: B. A. Windeatt, 'Julian of Norwich and Her Audience', *Review of English Studies*, n.s., 28 (1977), 1–17, a comparison between ST and LT which is most suggestive but does not explicitly discuss Julian's hermeneutics; Paul Molinari, *Julian of Norwich*, London, 1958 (cited as Molinari), which deals at length with Julian's classification of her visions (see further note 19), and with the question of their authenticity; and the lengthy introduction to Colledge and Walsh's edition, especially pp.67–71, which outlines their own hermeneutic assumptions, and pp.71–198, a richly controversial account of Julian's exegesis of her revelation.

4 Such a desire is most obvious in the many studies which emphasize either the authenticity of Julian's revelation or the orthodoxy of her book (for example, Molinari, Colledge and Walsh), but is also evident in what we might call the 'appreciations' of Julian that make up the bulk of writing on her (see Valerie Lagorio and Ritamary Bradley, *The Fourteenth-Century English Mystics: A Comprehensive Annotated Bibliography*, New York, 1981, most of items 530–619). It needs to be remembered that Julian studies have developed in proximity to a religious controversy about the worth of mysticism as a whole, and that the caution and occasional defensiveness of some writing on Julian is a response to real attacks on her authenticity and value – for which see, most recently, Andrew Ryder, 'A Note on Julian's Vision', *Downside Review*, 96 (1978), 299–304.

5 LT, ch.7, p.8; S1 omits 'mynde'; BL Sloane 3705 (S2), which seems to share an immediate ancestor with S1, reads 'enderstanding'.

as do fundamentalist readings of anything. The second reason is that, as so often elsewhere, Julian proves to have thought things out more clearly than her readers, and at a number of points in the revised version of the *Revelation of Love* displays a hermeneutic awareness that is at once sophisticated, individual, and impressively of a piece with the rest of her theology. The purpose of this paper is in fact to argue that hermeneutic enquiry is basic to Julian's enterprise in something of the sense it is to Chaucer's project in *The Canterbury Tales* or Langland's in *Piers Plowman*.[6] In different ways, all three writers find themselves concerned almost as closely with the question of how truth can be known and interpreted as they do with the nature of truth. As the passage from chapter 80 of the *Revelation of Love* quoted above makes clear, such a concern is of course integral to any spirituality that takes seriously Paul's dictum, '*nunc cognosco ex parte*',[7] an acceptable paraphrase of which would be 'in this life all knowledge is contingent': a dictum which we can also see in operation in the babbling heterogeneity of Chaucer's Canterbury pilgrims, and which is perhaps the only immovable truth uncovered by Will in all of his wanderings. Yet these same parallels also suggest something distinctively late medieval about Julian's belief that no knowledge beyond the merest 'ABC' can be obtained in this life. Between her remarks and the superficially similar ones, likewise quoted above, with which Richard of St Victor begins his wonderfully confident speculations on the Trinity lie all that separate the middle of the twelfth century from the last years of the fourteenth: the age of scholasticism, the rise of nominalism, the decline of the crusading ideal, the growth of ever more successful heresies, the advent of the Great Schism. Where Julian is apparently closer to Richard than to either Langland or Chaucer is in the assurance with which she can incorporate into her vision of life the second half of Paul's dictum: '*tunc autem cognoscam sicut et cognitus sum*' – 'but then I shall know even as I am known'.[8] It is this optimistic and intimate expectation of knowledge that is to come that distinguishes the *Revelation of Love* from most other products of the late medieval 'age of anxiety', and which enables Julian to resolve – and to do so with a remarkable intellectual coherence – most of the hermeneutic difficulties in which her long life's labour involved her.

---

[6] For hermeneutic enquiry in Chaucer, see, most recently, Carolyn Dinshaw, *Chaucer's Sexual Poetics*, Madison, 1989. The most thorough-going analysis of Langland in these terms is still Mary Carruthers, *The Search for St Truth: A Study of Meaning in 'Piers Plowman'*, Evanston, 1973.

[7] 1 Corinthians 13:12a, from *Biblia sacra iuxta vulgatam versionem*, ed. Bonifatio Fischer *et al.*, 2 vols, Stuttgart, 1983.

[8] 1 Corinthians 13:12b.

2

The essence of the hermeneutic problem which any reader of Julian faces, and which she faced in recording her experience, lies in the impossibility of distinguishing clearly between the revelation itself and the responses and reflections it provoked.[9] Very many years – certainly more than twenty and perhaps as many as forty – separate Julian's experiences in May, 1373 from the final account given in the Long Text. These years were presumably spent in meditation on those experiences, but this is not an altogether reassuring fact to the literal-minded reader; after all, intense thought on a single set of themes over a sustained period is hardly the best way to preserve those themes in their original form. Nor does the earlier Short Text (which I will not on the whole be considering here) provide as much help as we might like. Even if it really is the freshly immediate response to revelation that it has generally been taken to be – and I will argue elsewhere that it is not[10] – it differs so markedly and in so many respects from Julian's revision as to raise more difficulties than it settles. For example, most of the imagistic precision for which Julian has become famous – as when she likens the blood flowing down from Christ's forehead to pellets, herring-scales and rain falling off a roof, explaining gravely why each image is appropriate – is absent from the Short Text, even though she frequently states or implies in the Long Text that such images 'came to her mind' at the time of the revelation.[11] Is this absence because Julian for some reason suppressed material,

9 This is also the view of Roger Ellis in 'Revelation and the Life of Faith: The Vision of Julian of Norwich', *Christian*, 6 (1980), 61–71, (especially p.70), and of Marion Glasscoe in 'Means of Showing: An Approach to Reading Julian of Norwich', *Analecta Cartusiana*, 106, Salzburg, 1983, 151–77, especially pp.151–52). Contrast the opposite view of Colledge and Walsh, e.g. note to LT, chapter 51, line 80 (p.520), which holds that revelation and reflection are always carefully distinguished; see further section 4 below.

10 See an article in progress under the title of 'The Composition of Julian of Norwich's *Revelation of Love*', which presents evidence that ST dates from the first half of the 1380s at the earliest, and may have been completed after 1388: an argument that of course has a considerable impact on our dating of LT. The article is based on a paper 'A wyf ther was', given at the conference: Women in Middle English Literature, Liège, December 1990.

11 LT, ch.7, p.8: 'These iii come to my [mynde] in the tyme: pellots, for roundhede in the comynge out of the blode; the scale of heryng, [for roundhede] in the spreadeing in the forehede; the dropys of evese, for the plentioushede inumerable.' (Compare ST. chs 3 and 5, pp.210–11, 217–18). Another example of the passage which is far more detailed visually in LT is provided by the description of the dying and drying of Christ in chs 16 and 17, pp.18–20, with which compare ST, ch.10 (pp.233–35). See especially LT, p.19:
    And ferthermore, I saw that the swete skyn and the tender flesh, with the heere and the blode, was al rasyd and losyd abov from the bone with the thornys, where thowe it were daggyd on many pecys, as a clith that were saggand, as it wold hastely have fallen of for hevy and lose while it had kynde moysture. And

perhaps because it seemed too trivial and non-symbolic? Or has her memory of her 'mind' at the time of the revelation undergone that drift towards greater vividness that occurs when we tell an important dream many times, gradually fusing our sense of what we experienced with our understanding of what it meant and our desire to convey some of the force as well as the bare bones of the experience to our listeners? These may seem the tiresomely unanswerable questions of a precisionist – literary and theological scholars alike have tended to hop over them with little more than a backward glance – but their importance is real enough if we take Julian's own precision seriously. The passing of time is not an incidental feature of the Long Text; on the contrary, dates, numbers of years, Julian's own age, are carefully brought before us at the work's most crucial moments, as though they are of thematic significance.[12]

I will return later to consider the problem of time from Julian's own perspective, and to discuss the passage in the Long Text which effectively cuts the Gordian knot I am attempting here to tie. But the inseparability of divine revelation from human reflection and the hermeneutic tangles this inseparability creates are not, of course, the products merely of Julian's failure to record her experiences sooner than she did, or to do so with complete consistency on two different occasions. They are integral, rather, to the very qualities of the revelation itself which made it at once so time-consuming and so important to comprehend, assess and at last write down: to its experiential elusiveness and its structural complexity, its apparently endless profundity and its disconcerting, potentially perhaps even dangerous, theological optimism. I clearly cannot hope to discuss any of these qualities adequately in a paper of this size (and I will be giving Julian's theology in particular only a peripheral treatment), nonetheless, something must now be said about the nature of Julian's revelation, about the exegetical framework that she evolves in order to deal with it, and about how that framework is in practice applied.

that was grete sorrow and drede to me, for methowte I wold not for my life a sen it fallen . . . And than . . . it began to dreyen and stynte a party of the weyte and sette abute the garland. And thus it envyronyd al aboute, as it were garland upon garland . . .

This passage is instuctive in another sense also, sinse S1 here differs importantly from P (see Colledge and Walsh, vol.2, pp.362–63), as though the scribes of the two manuscripts, or of their ancestors, have felt free to develop this Passion meditation in their own directions. See Windeatt, *art. cit.*, for further examples of the relation between LT and ST.

12 References to the passing of time are introduced in the first chapter of exposition (ch.2, p.2), in the key chapter 51, almost at the centre of the work (p.56), and again in the last chapter (ch.86, p.102).

3

Whether or not she knew much or anything about mystical predecessors such as Bridget of Sweden, Mechthild of Hackeborn or Elizabeth of Schönau, the form of Julian's revelation presented her with an interpretive task which would have rendered their examples of limited usefulness.[13] As they have come down to us and conceivably came down to Julian, the experiences of these women seem to have been of a fairly direct kind: a succession of visions, often accompanied by celestial conversations, and sometimes also affecting the senses of smell, touch and taste, which in bald outline at least would not have been difficult to understand or record.[14] It is clear that Julian's experience was radically different: a disparate series of glimpses of Christ's Passion, strung like beads along her life-saving gaze at a crucifix, and interspersed with other, more abstract sights, as well as with a few pregnant words passed from Christ to her and sometimes back again. The power of this revelation must have lain more in its sense of latency than in any of its unspectacular external manifestations: in the way that it seemed to offer (as it still seemed to offer decades later) no more than 'as it were the begynnyng of an ABC' of 'our lordis menyng' – as though the entire revelation corresponded to the introductory *aleph* which some Cabbalists averred was all that God actually said to Moses on mount Sinai.[15] In my own view, though many will not agree, the lack of visual detail in the Short Text perhaps indicates that even the Passion scenes themselves originally had little of

[13] The works of all three writers were available in England by the fifteenth century. In view of Margery Kempe's intense awareness of Bridget, Julian probably knew at least of her, although not until some time after 1373. For Bridget, see Roger Ellis, 'Flores ad Fabricandum . . . Coronam': An Investigation into the Uses of the Revelations of St Bridget of Sweden in Fifteenth-Century England', *Medium Aevum*, 51 (1982), 163–86. For Mechtild, see *The Booke of Gostlye Grace of Mechtild of Hackeborn*, ed. Theresa A. Halligan, Toronto, 1979, pp.47–59. For Elizabeth, see Ruth J. Dean, 'Manuscripts of St Elizabeth of Schönau in England', *Modern Language Review*, 32 (1937), 62–71.

[14] Bridget's visions, for example, were set down immediately by her scribes, although the process of editing and organizing them into the structure that became the *Liber Celestis* was not completed until after her death. See Ellis, " 'Flores ad Fabricandum . . ." ', *op. cit.*, cited in note 13.

[15] See LT, ch.51, p.59. For the radical Cabbalist view of the handing down of the ten commandments (held, e.g., by Rabbi Mendel of Rymanow), see Gershom Scholem, *On The Kabbalah and Its Symbolism*, New York, 1965, p.30, who remarks:

> In Hebrew the consonant *aleph* represents nothing more than the position taken by the larynx when a word begins with a vowel. Thus the *aleph* may be said to denote the source of all articulate sound . . . To hear the *aleph* is to hear next to nothing; it is the preparation for all audicble language . . .

Similarly, to call one's own mature understanding of a revelation merely the 'begennynge of an ABC' involves a recognition that the revelation itself is still only a tiny part not of truth as such but of the preparation for knowing a truth that it can no more than dimly foreshadow.

the mesmerising clarity that so colours their presentation in Julian's revision; after all, her youthful request for more 'feleing in the passion of Christe', which she describes at the beginning of the work, surely implies that her imagination was not of the kind that found easy the sympathetic absorption in the events of Christ's death that Passion meditation demands.[16] This may, of course, be quite wrong. But even if it is, Julian's revelation has an imagistic sparseness and at least a surface fragmentariness to it that is largely untypical of the experiences of medieval women visionaries, and which must initially have been deeply confusing to its recipient. It is not surprising that her own earliest interpretation of her experience was that it was an attack of madness: 'Then cam a religious person to me and askid me how I ferid. And I seyd I had ravid today, and he leuhe loud and inderly.'[17]

The basic exegetical strategy which both versions of the *Revelation of Love* describe and apply in an attempt to articulate and circumscribe the complexities of Julian's experience is the familiar tripartite division of the 'shewings' into 'bodily sight', 'word formyd in my understonding' and 'ghostly sight': a division which is occasionally complicated by further categories, such as 'gostly in bodily lyknes' and 'more gostly without bodyly lyknes', but which by and large provides a serviceable framework.[18] Two of the three main terms, 'bodily sight' and 'ghostly sight', occur in other Middle English religious writings (for example, Walter Hilton's *Scale of Perfection*), where they characteristically derive (albeit indirectly) from Augustine's distinctions (in his commentary *De Genesi ad Litteram*) between 'corporeal', 'imaginative' and 'intellective' vision – his three categories sometimes being reduced to two under the influence, presumably, of the better known distinction between the corporeal and spiritual senses.[19] I know of no other women visionaries who use this Augustinian

---

[16] Compare LT, ch.51, pp.54–61 (part of which is discussed at length below), in which Julian confessedly extrapolates her vision with details she cannot be sure were originally there. With the exception of a few famous passages, the *Revelation of Love* is not rich in visual imagery.

[17] LT, ch.66, p.81.

[18] The basic tripartite distinction is made in LT, ch.9, p.11 (compare ST, ch.7, p.224), and reiterated in ch.73, p.88 (compare ST, ch.23, pp.272–73); the category 'gostly in bodily lyknes' is introduced in LT, ch.4, p.5, to describe Julian's first vision of Mary, and is mentioned again, with 'more gostly without bodyoy lyknes', at the beginning of LT, ch.51, p.54, at the beginning of the parable of the lord and servant.

[19] See Augustine, *De Genesi at Litteram*, Book XII, chp.6 ff. in PL 34, cols. 458ff. For discussions of the medieval influence of Augustine's distinctions, see J.-P. Torrell, *Théorie de la prophétie et philosophie de la conaissance aux environs 1230: La Contribution d'Hughes de Saint-Cher*, Spicilegium Sacrum Lovaniense, Études et documents, 40, Louvain, 1977. For Hilton's use of 'bodily' and 'ghostly' sight, see *Scale of Perfection* (e.g., in the modernization of Evelyn Underhill, London, 1923), Book I, chp10–11, and Book II, chp43—46, where the terms undoubtedly correspond to Augustinian 'corporeal' and 'intellectual' vision. The phrase 'gastelich sihðe' is also used in Book II of *Ancrene Wisse* (ed. J. R. R. Tolkien, Early English Text Society, O.S., 249, London, 1962, f.24a, 7) to describe contemplation by the spiritual

terminology,[20] and no other visionary material which combines 'bodily' and 'ghostly' sight with any of the almost polyphonic complexity of Julian's revelation (it is more common for them to be contrasted, as they are by Hilton, than to occur together in an integrated act of divine communication).[21] Nonetheless, by employing them Julian evidently intends to suggest the continuity between her revelation and visionary tradition, and to lessen both our and perhaps her own sense of the revelation's essential elusiveness and strangeness.[22]

The 'Augustinian' hermeneutic thus creates some basic categories which have the added benefit of being sanctioned by tradition. Yet as soon as we look in detail at the interpretive problems posed by Julian's revelation, it becomes clear how inadequate this exegetical device, taken on its own, must prove to be. For in practice Julian finds herself describing almost as many kinds of 'sight' and other divinely-inspired experiences, and invoking almost as many kinds of exegesis with which to interpret them, as her revelation can be separated into distinguishable visionary moments. The flexibility with which she deploys words depicting her apprehension of the revelation – words such as 'understood', 'showed', 'took', 'conceived' and especially 'saw' – indeed

senses, in a passage indebted to Gregory's *Moralia in Iob* and Book X of Augustine'e *Confessions*; see *Anchoritic Spirituality: 'Ancrene Wisse' and Associated Works*, trans. Anne Savage and Nicholas Watson, The Classics of Western Spirituality, Mahwah, 1991, pp.355–56, notes 58 and 63–66. In *The Chastizing of God's Children* (ed. Joyce Bazire and Eric Colledge, Oxford, 1957, 169.12–171.17), the term 'bodily' sight again has a strictly Augustinian sense, this time transmitted via Alphonse of Pecha's *Epistola Solitarii*, the source of this part of the *Chastizing*. In the light of these parallels, the insistence by both Molinari (pp.60–70) and Colledge and Walsh (p.87) that Julian's use of the term 'bodily sight' corresponds to Augustinian *intellectual* vision is unacceptable – especially if we recall that Julian's first 'bodily sight' of the bleeding head, and all subsequent sights in this mode, develop from her continuing gaze at a crucifix which is physically present throughout. Nor is Molinari likely to be right in assuming that Julian's terminology is subjectively descriptive rather than formally analytic; on the contrary, her careful attempts to distinguish different modes of vision using the accepted Middle English terminology suggests that she is almost certainly aware on some level of the Augustinian categories.

20　Note, however, that if Julian encountered Bridget's *Liber Celestis* (or *The Chastizing of God's Children*), she would have met this terminology in *relation* to Bridget's visions, albeit not in the visions themselves, in Alphonse of Pecha's *Epistola Solitarii*. (For the circulation of this work with the second edition of the *Liber*, see Roger Ellis, *The Liber Celestis of St Bridget of Sweden*, Early English Text Society, O.S., 291 (1988), pp.x–xii.)

21　See, e.g., *Scale of Perfection*, Book I, chapters 10–12, which admit the existence of genuine 'bodily sight', but focus the reader's attention on the capacity of such sensual visions to lead one away from true contemplation.

22　I will not mostly be concerned here with Julian's other category of revelatory modes, 'word formyd in my understonding', but it too can be linked to traditional mystical terminology. For example, Alphonse of Pecha (and after him *The Chastizing of God's Children*, 172.9–173.4, see notes 19 and 20) discusses the various kinds of mystical locutions, drawing on Book XVIII of Gregory's *Moralia in Iob*.

renders her own (or any other) system of categorization virtually useless for the purposes of detailed analysis. Nor does Julian seem to resist this flexibility; on the contrary, she seems determined to use the language of revelation in as wide a variety of ways as possible, almost as though she is deliberately working against the restrictions of her own circumscribing hermeneutic structure.

4

Consider first, for example, the opening of one of Julian's exegetical showpieces, the famous passage with which the series of revelations begins:

> In this sodenly I saw the rede blode trekelyn downe fro under the garlande, hote and freisly and ryth plenteously, as it were in the time of his passion that the garlande of thornys was pressid on his blissid hede. Ryte so, both God and man, the same that sufferd thus for me, I conceived treuly and mightily that it was himselfe shewed it me, without ony mene. And, in the same sheweing, sodenly the Trinite fullfilled the herte most of ioy. And so I understood it shall be in hevyn withoute end to all that shall come there. For the Trinite is God, God is the Trinite; the Trinite is our maker and keeper, the Trinite is our everlasting lover, everlasting ioy and blisse, be our lord Iesus Christ. And this was shewed in the first and in all; for where Iesus appereith the blissid Trinite is understond, as to my sight.[23]

This passage moves from the phrase 'I saw', which apparently signifies in a wholly literal sense that 'there appeared before my eyes', to the phrase 'as to my sight', in which the image of seeing is equally wholly figurative, meaning something like 'according to my divinely inspired interpretation'. Between these points there is a development from Julian's 'conceiving' what it is she is seeing and who it is that is showing it to her, to the joy she feels, to her understanding of an eternal theological truth about that joy, and to her generalizing of that truth – on the basis both of this showing and of those that follow – into the interpretive principle that 'where Iesus appereith the blissid Trinite is understond'. This principle is described as 'shewed', that is, 'manifested', in the revelation as a whole – although the physical sight of the blood has also been called a 'sheweing' – and the phrase 'as to my sight' which rounds the passage off is clearly intended to intensify, not qualify, one's sense that the revelatory process is still at work even as Julian sets out to record an experience that is far in her past.[24] Thus although the vision begins with the simple miracle of a sight of Christ's blood, every moment of this progression towards abstraction and generalization continues to be suffused with the language of revelation, and both

---

[23] LT, ch.4, p.4.

[24] While Middle English 'as to my sight' was doubtless sometimes used with the vague generality of the modern English 'in my view', the instances of similar phrases given in the Middle English Dictionary article on 'sight' mostly give the term real weight, as though it is more closely equivalent to 'in my *judgement*' (see especially definition 8 (b), where 'as to my sight' itself is not recorded). For obvious reasons, Julian's use of the term is likely to have been especially conscious and serious.

Julian's original response to what she saw and, indeed, her *present* response prove to form as vital a part of the whole picture as the vision of the blood itself. After all, it is her 'true and mighty' acceptance of the vision as it begins, and her much later identification of its deepest source as the Trinity rather than Christ alone, that renders the process of interpretation – of 'seeing' in a figurative as well as a visual sense – possible.[25] A term as crude as 'bodily sight' is hardly an adequate or accurate way of describing the delicate interaction of eye and mind, of memory, thought and feeling, of God and Julian, which blossoms upwards and outwards from a single visionary moment in the text.

It is true that once this 'blossoming' process is established, the more analytic parts of Julian's account are attributed to the visionary faculty of 'ghostly sight'. Yet even in the first revelation, the terminology associated with 'ghostly sight' is already used still more creatively, and more inconsistently, than that associated with 'bodily sight'. The term enters the work in an indirect and somewhat mysterious fashion. Looking at the 'bodily sight' of the Passion, Julian 'knew wele that it was strength enow to me, ya and to all creturers leving, ageyn all the fends of hell and ghostly temptation'.[26] Then, 'in this' (that is, either 'in' the Passion or 'within' Julian's knowledge of its efficacy), God 'browght our blissid lady to my understonding', where she is seen 'in the stature that she was wan she conceived with child', in a mode which is called 'ghostly in bodily likeness'. This expression, which is suggestive of a visual experience in a less concrete form than the vision of the blood, perhaps evocative of Augustinian 'imaginative vision', is made redundant after only a sentence by a shift to a more abstract kind of showing, a partial intuition of 'the wisedam and the trueth of hir soule' which 'caused hir sey full mekely to Gabriel: "Lo me, Gods handmayd" '. This would seem close to the category of 'intellectual vision'.[27] So likewise would the next visionary moment, which occurs 'in this same time', when Christ shows 'a ghostly sight of his homely loveing' in which Julian says she 'saw' (that is, more or less, 'realized') 'that he is to us everything that is good and comfortable for us'.[28] At this point, we appear to have reached the terminus of another such process of abstraction from the visual to the theological of the kind we saw growing out of the vision of the blood. But now, from 'in this' apparently wholly non-visual realization, Christ shows a new, partly visual image of 'a littil thing, the quantitye of an hesil nutt in the palme of my hand', which a 'general' voice

25 Contrast the equivalent passage in ST, ch.3, pp.210–11, which omits everything from 'And, in the same sheweing', presenting us with an incident and its immediate response ('I conseyvede treuly and myghttyllye that itt was hym selfe that schewyd it me') rather as the B and C texts of *Piers Plowman* builds on the A text's relatively simple notion of Dowel, Dobet and Dobest, turning them into no more than what John Alford calls 'primarily a rhetorical scheme for amplification' (*A Companion to 'Piers Plowman'*, ed. John A. Alford, Berkeley, 1988, p.46).
26 LT, ch.4, p.4.
27 LT, ch.4, p.5.
28 LT, ch.5, p.5.

tells Julian is 'all that is made', and which she considers 'with eye of my understondyng', seeing in it 'iii propertes' – that God makes it, loves it and keeps it. Here, Julian claims to 'see' the properties of the Trinity reflected in an image of the creation that is seemingly also 'seen', in a quasi-physical sense, lying in her hand. Evidently the process we are now involved with is not one of abstraction from images but of theological thinking through images; the line of development runs from Mary's 'wisedam and trueth' in anticipation of the Incarnation, through Julian's intuition of God's love for humankind, to her recognition that this love encompasses the whole of creation. Yet a further surprise is in store, for the long argument which follows from the vision of the 'littil thing', and which focusses now on the human response to God, instead of the divine response to humanity – on the need to approach God 'nakidly', turning away from the created order in an act of apophatic forgetting – is actually a meditation not on the 'litill thing' itself but on Julian's immediate reaction to it: 'methowte it might suddenly have fallen to nowte for littil'. Indeed, Julian treats this statement with much the intensity of attention she will later bestow on the words Christ 'forms in her understanding', returning to the words 'nowte' and 'litill' (for example, 'it needyth us to have knoweing of the littlehede of creatures and to nowtyn all things') as though they form part of the divinely inspired 'text' of her revelation.[29] Rather as in the account of the 'bodily sight', the revelation here expands to incorporate, perhaps even to become, Julian's response to it, which as she writes she further elaborates into a speech spoken by the soul to God (' "God of thy goodnesse give me thyselfe" ') that is also treated as part of the revelation – it is written 'as be the understonding that I have in this sheweing'.[30] It seems that the term 'ghostly sight' encompasses the entirety of words, thoughts and feelings that she associates with this complex succession of insights.

In the first revelation, the terminology associated with 'bodily' and 'ghostly sight' is thus already being stretched beyond its limits both by the complexity of the visionary experience itself and by Julian's desire to articulate that complexity as fully as possible. Yet the exposition of the first revelation is more systematic than most of what follows, in which an ever increasing variety of phenomena are assimilated into the categories of sight and showing. For example, at several

---

[29] LT, ch.5, p.5.
[30] LT, ch.5, p.6. The immediate context makes the 'revelatory' status of this speech clearer:
> Also our lord God shewed that it is full gret plesance to him that a sily soule come to him nakidly and pleynly and homely. For this is the kinde yernings of the soule by the touching of the Holy Ghost, as be the understondyng that I have in this sheweing: 'God, of thy goodnesse, give me thyselfe . . .' (LT, ch.5, p.6)

Logically, the word 'for' suggests that rather than being a meditative extrapolation of the 'showing' described in the first sentence, the speech actually is that 'showing' – as becomes clear if one substitutes 'so', 'thus' or even 'and'.

points and in various ways, Julian finds revelatory material in what she *does not* see. The main significance of the second revelation develops from her initial inability to decide whether it really is a revelation or not; here, her disappointment at seeing Christ's bleeding head on the point of turning back into a mere figure on a crucifix becomes a lesson about God's necessary absences, in spite of which 'he wille that we levyn that we se him continually', holding on by faith to the vision we cannot always keep in sight. This is a vision about the limitations of vision.[31] The third revelation centres attention on what is not there in a more radical way. After seeing 'God in a point' ('by which sight I saw that he is in al things'), Julian proceeds to the generalization, 'here I saw sothly that synne is no dede, for in al this was not synne shewid'. Here, Julian explicitly 'sees' an insight (and one which comes to be of considerable importance to her theology) *as a result* of its not being 'showed'.[32] Yet another kind of showing based on the absence of vision is revelation XI, in which Christ first offers Julian a sight of his mother (in the words, 'wilt thou se her?'), then fails to bestow this sight on her when she accepts it. 'Oftentymes I prayd this ["ya, good lord, if it be thy will"], and I wend a seen hir in bodily presens, but I saw hir not so', comments Julian, only to insist at once that 'Iesus *in that word* ["wilt thou se her"] shewid me a gostly sigte of hir', saving the revelation by retreating from a literal to a figurative reading of Christ's offer.[33]

In the later stages of the *Revelation of Love*, these 'apophatic' and oxymoronic ways of understanding visionary material develop into Julian's marvellously subtle discussions of the partiality of all earthly knowledge, such as the one from chapter 80 with which this paper is prefaced. Yet by the time we have reached revelation XI we have also encountered other uses of the language of vision that are almost as unexpected. Revelation VII, for example, is called both a 'showing' and a 'vision', but consists only of a sensation: a 'soveren gostly lekyng in my soule', which is alternately bestowed on Julian and withdrawn.[34] Revelation III contains a speech by God which Julian does not hear, but somehow extrapolates merely from seeing him 'in a point': 'And al this shewid

---

[31] See LT, ch.10, pp.11–13. In her account of this revelation, Julian also amplifies an 'answer' made in her 'reason' to her desire for more light: 'If God wil shew thee more, he shal by thy light. Thee nedith none but him.' Like the 'general voice' which identifies the nut-like 'thing' in revelation I, the source of this speech is not specifically identified as God.

[32] LT, ch.11, pp.13–14.

[33] LT, ch.25, pp.27–28.

[34] LT, ch.15, pp.17–18:
   And after this he shewid a soveren gostly lekyng in my soule . . . then the peyne shewid ageyn to my feling, and than the ioy and the lekyng, and now that one, and now that other . . . This vision was shewid me, after myn vnderstondyng, that it is spedeful to some soulis to fele on this wise.
   Contrast the *Scale of Perfection*, Book I, ch.10, which distinguishes between 'bodily appearing' and 'any other feeling in bodily wits . . . in sounding of ear, or savouring in the mouth, or smelling at the nose . . .'

he ful blisfully, meneing thus: "Se, I am God. Se, I am in althing." '[35] An integral part of the visionary content of revelation V is a speech made, apparently out loud, by Julian herself about the things she is 'seeing' in Christ's Passion, 'game, scorne and arneste'.[36] Revelation VIII even contains a curious passage in which a sentence from her own Short Text is seemingly treated in the same way, as visionary material requiring explication.[37] In later chapters of the Long Text, especially in the major digression between revelations XIV and XV (chapters 44–63) and the lengthy conclusion after revelation XVI (chapters 73–86), there are yet more new applications for the terms 'ghostly sight' and 'showing', this time to indicate things Julian has learned from the entirety of the revelation: for example, that 'I saw that God may done all that us nedith', or 'I had in parte touching, sight and feling in iii propertes of God, in which the strength and effect of all the revelation stondith'.[38] Indeed, the whole concluding movement of fourteen chapters is announced as a sustained exposition of 'ghostly sight': 'for the gostly syght, I have seyd sumdele, but I may never full tellen it. And therefore of this syght I am sterrid to sey more as God will give me grace.'[39] This grandly general application of the terminology of revelation finally moves it to a place where its original basis in an Augustinian conception of imaginative and intellectual vision is apparently almost forgotten.[40]

[35] LT, ch.11, p.14. After the speech, Julian concludes the chapter, 'Thus migtily, wisely and lovinly was the soule examynyd in this vision. Than saw I sothly that me behovyd nedis to assenten with gret reverens, enioyand in God.' That is, the speech is a fictional dramatization of the effect of the 'vision' on the soul, at the end of which it 'sees' the truth.

[36] LT, ch.13, p.16. Julian explicates part of her own speech (' "I se scorne that God scornith him and he shal be scornyd" ') rather as if it were a locution spoken by Christ [italics mine]:

> And I seid 'He *is* scornid', I mene that God scornith him – that is to sey, for he seeth him now as he shall done withoute end. For in this God shewid that the fend is dampnid. And this ment I when I seid, 'He *shall be* scornyd': at domysday generally of all that shal be savyd, to hose consolation he hath gret invye . . . .

[37] Thus I saw the swete fleshe dey, in semyng be party after party, dryande with mervelous peynys. And as longe as any spirit had life in Crists fleshe, so longe sufferid he peyne. This longe pynyng semyd to me as if he had bene seven night ded, deyand, at the poynt of out passing away, sufferand the last peyne. And than I said [*P reads 'say'*] it semyd to me as if he had bene seven night ded, it menyth that the swete body was so discoloryd, so drye, so clongen, so dedely and so petevous as he had be seven night dede, continuly deyand   (LT, ch.16, pp.18–19)

The third sentence here ('This longe pynyng' etc.) is an expansion of a passage of ST (ch.10, p.233) which is then explicated (somewhat clumsily) by means of further expansion in the next sentence. The formula 'that I said . . . it menyth' is most suggestive of the process of meditative amplification by which the sparseness of ST's accounts of Julian's 'bodily sights' acquire the far greater detail they possess in LT.

[38] LT, chs.75 and 83, pp.90 and 100.

[39] LT, ch.73, p.88.

[40] It would be possible, perhaps, to defend Julian's extremely broad use of 'ghostly sight'

5

Faced with a revelation which it took her a lifetime to begin to plumb and whose divine source made it by definition inexhaustible, Julian evidently felt it both appropriate and necessary to wield her basic exegetical tools in a comparably inexhaustible variety of ways. Medieval Biblical exegetes formalized their interpretive terminology into the celebrated 'four senses of Scripture', but nonetheless often pointed out the extraordinary capacity of God's word to exceed all attempts so to circumscribe it. For example, Gilbert of Stanford exclaims with awestruck poetry over the way that:

> Imitating the action of the swiftest of rivers, Holy Scripture fills up the depths of the human mind and yet always overflows, quenches the thirsty and yet remains inexhaustible. Bountiful streams of spiritual senses gush out from it and, merging into others, make still others spring up – or rather (since 'wisdom is undying'), they do not merge but *emerge* and, showing their beauty to others, cause these others not to replace them as they fail but to succeed them as they remain.[41]

If Julian continues to use her threefold exegetical system, it is with a similar belief in its final inadequacy and a similarly loving intention of letting her revelation 'fill up the depths of the human mind' by employing whatever means she can to make it speak. Indeed, the flexibility of her exposition, the variety of its strategies, and the rapidity with which it shuttles between particular moral points and far-reaching theological ones all suggest the influence of biblical exegesis – mediated, perhaps, mainly through preaching – on her writing and thought. It would even be possible, I think, to interpret many of her own interpretations using the framework of the tropological, allegorical and anagogical senses, and thus to regard the whole of the *Revelation of Love* as an

as a specialized development of the category of 'intellectual vision' as this is described in, for example, the last chapters of Book II of *The Scale of Perfection*, in which the soul 'sees' the truths of the Scriptures by intuition (see, Book II, ch.43), and then, presumably through the Scriptures, learns to contemplate the major doctrines of the Christian faith, 'seeing' the natures of souls (ch.45), of angels (ch.46), of the humanity and divinity of Christ (ch.46), and finally of the Trinity (ch.46). My point is that Julian's use of the terminology of revelation is so flexible that such parallels are likely to be almost accidental; she uses the terms as it suits her to, not according to any disciplined or learned idea of their meanings.

[41] '*Scriptura Sancta, morem rapidissimi fluminis tenens, sic humanarum mentium profunda replet, ut semper exundet; sic haurientes satiat, ut inexhausta permaneat. Profluunt ex ea spiritualium sensuum gurgites abundantes, et transeuntibus aliis, alia surgunt–immo, non transeuntibus (quia "sapientia immortalis est"* [see Widsom 1.15], *sed emergentibus, et decorem suum ostendentibus aliis, alii non deficientibus succedunt sed manentes subsequuntur.*' Gilbert of Stanford, *In Cant.* 20.225, quoted in Umberto Eco, *Semiotics and the Philosophy of Language*, Bloomington, 1984, p.150; the translation is my own. I am grateful to Anne Savage for drawing my attention to this passage, and to Eco's useful accompanying discussion.

intensely meditative commentary, rather along the lines of Bernard's *Sermones super Cantica Canticorum*.

Yet while the analogy between Julian's practice as an interpreter and those of a biblical exegete is a real one, it must not be allowed to blind us to a fundamental difference: that the revelation that constitutes the 'text' which Julian expounds is not a fixed entity – an immutable set of propositions or simple pictorial visions – but rather an interaction between a number of profoundly mysterious and (in their way) highly intellectual visionary moments and their actively-engaged recipient, the boundaries of which are by their very nature so fluid as to be impossible to chart. The consequences of this fluidity we have seen to be far-reaching indeed. For precisely the most distinctive and surprising thing about Julian's use of the language of revelation is her tendency to apply it so broadly that all her comments on the 'text' of her showings – both her brief responses and remarks as an actor in the drama and even her vastly extended meditations as its narrator – turn into further 'sights' and 'showings', thus in effect becoming 'text' themselves. Indeed, if we take all Julian's references to 'sight', 'showing', 'understonding' and so on seriously, it is hard to find any passage of the *Revelation of Love* which is not implicitly or explicitly treated as actually constituting (as distinct from merely commenting on) part of the revelation. It is as though the Biblical text in the centre of its manuscript page were literally to 'overflow' and to merge with the surrounding apparatus; or, to put the same point the other way around, as though the apparatus were to merge with the text, annexing its divinely-inspired status and authority, and forming a layered, composite text which engages in its own exegesis. It is true that Julian emphasises that her book is provisional and impossible to finish in this life, stating as she closes that 'this book is begunne be Gods gift and his grace, but it is not yet performid, as to my syte'.[42] Yet as I have pointed out, the *Revelation of Love* views such contingency as a condition of all earthly understanding whatever; one of the most theologically daring aspects of the work is its insistence that even the truth God revealed to the Church is provisional in very much the same way.[43] Within the limitations imposed by the present life, the words with which the Long Text opens are apparently meant to be applied literally not merely to the original 'showings', narrowly defined, but rather to the work as a whole: '*this* is a revelation of love'.[44]

---

[42] LT, ch.86, p.102; note again (see note 24) how much more pointed is Julian's use of the phrase 'as to my sight' than first appears.

[43] The provisional and temporary nature of the 'feith of holy church' is stressed throughout chs.44–47, where this faith is described as the 'lower dome' (the 'heyer dome' being the revelation), necessary only on account of the fallen state of human sensuality, which demands that we know ourselves sinners and worthy of wrath *even though* God is not in fact capable of such wrath (see especially LT, ch.45, pp.47–48). For an analysis, see Grace Jantzen, *Julian of Norwich*, London, 1987, pp.177–80.

[44] LT, ch.1, p.1.

6

At this point, I anticipate the objection that, after laying grave charges of fundamentalism against readings of Julian which ignore the hermeneutic complexities of her work, I am merely compounding the offence in my own way, by insisting with dogged persistence on a literalistic reading of her visionary language. Am I not pressing her uses of 'see', 'sight', even 'showing' and especially 'understanding' too hard by claiming that, taken *in toto*, they obliterate the distinction between revelation and commentary? After all, what purpose could it serve Julian to present her work in this audacious way, as though it were a direct equivalent of – rather than merely a vehicle for – the word of God? And how, in any case, could she justify such a presentation when she is writing at so many years remove from her original, authenticating experience? Further, if the *Revelation of Love* is indeed intended to be as well as merely to contain a revelation, why is it that Julian nonetheless maintains so much of the format of a 'text' with accompanying commentary, rather than fusing the two into a work that is overtly visionary in nature throughout?[45] I wish to end by considering some of the issues raised by these important questions.

First, Julian's purpose in presenting her work as somehow constituting an equivalent of her original revelation has to do with her fundamental understanding of the revelation's significance: that through it, God is announcing his nature anew not only to her but to Christian humanity as a whole. This understanding takes various forms during the course of the *Revelation of Love*. It is at its most daring in the chapters following the exposition of revelation XIII, in which Julian learns that 'al manner of thyng shal be wele':[46] a statement that opens up a gulf, which the rest of the work concludes is finally unbridgeable in this life, between what is at one point called the 'heyer dome' of the revelation and the 'lower dome' (or 'dome of holy church') of received Christian orthodoxy.[47] From this revelation on, indeed, the tension between the two

---

[45] Compare, for example, Hildegard of Bingen's *Scivias*, a series of visions, prophecies and expositions, all of which are presented as divine in their immediate origin, and as having been given in a timeless visionary moment, but which clearly incorporate the author's thought and reading during the ten years the work took to write. See the edition in Corpus Christianorum, Continuatio Medievalis, volumes 43–43a, by Adelgundis Führkötter, Turnhout, 1978.

[46] LT, ch.27, pp.28–29.

[47] LT, ch.45, p.48. As I understand Julian's argument, she clearly articulates the continuing *necessity* for both 'domes', but is unable to reconcile their *truth*, that is, how God views both. See especially LT, ch.45, p.48:

Than was this my desire: that I myte sen in God in what manner that the dome of holy church herin techyth is trew in his syte . . . wherby thei myte both be savid . . . And to al this I had non other answere but a mervelous example of a lord and of a servant–as I shal seyn after–and that full [mystely] shewid. And yet I 'domes' provides one of Julian's most fertile sources of 'ghostly sight' – for she assures us earlier that she was aware, throughout her experience, of 'the feith of holy church' which 'stode continualy in my sight' (a hermeneutic principle garbed like a personification out of *Piers Plowman*), 'willing and meneing never to receive onything that might be contrary therunto'.[48] Such tension can only be meaningful or productive, however, if Julian's experience can be regarded as being embodied in an authoritative and definitive form, accessible to all in the same way as the 'feith of holy church' itself. This, I believe, is one of the motivating forces behind the vital passage of hermeneutic reflection which occurs at the end of the first revelation and which is far more than the prolonged gesture of humility it appears to be. Chapter 8 of the Long Text, a kind of coda to revelation I, describes Julian's immediate response to it (a response that makes her say to those around her, ' "it is today domysday with me" ') by recalling how 'I was mekil sterid in charite to mine even cristen, that thei might seen and knowyn the same that I saw'.[49] Julian expounds this reminiscence (which, interestingly, she explicitly calls 'the gostly shewing of our lord God') in a celebrated passage where she states that 'all that I say of me I sey in the person of al myn even cristen', and counsels readers to:

> levyn the beholding of a wretch that it was shewid to, and mightily, wisely and mekely behold God, that of his curtes love and endles godenes wolde shewyn it generally in comfort of us al . . . For it is Gods will that ye take it with gret ioy and likyng as Iesus had shewid it on to you all.[50]

Here we are given two different hermeneutic instructions. First, we are to read every reference to Julian as indicating Christian humanity as a whole – the phrase 'in the person of', which derives from the technical language of Biblical exegesis, suggesting the formal nature of this instruction.[51] Second, it is God's will that we should 'take' – that is, appropriate – the revelation as though it is each of us who receives it, individually and affectively as well as in a merely representative sense. Chapter 9 elaborates the theological basis of these instructions, and concludes with a practical admission that readers will still need divine inspiration to 'take' Julian's exposition of her 'ghostly sight' in a manner

> stond in desire, and will into my end, that I myte be grace knowen these ii domys as it longyth to me . . . .

Instead of reconciling this opposition in a systematic theological way, as Colledge and Walsh's notes and summaries persistently suggest, the rest of the *Revelation of Love* seems to me, rather, to make theology out of the fully acknowledged impossibility of doing so.

[48] LT, ch.9, p.10.
[49] LT, ch.8, p.9.
[50] LT, ch.8, p.10.
[51] In medieval Biblical exegesis, the phrase *in persona* is a standard way of identifying the category of individual to whom a Biblical passage refers, or is being made to refer – sometimes a Biblical *auctor* being deemed to speak *in propria persona*, sometimes *in persona aliorum*. For discussion, see A. J. Minnis, *Medieval Theory of Authorship*, London, 1983, ch.3.

'more gostly and more swetely than I can or may telle it'.[52] Yet even bearing this qualification in mind, Julian's belief in the universality of her revelation makes logically inevitable the view of her own written account that she here implies. For if the showing was indeed made for all, it must be possible for her readers to appropriate it 'as Iesus had shewid it on to you all'. Moreover, through God's inspiration and her own lifetime of thought and prayer, her account of her experience must potentially have the same relation to her readers as the experience itself has to her. For the slow, deliberative and prayerful reader, the written *Revelation of Love* must be, or be meant to become, the showing.

The hermeneutic instructions given in this passage thus raise to the level of a principle what we have already seen to be Julian's practice both in revelation I and throughout her work. If God is described as 'showing' or Julian as 'seeing' many difficult and daring ideas that derive only in a convoluted way from the original revelation, we (I am using this word to designate the kind of reader Julian had in mind) are still obliged to 'take' such ideas to ourselves with as much of the force of revelation as we can. According to chapter 9, moreover, our success will even be a measure of our love for God: 'in as much as ye love God the better, it is more to you than to me'.[53] Yet on what basis can we as readers, or could Julian as a writer, have confidence that everything the *Revelation of Love* treats as revealed actually is so? On the face of it, after all, the work is obviously no more (and no less) than a movingly personal elaboration of a series of divinely-inspired but still inchoate ideas and images: an elaboration which it is tempting to assume (especially when we refer back to the Short Text) could as easily have been taken in quite different directions. Is there not even the danger that Julian's ubiquitous use of the terminology of revelation at such distant removes from her original experience will have the unintended effect of dissipating its power and authority, by making all references to 'sight' and 'showing' seem merely ornamental? With these questions we suddenly find ourselves back somewhere near our starting-point: the hermeneutic problem confronting readers who think of the *Revelation of Love* as a product not only of divine inspiration but of time and of human fallibility. Let us at last see, then, what Julian has to say that bears on this problem.

7

Julian's defence of the authenticity of her interpretation occurs at the hinge of chapter 51 of the Long Text, where she recounts her long failure to penetrate the 'misty example' of the lord and the servant, and the three 'propertes' which eventually in part alleviated her frustration, allowing her to comprehend at least

---

[52] LT, ch.9, p.11.
[53] LT, ch.9, p.10.

'the begynnyng of an ABC'. While the passage is familiar, the breadth of its application has not always been understood:[54]

> And thus in that tyme I stode mekyl in onknowyng. For the full vnderstondyng of this mervelous example was not goven me in that tyme – in which mystye example [the privities] of the revelation be yet mekyl hidde; and notwithstondyng this I saw and understode that every shewing is full of privities. And therfore me behovith now to tellen iii propertes in which I am sumdele esyd. The frest is the begynnyng of techyng that I understod therein in the same tyme. The ii is the inward lernyng that I have vnderstodyn therein sithen. The iii, al the hole revelation from the begynnyng to the end (that is to sey, of this boke), which our lord God of his goodnes bryngeth oftentymes frely to the syte of myn vnderstondyng. And these iii arn so onyd, as to my vnderstondyng, that I cannot, ner may, depart them. And be these iii as on I have techyng wherby I owe to leyvyn and trostyn in our lord God, that of the same godenes that he shewed it, and for the same end, ryth so of the same goodnes and for the same end he shal declaryn it to us whan it is his wille. For xx yeres after the tyme of the shewing, save iii monethis, I had techyng inwardly, as I shal seyen: 'it longyth to the to taken hede to all the propertes and condition that weryn shewed in the example, thow thou thynke that they ben mysty and indifferent to thy syte'. I assend wilfully with grete desire, [seeing] inwardly with avisement al the poynts and propertes that wer shewid in the same tyme, as ferforth as my witt and vnderstondyng wold servyn.[55]

The immediate context of this passage is limited. Three 'propertes' – Julian's memory of the 'example' as she originally saw it, her subsequent reflections on it, and her understanding of it in relation to the rest of her revelation – all combine, emboldened by her 'inward techyng', into the synthetic account that follows in the rest of the chapter. Although this account attempts to distinguish these 'propertes', the passage admits it to be an impossibility, seeming rather to shelter behind the 'inward techyng' Julian receives from God, as though this provided a fresh authentication of her thoughts, in spite of the confusion into which they have fallen. Yet there is more to the passage than this. First, Julian makes it clear that the hermeneutic 'propertes' she describes here are those she has brought not only to the key parable of the lord and servant but to the whole of her revelation; 'every shewing', not merely this 'misty example', is described as 'full of privities' – as the lengthy digression on 'the hole revelation' of which chapter 51 forms a part is indeed in the process of demonstrating. Second, these 'propertes' are far from being a casual grouping of modes of understanding. It is often noted that the Long Text constantly alludes to two triads: those of the

---

54 My analysis takes its own direction, but is somewhat parallel to those of Glasscoe, *art. cit.*, pp.168–69, and Colledge and Walsh, notes to ch.51, ll.76 and 80 (pp.519–20).
55 LT, ch.51, pp.55–56, S1 and S2 read 'iii propertes' for P's 'the privities', which is possible (as an early expression of the extent to which the meaning of the revelation is still latent), but lacks the clarity of P. P omits 'that is to sey of this boke' of S1 and S2 which resembles an unhelpful scribal gloss, and reads 'thre knowynges' for 'onknowyng' of S1 and S2; this makes very poor sense and is surely a nervous scribal emendation, rather than the 'clear example of P's superiority' to S1 and S2 that Colledge and Walsh claim it to be (note to ch.51, l.70, p.519).

human memory, reason and will on the one hand, and of the traditional attributes of the persons of the Trinity – respectively might, wisdom and love – on the other.[56] Julian uses such allusions – which operate within a cognitive framework most famously defined by Augustine's *De Trinitate* – to bring out her view that 'where Iesus appereith the blissid Trinite is understond', and also to insist on the intimacy of the image and likeness that unites God with the human soul. Chapter 44 of the Long Text, for example, states explicitly that God is:

> endles soverain trueth, endles severeyn wisdam, endles sovereyn love, onmade, and mans soule is a creature in God which hath the same propertyes made. . . it seith God, it beholdyth God and it lovyth God.[57]

What has gone unnoticed (or, at least, undiscussed) is the deliberate way that the 'made' and 'unmade' trinities parallel (and thereby implicitly correspond to) the hermeneutic 'propertes' that Julian describes in the present passage – the correspondences being as follows:

> *the begynnyng of techyng*/ Julian's memory/ Father/ might-truth
> *inward lernyng*/ Julian's reason/ Son/ wisdom
> *the hole revelation*/ Julian's will/ Holy Spirit/ love

These correspondences considerably enlarge the implications of what Julian is saying in this passage about the interpretation of her revelation. For if the process by which Julian experienced her revelation, reflected on it, and analysed its various parts in the light of the whole finds a parallel at each stage with the dynamic inner structure of the Trinity, it follows that the Trinity has been present at each of these stages. It also follows that the divine inspiration which produced her revelation has continued to aid her as she reflects on it and writes it down. Thus whatever relation in literal terms the written *Revelation of Love* has to the experience from which it grew, it can legitimately claim to be an authentic and inspired account of that experience. What proves this last conclusion for Julian is the very thing that seemed initially to cast doubt on the authenticity of her account: the fact that after twenty years and more it is impossible to distinguish between original experience and subsequent interpretation: 'these iii arn so onyd, as to my vnderstondyng, that I cannot, ner may, depart them'.[58] For rather than reading this situation as a sign of her own confusion, she sees it as evidence of the underlying unity inherent in each stage of her experience of the revelation, which both corresponds to and is a product of the unity that inheres in the Trinity itself. Just as the Trinity consists of three persons whose activities are ultimately indistinguishable, since they are united in a single godhead, so her revelation, and the book in which she embodies it, consist of three 'propertes'

---

[56] See, for example, Jantzen, *op. cit.*, ch.7. For a succinct account of the theological background, See J. P. H. Clark, '*Fiducia* in Julian of Norwich, II', *Downside Review*, 95 (1979), 214–29, especially p.225.

[57] LT, ch.44, p.47.

[58] LT, ch.51, p.56.

which are indistinguishably united in one showing. In other words, her written account of the 'revelation of love' is authentic not in spite of the fact that, but *because*, revelation and interpretation are impossible to disentangle.

This, then, is the 'trinitarian hermeneutic' which underpins Julian's interpretation of her revelation, allowing her to pronounce on it with confidence, and allowing her intended readers to treat her pronouncements as the constituent parts of God's 'showing' that she claims them to be. The thoroughness with which she reflects on all aspects of her experience here bears remarkable fruit, in a sophisticated analysis of the problem of time and human memory that turns what was at first sight a serious hermeneutic difficulty into her most important argument for the authority of her work. Nor is this argument in any sense merely a clever evasion of the problem; it is far too carefully integrated into both the structure and the theology of the *Revelation of Love* for that. By this point in the work, after all, we have encountered both the distinction between these three hermeneutic 'propertes' and the fact of their inseparability many times. For example, the passage at the beginning of the first revelation describing the 'bodily sight' of the blood quoted above proves to move schematically from Julian's memory of this sight ('the begynnyng of techyng'), to her understanding of it ('inward lernyng'), to her sense of its significance in relation to 'the hole revelation'; at the same time, the difficulty of separating experience and reflection even in this passage, especially in the subtle shift from 'I saw' to 'as to my sight', already implies the fact that 'these iii arn so onyd, as to my vnderstondyng, that I cannot, ner may, depart them'.[59] This combination – of a format that always seems *about* to be that of text and accompanying commentary, with slippages between the two that continually undo this distinction – is indeed, as we have seen, a virtual hallmark of Julian's exegetical practice. In the light of the 'trinitarian hermeneutic' such a combination takes on a thematic importance. On the one hand, it corresponds to the paradoxically triune nature of the godhead: in which, for example, the Father 'gives birth' to the Son as his Word, and the procession of the Spirit acts as a further 'stage' in the divine self-articulation, but in which all the persons are to be seen as constituting a single essence. On the other hand, it corresponds to the triadic structure of Julian's soul, which, until it is united with God in heaven, can only experience the truth partially, not as accomplished and completed revelation but as *process*. What Julian learns in chapter 51 is nothing like a full understanding of the 'misty example' (which is why attempts to show how this chapter resolves the tension between revelation and Christian orthodoxy not only fail but miss the point). Julian is only 'sumdele esyd' because at last she has learnt 'to leyvyn and trostyn in our lord God, that . . . he shal declaryn [his full meaning] whan it is his wille'.[60] She has learnt, in short, how to live *without* the full knowledge that even after her revelation she can only long for, never attain, in this life.

[59] *Ibid.*
[60] *Ibid.*

8

If the whole of the *Revelation of Love* is meant to be read as a species of divinely-inspired text, a revelation in its own right to the properly attentive reader, the truth it imparts turns out to be of an interestingly self-reflexive and provisional kind. As with *Piers Plowman*, which leaves us with the simple injunction 'lerne to love . . . and leef alle othere', the work can conclude by asserting a single, unifying meaning to all God has revealed through it: ' ''woldst thou wetten thi Lord's mening in this thing? Wete it wele: love was his mening.'' '[61] But also as with *Piers Plowman*, in which even the injunction to love must lead to the initiation of still one more pilgrimage, as Conscience walks 'as wide as the world lasteth' in search of Piers, the end of the *Revelation of Love* asserts simultaneously that full knowledge of that meaning is always in the future: 'this booke is begunne . . . but it is not yet performid'.[62] Indeed, in a certain way this prolonged deferral proves ultimately to be a condition not only of life but of love itself. 'Ere God made us, he loved us', says Julian, and plays with the idea of closure as she insists on its impossibility: 'which love was never slakid, no never shall'.[63] *Tunc autem cognoscam sicut et cognitus sum:*[64] even this lasting fullness, it seems, finally emerges not as a state but as a never-satiated process.

---

[61] *Piers Plowman*, ed. A. V. C. Schmidt, London, 1978, B XX, 1.208; LT, ch.86, p.102.
[62] *Piers Plowman* B XX, 1.382; LT, ch.86, p.102.
[63] LT, *ibid*.
[64] 1 Corinthians 13:126.

'WHO HAS WRITTEN THIS BOOK?':
VISIONARY AUTOBIOGRAPHY
IN LANGLAND'S C TEXT

KATHRYN KERBY-FULTON

'AH! LORD GOD! Who has written this book? I in my weakness have written it, because I dared not hide the gift that is in it.'[1]. Mechthild of Magdeburg's almost anguished question at the opening of her book of revelations captures the mingled feelings of compulsion, self-doubt and evangelism characteristic of medieval visionary writing. As Elizabeth Petroff has written: 'the self that comes into existence in the course of visionary experience is a writing self', and that sense of authorial responsibility for delivering an unpopular or unusual message to a suspicious public seems at times to have oppressed even the most self-confident visionaries.[2] From the standpoint of the medieval church, it was not the visions themselves that were a problem, but the publication of them. As William Christian writes of a female visionary in his study of *Apparitions in late Medieval and Renaissance Spain*:

> A seer who was deceived could not be blamed for being tricked, but was culpable if she or he communicated the false vision to others. Francisca would not have been punished if, even believing her visions, she had told no one but the priest. Her crime was in the publicity she gave the vision and the cult she encouraged by trusting her own discernment when it was at variance with that of the church.[3]

Christian also mentions another important aspect of medieval attitudes toward vision: whether a vision had actually occurred – the first thing a modern person would doubt – was rarely questioned in the Middle Ages, but the source of the vision was always under suspicion,[4] for even 'Satan himself disguises himself as an angel of light' (2 Corinthians 11:14). Therefore all visionaries were expected to undergo testing (*probatio*): 'Test the spirits to see whether they are of God' (1 John 4:1). Such testing involved a myriad of questions ranging from inquiry into the theological orthodoxy of the vision and its adherence to established visionary

---

[1] *The Revelations of Mechthild of Magdeburg*, tr. Lucy Menzies, London, 1953, p.3.
[2] *Medieval Women's Visionary Literature*, New York, 1986, p.27. For instances of visionary concern about publication or publicity see Mechtild of Hackeborn, *The Booke of Gostlye Grace*, ed. Theresa Halligan, Toronto, 1979, pp.586–588; and Kathryn Kerby-Fulton and Dyan Elliott, 'Self-Image and the Visionary Role in two letters from the Correspondence of Elizabeth of Schonau and Hildegard of Bingen', *Vox Benedictina*, 2 (1985), 204–223.
[3] Princeton, 1981, p.196, discussing Francisca la Brava.
[4] *Ibid.*, p.194.

conventions, to the visionary's mode of living, social standing, education, temperament and religious commitment. Furthermore, there is good evidence that the more sophisticated visionary writers recorded their experiences with such official criteria in mind.[5] Langland, too, I believe was aware of these issues.

At some point between the writing of the B and C texts Langland seems to have decided that his own work would come under such scrutiny. Notwithstanding the self-parodic element which his dreamer takes on at times, Will's visionary stance became increasingly important in the author's mind in this final version. The questions of poetic vocation which troubled him in B give way in C to questions of visionary vocation, and if that notion seems too grandiose consider the charismatic leanings of the poem, its explicit prophecies of the future, its Old-Testament style denunciations of abuse, and most important, its concern with teaching 'that which is necessary to salvation' (Thomas Aquinas's definition of prophecy).[6] By the time the C text was being written the poet already had an established denunciatory reputation, as the well known 'autobiographical passage' or *Apologia* shows:

> Thus y awakede, woet god, whan y wonede in Cornehull,
> Kytte and y in a cote, yclothed as a lollare,
> And lytel ylet by, leueth me for sothe,
> Amonges lollares of Londone and lewede ermytes,
> For y made of tho men as resoun me tauhte.   (C V.1–5)[7]

These lines exude a new self-confidence in his poetic stance (which he had explicitly doubted in B), but the self-confidence is harder to muster in the discussion of his manner of living which follows. The problem is that he looks, on the surface at least, too much like those he denounces, and the *Apologia* develops into an emotionally complex piece of self-justification, soul-searching and questioning of vocation. Showing a typically Langlandian preference for inner rather than external authority figures, Conscience and Reason act rather

---

[5] See for instance the editors' note regarding Julian's awareness of canonization requirements in relating her experiences, *A Book of Showings to the Anchoress Julian of Norwich*, ed. Edmund Colledge and James Walsh, Toronto, 1978, p.292, n.3, and Kathryn Kerby-Fulton, *Reformist Apocalypticism and Piers Plowman*, Cambridge, 1990, pp.118–125 on visionary awareness of conventions and validity issues. The best discussion of *probatio* is to be found in Eric Colledge, '*Epistola solitarii ad reges*: Alphonse of Pecha as Organizer of Brigittine and Urbanist Propaganda', *Mediaeval Studies*, 18 (1956), 19–49.

[6] See Paul Synave and P. Benoit, *A Commentary on the Summa Theologica II–II, Questions 171–178*, New York, 1961, notes to Q.171, a.3.c.

[7] All quotations from the C text of *Piers Plowman* are from the edition of Derek Pearsall, London, 1978; his notes V.1–108 (the *Apologia*) provide good guidance on critical and textual matters. All quotations from the B text are from the edition of George Kane and E. T. Donaldson, London, 1975. Latin translations, unless otherwise noted, are my own.

like probators, posing, as I shall argue, the kinds of questions recommended in treatises on visionary validation. The emphasis in these treatises on the need for all visionaries to submit their experiences to the judgement of expert, authoritative, spiritual advisers can hardly be overstated, and it is characteristic of Langland that he found a way to radically challenge authority just when he appears to be submitting to it: by choosing inner faculties as spiritual directors he makes a strong statement about the true nature of authority.

Although questions of visionary validation had concerned writers in earlier centuries,[8] there was a renewed interest in the problem of discernment of spirits in the later part of the fourteenth century. As Colledge has shown, the canonization process of Bridget of Sweden and its aftermath provoked a flurry of pamphlets on the subject, and I will be discussing three treatises associated with this controversy which provide a good sense of the range of medieval opinion on religious visions: the *Epistola Solitarii ad Reges*, written by Bridget's literary executor, Alphonse of Pecha between 1373 and 1379 in defence of her visions; chapters XVIII–XX of *The Chastising of God's Children* on visionary *discretio*, largely adapted from Alphonse's work shortly after 1382; and finally the *De Probatione Spirituum* of Jean Gerson written in 1415, a response to Alphonse provoked by reconsideration of Bridget's canonization at the Council of Constance.[9] Langland could have known either of the first two, but in what follows I will not be arguing a case for any of them as his sources. Rather, since they draw on standard passages in the Fathers and other authorities (like Hugh of St Victor and St Thomas Aquinas), I assume that their central assumptions were known to Langland in some form. The three works exhibit a wide range of opinion: both the *Chastising*-author and Gerson were much more suspicious of visions than Alphonse; the *Chastising*-author, writing in English, was apparently concerned in part with the threat to orthodoxy posed by the rise of the Wycliffite movement (it seems to have been written shortly after the sensational recantations of three Wycliffites in 1382), while Gerson was anxious about the

---

[8] See Barbara Newman, 'Hildegard of Bingen: Visions and Validation', *Church History*, 54 (1985), 163–175; and David Burr, 'Olivi, Apocalyptic Expectation, and Visionary Experience', *Traditio*, XLI (1985), 272–288.

[9] The *Epistola* is quoted from Gonzales Durante's edition of the *Revelationum S. Birgitte*, Antwerp, 1611, pp.576–590 (I have silently expanded all abbreviations in quotations from this edition). A new edition of the *Epistola Solitarii* had become available since this article was prepared for publication; it may be found in *Alfonso of Jaén: His Life and Works*, ed. Arne Jönsson, Lund, 1990. All quotations in this article have been checked against Jönsson's edition and the only differences are orthographical; however, Jönsson's work should form the basis of future scholarship on the *Epistola*. The *Chastising* is edited by Joyce Bazire and Eric Colledge, Oxford, 1957, whose notes indicate the many places where the author diverges from simply translating Alphonse's text; for Gerson's work see Paschal Boland, *The Concept of Discretio Spirituum in John Gerson's 'De Probatione Spiritum' and 'De Distinctione Verarum Visionum a Falsis'*, Washington, 1959 (any translations of Gerson are Boland's).

trend toward Church approval of 'false, imaginary or foolish visions', especially, it seems by women like Bridget.[10]

The decade that lapsed between the writing of the B and C texts of *Piers Plowman* saw the unfolding of dramatic events in England, most notably the social tensions of the Peasant's Revolt and the ecclesiastical strains of the growth of the Wycliffite movement. That these left their mark on the poet and on the poem is beyond doubt – rebel leaders had used the figure of Piers to support a radical cause, and a number of C text revisions suggest that Langland was trying to protect himself against a charge of unorthodoxy in an atmosphere of growing Wycliffite censorship.[11] How these tensions surrounding him relate to the marked emphasis on visionary, charismatic spirituality evident in the C text revisions is certainly not a subject which can be dealt with fully in a short paper; however, one aspect of these revisions will concern us here, that is changes associated with autobiographical passages in C in which Langland clearly felt the need to address the question of authorial vocation and visionary credibility. In the C text he frequently excises, distinguishes or softens Will's relationship with problematic groups: beggars, lollars (false clerics), lunatics, and the lowest rank of society, at the same time as a charismatic ideology drives him to idealise poverty.[12] The so-called 'autobiographical passage', or *Apologia* at the opening of C V is the centrepiece of a series of revisions which indicate that Langland was looking over his shoulder during this period, and it seems to function as evidence of a self-imposed *probatio*. This paper will explore the nature of these autobiographical revisions in the light of the conventions of visionary autobiography and authorial concern for credibility.

Critics of *Piers Plowman* have always been divided on the issue of the degree of autobiographical veracity in the poem.[13] The best known treatment of the problem is George Kane's 1965 'The Autobiographical Fallacy in Chaucer and

---

[10] Boland, *op. cit.*, p.28.

[11] I would like to thank Linda Olson for allowing me to cite her forthcoming essay, 'William Langland's Piers Plowman: Spiritual Revisions in the Age of Wyclif', and for her valuable comments on the present paper.

[12] On aspects of Langland's revision process see part iv of Kane and Donaldson's edition *op. cit.*, 'The C Reviser's B'; George Russell, ' "As They Read It": Some Notes on Early Responses to the C-Version of Piers Plowman', *Leeds Studies in English*, NS XX (1989), 173–188; Wendy Scase, 'Two Piers Plowman C-text Interpolations: Evidence for a Second Textual Tradition', *Notes and Queries*, Dec. (1987), 456–463 (further bibliography, p.457, n.3). Notes in Pearsall's edition also contain much information about C text revisions.

[13] The following works are cited in this paragraph: Kane's study was produced as the Chambers Memorial Lecture, London, 1965; Woolf, 'Some Non-Medieval Qualities of Piers Plowman', *Essays in Criticism*, 12 (1962), 111–25; Donaldson, *Piers Plowman: The C-Text and its Poet*, New Haven, 1949; Anne Middleton, 'The Audience and Public of Piers Plowman' in *Middle English Alliterative Poetry and its Literary Background*, ed. David Lawton, Cambridge, 1982, pp.101–123 (but see also her 'William Langland's "Kynde Name": Authorial Signature and Social Identity in Late Fourteenth-Century England' in *Literary Practice and Social Change in Britain,*

Langland Studies', which, in spite of its cautionary title, gives numerous reasons why the author of a fourteenth-century narrative poem must be considered as historically present in his poem. Rosemary Woolf had already labelled the apparent autobiographical authenticity of Langland's narrator as 'non-medieval', and E. T. Donaldson, in his superb book on the C Text, had taken the *Apologia* seriously enough to produce a detailed description of the ecclesiastical duties of unbeneficed clergy in an attempt to understand Langland's apparent mode of livelihood. He threw down a challenge to anyone who rejected its autobiographical status to show what purpose it was meant to serve if it was fictional (no one has yet been able to do so). However, more recent critics have, under the influence of New Critical and Deconstructionist ideologies, opted largely for the view that Will is entirely a fictive persona: thus Anne Middleton, in a recent stimulating essay sees the identification of Will with the writer as one of the 'acts of mistaken identity' committed by early reformist readers, (one by implication not committed by modern sophisticates) and David Lawton, in a Deconstructionist reading of the poem's persona, sees the dreamer as a discontinuous presence, arguing that Langland demonstrates 'the plurality of Will in the poem'.[14] However, all of these scholars are approaching the poem largely from the standpoint of its relation to secular dream vision literature, but as I have argued elsewhere, the poem calls for a broader treatment which considers the religious visionary tradition as well. Students of the poem who approach it from the latter standpoint immediately recognize elements of the genre of spiritual autobiography even amidst the narratorial quicksand of the poem's multiple 'I' speakers. A case in point is Denise Despres's recent discussion of the poem as a spiritual autobiography, pointing out that in the C Text Langland 'buttressed the autobiographical structure' by adding the *Apologia*, set in 'a world of specific places, Cornhulle and London'.[15] Like all spiritual autobiographies, the poem leaves out many things which a modern secular audience would consider mandatory to biography, and it doubtless reshapes much of the raw material of the author's life to fit a conventional or figural record, but recent research on the nature of religious visionary writing, and on the historically verifiable aspects of persona in medieval poetry suggests that we are wrong to mistake Langland's autobiographical signals for false signs. If nothing else, the results of the dialect study of the poem's manuscripts recently published by Professor Samuels, which show that the author of *Piers* had to have grown up in the Malvern area, ought to give pause to those who contend that nothing the 'I' speaker says is reliably connectable to the poet.[16]

1380–1530, ed. Lee Patterson, Berkeley, 1990, pp.15–82); David Lawton, 'The Subject of Piers Plowman', *Yearbook of Langland Studies* 1 (1987), 1–30.

[14] 'The Subject of Piers Plowman' *op. cit.*, p.2.

[15] Despres, *Ghostly Sights: Visual Meditation in Late-Medieval Literature*, Norman, Oklahoma, 1989, pp.122–7.

[16] M. L. Samuels, 'Langland's Dialect', *Medium Aevum*, LIV (1985), 232–247.

Indeed, it is the very specificity of certain self-referential passages in Langland that give the reader a strong sense of autobiographical authenticity, but the difficulties of accurately interpreting these details are considerable. Fortunately, two ground-breaking studies of the problem, Burrow's study 'Autobiographical Poetry in the Middle Ages' in relation to Hoccleve, and Dinzelbacher's *Vision und Visionsliteratur im Mittelalter* have provided us with some guidelines.

In his arresting study of Hoccleve, Burrow points out that 'medieval autobiographies, if ever there was such a thing', are not autobiographies, in our modern sense of a distinct genre.[17] Thus, works like *The Confessions* of St Augustine or the *Historia Calamitatum* of Abelard are, respectively, instances of the medieval genres of *confessio* and *consolatio*, and as such their autobiographical function is subordinated to their function as consolation or as confession (or so their writers would have us believe). Burrow also shows that in recognizing the practical purpose of Hoccleve's autobiographical writing (for example, his begging poems) and the historical accuracy, as judged by external evidence, of his self-reference, there are two lessons for modern readers: (1) that medieval writers turned to autobiography for specific, perhaps even practical purposes, (2) that medieval writers wrote autobiography in the form of some other genre. In the pre-Romantic period, subjectivity was of interest not for its own sake, but because it illuminated something else, for instance, conversion, in the case of Augustine, or financial need, in the case of Hoccleve.

The two genres most often discussed as conveyers of medieval autobiographical writing are *confessio* and *consolatio*, and certainly one finds elements of both in Langland's self-referential passages, but a third genre, *visio* is rather neglected in this regard, at least outside of the study of medieval women writers. As Peter Dinzelbacher has shown in his astonishingly comprehensive study of medieval vision literature, realistic or specific autobiographical detail is a reliable marker of actual experienced vision (*erfahrene Vision*), as opposed to fictionalized literary vision, in which the attributes of the 'I' speaker are those of an 'Everyman'.[18] So, for example, in a dream vision poem in which the 'I' speaker sets out for a walk on a May morning, it would be foolish to look for the year and the date in which the author had this experience; as Burrow says,

> For a competent reader the question of truth will not arise in this case. Here the conventional and the autobiographical can indeed be treated as mutually exclusive (393)

However, when Julian of Norwich writes,

---

[17] Burrow's study appears in *Proceedings of the British Academy*, LXVIII (1982), pp.389–412.

[18] *Vision und Visionsliteratur im Mittelalter*, Stuttgart, 1981, p.66. For a chart listing Dinzelbacher's criteria, and discussion, see Kerby-Fulton, *Reformist Apocalypticism*, *op. cit.*, pp.118–121.

> This reuelation was made to a symple creature . . . the yer of our lord a
> thousannde and three hundered and lxxiii, the xiij daie of May,[19]

Burrow's 'competent reader' would not look to poetic convention to illuminate
the May reference – the specificity of the date, and the lack of symbolic
resonance give it an air of veracity. Or, to take another example, the Dominican
visionary Robert of Uzès, who is always careful to establish the setting of his
visions, mentions that he saw a vision on the future state of the church in the
home of a certain Breton lord in the city of Orange, a detail which has no
obvious edificatory or allegorical value.[20] Why mention it at all? It seems to arise
out of an impetus to chronical rather than to fictionalize or even edify; the detail
enhances the sense of moment, and it lends realism, and therefore credibility to
the visionary's claim that God intervened at just that point in time.
Autobiographical elements in visionary literature clearly have an explicit
function. Most obviously, they signal real experience to the reader. And even in
instances in which such realistic details are fictional (a deconstructionist would
say that they are all 'narrative'), they have been created by the medieval author
for the same purpose, that is, to signal autobiographical authenticity.[21]

A final guideline, or note of caution, for interpreting autobiographical
elements in vision literature is that the reader should be aware of the conventions
peculiar to the genre; if an experience is to be accepted as authentic it must be
recorded in a fashion which reminds readers of other visions already accepted as
authentic. A case in point is one of the objections raised by interrogators of Joan
of Arc; noting that she had seen St Michael bow in one of her visions they
doubted its authenticity:

> when there is no indication that such a bow or greeting had even been made by
> angels or archangels to any holy man and not even to the Blessed Virgin.[22]

Langland's awareness of the conventions of religious vision is apparent in many
places throughout the poem in which he uses the kind of biographical visionary

---

[19] *Showings*, *op. cit.*, p.285.

[20] Robert's visions are edited by Jeanne Bignami-Odier, 'Les Visions de Robert d'Uzès,
O.P. (d.1296)', *Archivum Fratrum Predictorum*, 25 (1955), 258–310; see Visio X.

[21] This is perhaps the proper place to say a word about critical approach. New Criticism
taught us to read all first person reference as 'persona', and Deconstructionism is even
more dogmatic in its insistence that nothing, not even history, exists beyond narrative.
Although it can be useful to be reminded that all writing about the self is to some extent
fictionalized, since it is clear that some 'narratives' are intended by their authors and
received by their readers as more historically authentic than others, the Deconstructionist position becomes nearly irrelevant in a study like this. My approach here
involves questions of authorial intention, and especially the author's anticipation of,
and reaction to, reader response, in an attempt to better understand medieval attitudes
towards vision and visionaries. In this sense this paper has, like Burrow's study of
Hoccleve, more affinities with New Historicist approaches, although it makes no
pretentions to any particular theoretical approach.

[22] Christian, *op. cit.*, p.191.

settings Dinzelbacher finds characteristic of non-fictional vision literature, in which revelations typically occur during Mass (as in C XXI 1–8), or while praying in church (often before a crucifix, as in C V 105–8), or at home among family (as in C XX.470–8), as opposed to the idyllic garden or burbling stream setting (as in B Prol. 7–10) of fictional dream vision literature. In his C revisions Langland cancelled or modified his idyllic settings, and created some new religious ones, as for instance at the end of the *Apologia* where Will begins a new vision praying in church before the crucifix (V 105–8). Similarly, Will's waking on Easter morning, to the sound of bells, amidst his family (XX.470–78) makes use of a number of religious vision conventions (the holy day, the sound of the bells), but includes specific details of the names of family members (his wife 'Kitte' and daughter 'Calote' are named). For a medieval audience such a passage would signal visionary biography. In making our own judgement it is important to remember, as Burrow has shown, that the presence of conventional elements in no way rules out autobiographical authenticity; he suggests that one must beware of the 'conventional fallacy', the opposite type of logical error from the famous 'autobiographical fallacy' with which New Critics suppressed autobiographical interpretation for decades. The conventional fallacy involves the mistaken assumption that because an element in a text seems conventional it is therefore untrue – but all of us do and say conventional things every day. So, for example, in the *Apologia* Will mentions that he lives with his wife, Kit, in a cottage (C V.2) and critics are quick to point out that Kit is a conventional name for a wife at this time, implying that she may therefore be fictional; but one could argue the exact opposite – if the name was a common one, so much more reason for supposing the Langland's wife may have actually been called 'Kit'.[23]

Langland also uses the language of vision precisely, especially in descriptions of Will's emotions. The visionary's assessments of 'feelings' (we might note here Margery Kempe's extensive use of the word) were themselves evidence of true or false visions, as all the treatizes on the subject mention.[24] So, for instance, the *Chastising*-author, following Alphonse's seven tokens of true vision, gives as the second token 'to knowe a goode visioun' when the soul 'Feliþ hym fulfilled or rauyshed . . . wiþ a goostli swetnesse', which 'swetnesse of loue þe deuel may nat ȝiue'.[25] Earlier he had defined 'rauyshyng', which 'aftir seint austyn mai propirli be clepid a swounyng'.[26] Langland uses the word 'swoon' at the opening of the Tree of Charity vision in the B text, where, upon hearing the name of Piers Will 'swowned after,/ And lay longe in a louedreem' (B XVI.19–20), a very precise use of the visionary concept of ecstasy.

[23] See Pearsall's note to V.2 and VII.304; it would be easier to see 'Kitte' as a type name if she were not coupled with 'Calote' later in XX.470-8. What possible allegorical significance could Calote have?
[24] See the *Epistola*, p.586; *Chastising, op. cit.*, p.178; Christian, *op. cit.*, pp.193–4.
[25] *Chastising, op. cit.*, p.178.
[26] *Ibid.*, p.170.

Similarly, Langland seems aware that in true visions fear at the appearance of a holy figure should be followed by joy; thus one of Joan of Arc's visions was judged true because, following Thomas Aquinas, the probator noted that fear was followed by joy, adding that if the fear remains, 'the enemy is present'.[27] So too Will, upon seeing Lady Holy Church, is initially 'afeerd of here face, thow she fayre were' (C I.10), but later clings to her words and presence.

In any event it looks as if medieval readers of religious visionary poetry, like Langland's and Dante's, fully accepted its autobiographical implications: Ann Middleton notes that John But 'committed the autobiographical fallacy', viewing Will's visions as figuratively conveyed but authentic spiritual experience.[28] There has been relatively little reader-response-study of *Piers Plowman*,[29] but an exhaustive study of the illustrations of the *Divine Comedy* as reader-response suggests a similar pattern: Brieger has shown that during most of the fourteenth century the poem was accepted by its readers as an authentic otherworld journey, and toward the end of the century emphasis began to shift toward a strong interest in the autobiographical elements, in which Dante was seen as 'a great genius relating his personal experiences'.[30] It is easy to feel a sense of smug superiority over medieval readers whose naivety, we imagine, led them to read a poetic persona literally – but perhaps they knew something we do not. I suspect that they were much more familiar with the conventions and assumptions of both religious and secular vision literature, and that they recognized the author's autobiographical signals as evidence of the former. Of course, we can never know whether Langland actually experienced his visions in the literal sense, but what it behoves us to know is that he is invoking specific conventions that signal autobiographical religious vision to a medieval audience.

Such signals are especially plentiful in the *Apologia*, which fulfils most of the criteria established by Dinzelbacher as evidence of non-fictional vision. Four of these criteria are important for the study of visionary autobiography: (1) the narrator, far from being an 'Everyman' of fictionalized vision is identified very specifically in terms of his place of residence, his manner of dress and livelihood, his family, and even his reputation in the community. The description is not without its ironies, but these do not undermine the autobiographical impetus. (2) The vision occurs in a waking state and the

---

27 Christian, *op. cit.*, p.193.
28 Middleton, 'Making a Good End: John But as a Reader of Piers Plowman', in *Medieval English Studies Presented to George Kane*, ed. Edward Donald Kennedy et al., Wolfeboro, NY, 1988, 236–266.
29 See Russell, 'As They Read It', *op. cit.*, and his article, 'Some Early Responses to the C-Version of *Piers Plowman*', *Viator*, 15 (1984), 275–300. Carl Grindley, University of Victoria, is currently completing a dissertation on the annotations in Huntington MS 143.
30 P. Brieger, 'Pictorial Commentaries to the Commedia', in P. Brieger, M. Meiss and C. S. Singleton, *Illuminated Manuscripts of the Divine Comedy*, I, Princeton, 1969, pp.88–89.

visionary is disturbed by the experience, so disturbed that (3) the vision results in a change in the visionary's life, or at least profound penitence and soul-searching. Fictional visions occur during sleep, according to Dinzelbacher, and do not change or disturb the visionary's life. (4) The Episode occurs in a realistic setting (a hot harvest time), and ends in a common setting for experienced visions, in church, before a crucifix, not in the idyllic setting of fictional vision. According to the criteria established by Dinzelbacher, the *Apologia* does indeed look as if it were written to buttress a growing sense of spiritual autobiography, as Denise Despres says, but there is also specific evidence of the concerns of *discretio* in the visionary self-image.

Beginning with the criteria set out in the *Epistola*, Alphonse stresses that it is dangerous to condemn or approve any visionary without subtly examining three broad categories of evidence: the kind (including rank) of the persons (*de qualitate ipsarum personarum*), the manner of living (*de modo vivendi*), and the kind of subject or occasion of the visions (*de qualitate materiae visionum*).[31] These are tested, in the form of a myriad of questions which the probator must ask the visionary. The very first question concerns the person's status (lay or clerical) and commitment to the spiritual life: is the person '*spiritualis, vel an sit mundana, & saecularis?*' Does the person life under discipline, special obedience, the guidance of expert spiritual advisers, or does the person simply follow his or her own will? (in the *Chastising* translation: 'at his owne propir wil'). Other questions concern orthodoxy, stability (even stability of residence seems to be a concern, in the traditional monastic sense),[32] willingness to accept counsel, and perseverance in visionary experiences. Most questions are premised on the principle of Matthew 7:18, which teaches that good and evil may be distinguished 'by their fruits' and therefore scrutiny of the effect of the visions on the demeanour of the visionary is crucial, for instance:

> Is the visionary virtuous and penitent, and having frequent visions, is the person humble and long persevering, or a new convert (*novitia*)? Does the person have good natural and spiritual understanding, and discretion of judgement, or is his mind capricious, unpredictable or given to fantasy?[33]

Gerson echoes these concerns very nearly, and adds:

> Moreover, it is very important to investigate the personality of the individual, his education, habits, likes, associates; also whether he is rich or poor

(the concern here is to isolate unscrupulous motives).[34] These questions go a long way toward explaining the peculiar strategy of questioning on the part of

---

[31] *Epistola, op. cit.*, p.578.

[32] Note the care with which Alphonse discusses Bridget's movements, *Epistola, op. cit.*, p.579.

[33] *Epistola, op. cit.*, p.578 (my translation hides the repetitiveness of Alphonse's style). For a fuller list of the questions and a summary of the entire treatise see Edmund Colledge's article *Medieval Studies* 18 (1956) *op. cit.*

[34] Boland, *op. cit.*, pp.30-31.

the allegorical spiritual advisers of the *Apologia*; Conscience and Reason behave very much as probators concerned with establishing status, vocation, stability, and degree of perseverance of their visionary, Will.

These elements of spiritual testing appear in the *Apologia* in close connection with the kind of self-portrait one finds in conversion autobiography, that is, where the converted author casts a jaundiced eye back over the pre-conversion self (for example, the rather acidic tone that the older Augustine uses to blight his own pre-conversion self-portraits).[35] At the beginning of the *Apologia*, which seems to be a kind of flashback to younger or pre-conversion days, Will describes himself as lazy ('y hadde myn hele/ And lymes to labory with and loyede wel fare/ And no dede to do but to drynke and to slepe') and rather a daydreamer ('romynge in remembraunce') when in a hot harvest time he is 'apposede' by Reason (V.8–9). This is not a flattering self-portrait, but medieval confessional autobiography never paints flattering portraits, especially of the pre-conversion state. The problem is one of establishing status and vocation:

> 'Can thow seruen,' he sayde, 'or syngen in a churche,
> Or koke for my cokeres or to þe cart piche,
> . . .
> Or eny other kynes craft þat to þe comune nedeth,
> That þou betere therby þat byleue the fynden?'   (V.12–21)

Reason's questions seem initially concerned to establish whether Will is a cleric or lay person, a line of questioning that will be strenuously pursued in the rest of the passage, and eventually broadened into questions about his commitments to the spiritual life generally. Reason's heavy emphasis on opportunities for agricultural labour (8 lines), and the comparatively short list of clerical possibilities (1 line) suggests that the nature of Will's clerical status is in doubt to the casual observer, and, as Donaldson has shown, this is exactly the grey area in which clerks in minor orders found themselves.[36] It takes some eighty lines for Will to assert his right to wear the long clerical robes which were so dubiously introduced in the first lines, as well as to justify his manner of breadwinning, which, it seems, is hard to distinguish from begging. When Reason challenges him about his *modus vivendi* – he neither serves the church officially, nor labours manually, nor has lands to live upon, nor is he crippled, and worst of all he appears to lead the 'lollarne lyf' of the false hermit – he is provoked to tell his life story: his family was supporting his education, but since they died he has never been able to find a life he liked so well 'but in this longe clothes' (V.40–41). Such a narrative of youth and education is, according to Orme, highly unusual in this period.[37] This type of specificity, according to Dinzelbacher, would likely indicate authentic autobiography, and according to

---

35 On the influence of Augustine's *Confessions* see Pierre Courcelle, *Les Confessions de Augustine dans la Tradition Littéraire*, Paris, 1950.
36 Donaldson, *Piers Plowman: The C Text*, op. cit., ch. VII.
37 Nicholas Orme, 'Langland and Education', *History of Education*, 11 (1982), 251–66.

Burrow, one should consider whether there is a practical reason for the inclusion of such details. Probators were specifically instructed to enquire about the visionary's social class and education, and here they serve to establish intellectual and social credibility, as well as functioning to lay to rest the kind of association with rebels, fanatics and dissolutes that may have worried Langland after the Peasant's Revolt. Will goes on to assert that he does indeed have a vocation, that is, a clerical one, and in an adroit response to Reason's valorizing of manual labour, he declares that the tools ('lomes') that he labours with, and by which he deserves livelihood, are his *pater noster* and his primer, his Psalter and his seven psalmes (V.45–7), by which he says prayers for the souls of those who 'fynden me my fode' on a monthly basis. Reason had earlier implied that he did nothing to better the lives of those who supported him (V.21), but, like all intellectual labourers, Will defends himself by saying that while it may look as if he is a social parasite, he is actually providing a needed service. Praying is a form of legitimate labour; his manner of life is distinguishable from begging (V.48–9). In a society in which prayer was a legitimately purchasable commodity, this is not so odd. However, Conscience is not impressed with the fact that it is an unsupervised form of living and impugns it as a probator would:

> Quod Consciences, 'By Crist, y can nat see this lyeth;
> Ac it semeth no sad parfitnesse in citees to begge,
> But he be obediencer to prior or to mynistre.'   (V.89–91)

The remark is pointedly plain: an obediencer is a member of a religious order, or one who owes obedience; Will's practice is not externally verifiable. But the objection is really to the way 'it semeth', rather than to what it is (Conscience does not impugn praying for a living, and although his bluntness is comical, the passage may not have seemed as cutting to a medieval audience as one might think). Langland has always prioritized internal over external regulation, and this may be his concern here as well. And who could have a better spiritual supervisor ('prior' or 'mynistre') than Conscience? The problem he raises, then, seems to be with the way it looks, which is precisely the concern of a defender or apologist for visionaries, as one sees in Alphonse.

As we have seen, visionary credibility rested heavily on the issue of the seer's social status and manner of life. Gerson stresses that the rich were suspect as visionaries, as were the very poor, and possible motives for deception had to be explained always (Christian cites the instance of a poor man for whom a job as shrine tender would be preferable to manual labour).[38] Interesting in this regard is the data Christian gathered on fourteen Spanish visionaries, male and female, who were believed by the authorities: all were peasants or rural craftsmen, but none were from the ranks of the truly poor. Only one was an adult day labourer (who was eventually whipped), and none was a beggar. Apparently God called the simple and the humble as spokesmen, but not the dissolute. That the poet is

---

[38] Christian, *op. cit.*, p.199.

anxious to distinguish himself from the lowest members of society becomes abundantly, even, to modern ears, offensively evident as the passage continues. He launches into an attack on current practices of allowing bastards and bondmen's children to become priests (and shoemaker's sons to become knights): 'Hit bycometh for clerkes Crist for to serue/ And knaues vncrounede to carte and to worche' (V.61–2). Although much in the long passage (V.53–81) is justifiable criticism of simoniacal and other corrupt practices, and much more is justifiable in terms of medieval social ideology (however offensive it seems to us), there is more than a touch of social insecurity here as well. Will protests loudly against the upward mobility of society's lowest elements (a new emphasis in the C text), and everything he has said – implicitly or explicitly – declares him to be a respectably born man down on his luck, who has forged the best system of livelihood he can for himself in the face of his misfortunes, education, inclinations, social rank and evangelical ideology. Whether or not he would pass *probatio* (his 'pugnacious self-justification' would not have impressed most probators), he has managed to establish that the vocation to which he has been called is clerkly (one probable self-portrait in B describes him as speaking 'clergially' (Prol.124)), even if his actual status within this estate is uncertain.

The *Apologia* was clearly added to the C text to clarify a few things about the author – to set the record straight, with a little 'pugnacious self-justification', or at least as much as the genre would allow (one is reminded of Abelard's *Historia*, which is officially an *epistola consolatoria*, but is actually largely self-justification).[39] Missing from this self-portrait is the element of madness or foolishness which is present in a number of embryonic self-portraits throughout the poem, especially in B. All the treatises on *probatio* stress the importance of soundness of mind; the *Chastising*-author, translating Alphonse, writes that the probator should enquire 'wheþer he be liȝt in kynde, or liȝt of frealte in chiere, in worde or in dede, or ellis wheþer he haue fieble vndirstondyng, or wheþir he haue a sad knowyng or feelyng, or ellis a sodeyn wit for fantesie'.[40] Furthermore, all the treatizes express the distrust of the imagination found in numerous authorities (Alphonse cites Augustine and Aquinas) and often registered in mystical works.[41] Demons can operate at the first two levels of vision (corporeal and imaginative), but not at the level of intellectual vision (according to Alphonse, who is citing Aquinas, *Daemones, inquit, ea quae sciunt hominibus manifestant, non quidem per illuminationem intellectus, sed per aliquam imaginariam visionem*[42] (Demons, he says, manifest those things they know not through intellectual illumination, but through some imaginary

---

[39] Pearsall, *C Text, op. cit.*, note to V.1.

[40] *Op. Cit.*, p. 175.

[41] See Alastair Minnis, 'Langland's Ymaginatif and late-medieval theories of Imagination', in *Comparative Criticism: A Yearbook*, ed. E. S. Shaffer, Cambridge, 1981, 3, pp.71–103.

[42] *Epistola, op. cit.*, p.586.

vision, or even by communicating through sensory things.) The forerunner in the B text of the C *Apologia* is the famous passage in which Imaginatif confronts Will with the question of vocation: 'And þow medlest þee wiþ makynges and my3test go sey þi sauter,/ And bidde for hem þat 3yueþ þee breed' (B XII.16–17) for there are already enough books on Dowell. This passage disappears in C, but two of its lines (16,17) are echoes in the C *Apologia* (V.47,48), suggesting that Langland did specifically reword the B confrontation with Imaginatif on the subject of poetic vocation into the C confrontation with Conscience and Reason on the subject of prophetic vocation. In doing so he has shifted the personified mental faculties to a higher plane of respectability. Although the *vis imaginativa* was thought by some authorities to play a special role in the charism of prophecy, one senses that Langland wanted mental faculties of more impeccable credentials to personify in C's more earnest *Apologia*. Again, there is a concern with how things look, and this concern is at odds with the charismatic impetus in the poet, who shared with a thinker like Alphonse a passionate belief in visionary experience, but a painful sense that it was suspect.

Alphonse's concern in the *Epistola* is with the reception of Bridget's visions in the sophisticated world of the court, a world of which Alphonse had firsthand experience, and which he knew to be dominated, in religious matters, by learned court clerics, 'doctors in both laws, no doubt, of the type that will dismiss the *Revelations* as the vapourings of a mere woman'.[43] Alphonse himself is a traditional monastic thinker with practical experience of the spiritual life (in his own description of the ideal probator, of *sentimentorum consolationum, et visionum mentalium spiritualiter, aut intellectualiter sibi diuinitus infusorum*[44] – feelings of consolation, and of mental visions divinely infused, spiritually or even intellectually), having counselled a host of visionaries including St Catherine of Sienna, St Bridget and St Katherine of Sweden, and the Blessed Clara Gambacorti – an impressive *curriculum vitae*. Few today, Alphonse laments, with a significant glance in the direction of the scholastics and canon lawyers, have the requisite qualities to discern spirits and judge visions justly; many blindly condemn visionaries out of hand (*ex abrupto*).[45] Then, in a display of the charismatic-evangelical fervour which permeates reformist visionary thought like Bridget's and Langland's, he focusses especially on the scorn of *simplices personas spirituales, idiotas, & sexum foemineum quasi ignarum & leuis capacitatis & reputationis*[46] (simple religious people, unlearned and of the feminine sex, as if they are ignorant, and of little ability and consideration) as being unworthy of visions. Such scoffing sophisticates miss the point that God

---

[43] Colledge, *Epistola, op. cit.*, p.49.
[44] *Epistola, op. cit.*, p.576.
[45] *Idem.*
[46] *Ibid.*, p. 577.

has often chosen the weak (*informa mundi*) in order to confound the wise:[47] did he not make a shepherd his prophet, and fill young simple ones (*iuuenes idiotas*) with the spirit of prophecy? Were not fishermen rather than learned ones (*doctores*) his apostles? Numerous passages in *Piers* pose exactly the same charismatic ideology, and, like Langland, Alphonse struggles to find a balance between a heartfelt belief that God will choose unlikely vessels as his prophets, and the need to show orthodoxy and discretion (*discretio*). In the chapters that follow, Alphonse does all he can to dissociate the true visionary from the lunatic, while preserving the dignity of the *idiota* – not an easy task, and one which Langland began to handle with discretion only in the C Text.

A few instances will have to suffice. In the B Prologue a lunatic ('a leene þyng wiþalle') kneels before the king and 'clergially' warns him of his own eschatology in an almost Brigittine fashion, urging him to rule justly (B Prol.123). In the C text the lunatic disappears and the impersonal Kynde Witt speaks the lines (C Prol.147). A second, more complex instance of this sort of revision occurs in Langland's reworking of the opening of B XV in which Will, frustrated by his inability to find Dowell, depicts himself as a fool:

> And so my wit weex and wanyed til I a fool weere.
> And some lakkede my lif – allowed if fewe –
> And lete me for a lorel and looþ to reuerencen
> Lordes or ladies or any lif ellis.   (B XV.3–6)

Describing his refusal to greet anyone he meets, no matter how rich, he ends 'and in þat folie I raued/ Til reson hadde ruþe on me and rokked me aslepe' (10–11). In the C text this passage disappears, but a new passage on 'lunatyk lollares' was created in Passus IX: drawing upon the Pauline notion of the holy fool and the Franciscan notion of *joculatores Domini*, Langland created one of his most charismatic protraits of lunatic wanderers endowed with a holy carelessness of worldly comforts, acting as God's 'priue disciples' or 'munstrals of heuene' (one of the positive images of minstrels, distinct from many negative ones in C). Like Will in the B text these lunatics 'madden as þe mone sit', and refuse to greet anyone, no matter how important ('And thauh a mete with the Mayre ameddes þe strete,/ A reuerenseth hym ryht nauht, no rather then another'. (IX.122–3)) This indifference, and the fact that they beg without a bag, connect them both with Christ's apostles and with Will himself, although the connection is so oblique that only a reader who knew the poem well, or who had a keen interest in charismatic ecclesiology, would pick up the connections. I suspect that these were the only readers Langland wanted making such a connection.

---

[47] Alphonse's ideas about women visionaries in this passage are reminiscent of Hildegard of Bingen's, whose works he might have known. See Kerby-Fulton, *Reformist Apocalypticism, op. cit.*, pp. 64–75.

Through a study of some of the C revisions one gets a sense that Langland was looking over his shoulder during the creation of his last version. We know that he never finished the ambitious process of revision of which some C passages bear evidence, and we do not know precisely what motivated all the re-writing he did do, but I hope that I have shown that there is a movement towards *discretio* in C's self-referential passages. Medieval reading habits suggest that his audience probably read these passages autobiographically, and no matter what we as modern readers decide about their historical authenticity, we can see that Langland strove to stabilize the visionary self-image he presents in C, yet without compromising the charismatic passions which attracted him to the genre. This is precisely the balance between charism and *discretio* that Alphonse hoped to achieve in the *Epistola*. Such treatises, whether Langland knew these particular ones or not, have much to tell us about medieval theological responses to contemporary visionary writing, and such responses could not but have shaped Langland's thinking about self-representation.

THE MYSTIC THEOLOGY OF THE THIRTEENTH-CENTURY MYSTIC, HADEWIJCH, AND ITS LITERARY EXPRESSION

SASKIA MURK JANSEN

THE HISTORICAL FIGURE OF HADEWIJCH is shadowy in the extreme. A fourteenth century note on the fly-leaf of manuscript Ghent University Library 941 calls her *Hadewijch de Antverpia*, 'Hadewijch of Antwerp', but by the early seventeenth century the Bollandists (a group of Jesuit scholars compiling the *Acta Sanctorum*) were unable to trace any reference to Hadewijch in Antwerp or in Brussels in the environs of which city most of the Hadewijch manuscripts originated.[1] The texts ascribed to Hadewijch survive in five closely related manuscripts and comprise fourteen *Visions*, a curious text known as the *List of the Perfect Ones*, thirty-two *Letters* and forty-five *Stanzaic Poems*. The manuscripts also contain a second collection of poems known as the *Mengeldichten* – the *Poems in Mixed Forms*.[2] The first sixteen *Mengeldichten*, fifteen of which are in rhyming couplets, should more properly be described as *Epistolary Poems* – they are closely related to the prose letters, two of which start with a passage in rhyming couplets. These poems survive in four of the five Hadewijch manuscripts and have generally also been attributed to Hadewijch. There have been doubts expressed, largely on account of the perceived lower poetic quality of these poems compared with the *Stanzaic Poems*, but my research using quantitative statistical analysis of language has shown that such

---

[1] The main Hadewijch manuscripts are Brussels Koninklijkebibliotheek 2879–80 (MS.A), Brussels Koninklijkebibliotheek 2877–78 (MS.B), Ghent Universiteits-bibliotheek 941 (MS.C), Brussels Koninlijkebibliotheek 3093–95 (MS.D) and Antwerp Ruusbroec-genootschaps Bibliotheek 385ii (MS.R). MSS A and B originated in Brussels probably between 1375 and 1383; MS.C comes from the monastery of Bethleem near Leuven in the second half of the fourteenth century; MS.D was probably copied in the monastery of St Paul in Zonien near Brussels (known as the Rooklooster) in the second half of the fifteenth century: MS.R is a paper codex from the first quarter of the sixteenth century.

[2] The standard editions of these texts are those prepared by J. Van Mierlo between 1924 and 1952. *Hadewijch Visioenen*, 2 vols, Ghent, 1924; *Hadewijch Strofische Gedichten*, 2 vols, Antwerp, 1942; *Hadewijch Brieven*, 2 vols, Antwerp, 1947; *Hadewijch Mengeldichten*, Antwerp, 1952. The only available translation, (*Hadewijch The Complete Works*, tr. Mother Columba Hart, Classics of Western Spirituality, London, 1980) is not sufficiently reliable for academic purposes. A new English edition with a facing page translation to be published by Peeters in Leuven, is currently in preparation.

doubts are unfounded.[3] The other *Mengeldichten*, numbers 17–29 in Van Mierlo's edition, have hitherto not been attributed to Hadewijch. These poems have been considered as a single group and have been attributed to a late thirteenth- or early fourteenth-century author, while Hadewijch is presumed to have been active circa 1240–1250. However if, as Van Mierlo suggested, poems 17–29 are considered as two separate collections consisting in one case of poems 17–24 and in the other of poems 25–29, an analysis of the poetics, theology and language of the two collections in comparison with those of the *Stanzaic Poems* and the *Epistolary Poems* reveals that, although poems 25–29 contain elements which could suggest an author later than Hadewijch, poems 17–24 should more properly be attributed to a contemporary of Hadewijch's who was very familiar with her work, with the poetics governing the composition of the *Stanzaic Poems*, and with Hadewijch's definition of the mystic experience, and who also enjoyed an awareness of union with God. The nature of the experience related in poems 17–24 as well the description of it are equal to the best of Hadewijch. We are therefore faced with a choice – we can either posit a second, highly gifted mystic poet within Hadewijch's immediate circle who remained anonymous, or we can accept the possibility of her authorship of these poems. The most straightforward solution is that these texts should properly be attributed to Hadewijch as well.[4] To sum up: the texts which should, in my opinion, be attributed to Hadewijch are therefore the fourteen *Visions*, the *List of the Perfect Ones*, thirty-two *Letters* in prose, forty-five *Stanzaic Poems*, sixteen *Epistolary Poems* and the *Mengeldichten* 17–24, the *Lyric Poems*. In addition to the poems 25–29, two of the manuscripts also contain another text of uncertain authorship – a short prose piece known as the *Twee-Vormich Tractaetken*, the *Small Two-fold Tract*. Like the Poems in *Mixed Forms*, this tract has been largely overlooked in the past.

The *List of the Perfect Ones* which I described just now as a rather curious text is the principal source of information by which scholars have sought to date Hadewijch's literary activity. It occurs at the end of the *Visions*, almost as an appendix, and presents a list of those who, according to Hadewijch, have received the eighth 'gift of love'. As well as Biblical and historical figures she lists many contemporaries – unfortunately for us she does so in less than helpful ways such as 'three Béguines and two nuns', 'In Paris there lives a forgotten master alone in a small cell', and 'In England .ix. five hermits, .ij. anchorites and .ij. noble ladies'. However, two of the references have proved more helpful. The author mentions a Béguine whom a certain 'Master Robert' had killed on account of her righteous love. Titus Brandsma has suggested that this 'Master

---

[3] S. Murk Jansen, *The Measure of Mystic Thought: a study of Hadewijch's Mengeldichten*, Göppinger Arbeiten zur Germanistik, 536, Göppingen, 1991. The Appendix also includes a detailed description of the Hadewijch manuscripts.

[4] The authorship debate and the evidence for this conclusion are described in Murk Jansen, *The Measure of Mystic Thought, op. cit.*

Robert' may have been Robert le Bougre, a particularly unsavoury inquisitor inflicted on Flanders in the 1230s.[5] Brandsma has identified the Béguine as probably a certain Aleydis whom Robert le Bougre had burned at the stake in 1236. If these identifications are correct they give the *terminus post quem* for the *List*, if for nothing else. Another entry refers to hermits living on the walls of Jerusalem. In view of the international nature of the references in the rest of the List there is no reason to suppose that the author is referring to a Jerusalem other than that in the Holy Land. As Jerusalem was finally lost to the Khorezmians on 23 August 1244, with the subsequent brutal massacre of all Christians in the environs, this entry provides the *terminus ante quem*. Allowing for a certain time lapse for the information to reach the author, it seems unlikely that the *List* would have been written much later than 1250. There remains the vexed question of the authorship, but failing any evidence to the contrary it is generally accepted as genuine. According to the *List* then, Hadewijch was writing just before the middle of the thirteenth century and this is certainly the impression given by her language. There is no way of dating language exactly, but Hadewijch's language is clearly closer to that of the Cistercian nun Beatrijs of Nazareth who died in 1268 than that of Ruusbroec who died just over a century later.[6] The nature of Hadewijch's mystic theology also suggests a date around the middle of the thirteenth century rather than very much later. Her writings stand in the Augustinian tradition of contemplative monastic theology, based on experience rather than on speculation and show little or no trace of the scholastic theology which was to gain currency in the late thirteenth century. Her theology resembles that of Bernard of Clairvaux and the Victorines more than that of Eckhart or Marguerite Porete.[7]

The very few personal remarks Hadewijch lets fall in her *Letters* and in the *Epistolary Poems* suggest that she was not a member of a convent, but that she lived in a rather less stable community as an early Béguine. The Béguines were a movement of lay religious women which came into prominence in the first half of the thirteenth century. It has been convincingly argued that the Béguines were

---

[5] Titus Brandsma, 'Wanneer schreef Hadewijch hare visioenen?', *Studia Catholica*, 2 (1926), 238–256.

[6] Beatrijs wrote one text, the *Seuen manieren van heiliger minnen*, which is written in rhythmic prose not unlike that of Hadewijch. *Beatrijs van Nazareth Van Seuen Manieren van Heileger Minnen*, eds. H. Vekeman and J. Tersteeg, Klassiek Letterkundig Pantheon 188, Zutphen, 1970. Currently no translation into English is available, though extracts have been translated with varying degrees of accuracy in the following recent anthologies: *Beguine Spirituality*, Fiona Bowie, London, 1989; *Women Mystics in Medieval Europe*, Emilie Zum Brun and Georgette Epiney-Burgard, New York, 1989. See also R. De Ganck, *Beatrice of Nazareth and the thirteenth-century mulieres religiosae of the Low Churches*, 3 vols, Kalamazoo, 1991.

[7] Marguerite Porete died at the stake in 1310 for disseminating her work *Le mirouer des simples ames*. Marguerite Porete, *Speculum simplicium Animarum*, eds R. Guarnieri and P. Verdeyen, Corpos Christianorum Continuatio Medieualis LXIX, Turnhout, 1986.

a development of the laysisters of the Premonstratensian and Cistercian orders.[8] There was a dramatic increase in the number of lay religious women in the Low Countries and in Germany during the early thirteenth century which coincided with the restriction of entry of women into established orders and the desire to live a life of apostolic poverty in the world as illustrated by the inception of the Franciscan and the Dominican orders. The evidence shows that, like Francis and Dominic, the overwhelming majority of early Béguines came from the nobility and from the wealthy urban patriciate.[9] These women took vows of chastity and obedience, though not of stability, and the vows could be revoked if a Béguine chose to marry or to enter a convent. The property with which they entered life as a Béguine, often the house in which they lived, reverted to them if they changed their way of life. The life of the early Béguines was quite different from the impression given by the large and beautiful Béguinages in Antwerp, Bruges and other cities in the Low Countries. Some of the early Béguines lived alone, either within their families or in separate houses, others lived in small groups of like-minded women. The size and composition of such groups will have fluctuated as the reputation of the Mistress attracted new members, while others left to join a convent or to re-enter the world. Béguines tended to cluster around Dominican and Franciscan convents, to do for the strictly enclosed nuns of these orders what these were unable to do for themselves.[10] The evidence suggests that the priests responsible for the spiritual welfare of the Béguines were largely from these orders as well.[11] It is thought that Hadewijch may have lived in such a small group of women, and with her intellect, her powerful personality and her mystic gifts she may well have had some authority within it. However, in her *Letters* and *Epistolary Poems* Hadewijch is giving spiritual direction to correspondents at least some of whom are elsewhere at the time of her writing. There are also suggestions in her letters that there may have been a time when she was living in less congenial circumstances.[12] However, as we have no

---

[8] Carol Neel, 'The Origins of the Beguines', in *Sisters and Workers in the Middle Ages*, eds J. Bennett, E. Clark, J. O'Barr, B. Vilen, S. Westpahl-Wihl, Chicago, 1989, pp.240–260.

[9] H. Grundmann, *Religiöse Bewegungen im Mittelalter*, second edition, Hildesheim, 1961. There may of course have been socially or economically disadvantaged women who became Béguines at this period, but the available evidence does not mention them.

[10] Isabel Grübel, *Bettelorden und Frauenfrömmigkeit im 13. Jahrhundert*, Kultur-geschichtliche Forschungen 9, Munich, 1987, pp.93–109.

[11] See Grundmann, *op. cit.*, p.312, Grübel, *op. cit.*, p.59. See also J. B. Freed, *The mendicant orders in German society 1219–1273*, Princeton, 1969. The evidence suggests that the Dominicans became more quickly and deeply involved with the care of women than the Franciscans. There is perhaps a correlation between the fact that the Dominican order appears to have been more attractive to the upper classes than the Franciscan, and that the early Béguines were largely drawn from the same social group.

[12] See for example, letter 21 and letter 25. That her correspondents were living elsewhere see for example epistolary poem 6:7–8.

evidence about Hadewijch external to her writings, any speculation about the details of her life must remain precisely that – speculation.

One of the pitfalls facing Béguines was the Church's objection to women teaching or even in some cases talking about matters of theology and its speed in levelling accusations of heresy against those who did so outside its framework. Many women at this period employed variations on the humility topos as a way of preempting criticism. For example, Mechtild of Magdeburg, a mystic who lived many years as a Béguine in Magdeburg before choosing to end her life as a Cistercian nun at the convent of Helfta, writes how she had been warned that her book would be burned. She subsequently seeks justification for her writing from God and describes a conversation between herself and God in which she says:

> Alas Lord, were I a learned man, and you had worked this miracle in me, it would forever bring you glory. But how can anyone believe that You have built a golden house in this filthy slough?

and God replies:

> Whenever I bestow a special grace I always sought for the lowest, the least, the best concealed place . . . It is a great honour for me and strengthens holy Christianity significantly that the unlearned mouth teaches the erudite tongues about my Holy Spirit.[13]

Hadewijch was clearly also aware of the danger and justifies herself and her audience in a number of rather subtle ways. Unlike Mechtild of Magdeburg, Hadewijch does not lament the fact that she, a mere woman, should be called upon to write about God. Rather, in her first epistolary poem she describes Mary Magdalene as the great example, and she specifies the way in which her example is to be followed by a paraphrase from John 20 'I have seen the Lord, and he said these things to me' (*Epistolary Poems* 3:62). These words echo Jesus' exhortation to Mary Magdalene after his resurrection 'Go to the brethren and tell them what you have seen.' The example Hadewijch urges on her audience is to follow that instruction from Jesus and to become an apostle according to Paul's definition – one who has seen the risen Lord and bears witness to him. Hadewijch's description of Mary Magdalene as the great example may have been in part a gesture of respect to the Dominican Order which had chosen Mary Magdalene as their patron saint because she was the 'apostle to the apostles', having been given this command to preach by the risen Jesus, but in this Hadewijch is also claiming for herself the ultimate authority for her actions. In the Lyric Poems Hadewijch again identifies herself and her audience with the apostles. In a stanza referring to the image of the head and the feet of Christ, she writes:

---

[13] *Das fliessende Licht der Gottheit*, Book 2:26. *Mechtild von Magdeburg, Das fliessende Licht der Gottheit*, ed. Hans Neumann, 2 vols, Zurich, 1990–91. Translation taken from *Mechtild von Magdeburg, Flowing Light of the Divinity*, tr. C. Mesch Galvani, ed. S. Clark, New York, 1991.

Dies houets noed
Was soe groot
Alst hen wael sceen,
Wat soudense rouwe
In haer ontrouwe
Claghen die teen? ` (*Lyric Poems* 19:157–162; VM18:271–276)[14]

(Since the head's suffering was so great in order that they might
receive the benefit, what cause have the toes to lament in their
unfaithfulness?)

The head and feet of Christ were variously interpreted as the divinity of Christ
and his incarnation, or as Christ himself and his apostles on earth. By using the
word *teen* 'toes' (which was necessary to complete the rhyme) Hadewijch is able
to make the identification between herself and her audience and Christ's apostles
with humility.

There is one important aspect of Hadewijch's writing that can too easily be
obscured in translation, namely the ambiguity and plurality of the word *minne*
(love) which Hadewijch uses for the divine. The debate that has raged about the
precise meaning of the word in Hadewijch is witness to its ambiguity. Some
scholars have argued that *minne* refers to God the Son, and indeed in the
Stanzaic Poems Hadewijch identifies the two. In poem 29 she writes:

Die vader van anebeghinne
Hadde sinen sone die minne
Verborghen in sinen scoet   (*Stanzaic Poems* 29:41–43)

(The Father from the beginning had his Son, love, hidden in his lap).[15]

However, in the *Letters* she identifies *minne* equally clearly with the Holy
Spirit.[16] *Minne* has also been interpreted as a quality of God, as the
personification of man's love for God, or even as the personification of the
experience of a relationship. The difficulty that all such definitions encounter,
and the reason that the debate generated some heat, is that it is always possible to
quote passages where a particular definition is clearly out of the question. To
argue, as some scholars have tried to do, that Hadewijch must have meant one
thing or another on the basis of twentieth-century dogmatic theology, brings us
no closer to Hadewijch's thought.

An analysis of the way Hadewijch uses language reveals the frequency with
which she uses homonyms to create apparent paradoxes and plurality of
meaning. I submit that Hadewijch employs the same technique with respect to

---

[14] The numbering of the *Poems in Mixed Forms* (*Epistolary Poems*, *Lyric Poems* and
Further Poems) is that of the new Hadewijch edition published by Peeters which
follows the numbering of texts in MS.B. Where this number is different from that in
Van Mierlo's edition I also give the number in that edition preceded by VM. Van
Mierlo's numbering does not follow that of any one manuscript.

[15] I chose to translate the word *schoot* here as 'lap' rather than as 'bosom' which is the
more usual English term because in Middle Dutch it includes the meaning 'womb'.

[16] See for example letter 28.

the word *minne*. When analysing Hadewijch's work it should be remembered
that all her poetry, and her prose, was intended to be heard, not read silently as
we do now. When listening to a text being read aloud, one is aware of what has
gone before but, unlike the reader, the listener has no inkling of what is to come.
The moment a word is spoken you can interpret it only in the light of what has
already been said, although what follows may cause you to re-interpret the word
subsequently. When such re-interpretation occurs the first interpretation may
inform the second and both meanings may continue in some sense to be present
simultaneously. One example of this in Hadewijch occurs in epistolary poem 13.
This poem is a sequence of one-line paradoxes arranged in rhyming couplets. In
one couplet Hadewijch exploits the ambiguity of a homonym to create a third
paradox between the two lines:

> Omme hare quelen dat es ghesonde
> Hare helen openbaert hare conden   (*Epistolary Poems* 13:10–11)
>
> (To suffer for her, that is healthy; Her healing reveals her knowledge *or* Her
> hiding reveals what can be known about her.)

The verb *helen* can mean either 'to hide' or 'to heal'. The second reading given
is clearly the primary one intended, but because of the context of the previous
line the meaning 'to heal' springs first to mind and creates the additional paradox
that whereas to suffer for *minne* is good, her healing is also good. An example of
a different kind of duality occurs in lyric poem 26, where Hadewijch develops
the image of *Minne* as a tavern keeper. She writes:

> Si es melde mede
> Ende scinct van vollen
> Maer die met hare drincken
> Doetse op een wincken
> Bloet vertollen   (*Lyric Poems* 26:14–18; VM24:74–96)
>
> (She is also generous and pours full-measure; but those who drink with her
> she causes at a wink to pay [in] blood).

The homonym of the verb *scinken* (to pour) means 'to cause pain' so the lines
could also be translated as 'She is generous too, and causes full measure of
pain'. A frequently recurring example of ambiguity is the word *doghet* and its
cognates, which mean 'virtue', and its homonyms which mean 'suffering'.
Whenever the word occurs, both meanings are to some extent present. For
example:

> Soe seldi altoos met bernende sinne
> Soeken nuwe dogen om minne
>
> . . .
>
> Siet in wat dogene ic hebbe gelegen
> Dat u ongereet ware to dogene
> So begeert dan dogen om te hoegene   (*Epistolary Poems* 5:19–20, 30–32)
>
> (So shall you always, with passionate longing, seek new virtue [suffering]
> for love . . . See in what suffering [virtue] I have lain, which you were not

prepared to suffer [practice], so then desire virtue [suffering] so that you
may rise higher.)

These few examples show some of the ways in which Hadewijch exploits
plurality of meaning and ambiguity in her writing. It seems likely that Hadewijch
consciously exploited the word *minne* in the same way, and that some or all of
the possible interpretations of the word inform the meaning in a given context.
That Hadewijch sought the ambiguity to give greater depth and nuance to her
writing is suggested by the fact that it can be difficult to determine the
grammatical function of the word *minne* in a sentence – the word could be a
noun, a verb, or even part of an adverbial phrase. The classic example of this is
the final stanza of no. 15 of the *Epistolary Poems*:

> Ay minne ware ic minne
> Ende met minne
> minne u minne
> Ay minne om minne
> gheuet dat minne
> de minne al minne volkinne (*Epistolary Poems* 15:63–68; VM15:49–52)

> (O love, were I love, and with love, love, to love you, O love for love give
> that love which love fully recognises as love).

The uncertainty concerning exactly what or who Hadewijch is referring to by the
word *minne*, whether to God or to the experience of loving, enables her to say
things about her experience of God which could perhaps not be said otherwise.
For example in epistolary poem 16 she names *minne* as hell and writes:

> Dats hille na den wesene dat es minne
> Want si verderuet ziele ende zinne
> Soe datse meer vercoeueren en mogen
> Noch te anderen zaken en dogen
> Dan verloren te sine in storme van minnen
> Met liue met ziele met herte met sinnen
> Bliuen de minnende in de hille verloren
> Wie dat wilt wachtere hem voren (*Epistolary Poems* 16:199–206)

> (That is hell according to the being that is love, because she destroys soul
> and sense so that they can never recover, nor be good for anything else
> except to be lost in the storms of love With life, with soul, with heart, with
> sense the lovers remain lost in hell; who wishes that, be wary of it.)

Given the plurality of meaning elsewhere in the Hadewijch texts it does justice
neither to the complexity of Hadewijch's mystic experience nor to the subtlety of
her expression of it, to dismiss this as a literary topos describing the human
experience of love.

Another aspect of Hadewijch's use of the word *minne* for the divine is that the
noun is feminine and is therefore necessarily accompanied by the feminine form
of adjectives and feminine pronouns. That this female-ness is not a kind of
linguistic accident with no further content or meaning is shown by Hadewijch's

on several occasions referring to *Minne* explicitly as 'Lady Love'.[17] This device of course works particularly well in the *Stanzaic Poems* which are written using the form and conventions of the courtly love-lyric. Almost every poem begins with a classic *Natureingang* and most of them describe the hard lot of the lover languishing in unrewarded loving service of a demanding lady. Not perhaps very remarkable, except that the (male) lover is the persona of Hadewijch herself and the demanding fickle lady represents God. In stanzaic poem 17, for example, Hadewijch writes:

> Wat mach hem bliscap ommeuaen
> Die minne in hachten heeft inghe ghedaen
> Ende die de wijdde van minnen woude ommegaen
> Ende vri ghebruken in trouwen?
> Meer dan sterren anden hemel staen
> Heuet die minne dan rouwen.
>
> Dat ghetal diere rouwen moet sijn ghesweghen.
> Die grote sware waghen bliuen onghesweghen,
> Daer ne gheet gheen ghelike jeghen
> So eest best dat mens begheue.
> Al es mijn deel cleine ic hebber verdreghen
> Mi gruwelt dat ic leue.
>
> Hoe mach hem gruwelen ende rouwen tleuen
> Die sijn al heuet op al ghegheven
> Ende in donckeren dole wert verre verdreuen
> Daer hi meer ne waent doen kere
> Ende in onthopenden storme al wert tewreuen
> Wat rouwen gheliket dien sere? (*Stanzaic Poems* 27:13–30)

(How can joy surround him whom love has tightly imprisoned, and who wanted to travel the wide expanse of love and freely enjoy it? Love then causes more sorrows than there are stars in heaven. The number of these sorrows must be unspoken, the great weighty burdens remain unweighed. There is nothing which can compare with it, so it is best not to attempt comparison. Even though my part is small, I shudder that I live. How life can cause him to shudder and to suffer who has risked his all for all and is driven far off to wander in the dark whence he fears never to return, and is crushed in a storm of despair; what suffering can be compared to that pain?).

In stanzaic poem 22 she writes:

> Van minnen claghic ghene pine
> Mi staet altoes haer onderdaen te sine
> Daer sijt ghebiedet lude ende stillekine
> . . .
> Hets een wonder onuerstaen
> Dat mijn herte dus heuet beuaen
> Ende doet dolen in ene wilde woestine

---

[17] For example lyric poem 26:25 (VM24:85), and *Stanzaic Poems* 2:19 and 11:13.

Soe wrede wuestine wert nie ghescapen
So die minne in haer lantscap can maken.   (*Stanzaic Poems* 22:23–30)

(I do not complain that love causes me pain, my role is always to be
subservient to her when she commands loudly or quietly . . . It is an
uncomprehended wonder that has thus captured my heart and causes me to
wander in a wild desert. No desert as cruel as that which love can make in
her landscape was ever created).

The relationship described by Hadewijch is not a very comfortable one, and is
far removed from the loving serenity of Julian of Norwich's vision.[18] However it
would be wrong to infer that she never experienced the joy of mystic union with
God. The central element of Hadewijch's mystic theology is paradox. In the
Lyric Poems she describes the experience of union with God as *vercrighen in
ontbliuen* 'to obtain within lack'. In *Visions* (no. 13) she defines this experience
as the eighth, the highest, gift of love:

Wat die minne gheuet dats ghesuert ende vertert ende verslonden watse nempt dats
rike ghemaket van groter ghewout van ghebrukene dies manens der minnen alle
uren groot effens hare seluen.

(What loves gives is soured, consumed and swallowed up; what she takes that
becomes riches by the great strength of the experience of desire for love which is
every hour as great as herself).

That is to say: the absence of love causes the lover to desire love more and more
until the magnitude of that desire becomes comparable to the magnitude of love's
love for man, and only in the greatness of desire is unity of love possible.

Suffering (defined elsewhere by Hadewijch as the consciousness that all that
one has of love falls short of love itself, in other words, the consciousness of the
absence of love) is the means by which man is transformed and this
transformation is the experience of union with God. As the passages quoted
above show, Hadewijch uses images of imprisonment, bondage, torture and
darkness to describe this suffering, and the experience of union is described in
terms of space and light – for example the space longed for by the lover in
stanzaic poem 17 (see above). It is particularly in the *Lyric Poems* that
Hadewijch describes and illustrates the ultimate gift of love – the realisation of
obtaining the joy of union within, and by means of, the consciousness of lack.
She writes:

Alle dinge
Sijn mi te inge
Ic ben soe wijt

---

[18] Something analogous to Julian's vision may be found in the work of Gertrude the
Great of Helfta. Accepted into the convent at the age of five, Gertrude's experience of
life will have been very different from that of the Béguines Hadewijch and Mechtild,
and this may explain the contrast between their vision of their relationship to God and
her own. She wrote in Latin but some of her work is available in translation: *Gertrude
the Great of Helfta: Spiritual Exercises*, trans. G. J. and J. Lewis, Kalamazoo, 1989;
The Life and Revelations of St Gertrude, trans. a religious Poor Clare, London, 1865.

Om een ongescepen
Hebbic begrepen
In eweghen tijt

Ic hebt ghevaen
Het heeft mi ontdaen
Widere dan wijt
Mi es te inghe al el
Dat wetti wel
Ghi dijs oec daer zijt.   (*Lyric Poems* 21:13-24)

(All things are too confined for me. I am so wide, for I have encompassed an uncreated one in eternity. I have it, it has undone me wider than wide. All else is too confined for me, that you know well, you who are there also.)

WORK AND WORK ETHICS IN
THE NUNNERY OF SYON ABBEY IN
THE FIFTEENTH CENTURY

ULLA SANDER OLSEN

SOME TIME BETWEEN 1342–1349, during a stay in Vadstena, Sweden, St Bridget is believed to have received, directly from Christ himself, the Rule for the monastic order which she wanted to found, i.e. an order for nuns with a group of priests attached to it.[1] This rule was not confirmed by the Pope until 1378, and then only as Constitutions to the Rule of St Augustinus, since the foundation of new orders was no longer allowed. As the so-called *Revelationes Extravagantes*[2] prove, St Bridget was aware that her Rule in some respects needed complement.[3] She therefore allowed one of her secretaries, Prior Petrus Olavi from Alvastra, to complete and define the Rule, adapting it to already extant statutes for monks and nuns, principally of the order of St Benedict and St Bernard (*Rewyll*, ch.23).[4] He also used some

---

[1] For an English text of the Rule of St Bridget, see *The Rewyll of Seynt Sauioure and other Middle English Brigittine Legislative Texts*, (vol. 2: The MSS. Cambridge University Library Ff.5.33. and St John's College Cambridge 11) ed. James Hogg, Salzburger Studien zur Anglistik und Amerikanistik, 6, Salzburg, 1978. Hereafter *Rewyll* [= MS Ff.5.33, Middle-English in 24 chapters]. On the development of the Rule, see *Den heliga Birgitta Opera Minora I: Regula Salvatoris*, ed. Sten Eklund, Stockholm, 1975, SSFS Ser. 2, Bd. VIII:1, pp.21-26.

[2] *Den heliga Birgittas Reuelaciones Extrauagantes*, ed. Lennart Hollman, Uppsala, 1956, SSFS Ser. 2, Bd. V.

[3] Chapters 1–46, 74, and 113–115 concern the foundation in Vadstena.

[4] Eklund, *op. cit.*, p.132 (cap. 26): *Episcopus, in cuius dyocesi monasterium est, erit tam sororum quam fratrum pater et visitator . . . Princeps regni seu terre, in qua est monsterium, erit responsalis et defensor in omnibus necessitatibus. Papa vero super vtrumque . . . erit eorum tutor caritatiuus; 'Quicumque monasterium huius religionis construere voluerit, nullatenus sine voluntate et licencia pape hoc presumat. Deinde istis constitucionibus per papam confirmatis inquirantur aliqui deuoti fratres de regulis Benedicti vel Bernardi, qui istis constitucionibus addendo inscribant, quomodo excessus sunt emendandi in monasterio et quomodo sepeliende sunt persone monialium et fratrum ibi moriencium et qualiter visitabit episcopus et pro quibus casibus ingrediatur monasterium episcopus vel alie persone vtputa medicus vel magistri, qui aliqua debeant laborare et reparare in monasterio etc. Addatur eciam de forma eleccionis abbatisse, de modo institucionis officialium et exprimantur loca, in quibus silencium est seruandum, sicut ecclesia, chorus, refectorium, dormitorium et alia loca, in quibus silencium seruandum est. Et omnia alia necessaria ad obseruanciam regularem, que in hiis constitucionibus non continentur, ad earum perfeccionem et roboracionem assumantur de regulis supradictis.*

of *Revelationes Extravagantes* for his Additions to the Rule (52 chapters).[5]

From the context of the chapter above-mentioned (*Rewyll*, ch.23) one may suppose that it also refers to the foundation of new monasteries in different countries, who 'are to develop their own links with other religious and secular authorities', (which might probably also be a condition for their survival) 'a context which leads one to suppose that St Bridget expected each new house, similarly, to develop its own volume of additional legislation'.[6] The Syon Additions for the sisters (59 chapters) can thus be considered the additional legislation for the English Bridgettines[7] in line with the Vadstena Additions, to which I add not only the Additions of Prior Petrus (also called the Constitutions to the Rule of St Bridget) but also the so-called *Lucidarium Sororum* (49 chapters), a book of customs developed in the nunnery of Vadstena in the 15th century, also drawing on *Revelationes Extravagantes*.[8]

---

[5] The Additions of Prior Petrus are edited in Old Swedish under the title 'Constitutiones' in *Heliga Birgittas Uppenbarelser*, ed. G. E. Klemming, Bd. 5: Bihang, 15–55. Hereafter Add. P.Petrus. Latin text in *Dokumente und Untersuchungen zur inneren Geschichte der drei Birgittenklöster Bayerns, 1420–1570*, ed. Tore Nyberg, Quellen und Erörterungen zur Bayerischen Geschichte, N.F. 26/2, München, 1974, pp.42–110, nr.223. For a comment on these Additions, see Torvald Höjer, *Studier i Vadstena klosters och birgittinordens historia intill midten af 1400-talet*, Upsala, 1905, pp.71–78; and Tore Nyberg, 'Prior Petrus författarskap till Vadstena klosters tilläggsstadgar', *Nordisk tidskrift för bok- och biblioteksväsen*, 53 (1966), 47–54.

[6] Roger Ellis, *Syon Abbey: The Spirituality of the English Bridgettines*, Analecta Cartusiana, 68/2 (1984), p.52. *Ibid.*, p.77; Ellis sums up the sources of the Syon Additions known to him, i.e. the Rules of St Bridget, St Augustin and St Benedict, the Cistercian constitutions and the Additions of Prior Petrus. Other sources (*ibid.* n.27) are listed in M. B. Tait, 'The Brigittine Monastery of Syon (Middlesex) with Special Reference to its Monastic Usage', (unpubl. D.Phil thesis), Oxford, 1975, which I at the present moment have had no opportunity to consult.

[7] *The Rewyll of Seynt Sauioure. Vol. 4: The Syon Additions for the Sisters from the British Library MS. Arundel 146*, ed. James Hogg, Salzburger Studien zur Anglistik und Amerikanistik, 6, Salzburg, (1980). Hereafter *Syon Add.* For still extant MSS copies, see Ellis, *op. cit.*, p.53.

[8] Edition in Old Swedish in Klemming, *op. cit.*, 57–106. Hereafter *Luc. Sor.* On the General Chapter in Gnadenberg, Bayern, 1487 (to which Syon Abbey sent its apologies *per Apostolicum Breve plumbatum*, see below n.21) the assembly solemnly declared *quod in omnibus vivendi observantiam in Regula S.Salvatoris per modum constitutionum traditam ab Urbano VI. & Martino V. summis Pontificibus confirmatam, nec non Regulam S. Augustini & additiones Prioris Petri dudum acceptatas & sigillatas in quantum dictae Regulae S. Salvatoris non contrariantur personae utriusque sexus nostri Ordinis uniformiter observabunt & et pro posse observari faciant & procurent.* Concerning different points in daily regular life the brothers must refer to *Liber Usuum* and the sisters to *Lucidarium Sororum: Item Sorores omnino se conforment in Choro, Refectorio & coeteris officiis Caeremoniis contentis in Libro earum, qui Lucidarium intitulatur*, see Carl Friedrich Wilhelm, Freiherr von Nettelbla, 'Vorläufige kurzgefasste Nachricht von einigen Klöstern der H. Schwedischen Birgitte ausserhalb Schweden besonders in Teutschland mit Urkunden und Kupferstichen', Frankfurt, 1764, *Anhang von Urkunden, Nr. 29: Capitulum Montis-Gratiae celebratum sub*

But let us see what the Rule of St Bridget says about manual work in the nunnery (*Rewyll*, ch.20, 'That the sustres be not ydel but laboure in dewe tyme'):

> So the susteris yche tyme that they are not at dyvyne s[er]uice or redyng. and it be suche tyme yat they may lefully trauayle: tha[n]ne must they also laboure w[y]t[h] her hondye that as they serue god w[y]t[h] the mouth. so they serue also wyth other me[m]brys, . . . that by bodely laboure they shulde be more able to sp[irit]uel laboure.

The life and work of St Mary, Christ and his apostles are held forward as examples to the sisters.[9] After the Rule the most important legislative document was the Additions of Prior Petrus, confirmed, for the first time, in 1384 by Nils Hermansson, Bishop of Linköping.[10]

To the medieval convents there was usually attached a staff of servants, conversi/conversae or lay sisters/lay brothers respectively, to do the heavier work in the big self-sufficient household, which generally constituted a medieval monastery. Whereas St Bridget's Rule allowed the male convent to take in eight lay brothers to serve the thirteen priests and four deacons, no provisions were made for lay sisters in the nunnery, which meant that St Bridget actually expected the sixty nuns to do all sorts of domestic work themselves.

In this spirit chapter 19 (*De labor sororum*) of the Additions of Prior Petrus is written. The work should be distributed by the Abbess according to skills and so that no one should be spared more than the other except in case of poor health or service in the choir. Those who were not accustomed to it, should be spared a little, till they had adapted themselves. No sister should be excused from manual work. The text here mentions work in kitchen, bakery, brewery, dairy, spinning- or weaving-mill. It was finally stressed once more that no sister should

---

Innocentio VIII. *Anno 1487*, 162–184, pp.167–168, 171. The Bridgettine legislative documents, preserved in 15th–17th century MSS, from the Dutch monastery Marienwater, founded 1434, which obviously followed the Vadstena-tradition and the General Chapter in Gnadenberg, contain generally: The Rules of St Augustin and St Bridget, the Additions of Prior Petrus, Lucidarium Sororum, Culpae, *Declarationes* [of dubious passages in the statutes], and *Ordinarius* [liturgical prescriptions]; these documents are sometimes collected in one volume, but are also found separately, see Ulla Sander Olsen, 'Et klosterbibliotek, Marienwater, fra ca. 1434–1713 : Forsøg på en rekonstruktion', (unpubl. paper, Danmarks Biblioteksskole), København, 1977, pp.44–46. It seems to me that the Syon Additions represent an attempt to unite all these elements above-mentioned in one text; they can be said to correspond roughly to locally adapted versions of Culpae (ch.1–7), the Additions of Prior Petrus/*Lucidarium Sororum* (ch.14–27, 45–59), and *Ordinarius* (ch.28–44). For a recent edition of Culpae, see *De Culpis*, ed. Christer Henriksén, Studia Seminarii Latini Upsaliensis, 1, Uppsala, 1990.

9 Eklund, *op. cit.*, p.128 (cap. 23). For the work and work ethics in the Bridgettine nunneries of Scandinavia, see Ulla Sander Olsen, 'Arbejdspraksis og arbejdsethos i birgittinernes nonnekonvent', in *Birgitta, hendes værk og hendes klostre i Norden* (Symposium, Mariager, 8.–11. marts 1990), Odense, 1991 (in printing).

10 The text is printed in Nyberg, 'Prior Petrus', *op. cit.*, pp.50–51.

be excused from work in the kitchen, except the Abbess, the Prioress and the sick.[11]

In the first monastery of the order in Vadstena, Sweden, founded about 1370,[12] the sisters, mostly of noble family, were not very happy with these prescriptions, obliging them to do domestic work, which in their opinion was too hard for them and disturbing to their devotional life and, probably most important of all, in their homes was assigned to servants.[13] However, in the beginning these prescriptions seemingly were observed. The still preserved Vadstena Diary has an entry about a sister, deceased 1402, who despite her noble origin was always industrious and humble and worked very hard in the kitchen.[14] Other entries, from the beginning of the fifteenth century, on the contrary, show that a considerable part of the hard manual work in brewery, bakery and weaving mill was done outside the enclosure by the so-called 'sorores ab extra', pious women, often widows, assimilated into the monastery by private vows.[15]

A revised text of the Additions of Prior Petrus was confirmed in 1420 by Knut Bosson, Bishop of Linköping,[16] this time with an important appendix to the notorious chapter 19, namely chapter 35 of *Revelationes extravagantes*, allowing the Abbess, if the necessity and the place demanded it, to take in four kitchen sisters, who should live inside the enclosure but not belong to the community. Their tasks were to look after the fire, to carry wood and water, to empty the dustbins and to help less strong sisters with their work. The reasons given for this moderation of the nuns' manual work are that some sisters were old and weak, some less accustomed to labour, and other more dedicated to meditation.[17] The sisters' work in bakery and brewery was omitted in the text.[18]

---

[11] Nyberg, *Dokumente, op. cit.*, pp.89–90.

[12] For the history of Vadstena monastery in the fifteenth century, see Höjer, *op. cit.*; and Tore Nyberg, *Birgittinische Klostergründungen des Mittelalters*, Bibliotheca Historica Lundensis, 15, Lund, 1965. An excellent but more popular history of the convent and its daily life is Andreas Lindblom, Vadstena Klosters öden, Vadstena, 1973.

[13] See Birgit Klockars, 'Kvinnans roll under medeltiden', *Credo*, 50 (1969), 123–127, and Eileen Power, *Medieval English Nunneries c. 1275 to 1535*, Cambridge, 1922, pp.4ff.

[14] *Diarium Vadstenense, the Memorial Book of Vadstena Abbey*, ed. Claes Gejrot, Acta Universitatis Stockholmiensis, Studia Latina Stockholmiensia, 33, Stockholm, 1988, p.139, nr.114.

[15] Gejrot, *op. cit.*, p.156, nr.174, April 4, 1409; p.160, nr.197, April 4, 1411; p.184, nr.357, Nov. 11, 1424. *Revelationes Extravagantes*, cap. 33, (Hollman, *op. cit.*, pp.147–148) gives permission to employ four *fratres ab extra* to assist the monastery in its relationship with the surroundings; in analogy with this also *sorores ab extra* were engaged. See *Wadstena kloster-reglor*, ed. Carl Ferdinand Lindström, SSFS, 2/1, Stockholm, 1845.

[16] Höjer, *op. cit.*, p.77.

[17] Hollman, *op. cit.*, pp.150–151.

[18] Nyberg, *Dokumente, op. cit.*, p.90.

On Dec. 1, 1422, Pope Martinus V confirmed the Abbess's right to take in these *focariae* or kitchen sisters. The general chapter of Vadstena in 1429 again treated the question of the sisters' work in the kitchen, and it was decided that the sisters, in turn, should supervise the work of the *focariae* and other servants.[19]

When Syon Abbey was founded in 1415, the English sisters who entered, just like their sisters in Vadstena, refused to observe the original Additions of Prior Petrus, declaring that they would not take upon them the hard work above-mentioned, nor observe any other additions to the Rule of St Bridget. A committee of theologians decided in 1416 against the sisters' claims to be discharged from domestic work.[20]

On Febr. 2, 1422, Martinus V issued the great Bull of Privileges for the English Bridgettines, called *Mare Magnum Anglicanum*, which made Syon Abbey independent of the other Bridgettine monasteries and of all centralizing authorities within the order.[21] They could now proceed to make their own Additions. These Additions must thus have their origin after the issue of *Mare Magnum Anglicanum* or *Bulla Reformatoria*, which they cite, and before January 1473, when Bishop Thomas Kempe formally published them.[22]

As we have seen the adoption of *Extrav.* 35 sanctioned the creation of a small group of lay sisters (*focariae*) to assist the choir sisters. In the Vadstena legislation their reading and prayers are prescribed in the Additions of Prior Petrus ch.17, and in ch.25 of *Lucidarium Sororum*. Special statutes were made for them.[23]

In the Syon Additions neither *focariae* nor lay sisters are mentioned. There are traces of evidence that the Syon sisters, despite lack of legislation in this respect, had indeed profited from the short period (1420–1422) when the only Additions to the Rule were those of Prior Petrus, to introduce *focariae* or kitchen sisters. Although the Syon Additions do not mention them, they might have had their own statutes, just like those in the motherhouse of Vadstena. In 1539, at the suppression of Syon, four lay sisters are listed, a surprisingly small number for a

---

[19] Höjer, *op. cit.*, p.78.

[20] *Ibid.*, pp.76–77. David Knowles, *The Religious Orders in England, vol. 2: The End of the Middle Ages*, Cambridge, 1955, p.178, says that at this or a following meeting the committee 'made from the Rule of St Benedict and the Cistercian constitutions, additions of their own to supplement the Bridgettine rule for England only. These were embodied in the directory of Syon and remained in force even after the dissolution of the house'. However, these Additions are rather a book of customs like *Lucidarium Sororum*, i.e. everyday experiences, also adopted from other orders (see n.6 above), which in due time have been committed to writing. For their dating, see text below.

[21] See Höjer, *op. cit.*, pp.193f. and 256; and Hans Cnattingius, *Studies in the Order of St Bridget of Sweden, 1 : The Crisis in the 1420s*, Acta Universitatis Stockholmiensis, 7, Stockholm, 1963, pp.150ff. In virtue of this Bull, Syon was not represented on the general chapters in Vadstena, 1429, and in Gnadenberg, 1487, where the common legislation for the whole order was treated (see n.8 above).

[22] Ellis, *op. cit.*, p.53.

[23] Edited in Lindström, *op. cit.*, pp.2–29.

big and rich monastery, but exactly the allowed number of focariae.[24] However, the lay sisters did not receive formal acknowledgement in Syon's legislation until 1607, when the Lisbon Rule extended the original provisions for the lay brothers so as to include them too.[25]

The abbess, the central figure in a Bridgettine monastery, was the head of both convents and had the care for all temporal matters. From her 'All necessaries are to be hopyd . . . that ys to sey regulere clothynge. beddynge and instrume[n]tys of werke' (*Rewyll*, ch.1).[26] Since it would obviously surpass her strength to do everything personally, a number of officers were appointed, to assist her (*Syon Add.*, ch.13).

This chapter, titled 'How officers schal be put in and take oute', sums up the different offices, which the sisters could hold: 'a pryores,[27] the serches, the chauntres, and subchauntresses, the sexteyne and vndersexteyn, the treseres, and vndertreseres, the chambres, and vnder chambresse, the celeres, the fermeres, the keper of the waschyng howse, the keper of the garden and of the frutes therof, the keper of the butry and the freytour, the keper of the whele, the keper of the cloyster and dortour dores, with al such other officers'. In the text of the Syon Additions other offices are mentioned, e.g. the mistresses of novices (*Syon Add.*, chs.16 & 17) and some services which the sisters performed in turn, e.g. in the choir and in the refectory (serving at the table, reading aloud during the meals, *Syon Add.*, chs.50 & 52).

The officers were allowed to have one or more helpers. That means that 30–35 sisters out of the prescribed number of sixty had special duties to perform in the community every day, besides their attendance of choir services, Holy Masses in the church and their other spiritual exercises and devotional reading. With allowance for about ten sisters being too old or weak for work, that leaves us with about fifteen sisters who had no assigned daily duties in the household, except perhaps those which they performed in turn.[28]

---

[24] See G. J. Aungier, *The History and Antiquities of Syon Monastery*, London, 1840, p.90. *Ibid.* pp.51–52, 81–82; there are lists of nuns and monks, where no lay sisters are found, which however is not strange, since these lists were made on occasion of the election of a new confessor-general (1428) and a new abbess (1518), and *focariae* had no vote, as they did not belong to the community; note, however, that the lay brothers are listed at the election of the new confessor-general in 1428. In 1622, when Syon dwelt in Lisbon, three 'kitcheners' are listed, *ibid.*, p.*100. See also *The Bridgettine Breviary of Syon Abbey from the MS. with English Rubrics F.4.11 at Magdalene College, Cambridge*, ed. A. Jeffries Collins, Henry Bradshaw Society, 96, Worcester, 1969, p.xlii and n.1., who rejects the view that there should have been lay sisters in Syon.

[25] Ellis, *op. cit.*, p.126.

[26] Eklund, *op. cit.*, p.105 (cap. 2).

[27] In Syon the prioress was appointed by the abbess on advice from the confessor-general and the eldest sisters (*Syon Add.* ch.55), whereas the prioress, according to Add. P.Petrus, ch.15, should be chosen by the whole convent.

[28] Ruth Rajamaa, *Nunnornas ämbets- och arbetsuppgifter i Vadstena kloster: Beskrivning på basis av notiser i klostrets diarium 1344–1545*, PH-gruppen, Gruppen för

All clothes and food were provided for the sisters and brothers by the chambress and celleress (*Syon Add.*, ch.48). Accordingly their accounts contain a complete picture of the communal housekeeping. Celleresses', chambresses' and sacrists' accounts survive for Syon. They throw an interesting light on the provision of clothes and other necessities for the convent.[29] Even if the sisters, at least according to the Vadstena legislation, were supposed to perform a considerable amount of domestic work themselves, it appears from the accounts from both Vadstena[30] and Syon, that much of this sort of work was done by servants or lay workers outside the convent. Shortly before the suppression of Syon in 1539, the preserved accounts of the chambress, sister Bridget Belgrave, reveal to us (f.i.) that the sisters of Syon did not spin and weave themselves, but had it done for them.[31]

The principal task of the celleress was the care for food and drink for both communities and for food and drink, clothes and wages for the 'seruantes of housholde outewarde'. She must also ordain

> for all necessaryes longynge to al houses of offices, concernyng the bodyly fode of man, in the bakhows, brewhouse, kychen, buttry, pantry, celer, freytour, fermery, parlour, and suche other, both outwarde and inwarde, for straungers and dwellers.

It is here impossible to discern from the text if all these sorts of workshops and rooms were found both inside and outside the enclosure, or if some, e.g. the bakery and the brewery, were only outside.[32]

While the Syon Additions treat some of the monastic offices rather thoroughly,[33] and while they often go into the smallest detail concerning the

---

pedagogikhistorisk forskning och tolkningsteori, Rapport nr. 3, Stockholm, 1987, p.11, estimates, from the Additions of Prior Petrus and *Lucidarium Sororum*, that in Vadstena 20–25 sisters always had special duties to perform for the community. This should leave about 25 sisters free to do any other work, to which the Abbess might assign them.

[29] Cf. Power, *op. cit.*, pp.136–137.

[30] See *Vadstena klosters jordebok, 1500, jemte tillägg ur klostrets äldre jordeböcker*, ed. Carl Silfverstolpe, Historiska handlingar, XVI:1, Stockholm, 1897; 'Vadstena klosters uppbörds- och utgiftsbok, 1539-70', in *Antiqvarisk tidskrift för Sverige*, 16 (1895–1898), 1–207; Lars-Arne Norborg, *Storföretaget Vadstena kloster: Studier i senmedeltida godspolitik och ekonomiförvaltning*, Bibliotheca Historica Lundensis, 7, Lund, 1958.

[31] The accounts of the chambress, Sister Bridget Belgrave, 1536/37 are printed in *The Myroure of Oure Ladye*, ed. from the Original Black-letter Text of 1530 with Introduction and Notes by John Henry Blunt, Early English Text Society, E.S. 19, London, 1873, pp.xxvi–xxviii.

[32] The accounts af the celleress, Sister Agnes Merett, 1536/37 are printed *ibid.*, pp.xxix–xxxi. Even if these accounts (see also n.31 above and n.39 below) date from the sixteenth century, they might be significant also for the preceding century.

[33] On occasion of the description of the tasks of the infirmaress, *Syon Add.* ch.57, Power, *op. cit.*, p.134, calls the author of the Additions 'a person of all too vivid imagination'; about the duties of the chambress, ch.56, Blunt, *op. cit.*, p.xxv, declares that 'none except a feminine pen can enumerate them'.

sisters' behaviour, from their rising early in the morning till they lie in their beds in the evening, there is no special chapter on domestic work. In fact they say very little or nothing about the work of those sisters, who had no offices. Still, one of the objects for the bishop's examination at his regular visitation of the monastery every third year was, 'How sustres be occupyed, whan they be not atte dyuyne seruyse, nor at other conuentualle obseruances' (*Syon Add.*, ch.10, pnt. 10).

Here it is helpful to refer to *Lucidarium Sororum*, which contains two chapters, (22 and 23) with more direct suggestions as to the sort of work, with which the Bridgettine nuns might fill their working hours, outside church and choir. First of all provision of a big common workshop, with large windows to let in sufficient light and with comfortable chairs, was recommended. Here all the sisters, even the abbess and the prioress, were expected after dinner, about 10 a.m. till Vespers about 3 p.m.[34]

Seated in groups in this workshop, supervised by the abbess or her deputy on a small platform, the sisters should perform the work, which the abbess had assigned to them: copying, correcting or illuminating manuscripts, probably also binding them, or doing different sorts of needlework, making or repairing clothes for both sisters and brothers. During the work they were allowed to talk in low voices on edifying subjects. This probably, also afforded the opportunity for the sisters, who were occupied with more artistic work, to seek advice and inspiration from each other. Every Saturday at a fixed time the sisters should go to the chapter-room and show the Abbess their needlework, how much they had done during the week.

Naturally, the holders of offices and the sisters who in their turn were occupied with the household first joined their sisters in the common workshop after having done their duties in the assigned places. Add. P. Petrus, ch.18, provides for two or four *custodes*, who during the working hours when the sisters were allowed to speak, should go around the convent to ensure that the sisters behaved in a religious way. The corresponding text about the 'serches' in the Syon Additions (ch.55) has nothing about this manual work. St Bridget herself knew the value of silence for a life of prayer, but still she modified such a prescription and allowed a modest conversation during certain types of work which could not otherwise be done properly, 'ffor all thynges owyn to be doo resonably' so that there should be no occasion for slander (*Rewyll*, ch.5).[35]

---

[34] Some attempts have been made to reconstruct the working day in a Bridgettine nunnery, they estimate from 3 to 6 hours for manual work. See f.i. Collins, *op. cit.*, pp.xivff., for the estimated time for the divine services. Lindblom, *op. cit.*, p.83, is more specific, although he makes some reservations concerning the exact hours. He places dinner at 9 a.m. and leaves time for manual work from 11 a.m. to 2.30 p.m., – only three and a half hours. St Birgitta herself followed a strict, almost monastic, schedule together with her companions in Rome, see Hollman, *op. cit.*, pp.187–189, cap. 65.

[35] Eklund, *op. cit.*, p.109 (cap. 6).

Quite a lot is known about these typical monastic and female activities in the Vadstena monastery. The question to be asked is whether the sisters of Syon followed the good examples of their Swedish sisters. In the Syon Additions a common workshop is not among the rooms, which are summed up as the cellaress' responsibility, nor is it mentioned anywhere else, which, however, does not prove that it did not exist. Whereas sisters from Syon are known as owners of manuscripts and books, and manuscripts and books have been produced for them, no copyists among the sisters are known by their names, as far as I know.[36] The Vadstena diary, however, mentions a few copyists and illuminators, and even a translatrice, which shows that at least some of the sisters knew foreign languages.[37]

The Syon-chantress had not only the care of the books for the divine service, chapter-room and refectory, she also had to see that these books were corrected, if necessary, so that e.g. all the choir books had the same text and the same music notes. She also had to keep the profession-register and the obituary up-to-date (*Syon Add.*, ch.45).[38]

In this connection it is also interesting to have a look at the Syon-sacristans' accounts, which show expenses for materials which obviously could be used for embroidery, maybe even for writing and illuminating manuscripts within the convent. The sacristan was probably also the librarian,[39] although the Syon Additions do not say much about it except that the sacristan should also provide various equipment for writing: 'penners, pennes, ynke, ynke hornes, tables and

---

[36] The preserved manuscripts and books from Syon Abbey are listed in *Medieval Libraries of Great Britain: A List of Surviving Books*, edited N. R. Ker, 2nd ed., London, 1964, pp.184–187. For Syon sisters, who have owned or better used manuscripts see e.g. Collins, *op. cit.*, p.xxxiv ff. (Elizabeth Yate, Dorothe Slyght, Elizabeth Edwards, Elizabeth Montoun/Mounton/Mountayne, Anna Bowys, Eleanor Fettiplace), and *Rewyll*, Introduction, p.iii–iv, n.5. For the literary work of the brother convent, see James Hogg, 'The Contribution of the Brigittine Order to Late Medieval English Spirituality', *Spiritualität Heute und Gestern. Internationaler Kongress von 4. bis 7. August 1982*, *Analecta Cartusiana*, 35 (1983), 153–174, with further literature.

[37] In the Vadstena nunnery three authoresses (Abbess Ingeborg Gerhardsdotter, Abbess Margareta Claesdotter, Abbess Anna Fickesdotter Bülow, see Carl Silfverstolpe, *Klosterfolket i Vadstena, Personhistoriska anteckningar*, Stockholm, 1898, abbesses nos.6, 10, 13) are known, one translatrice (Kristina Elofsdotter, *ibid.*, nun no.270), eight copyists (*ibid.*, abbess no.14, nuns nos.20, 45, 177, 207, 212, 215, 277), five owners or users (*ibid.* abbesses nos.10 and 12, nuns nos.223, 266, 314), and three sponsors (*ibid.* nuns nos.215, 251, 272). For the library of Vadstena, see Vilhelm Gödel, *Sveriges medeltidslitteratur. Proveniens före Antikvitetskollegiet*, Stockholm, 1916; *Birgitta-utställningen*, 1918, ed. Isak Collijn och Andreas Lindblom, Uppsala, 1918; *Vadstena klosters bibliotek: Ny katalog och nya forskningsmöjligheter*, ed. Monica Hedlund and Alf Härdelin, Acta Bibliothecae R. Universitatis Upsaliensis, 29, Stockholm, 1990.

[38] No similar duties are assigned to the Vadstena-chantress, who has not got a special chapter in Add. P.Petrus or *Luc.Sor*.

[39] See Mary Carpenter Erler, 'Syon Abbey's Care for Books: Its Sacristan's Account Rolls 1505/7–1536/6', in *Scriptorium*, 29 (1985), 293–307, p.297.

suche other as the abbesse assygneth her' (*Syon Add.*, ch.48). In 1482 the abbess of Syon employed a bookbinder who should bind, repair and make books,[40] but, as has been pointed out, one man might bind about thirty books a year, but he could not have written that many himself.[41] It is possible, that the sacristan's purchases were also for the copying work of the brothers and sisters.

The Rule of St Bridget says about the work of the sisters that 'this labour shal not be to ony vainte of the worlde. nor to ony p[ro]pir lucre. but as the laboure of the modir of god for the worship of god and of chirches and profitte of the pore' (*Rewyll*, ch.20).[42] In Vadstena it was one of the tasks of the four or more sacristans (*Luc. Sor.*, ch.42) to sew and embroider the church ornaments. In this connection they were given the dispensation in the Rule which, forbidding the sisters even to touch money, yet makes the exception 'but if it happely be nede to towche golde or syluyr for wevyng of ony werke and ʒet not that w[y]t[h]oute cownseyle & licence of the abbes' (*Rewyll*, ch.1).[43] St Bridget limited the ornaments in the monastery church, fearing that it should appear too rich. (cf. *Rewyll*, ch.18).[44] The Vadstena nuns, therefore, when their own church was provided for, also found time to make church ornaments, on commission, for the churches of the surrounding area, quite in accordance with the chapter of the Rule cited above.

Many beautiful works of embroidery from the nunnery of Vadstena (30–40 items) are known; and very skilled work has been preserved from the Bridgettine monastery of Nådendal in Finland.[45] It has been suggested that the so-called style III from the nunnery of Vadstena may have been inspired by the English art of embroidery through the connections with Syon Abbey.[46] As far as

---

[40] See Robert Jowitt Whitwell, 'An Ordinance for Syon Library, 1482', *English Historical Review*, 25 (1910), 121–123.

[41] Erler, *op. cit.*, pp.306–307.

[42] Eklund, *op. cit.*, p.128 (cap. 23).

[43] *Ibid.*, p.105 (cap. 2).

[44] *Ibid.*, p.127 (cap. 21).

[45] See Agnes Branting, 'Väfnader och broderier', in Collijn, *op. cit.*, 77–102, ch.5; Agnes Branting and Andreas Lindblom, *Medieval embroideries and textiles in Sweden*, 2 vols, Stockholm, 1932 (Swedish ed. 1928–1929); Agnes Geijer, 'Kyrklig textilkonst', in *Linköpings stift i ord och bild*, (1949), 219–230; Inger Estham, 'Medeltida textilier', in *Vadstena klosterkyrka, 2: Inredning*, Aron Andersson, Sveriges Kyrkor, Östergötland, bd. 194, Stockholm, 1983, 107–122; Inger Estham, 'Birgittinska broderier', in *Den ljusa medeltiden. Studier tillägnade Aron Andersson*, Museum of National Antiquities, Studies, 4, Stockholm, 1984, 25–42.

[46] Branting, *Väfnader, op. cit.*, p.80, suggests that the Vadstena sisters, who helped to found Syon, learnt to embroider after the English method, which they, at their return, taught the sisters in Vadstena. However, it is not quite certain that these pioneers returned to their motherhouse; neither their day of return nor that of their death is entered in the Vadstena Diary. See, however, Silfverstolpe, *Klosterfolket, op. cit.*, p.32, nun no.53, where a letter from Vadstena to Syon is mentioned, yet without source, indicating that the Swedish nuns did return home. At any rate, in 1428 they were still in England, see Aungier, *op. cit.*, p.51. But still it is possible that through

I know only a thirteenth-century cope, which belonged to Syon Abbey, has been preserved.[47]

Of course, not all the sisters had a skilled and artistic hand, but many other sorts of female handwork thrived in the Bridgettine convents. Just as it was common in the convents of other orders, the Bridgettines may have produced little things, purses, pincushions, gloves, mittens etc. to give to friends, relatives or benefactors of the convent. It does not seem that the work of the sisters was done in order that they should thereby maintain themselves, since the convent had to be sufficiently endowed from its foundation (see below). However, after the Reformation, when the convents were dying out, the Scandinavian nuns in some cases were forced to work for their living.[48]

As we have seen the Bridgettine nuns also worked for the brothers in the male convent. The abbess took care of the administration, the sisters' kitchen provided them with their meals. In Syon it was the lay brothers' task to prepare at least part of the meals, e.g. "make fyre, dresse potage' (*Syon Additions, for the Brethren*, ch.52).[49] The sisters also looked after the monks' wardrobe, and sewed and repaired the monastic habits, which work must not be left to people outside the convent (*Lucidarium Sororum* ch.46). It fell to the sisters concerned to provide the brothers with whatever they needed. Through this arrangement, and through the fact that a staff of servants (namely eight lay brothers and probably two *focarii*)[50] were allowed inside the enclosure, the necessary peace and time for study and prayer were guaranteed to priests whose duty it was to teach both the sisters and the people who visited the common church, and to administer the Sacraments.[51]

---

their connections with England the sisters in Sweden may have been influenced by the English art of embroidery; see also Geijer, *op. cit.*, p.228, (who, moreover, mentions two late-medieval English copes, which came to Sweden, perhaps as spoils of war, in the seventeenth century, one in the church of Fogdö in Södermanland, the other in the church of St Olav in Norrköping).

[47] Aungier, *op. cit.*, p.97, n.1, who speaks of 'three copes of rich stuff'; Power, *op. cit.*, p.256; Branting, *op. cit.*, p.80.

[48] See Birgit Klockars, *I Nådens Dal : Klosterfolk och andra c.1440–1590*, Skrifter utg. av Svenska Litteratursällskapet i Finland, 486, Helsingfors, 1979, p.185.

[49] *The Rewyll of Seynt Sauioure, vol 3: The Syon Additions for the Brethren and the Boke of Sygnes from the St. Paul's Cathedal Library MS.*, ed. James Hogg, Salzburger Studien zur Anglistik und Amerikanistik, Bd. 6, Salzburg, 1980, p.119, ch.52. In order to compare 'the boke of sygnes', *ibid.*, pp.134–144, with the Vadstena tradition in this respect, see Axel Nelson, 'Teckenspråket i Vadstena kloster', in *Nordisk tidskrift för bok- och biblioteksväsen*, 22 (1935), 25–43, pp.35–42: *Ars signandi secundum usum Monasterii Vastenensi*.

[50] See Hollman, *op. cit.*, p.151 (cap. 35).

[51] That the Bridgettine monks really appreciated the peace and quiet, which they enjoyed through the work of the sisters, appears from a tract written by Father Severinus of Koblenz, where the author refers to this fact as an extra advantage for the men who might want to join the order! This tract is edited in Tore Nyberg, 'Kvinder og mænd i birgittinerordenen: En middelalderlig tolkning af opgavefordeling og æresfortrin',

But hard work was not the rule for all twenty-four hours in a Bridgettine nunnery. In order to prevent certain sisters becoming rather too attached to their work, *Lucidarium Sororum* (ch.28) forbade the sisters to do any manual work after Compline. The General Chapter of Gnadenberg, 1487, also tried to moderate exaggerated love of working, forbidding the sisters to perform manual work in the church during the divine services![52] Even if these prohibitions are not in the Syon legislation, they might apply to the English Bridgettines, too.

It may be surprising, that the Syon Additions, unlike the Vadstena legislation, had no special chapters on the work of the sisters. The fact that the Syon legislation in this respect apparently was able to manage with the general prescriptions of the Rule, and only made provision for the necessary offices in the community, had, of course, the advantage that the sisters were not fixed in certain categories of work, but could easily adapt to changing times and places. It is questionable whether most fifteenth-century nuns thought of this, but for Syon on its later wanderings on the Continent it was undoubtedly a circumstance, from which it could benefit.

St Bridget's prescriptions for the manual work of her sisters and her view on poverty, personal and common, stand together. The most common complaint against the old monastic orders was that they had become too rich, with all the obvious consequences. They had fallen victims to their own success, since the industry and labour of their predecessors in many cases had made the convents large scale enterprises with a vast staff of lay servants to work all days of the year, in order to keep up with the demands.[53] St Bridget founded her order as a gesture of reform – a reaction against the extant orders of her time; instead she employed the allegory of the neglected vineyards, which need replacement (*Rewyll*, Prologue).[54]

Although both the Vadstena and the Syon monasteries in their time were reckoned among the richest convents of their respective countries, that had

---

Middelalder, metode og medier : Festskrift til Niels Skyum-Nielsen på 60–årsdagen den 17. oktober 1981, Odense, 1981, pp.195–222. However, there might sometimes have been disagreement in Vadstena between the two convents about the work of the sisters, according to an entry in the Vadstena Diary, Gejrot, *op. cit.*, pp.215–216: *Anno Domini mcdxlvii. Sorores assumpserunt sibi onus locionis vestimentorum fratrum generaliter secundum ordinacionem suam et vicissitudines faciendum.*

[52] Nettelbla, *op. cit.*, p.171, pnt. 21: *Item Sorores ex facili causa se a Choro non absentent, nec de horis exeant, nisi necessitate cogente & cum Licentia, nec manualia opera in Ecclesia tempore divinorum excerceant, cantus earum fiat in gravitate juxta additiones Domini Petri*; it must be added that the monks in their turn were forbidden to bring books to the choir in order to read or study during the divine services: *nullus in Chorum apportet librum ad legendum vel studendum sub horis vel Missa*! *Ibid.*, p.168, pnt. 4.

[53] Cf. Jacques Dubois, 'Le travail des moines au moyen âge', *Le travail au moyen âge : Un approche interdisciplinaire : Actes du Colloque international de Louvain-la-Neuve, 21–23 mai 1987*, ed. Jacqueline Hamesse et Colette Muraille-Samaran, Louvain- la-Neuve, 1990, 61–100, p.99.

[54] Eklund, *op. cit.*, pp.102–103, Prologus ch. II.

certainly not been the intention of the foundress of the Bridgettine order. In her rule she emphasizes the poverty of the monastery and the personal poverty of every member in particular. Two important elements here, namely the endowment and the manual work of the sisters, are very closely connected with this ideal. The nuns in the medieval convents were almost exclusively recruited from the upper classes, who were able to bring a sufficient dowry.[55] St Bridget prescribed that only the first sisters, who entered should bring a dowry big enough to maintain them during their lifetime. At the death of a sister her place and its incomes should be given to another, who thus should not bring any dowry, which means that anybody, who felt the vocation to the monastic life in a Bridgettine convent, could be accepted regardless of social standing. 'Persones that are pore at al. must be receyued frely', (Rewyll, ch.17).[56] This also ensured the common poverty of the convent as a whole.

As an extra precaution against eventual accumulation of riches, the Rule prescribed that the abbess, every year before All Saints' day, was obliged to present her accounts to both communities; a sum was set aside to meet the expenses of next year, and the surplus given to the poor on All Souls' day (ibid.). Every day the Bridgettines lived with the poor as it were next to them, by virtue of the prescription that the left-overs from the table of both communities should be given daily to the poor, as also the share of food and clothes of a deceased member the first week after his or her death (ibid.).

St Bridget's severe view on personal property appears from a text in her Revelations, Liber V, interrogacio septima,[57] in which Christ answers the question of whether it is allowed to be proud of riches:

> The world was created in order that man should be able to support his body by his work and through humility return to God . . . whatsoever you own more than is necessary for your living, you have as it were usurped. Because all temporary things should be common and charitably be equal for all the needy.[58]

St Bridget thus admitted everybody's right to have the necessities for his/her living. It was not her intention that the members of her order should suffer any deprivation. As on her journeys she may have seen the lack of discipline in over wealthy convents, so she may also have seen convents, where the inhabitants were too poor and starved to perform their monastic duties properly. Despite the many fasting days which she prescribes for the members of her order, she admonishes them again and again to take care of the body. The abbess must have

---

[55] See n.13 above.
[56] Eklund, op. cit., pp.124–126, (cap. 20).
[57] Sancta Birgitta Revelaciones Book V, Liber Questionum, ed. Birger Bergh, SFSS, ser. 2, Bd. VII:5, Uppsala, 1971, pp.11–112.
[58] Cf. the abridged text in The Liber Celestis of St Bridget of Sweden: The Middle English Version in British Library MS Claudius B i, together with a life of the saint from the same manuscript, vol. 1: Text, edited by Roger Ellis, Early English Text Society, 291, Oxford, 1987, p.373.

compassion on those 'whiche are vnderstonde to be very febyll to fulfylle there offices while they faste' (*Rewyll*, ch.8).[59] The sisters must follow the example of St Mary, who

> departyd all hir tyme in thre tymes. oon in whiche she prayed god wyth hir mowthe. Another in whiche she seruyd hym w[y]lt[h] hir hondys. and the thridde hauynge co[m]passion to the infirmity of the body. (*Rewyll*, ch.20)[60]

The body they should attend to as to 'a seke beste. as it may stonde in the s[er]uise of god' (*Rewyll*, ch.24).[61]

A practice or bad habit, which St Bridget might also have encountered in many convents of her time was that the nuns were allowed to work for themselves and for others and to keep the wages, in stead of giving them to their community.[62] Consequently she forbids her nuns to work for themselves or for worldly honour, but in obedience to the abbess, for God's glory, and for the churches and the poor, in imitation of Christ and his Apostles (*Rewyll*, ch.20).[63] The personal poverty of every member of the order is emphasized once more in the prohibition against accepting anything as their own from whomsoever, 'ffor as of a sparkel ys genderyd fyre: so of p[ro]pirte da[m]pnac[i]on which departyth the praysable vnite in the monastery' (*Rewyll*, ch.16).[64]

St Bridget goes so far in her interpretation of the vow of poverty (*Rewyll*, ch.1),[65] that she forbids her nuns even to touch gold and silver, even the smallest coin, except in connection with certain activities (e.g. embroidery) and offices (e.g. the treasurer and the sacristan), when the abbess may dispensate. This should be seen in relation to the almost universal custom, or rather bad habit, in the later middle ages that the nuns were paid a money allowance instead of food and clothing, a practice which deprived the office of chambress of nearly all its duties and possibly accounts for the rarity of chambresses' account rolls. As we have seen this did not apply to the Syon monastery.[66] A really poor person has to work with his hands for his living. Thus the sixty nuns should work with their hands, but not for their living, which they rightfully might expect from the abbess, but in imitation of Christ and his saints and to the greater glory of God. Their daily programme should be the ancient programme of monastic life: *Opus Dei*, *Lectio Divina* and *Labor*. Monastic history is largely the history of the relations between these three elements.[67] Also in the Bridgettine legislation we see attempts to find the

---

[59] Eklund, *op. cit.*, p.111 (cap. 9).
[60] *Ibid.*, p.128 (cap. 23).
[61] *Ibid.*, p.129 (cap. 24).
[62] For examples, see Power, *op. cit.*, ch.8.
[63] Eklund, *op. cit.*, p.128 (cap. 23).
[64] *Ibid.*, p.123 (cap. 19).
[65] Cf. *ibid.*, p.105 (cap. 2).
[66] See Power, *op. cit.*, p.136 and ch.8.
[67] Cf. Dubois, *op. cit.*, p.61.

balance between spiritual and bodily work. *Opus Dei*[68] is the principal task of the Bridgettines, put in the first place in the important chapter on the work of the sisters (*Rewyll*, ch.20).[69]

The same Rule admonishes the sisters that they should not have superfluous riches in their church, 'for they shall kepe to them for tresoure neyther golde ne syluyr or p[re]ciouse stones. but the grace of god wyth contynuell studyes. deuote p[ra]yers and godly praysynges' (*Rewyll*, ch.18).[70] Here *Lectio Divina* has the principal place.[71] However, in Add. P. Petrus, ch.6, it is said, that whenever the sisters are not doing manual work, they should read or pray or attend the divine services, unless the abbess orders otherwise, which apparently places *Labor* above *Lectio Divina* and *Opus Dei*, but obedience above all. Yet *Labor* has not its ends in itself: 'by bodely laboure they shulde be more able to spiritual laboure' (*Rewyll*, ch.20),[72], that is, through the interaction between body and spirit manual work should also become a spiritual activity.

[68] For editions of the Brigittine Breviary, see Collins, *op. cit.*, p.1; and *Den heliga Birgitta och den helige Petrus av Skänninge Officium parvum beate Marie Virginis. Vår Frus tidegärd*, utg. med inledning och översättning av Tryggve Lundén, 2 vols, Acta Universitatis Upsaliensis, Studia Historico- Ecclesiastica Upsaliensia, 27, Lund, 1976. For an English translation, see Blunt, *op. cit.* On this happy combination of *Opus Dei* and *Lectio Divina*, see Ann M. Hutchison, 'Devotional Reading in the Monastery and in the Late Medieval Household', *De Cella in Seculum : Religious and Secular Life and Devotion in Late Medieval England*, ed. Michael G. Sargent, Cambridge, 1989, pp.215–227.

[69] Eklund, *op. cit.*, p.128 (cap. 23).

[70] *Ibid.*, p.127 (cap. 21).

[71] Blunt, *op. cit.*, p.64; cf. Hutchison, *op. cit.*, p.221.

[72] Eklund, *op. cit.*, p.128 (cap. 27).

SYON MS 18 AND THE MEDIEVAL ENGLISH MYSTICAL TRADITION

VERONICA LAWRENCE

SYON MS 18 is an anonymous, undated manuscript held at Syon Abbey in Devon. The questions and problems that it poses about authorship and dating are important because of the nature of the contents of the work. The manuscript is a work of religious instruction intended for a monastic audience. It contains certain features in common with works in the English medieval mystical tradition, especially *The Cloud of Unknowing* and other works by the *Cloud*-author. This paper will examine Syon MS 18 in the context of the English medieval mystical tradition but will begin by describing the contents and appearance of the text and make some suggestions about dating and authorship.

Syon MS 18 is written in the mirror or *speculum* tradition. It is entitled *A looking glace for the religious* and begins,

> Dearly beloued, you couet to haue some spirituall looking glasse, wherein you may behoulde your selfe, and perfitly see through your beauties and deformities.[1]

It ends

> A lookinge glace you did couete to haue, see whether you haue receaued a lookinge glace or not . . .[2]

The author presents mirror images of both the 'unfaithful' and the 'faithful' servant of God. The unfaithful servant serves God in prosperity and abandons Him in adversity. He is wilful and interprets 'inward sweetness and consolation' and 'the infusion of sensible deuotion' as signs of holyness. These are not necessarily signs of holyness, the author tells us, and could lead the recipient to pride:

> for when they feele themselues pleasantly, tickled with inwarde solac[e]. by and by they take in hande to iudge and controwle, yea and to dispise others: nowe they esteeme themselues as saints, and secretarys of god: They would marvuelous faine haue. yea and they looke for reuelations from heauen, and they are much desyrous of mirracles to be shewe[d], ether by themselues, or vppon themse[lue]s, wherby others myght knowe the hollynes, which these men weene they haue, and yet haue it not: thus commonly vanishe they awaye in there owne vayne thoughts, which greedely gape for sensible grace, rather then the giuer of grace . . .[3]

---

[1] *A looking glace for the religious*, ed. Veronica Lawrence, Salzburg Studies in English Literature: Elizabethan & Renaissance Studies; 92:18, Salzburg, 1991, p.1.

[2] *Ibid.*, Conclusion, pp.95–96.

[3] *Ibid.*, ch.3, p.7.

The faithful servants of God, however, do not seek after spiritual consolation but seek to honour God. They shun ownership and remain constant in their love of God regardless of their fortune:

> No inwarde cloudynes. no difficulty of feelinge, no couldnes of affections. no drynes of hart no downcast of courrage, no slumber of spirite, no distresses of temptations, to be shorte no miseris of this lyfe, whatsoeuer they be, nor good successe of prosperitys cane throwe them downe forthof there place.[4]

Their foundation is the rock of the love of God and they derive their greatest comfort from doing the will of God. They are at peace because they try to avoid whatever would displease God and attempt to do the will of God no matter what may befall them.

The *Looking glace*-author does not believe, however, that sensible devotion is necessarily harmful:

> Yet that same neuerthelesse is also much profitable. if we vse it discreetly[: an]d those faythfull seruants (for so I tearme them [st]ill) whome our sauiour Iesus caulleth not his seru[a]nts but his frinds. those same faythfull seruants (I saye) seeke also for that effectuall and most sauory sweetnes of grace: they seeke for that ioyfull mirthe of Saluation. which commeth by our lord; they seeke for his amiable countenance and most sweete imbracinge . . .[5]

They see spiritual consolation as a gift from God and seek it for entirely different reasons than those of the unfaithful servant of God. They wish to be made more fervent, to be cleansed from sin and to please God better. They seek spiritual consolation as a means to this end rather than as an occasion for self-adulation. They are thankful to be recipients of it but do not depend upon it:

> They are euery waye happy and blessed, fo[r th]e lesse they sticke to these giftes. so much the rather do they r[e]ceaue giftes . . .[6]

They put their trust in 'the freedome of the childern of God, (which they haue obtayned, throughe the blood of christe)',[7] rather than in any good works that they may do.

The *Looking glace*-author concludes this section of the work by exhorting his readers to choose which reflection in the mirror they would like to emulate and which they would prefer to shun:

> Nowe thowe for thy parte, (dearly beloued) sith thow knowest the difference, betweene faythfull and vnfaythfull seruants, enforce thy selfe with all diligence, to be one of the number of these, wherof perhappes thow art not. and endeuour to be non of that sorte, wherof perhaps thow art one . . .[8]

The author also expresses a realization of the narrowness of the picture that he is painting. The world is not neatly divided into black and white, good and bad,

---

[4] *Ibid.*, ch.3, pp.7–8.
[5] *Ibid.*, ch.3, p.9.
[6] *Ibid.*, ch.3, p.10.
[7] *Ibid.*, ch.3, p.11.
[8] *Ibid.*, ch.3, p.11.

faithful and unfaithful servants. There is a grey area in between which is also to
be shunned. Those who are neither faithful nor unfaithful pretend to be devout
but in reality have their minds on the things of this world:

> These beinge drowned in a certaine diepe gulfe of mischiefes. do scant[ly] thinke
> of there owne saluation: such they be t[h]is daye as they weare yesterday, such they
> co[m] forth of the quyer. as they went in: that is v[n]cleane, lukewarme, lasye,
> waueringe, o[u]t of all forme and fashion, without feare, without reuerence; these
> with the holly wordes, whi[c]h they vtter forth of a [p]oluted mouth, do
> exa[s]perate, rather the[n] prayse god . . .[9]

The *Looking glace*-author expresses regret that these religious had ever entered
the monastery and suggests that they would have been better off outside the
cloister. He feels that they have no place in the monastery, that they are
freeloaders there under false pretenses:

> Sith they would needes more and more waxe vncleane, they should haue tarryed in
> the channell of filthynes, and not haue presumed to come from thence, into the
> sanctuarys of cleanes: they might by there filthy liuing in the world, haue
> purchased one single hell. where as nowe by there loose conuersation in
> monasterys, they make themselues worthy. to haue double punnishment, of towe
> hells: but of these matters [mu]ch to say. it is not my intente, therefore my talke
> must retourne to you again . . .[10]

He is true to his word. He never elaborates on why the servant who is neither
faithful nor unfaithful is worthy of 'towe hells'. This line concludes the 'mirror'
section of the work. Having described to the reader the image of 'a right
religious person',[11] the author then provides guidance to the religous so that it
may become his image.

In the chapters that follow, the author describes certain religious exercises that
would help a religious to attain the image that he seeks in the looking glace.
These exercises include reading, prayer and meditation, especially meditation on
the passion of Christ. They also include 'a laudable ydlenes' which the author
distinguishes from 'sinfull ydlenes.'[12] These exercises will help the reader to
attain 'quietnes a[n]d freedome of mynde'[13] and to get compunction. The author
gives examples of the ways in which the reader ought to meditate and the
subjects on which to meditate, using as his source the practice of a Benedictine
monk of his acquaintance. He divides the exercises that he gives into two
groups: one for beginners and one for the more advanced. He makes the work
accessible by defining words that he uses, such as aspiration, and by presenting
concepts in a way that would be easy to remember: 'tow sortes of ydlenes',[14]

---

[9] *Ibid.*, ch.3, p.12.
[10] *Ibid.*, ch.3, pp.12–13.
[11] *Ibid.*, ch.1, p.1.
[12] *Ibid.*, ch.4, p.14.
[13] *Ibid.*, ch.4, p.13.
[14] *Ibid.*, ch.4, p.13.

'tow kindes of feare'.[15] He explains how the reader ought to go about examining his conscience and remembering his past sins and how often he ought to do this. He describes to his readers how they ought to behave when engaged upon spiritual exercises and recommends moderation, for instance:

> Good and sweet (no doubte) is the breade of weepinge teares, but there be such which with that breade, oftentymes oppresse rather then refreshe the soule: For they linger and abyde so longe, in weepinge and waylinge, in so greate confraction, and breakinge of mynde, and in so vehemente cogitation of spirite and body, vnder these ouer farr stretched, or strayned exercyse . . .[16]

The opposite of 'quietness and freedom of mind' is 'tediousnes and trouble of mynde'[17] and the *Looking glace*-author provides advice about how this state may be avoided. He describes how God works in his disciples, first by visiting, comforting, brightening and beautifying them, refreshing, alluring and drawing them after Him, 'thus as it weare with mylke feedinge his newe loue'.[18] Afterwards, he allows them to face adversities, 'the sownde meate. and stronge dyet of afflictions'[19] in order to test their spirit:

> he doth purifye her, he bringeth her, he breaketh and tameth her, he worketh, heweth and cutteth her square. he instructeth her. he playneth her. he maketh he [*sic*] sleeke and smoothe, he adorneth and trimmeth her.[20]

During this time of trial, the *Looking Glace*-author exhorts his readers to patience and humility and recommends that they attend to their spiritual exercises during this time 'with most special diligence'.[21] He then counsels his readers on how they may avoid temptations 'before they haue possession of thy intrayles',[22] before the Devil 'that false iuglinge marchant',[23] can enter. He describes the sort of temptations that might be likely to assail the religious: vainglory, 'pryuat selfe-lykinge',[24] high-mindedness and pride. Gifts and grace from God are to be used to fight the Devil through patience and humility rather than allowing them to be used as a means whereby the Devil may enter. He advises his audience on what their outward behaviour ought to be and expresses dismay at the way in which many religious comport themselves:

> For this is there behauiour. if occation happen, that they must goe abroade out of the cloyster, or com in the sight and company of seculars, a man may wonder to see them, ouerthrowe themselues in follye and nycenes, rushing headlonge in into dotinge toyes. and superfluous curiousity. desyrous to put on such and suche

---

[15] *Ibid.*, ch.6, p.31.
[16] *Ibid.*, ch.7, p.48.
[17] *Ibid.*, ch.8, p.51.
[18] *Ibid.*, ch.8, p.53.
[19] *Ibid.*, ch.8, p.53.
[20] *Ibid.*, ch.8, p.54.
[21] *Ibid.*, ch.8, p.55.
[22] *Ibid.*, ch.9, p.57.
[23] *Ibid.*, ch.9, p.61.
[24] *Ibid.*, ch.9, p.59.

vnseemly garments. so and so mishapte coates. and girkines. such raggs and faggs, and other ill fauored attyre: And as for such apparell aggreable. with the appointmente of there owne rule, and with the ordinances of there father, that they are shamed to weare . . .[25]

and:

. . . very glade are they, to absent them selues from deuyne seruice, and from other actions, and exercyses of there couente: they leape and daunce for ioye, to get delitious and superfluous meate or drinke: they attende busily for occation, to passe ouer the tyme friuolously, with toyes and tryfles: They couet much to solace themselues. with disordered laughinge, they bourne with desyre to heare of worldly matters, to see vayne and vnprofitable sights, to take in all curious toyes, yea and applye them to there owne perticular vses: And as for pryuate selfe lykinge, fond and vnseemely mirthe. ydlenes, lighte talke. vayne bablinge, fables vncomely bahauiours, ill fashioned gestures, and other such lyke vices, they accompt to be ether no faults at all, or skant to be faults. and without scruple of conscience, they allowe and committe them . . .[26]

He tells his readers to wear plain apparrell, temper their sight, let their pace be neither too quick nor too slow, have a cheerful countenance, only laugh 'modestly and religiously',[27] speak neither too loudly nor too softly and to prefer silence to talk. He advises them on how to comport themselves in a disagreement of opinion and how to treat gossip and detraction. He encourages his readers to be like Martha in doing their work 'with good discretion, deuotion and courage. wisely zealously, readely & chearfully'[28] but, at the same time, turning their minds ever to God, as Mary did. He then gives

a breife methode or shorte waye to perfection by mortefyinge of a mans selfe. and by renowncinge propriety. and of the proffits thereof[29]

and then describes the state of perfection and exhorts his readers to seek it. Finally, he concludes with a brief rule for the examination of conscience at bedtime.

It is impossible to say when this treatise was written. Syon MS 18 seems to be the only extant version. The author never identifies himself in it. The text of the treatise nowhere makes reference to any event that might assist in the dating of the work although the critical comments about the religious of his day suggest that the work originated in pre-Reformation times. There may be an element of translation about it. James Hogg has suggested that *A looking glace* constitutes a version of Abbot Blosius' *Speculum Monachorum*.[30] This suggestion requires further examination.

---

[25] *Ibid.*, ch.10, p.65.

[26] *Ibid.*, ch.10, p.79.

[27] *Ibid.*, ch.10, p.67.

[28] *Ibid.*, ch.10, p.71.

[29] *Ibid.*, ch.11, p.80.

[30] *Richard Whytford's The Pype or Tonne of the Lyfe of Perfection: with an introductory study of Whytford's works*, ed. James Hogg, Salzburg, 1979–1989, 5 vols, Vol.1, p.62.

The handwritten catalogue at Syon Abbey attributes the work to the early sixteenth-century English Bridgettine author of devotional literature, Richard Whitford of Syon. A few details of his life will be provided at this point to give some context to a discussion of his possible authorship of *A looking glace*. Whitford, who was probably born in north Wales, spent some time at the University of Cambridge, where he was elected Fellow of Queens' College. Between 1498 and 1500, he was in Paris as chaplain, tutor and confessor to William Blount, fourth Lord Mountjoy. From 1500 to 1504, he returned to Cambridge, during part of which time he acted as treasurer of Queens' College. At some point before his entry into religious life, he may have been chaplain to Bishop Foxe of Winchester.[31] Two letters from Erasmus to Whitford survive, one dated 1499 and the other dated 1506.[32] The latter reveals that Whitford was held in high esteem by both More and Erasmus. The date of Whitford's entry into Syon Abbey is unknown. He remained there until the House was dissolved in 1539. Shortly before its dissolution, he is mentioned in several letters written to Thomas Cromwell by his officer, Thomas Bedyll.[33] In these letters, Bedyll sees Whitford as stubborn, uncooperative and outspoken. Whether Whitford eventually accepted the King's supremacy is unknown. He was given a pension of eight pounds a year by the Crown upon the dissolution of Syon, the last recorded payment of which is dated April 5, 1542.[34] He probably died shortly thereafter.

A looking glace is one of a large number of works attributed to Whitford. Of all those which do not make mention of the author's name somewhere in the text, it is the best candidate for inclusion in the *corpus* of his writings. *A looking glace* contains a number of features in common with authentic Whitford texts. Similar criteria may be used to those described by Phyllis Hodgson in her discussion of the connections between works ascribed to the *Cloud*-author: 'selection of subject matter, repeated emphases, distinctive presentation and the imprint in each of the same personality.'[35] As in the case of many of Whitford's writings, *A looking glace* begins with an explanation of the reason for its composition and was written in answer to a request. The author professes himself unworthy of the task but agrees to answer the request to the best of his ability. The *Looking*

---

[31] William Roper, *The Lyfe of Sir Thomas Moore, knighte*, ed. E. V. Hitchcock, Early English Text Society O.S., 197, London, 1935, pp.7–8. No other contemporary documentary evidence corroborates this.

[32] *Opus Epistolarum Desiderii Erasmi Roterodami*, ed. P. S. and H. M. Allen, Oxford, 1906, Vol.1, pp.226, 422–3.

[33] *Letters Relating to the Suppression of the Monasteries*, ed. T. Wright, London, 1843, p.48; *Calendar of State Papers, Foreign and Domestic, of the Reign of Henry VIII*, ed. J. S. Brewer, J. Gairdner and R. H. Brodie, London, 1830, Vol.1, p.422.

[34] Augmentation Office, Miscellaneous Books (Monastic Pensions), CCLII, fo.xi, in the Public Record Office.

[35] *The Cloud of Unknowing: and related treatises*, ed. Phyllis Hodgson, Salzburg, 1982, p. xii.

glace-author refers to himself as 'your wretched brother'[36] and Whitford frequently calls himself 'the wretch of Syon'. The tone of both authors is one of reassurance and encouragement. Both Whitford and the *Looking glace*-author describe spiritual exercises that involve using the faculty of the imangination. The vocabulary and phraseology employed by the author of *A looking glace* is frequently similar to that found in Whitford's writings. The use of simile and alliteration figures prominently in both. Themes and preoccupations similar to those found in Whitford's writings may also be found in *A looking glace*. Both authors, for instance, recommend to their readers meditation on Christ's Life and Passion as a means to counteract temptation. Both Whitford and the author of *A looking glace* also recognize that a practice that is spiritually beneficial to one person may not necessarily benefit another. The *Looking glace* author writes, for instance:

> . . . wherein if thou feelest. that looking vppon a booke doth hurte and hinder thy vnderstanding. so as thereby it is lesse able, to approche to god, and to be vnited vnto him, then look not vppon a booke: on the other syde, if thou perceauest. that lookinge vppon a booke doth helpe, and further thyne exercyse, looke then on a booke and spare not . . .[37]

Whitford expresses a similar opinion on the subject of deliberation over sins past:

> Thus have we shewed you, that although the recounte, and remembraunce of synnes past: may be good vnto some persons: yet not vnto all . . .[38]

The similarity between the two approaches is exemplified quite clearly by comparing the following two passages. Whitford, in *A werke for housholders*, writes:

> For the commune prouerbe is, that a great benefyte or gyfte is worse than loste vpon suche vnkynde persones that done not remember it, ne gyue due thankes therfore.[39]

and in *A looking glace*, one finds the following passage:

> . . . But take heede that t[h]ou neglecte not to give thanckes for [t]hose thinges which thou receauiste, for of all thinges forgetfullness of be[n]efitts receaued. and ingra[t]itude, di[s]please god exceedingly . . .[40]

Finally, the brief rule provided by the author of *A looking glace* for an examination of conscience at bed-time is very similar to that provided by Whitford in *A werke for housholders*.[41]

---

[36] Lawrence, *op. cit.*, Conclusion, p.96.
[37] *Ibid.*, ch.5, pp.30–31.
[38] Richard Whitford, *Dyuers holy instrucyons and teachynges very necessarye for the helth of mannes soule*, Myddylton, 1541, Fol. 64b. (*RSTC* 25420)
[39] Hogg, *op.cit.*, Vol.5, p.53, l.29–p.54, l.2.
[40] Lawrence, *op.cit.*, ch.4, p.19.
[41] Hogg, *op.cit.*, Vol.5, p.8, l.13–p.10, l.21.

Whether or not Whitford was the author of *A looking glace for the religious*, the work undoubtedly had some connection with Syon Abbey. Although little can be discovered of its history, the unique manuscript is held at Syon. The association with Syon may have been a long one, possibly commencing with the composition of the work. There are a number of aspects of the work which suggest that its intended audience may have been at least in part female. The image of the mirror or looking glass is traditionally identified more often with women than with men. A woman may, therefore, have been more likely than a man to request a looking glass. The request for a looking glass that resulted in the composition of the work brings to mind some of the requests to which Whitford was responding in the composition of a number of his works. He begins *A dayly exercyse and experyence of dethe* by explaining that

> This lytle tretie, or draught of deth, dyd I wryte more than .xx. yeres ago at the request of the reuerende Mother Dame Elizabeth Gybs whome Iesu perdon then Abbes of Syon. And by the oft callyng vpon and remembraunce of certeyne of hyr deuout systers.[42]

The Pype or Tonne of the Lyfe of Perfection begins,

> Good deuout religious daughter: you haue often and instantly required me to write vnto you & vnto your systers some good lesson of religion.[43]

There is, therefore, a precedent for the request for spiritual guidance in written form from the female members of the Syon community. Although the soul is traditionally referred to as female, the constant references to 'she' in the *Looking glace*'s description of how God tests the souls of his servants adds a female element to the work. Finally, when castigating the religious of his day, the *Looking glace*-author refers to both monks and nuns:

> And thus comming forthe abroade after this sorte, not as humble monkes or nunnes. but as delicate and gallant courtyars. with a prodigious shewe, and monstrous spectacle, contrary to the course of there profession: They giue to wise men greate cause of sorrowe and indignation, and do minister to the deuill, occation of laughter & mockery, declaringe euidently by this shamfull absurdity. what manner of people they are at home. secretly within themselues: to witt, proude, wanton, dainty, and full of vayne glorye: O monkes and nunnes, to to [sic] farre estraunged from true religion, o monkes not munkes, o munkes of the deuill: o nunnes not nunnes. o Religious not religious, but sacrilegious [sic] . . .[44]

and

> O vnhappy monkes. O wretched nunnes. o made monkes, o dotinge nunnes, o monkes not monkes. o nunnes not nunnes, o religious irreligious . . .[45]

Although these suggestions are far from proof that *A lookinge glace* was intended for a female audience or for the Syon sisters in particular, it does raise

---

[42] *Ibid.*, Vol.5, p.64, ll.3–7.
[43] *Ibid.*, Vol.2, Preface, p.3.
[44] Lawrence, *op.cit.*, ch.10, p.65.
[45] *Ibid.*, ch.10, p.80.

the question of the type of audience for whom the work was written and intended.

The manuscript consists of 116 pages. Originally, it would have been composed of 124 pages but eight are now missing. The manuscript is also quite badly worm-eaten and contains a large number of *lacunae*. Fortunately, it is not usually too difficult to guess at the missing words or letters.

The text of the manuscript is written in dark brown ink. Occasionally another hand, using a lighter brown ink, has inserted words into the text, usually in a clumsy attempt at correction. The handwriting of the body of the text, a flowing italic script, is tidy and legible and is probably of the seventeenth century. The handwriting of the manuscript does not, in fact, help us to date the text. The types of error that one finds in the manuscript indicate that it is a copy rather than the original text. It is impossible to say how much earlier the original was written but, as has already been stated, the content of the work suggests that it is pre-Reformation. This would fit in well with the possibility of Whitford's authorship of the piece. If, however, it is established that *A looking glace* constitutes a version of the *Speculum Monachorum*, Whitford's responsibility for the work would be less likely because of problems arising from the dating of Abbot Blosius' work.

Little work has been done on *A looking glace*. This may in part be explained by the fact that, until recently, the text only existed in unprinted form and anyone wishing to consult it had to make the journey to Syon Abbey in South Brent, Devon, in order to do so. No work has been done until the present on discussing *A looking glace* in the context of late medieval devotional works in general (aside from Whitford's writings) or of the medieval mystical tradition. In some respects, it bears a resemblance to *The Cloud of Unknowing* in terms of the methodical approach, teaching method and images that it uses. Although it is impossible to show that the *Cloud*-author directly influenced the writing of *A looking glace for the religious*, enough evidence may be gathered to show that *A looking glace* belongs to the same tradition as does *The Cloud of Unknowing*.

Phyllis Hodgson in the introduction to her edition of *The Cloud of Unknowing and related treatises* writes of the *Cloud*-author and Walter Hilton:

> Their lucid instructions prove them both adept in psychological analysis, pathfinders in introspection and recollection, men of learning, creatively eclectic in their use of their common traditional sources, displaying richly those qualities for which medieval English mystical prose is renowned, e.g. practical moderation in their counsel about physical asceticism, a sensitive understanding and a sympathy combined with down-to-earth outspokenness, a master of pithy and at times lofty eloquence in the vernacular.[46]

Although the writings of both authors have many of these features in common, the *Cloud*-author intended *The Cloud*, *The Book of Privy Counselling* and *The Epistle of Prayer* for a much more exclusive audience than that of the *Looking*

---

[46] Hodgson, *op.cit.*, p.ix.

glace. The *Looking glace*-author nowhere limits his readership as does the *Cloud*-author in his prologue:

> I charge þei & I beseche þee, wiþ as moche power & vertewe as þe bonde of charite is sufficient to suffre, whatsoeuer þou be þat þis book schalt haue in possession, ouþer bi propirte oþer by keping, by bering as messenger or elles bi borrowing, þat in as moche as in þee is by wille & auisement, neiþer þou rede it, ne write it, ne speke it, ne ȝit suffre it be red, wretyn, or spokyn, of any or to any, bot ȝif it be of soche one or to soche one þat haþ (by þi supposing) in a trewe wille & by an hole entent, purposed him to be a parfite folower of Criste, not only in actyue leuyng, bot in þe souereinnest pointe of contemplatife leuing þe whiche is possible by grace for to be comen to in þis present liif of a parfite soule ȝit abiding in þis deedly body; & þerto þat doþ þat in him is, &, bi þi supposing, haþ do longe tyme before, for to able him to contemplatiue leuyng by þe vertuous menes of actiue leuyng.[47]

The *Cloud*-author directs his work only at those aiming to attain 'þe souereinnest pointe of contemplatife leuing'. This can only be attained through putting aside the usual aids to devotion:

> ȝe, & ȝif it be cortesye & semely to sey, in þis werk it profiteþ litil or nouȝt to þink of þe kyndenes or þe worþines of God, ne on oure Lady, ne on þe seintes or aungelles in heuen, ne ȝit on þe ioies in heuen . . .[48]

and covering them in a cloud of forgetting:

> & þerfore, þof al it be good sumtyme to þink of þe kyndnes & þe worþines of God in special, & þof al it be a liȝt & a party of contemplacion: neuerþeles in þis werk it schal be casten down & keuerid wiþ a cloude of forȝetyng.[49]

The audience to whom the *Looking glace*-author directs his work is not yet aspiring to this level of contemplation as is the case in *The Epistle of Discretion*. In the sixth chapter of *A looking glace*, the author provides

> sondrye other goodly examples for matter and forme. of meditation. and aspyration, more apte for beginners, then the former weare.[50]

Even the exercises that the *Looking glace*-author provides for his more advanced readers involve imagining each day some part of Christ's passion. Nevertheless, both the author of *A looking glace* and the *Cloud*-author constantly have their audience at the forefront of their minds. Both constantly imagine to themselves what their readers are thinking and how their audience will respond to their message. This psychological awareness is manifested by the imaginary conversations that both the author of *A looking glace* and the *Cloud*-author hold with their readers. The *Looking glace*-author tells his readers to 'Sett thy selfe without dissimulation, beneathe all men and women'. He then imagines his readers' response to this:

[47] *Ibid.*, p.1 ll.8–21.
[48] *Ibid.*, ch.5, p.14, ll.4–7.
[49] *Ibid.*, ch.6, p.14, ll.23–26.
[50] Lawrence, *op.cit.*, ch.6, p.31.

And howe shall I doe that (sayest thou) sithe a greate nomber therebe, which hauinge caste awaye all feare, and there with all shamfastnes and modestye. do liue wickedly, which I nether doe nor mynde to do. what and shall I submitt my selfe, as inferior to him, shall I preferr them . . .[51]

To this objection, the *Looking glace*-author responds:

say I: For if thou wilt thinck with thy selfe, that they which to day. are the worst of all other, may be to morrow mor perfecte then thy selfe.[52]

The *Cloud*-author has similar conversations with the reader. When he tells his reader that he must give an account to God of how he spends his time, he imagines the reaction to this:

Bot soroufuly þou seist now: 'How schal I do? & siþ þis is soþ þat þou seist, how schal I ȝeue acompte of iche tyme seerly. I þat into þis day, now of foure & twenty ȝere age, neuer toke hede of tyme? ȝif I wolde now amende it, þou wost wel, bi verrey reson of þi wordes wretyn before, it may not be after þe cours of kynde ne of comoun grace, þat I schuld mowe kepe or elles make aseeþ to any mo tymes þan to þoo þat ben for to come. ȝe, & moreouer wel I wote, bi verrey proef, þat of þoo þat ben to come I schal on no wise, for habundaunce of freelte & slownes of sperite, mowe kepe one of an hondred; so þat I am verrely conclude in þeese resons. Help me now, for þe loue of Iesu!'[53]

The *Cloud*-author replies, 'Riȝt wel hast þou seide "for þe loue of Iesu". For in þe loue of Iesu þere schal be þin help.'[54]

The *Looking glace*-author also shares the *Cloud*-author's counsel of moderation in physical ascetism. We have already seen the way in which the author of *A looking glace* advises restraint in weeping. He also gives gentle counsel to the religious who, while pursuing his or her religious exercises is overcome with sleepiness:

If drowsy disposition to stirr thee to sleepe, doe somwhat molest thee out of season, and if thou feelest thy selfe there with sore oppressed. thou shalt benefitt thy selfe mor perhappes, (so as tyme and place permitt thee) is a pretty litle whyle by the waye, in the honor of god, thou leanest downe thy heade, and takest a nappe, then thou shouldest doe, if thou wilt stryue with it by extremyty . . .[55]

Although the *Looking glace*-author does not think that exhaustion assists in one's spiritual exercises and suggests a sympathetic remedy to the situation, he is also firm in saying that his readers should not take advantage of and misuse his kindly advice:

As for suche as knowe not the waye to be temperate, in eatinge, drinkinge, and in the vsage of the sences, if they fly to the aforesayed remedy against drunkenes, they haue neede to take heede, for it is to be feared, least thereby they encrease,

---

51 *Ibid.*, ch.9, pp.59–60.
52 *Ibid.*, ch.9, p.60.
53 Hodgson, *op.cit.*, ch.4, p.11, ll.30–40.
54 *Ibid.*, p.12 ll.1–2.
55 Lawrence, *op.cit.*, ch.8, p.55.

> rather then deminishe there disease: and so fallinge into a deepe and longe sleepe,
> doo leese much tyme pityfully by lasynes . . .[56]

The *Looking glace*-author is, therefore, in tune with the approach of the medieval English mystical writers in his sympathetic and empathic approach to his readership, in both his moderation and in his firmness.

A comparison of the sources used by the *Looking glace*-author with those found in the writings of the medieval English mystics is difficult to make at the present time because no work has been done on the identification of the *Looking glace*'s sources. *A looking glace* occasionally identifies a source with a note in the margin. For instance, beside the line,

> Therefore in thy intention and purpose, touchinge thy outward affayers, loue to be
> not only vprighte and harmlesse, as Martha was, but also single harted, cleare, and
> playne as Marie was,[57]

a note in the margin reads 'Luc. 10'. There are very few of such marginal notes and they are all without exception references to the Bible. There are undoubtedly many hidden references embedded in the text. One finds, for instance, the phrase 'our Sauiour . . . had not any thinge whereuppon to leane his heade',[58] a reference to Matthew 8:20, without any note beside it in the margin. The identification of such hidden references would be necessary before a comparison of sources could be made.

A line from *The Cloud of Unknowing* that is frequently quoted relates the journey of the individual towards the cloud of unknowing:

> & þou schalt step abouen it [the cloud of forgetting] stalworþly, bot listely, wiþ a
> deuoute & a plesing stering of loue, & fonde for to peerse þat derknes abouen þee.
> & smyte apon þat þicke cloude of vnknowyng wiþ a scharp darte of longing loue,
> & go not þens for þing þat befalleþ.[59]

The 'scharp darte of longing loue' finds a resonance in *A looking glace* when the author describes the meaning of the term aspiration:

> Now by this tearme of aspyration, (as by the rules before sett downe. thou mayst
> well perceaue) I meane a kinde of very briefe and shorte orisons. or prayers.
> hurling out sharpe darts of zeale, or rather feruente desyres. breathinge out flames
> of deuotion: or else lyuely and amorous affections to god: (And they may be cauled
> acclamations. sithes. and outcryes. full of zeale and feruencye. made to God by
> waye of prayer . . . [*sic*][60]

The *Looking glace*-author does not use the image of the cloud but on a number of occasions, uses words such as 'cloudiness' or 'cloudy'. When describing the faithful servants of God, the *Looking glace*-author, as has been seen, indicates

---

[56] *Ibid.*, ch.8, p.56.
[57] *Ibid.*, ch.10, p.72.
[58] *Ibid.*, ch.3, p.5.
[59] Hodgson, *op.cit.*, ch.6, p.14, ll.27–30.
[60] Lawrence, *op.cit.*, ch.5, p.31.

that 'No inwarde cloudynes . . . can throwe them down forthof there place.'[61]
When describing how God tests his servants, the *Looking glace*-author writes:

> Then by and by aduersytys on euery syde begine to rouse, outwardly men moleste
> her [that is, the servant's soul], inwardly passionat affections trouble her, paynes
> without afflicte her, pusillanimity within casteth her downe, infirmitys do greeue
> her bodly, [sic] darknes doth obscure and ouercloude her mynde: her outwarde
> sences are oppressed, her inwarde powers are dryed, vp . . .[62]

This 'cloudiness of mind' will prevent the soul of God's servant from having the
ability to attend to her religious exercises as had previously been her wont:

> So longe as such a tempest doeth endure, it wilbe somwhat hard for thee, to attend
> diligently at deuyne seruice. through to muche inconstancy. or clowdynes and
> trouble of mind; yet for all that be thou a patient longe sufferer, and in a quyet
> manner, doo all that in thee lyeth chearfully . . .[63]

Self-evidently, the *Cloud*-author's references to clouds, his contrast between the
cloud of unknowing and the cloud of forgetting and the way in which the entire
work is built around the image of the cloud of unknowing are much more
interesting and creative than are the few rather conventional references to
'cloudiness' that one finds in *A looking glace*. No resonance may be found here
as the two authors are using their references on different levels. In *The Cloud of
Unknowing*, the cloud references are rich and complex. The cloud of unknowing
is something toward which one should aspire. In *A looking glace*, cloudiness is
always something internal, usually related to a state of mind. It is the opposite of
one's internal state when 'thy inwarde parts wax cleare' and is something to be
avoided if possible.[64]

We have already seen how the *Looking glace*-author urges his audience not to
rely too heavily on 'spiritual consolation' and 'ghostly sweetness'. The *Cloud*-
author has much the same message for the reader:

> & herby maist þou see þat we schulde directe alle oure beholdyng vnto þis meek
> steryng of loue in oure wille. & in alle oþer swetnes & counfortes, bodily or
> goostly, be þei neuer so likyng ne so holy (ȝif it be cortesie & seemely to sey) we
> schuld haue a manner of rechelesnes. ȝif þei come, welcome hem; bot lene not to
> moche on hem for ferde of febelenes; for it wol take ful mochel of þi myȝtes to
> bide any longe tyme in soche swete felynges & wepynges. & parauenture þou
> mayst be steryd for to loue God for hem. & þat schalt þou fele by þis: ȝif þou
> grocche ouermoche when þei ben awey. & ȝif it be þus, þi loue is not ȝit neiþer
> chaste ne parfite. For a loue þat is chaste & parfite, þof it suffre þat þe body be fed
> & counfortid in þe presence of soche [swete] felynges & wepynges, neuerþeles ȝit
> it is not gruchyng, but ful wel apayed for to lacke hem at Goddes wille.[65]

---

[61] *Ibid.*, ch.3, pp.7–8.
[62] *Ibid.*, ch.8, pp.53–4.
[63] *Ibid.*, ch.8, p.55.
[64] *Ibid.*, ch.8, p.51. See also p.41 where it is considered the greatest joy 'to looke vppon
the god of gods in Syon, and to see him not vnder a clowde, not by waye of ridle, or of
obscure parable, but face to face to behould him . . .'.
[65] Hodgson, *op.cit.*, ch.50, pp.51–52, ll.36–9.

The *Looking glace*-author describes how God at first bestows spiritual consolation plentifully upon his followers but later withdraws it at times to test them. The *Cloud*-author writes that the spiritual comforts that God bestows vary from individual to individual. According to the *Cloud*-author, God bestows spiritual comfort and consolation as it is needed:

> For som creatures ben so weike & so tendre in spirit, þat bot ʒif þei were sumwhat counfortid by feling of soche swetnes, þei miʒte on no wise abide ne bere þe diuersete of temptacions & tribulacions þat þei suffre & ben trauaylid wiþ in þis liif of þeire bodily & goostly enmyes . . . & also, on þe toþer partye, þer ben sum creatures so stronge in spirit, þat þei kun pike hem counforte inowʒ wiþinne in þeire soules, in offryng up of þis reuerent & þis meek steryng of loue & acordaunce of wille, þat hem nedeþ not mochel to be fedde wiþ soche swete counfortes in bodely felynges.[66]

Both the *Looking glace*-author and the *Cloud*-author see these spiritual consolations in terms of God feeding his servants. Both use the image of feeding: 'hem nedeþ not mochel to be fedde' in the *Cloud* and 'thus as it weare with mylke feedinge his newe loue' in *A looking glace*. The *Looking glace*-author, however, also sees the withdrawal of spiritual consolations as a feeding of a different sort, 'with the sownde meate, and stronge dyet of afflictions'. The transition from milk to meat suggests that the afflictions that God's servants have to endure are part of the growing process. The relationship between God and his servants is likened to that of a mother weening her child. This image is another indication of a female presence in the work.

The time of trial and testing, during which God has withdrawn his spiritual consolation, is described in both *A looking glace* and *The Book of Privy Counselling*. In *A looking glace*, the author describes the state of disarray in which God's servant finds himself:

> So longe as such a tempest doeth endure, it wilbe somwhat hard for thee, to attend diligently at deuyne seruice. through to much inconstancy. or clowdynes and trouble of mynde.[67]

In *The Book of Privy Counselling*, the state in which the servant of God finds himself when God has withdrawn his tokens of grace are likened to a boat tossed about in a tempest:

> For sodenly, er euer þou wite, alle is awey, & þou leuyst bareyn in the bote, blowyn wiþ blundryng, now heder now þeder, þou wost neuir where ne wheder[68]

and the individual's inner state is described in terms of a storm: 'Many grete stormes & temptacions, parauenture, scholen rise in þis tyme, & þou wost neuer wheþer to renne for socour.'[69] The *Cloud*-author and the *Looking glace*-author both encourage their readers to have patience because this state of affairs will not

[66] *Ibid.*, p.52, ll.13–25.
[67] Lawrence, *op.cit.*, ch.8, p.55.
[68] Hodgson, *op.cit.*, p.96, ll.11–14.
[69] *Ibid.*, p.96, ll.4–5.

endure forever and help is around the corner. The *Looking glace* author writes: 'The nighte will passe ouer, darknes will shrincke awaye. and the daye will springe againe . . .'[70] In *The Book of Privy Counselling*, one finds the following words of comfort:

> ȝit be not abascht, for he schal come, I behote þee, ful sone, whan hym likiþ [to leþe þee] & douȝtely delyuer þee of alle þi dole, fer more worþely þen he euer did before.

The 'tokenes of grace', 'alle þees sensible swetnes, þes feruent felynges & þees flawming desires' will return again:

> He schal loke up, parauenture riȝt sone, & efte touche þee wiþ a more feruent stering of þat same grace þan euer þou feltest any before.[71]

The servant of God is alternately cast down and lifted up, as the *Looking glace*-author describes:

> Nowe the brydgroume hydeth himselfe. from the sowle, nowe againe he sheweth himselfe to her, nowe as it weare he forsaketh, and leaueth her in darknes, and in horor of death: nowe againe he calleth her backe to a delectable sence and feelinge of lighte . . .[72]

God does this in order to 'trye and prooue the soule',[73] to 'priuely proue þee & worche þee to his owne werk'.[74] He shapes and forms the will of his servant to His own will. The *Looking glace*-author describes this process in terms of 'hewing', 'cutting' and 'plaining'.[75] The *Cloud*-author writes that 'alle þis he doþ for he wil haue þee maad as pleying to his wille goostly as a roon gloue to þin honde bodely.'[76]

The *Looking glace*-author and the *Cloud*-author share a concern for the adoption of seemly behaviour among religous. The *Looking glace*-author, as has been shown, is quite colourful in his description of certain religious who abandon their habits outside the cloister and adopt the dress of seculars. Even within the cloister, many depart from an ordered existence with their 'ill fashioned gestures' and 'disordered laughinge'.[77] Even in reading must order and sequence be followed, 'Re[ad]e I saye not confusely not heere and there, but i[n or]der and in due course'.[78] The *Cloud*-author too is colourful in his descriptions of the 'ill fashioned gestures' of certain religious:

> For som men aren so kumbred in nice corious countenaunces in bodily beryng, þat whan þei schal ouȝt here, þei wriþen here hedes onside queyntely, & up wiþ þe

---

70 Lawrence, *op.cit.*, ch.8, p.55.
71 Hodgson, *op.cit.*, p.96, ll.30–31, 8–10.
72 Lawrence, *op.cit.*, ch.8, p.54.
73 *Ibid.*, ch.8, p.54.
74 Hodgson, *op.cit.*, p.96, ll.22–25.
75 Lawrence, *op.cit.*, ch.8, p.54.
76 Hodgson, *op.cit.*, p.96, ll.19–20.
77 Lawrence, *op.cit.*, ch.10, p.79.
78 *Ibid.*, ch.4, p.17.

chin; þei gape wiþ þeire mouþes as þei schulen speke, poynten wiþ here fyngres, or on þeire fyngres, or on þeire owne brestes, or on þeires þat þei speke to. Some kan nouþer sit stille, stonde stylle, ne ligge stille, bot ȝif þei be ouþer waggyng wiþ þeire fete, or elles somwhat doyng wiþ þeire handes. Som rowyn wiþ þeire armes in tyme of here spekyng, as hem nedid for to swymme ouer a grete water. Som ben euermore smyling & leiȝing at iche o er worde þat þei speke, as þei weren gigelotes & nice japyng jogelers lackyng kontenaunce.[79]

Both the *Looking glace*-author and the *Cloud*-author have very little patience with dissemblers or hypocrites. The *Looking glace*-author describes them as unchanging from day to day, leaving the choir in the same spiritual state as that in which they entered and exasperating God with holy words that do not emanate from the heart.[80] The *Cloud*-author describes the ridiculous facial gestures and tones of voice of the hypocrite in the following words:

> Some sette þeire iȝen in þeire hedes as þei were sturdy scheep betyn in þe heed, & as þei schulde diȝe anone. Som hangen here hedes on syde, as a worme were in þeire eres. Som pipyn when þei schuld speke, as þer were no spirit in þeire bodies; & þis is the propre condicion of an ypocrite.[81]

The *Cloud*-author recommends that his disciple, when he is called to God and has lifted up his heart to God 'wiþ a meek steryng of loue', concentrate on a single word of one syllable:

> & ȝif þee list haue þis entent lappid & foulden in o worde, for þou schuldest haue betir holde þerapon, take þee bot a litil worde of o silable; for so it is betir þen of two, for euer þe schorter it is, þe betir it accordeþ wiþ þe werk of þe spirite. & soche a worde is þis worde GOD or þis worde LOUE. Cheese þee wheþer þou wilt, or anoþer as þe list: whiche þat þee likeþ best of o silable. & fasten þis worde to þin herte, so þat it neuer go þens for þing þat bifalleþ.[82]

This single word will be 'þi scheeld & þi spere'.[83] With this word, 'þou schalt bete on þis cloude & þis derknes abouen þee'.[84] The *Looking glace*-author shows a similar form of prayer in action when he describes the spiritual exercises of the Benedictine brother. The brother prays as follows:

> O my God, O sweete delyghte of my soule, O my comfort, O my lyfe. O my loue, O my desyre. O my treasure. O all my good. O my beginninge and my ende, O that my soule mighte enioye thee. O that it might be hard, and faste bound with the loue of thee, O that it weare perfectly vnited vnto thee . . .[85]

This sort of prayer, composed of short bursts of simple words as if they were breaths of air, is repeated further on: 'O my god, O my loue, O my whole

---

[79] Hodgson, *op.cit.*, ch.53, p.55, ll.1–12.
[80] Lawrence, *op.cit.*, ch.3, p.12.
[81] Hodgson, *op.cit.*, ch.53, p.54, ll.16–20.
[82] *Ibid.*, ch.7, p.15, ll.30–36.
[83] *Ibid.*, ch.7, p.15, ll.37.
[84] *Ibid.*, ch.7, p.15, ll.38–39.
[85] Lawrence, *op.cit.*, ch.5, p.27.

desyre, O my vniversall good . . .'[86] The *Looking glace*-author describes this form of prayer as 'aspyrations, earnest cryes and sighthes to god'. The Benedictine brother used to pray often in this fashion 'knowinge that by exercyse of aspyrations. the spirite of man, is moreffectually vnited to the spirit of god'.[87]

Other resonances exist between *A looking glace* and *The Cloud of Unknowing* in their doctrine and their style. Both distrust learning and curiousity for its own sake. The fifty-sixth chapter of *The Cloud* is entitled 'How þei ben disseiued [þat] lenen more to þe coriouste of kyndely witte. & of clergie leerned in þe scole of men, þan to þe comoun doctrine counsel of Holi Chirche.'[88] The *Looking glace*-author advises his disciple to:

seeke not for curiousity. nor for superfluous intelligence and scien[c]e: nor yet for ornamente and eloquence of words: for the kingdome of god, consisteth [no]t in pleasant grace of speeche, but in hollynes of lyfe.[89]

The *Looking glace*-author warns against too vehement spiritual exercises when he advises against over-much weeping.[90] The fifty-eighth chapter of *The Cloud* is entitled, 'þat a man schal not take ensaumple of Seinte Martyn & of Seinte Steuen, for to streine his ymaginacion bodily upwardes in þe tyme of his preier'[91] and the fifty-ninth chapter, 'þat a man schal not take exsaumple at þe bodily assencion of Criste, for to streine his ymaginacion upwardes bodily in þe tyme of preier'.[92] Both frequently use alliteration for emphasis. To give but one example from each, one finds in *A looking glace* the line:

thus commonly vanishe they awaye in there owne vayne thoughts, which greedely gape for sensible grace, rather then the giuer of grace.[93]

In *The Cloud*, one finds the line: 'lache not ouer-hastely, as it were a gredy grehounde'.[94] The prologue to *The Cloud of Unknowing* concludes with the line,

Of þe whiche chapitres, þe last chapitres of alle techeþ som certeyn tokens by þe whiche a soule may verrely preue wheþer he be clepid of God to be a worcher in þis werk or none.[95]

At the end of *A looking glace*, one finds the following line: 'A lookinge glace you did couete to haue, see whether you haue receaued a lookinge glace or not.'[96]

Although *The Cloud of Unknowing* was directed at an audience more spiritually advanced than that of *A looking glace*, there can be little doubt that

---

[86] *Ibid.*, ch.5, p.28.
[87] *Ibid.*, ch.5, p.28.
[88] Hodgson, *op.cit.*, p.5, ll.39–41.
[89] Lawrence, *op.cit.*, ch.4, p.15.
[90] *Ibid.*, ch.7, p.48.
[91] Hodgson, *op.cit.*, p.6, ll.4–6.
[92] *Ibid.*, p.6, ll.7–9.
[93] Lawrence, *op.cit.*, ch.3, p.7.
[94] Hodgson, *op.cit.*, ch.46, p.48, ll.28–29.
[95] *Ibid.*, p.2, ll.14–17.
[96] Lawrence, *op.cit.*, Conclusion, pp.95–96.

they both belong to the same tradition. The similarity in doctrine and recommended practice is great. Both authors warn against similar obstacles and stumbling blocks in their disciples' journey on the road to perfection. Both *A looking glace* and the writings of the *Cloud*-author were composed in a like tone and spirit and there appears to be very little that the author of *Alooking glace* has written that would jar with, or contradict, anything found in the writings of the *Cloud*-author. For both, communication is paramount and they have their audiences constantly to the forefront of their minds. Both use colourful descriptions and examples to hold their readers' attention and similarities may even be found in the turn of phrase, literary conventions and imagery used by both. Although there is no proof of any direct influence of the writings of the *Cloud*-author on the composition of *A looking glace*, there can be little doubt that a kinship between the works does exist.

MARGERY KEMPE:
A SCANDINAVIAN INFLUENCE
IN MEDIEVAL ENGLAND?

GUNNEL CLEVE

IMITATIO SEEMS TO BE ONE of the core elements of medieval spiritual life. In most cases it is an *imitatio Christi*, but there were people who were unable to devote their lives full time to such a religious life as the church favoured above all other variants. For this reason we find a number of people searching for acceptable and accepted models among religious people, people wanting to adopt an *imitatio sanctorum* when they felt that a total commitment was denied to them. The situation must have been particularly difficult for married women as their husbands, according to the custom and the law of the time, were placed between themselves and Christ, and their first duty was to their husbands, and only through him to Christ. This is the situation Margery Kempe found herself in, when she first became aware of her vocation and needed a model for a religious life that was feasible in her particular circumstances.

Margery Kempe was, as we know, the daughter of one of the highly esteemed citizens of Kings Lynn. Her father had been mayor of that city and twice elected member of Parliament. Margery Kempe was very conscious of the status her family conferred upon her person, and probably occasionally considered her marriage a *mésalliance*. Margery Kempe had been married for some time when she first became aware of a special vocation. She was not, however, prepared to change her life as yet, and put off her personal decision to some time later. When all her business enterprises failed, she was finally prepared to reconsider the stirring towards a spiritual life that she had felt repeatedly.

Most modern studies of Margery Kempe refer to the fact that she was acquainted with St Bridget of Sweden and her *Revelations*. Birgitta had married early, but very reluctantly: she was obviously aware of God calling her to a different type of life. She had borne her husband eight children and was, by Margery's contemporaries, considered a saint, in spite of all this. Margery could not compete with Birgitta in social status; Birgitta was related to the royal house and married to one of the most influential men in their part of the country. But Margery was not concerned with the social status of Birgitta. To Margery, Birgitta's matrimony and child-bearing combined with the sanctity accorded to her were obviously much more important. As Margery Kempe's sense of vocation became more manifest, she found in Birgitta one of the rare examples

163

that she could use as a model for her own aspirations, whether this approach was a consciously chosen one or not.

There is evidence that Birgitta's revelations were known in England within, at most, thirty-five years of her death, and perhaps even as early as 1391 or thereabout.[1] Most modern studies of Margery Kempe's *Book* refer to the fact that she was acquainted with Birgitta's *Revelations* and probably also the saint's life.[2] Clarissa W. Atkinson distinguishes three different facets of influence:

> Birgitta and her writings served as personal and religious as well as literary models for both Margery Kempe and her scribe.[3]

Margery Kempe herself refers several times to St Bridget and to 'Bride's book' in her autobiography. She lists a number of books that she had heard people reading from at the beginning of her book:

> Sche told hym how sum-tyme þe Fadyr of Hevyn dalyd to hir sowle as pleynly and as veryly as o frend spekyth to anoþer be bodyly spech; sum-tyme þe Secunde Persone in Trinyte; sum-tyme all thre Personys in Trinyte & o substawns in Godhede dalyid to hir sowle & informyd hir in hir feyth & in hys lofe how sche xuld lofe hym, worshepyn hym, & dredyn hym, so excellently þat sche herd neuyr boke, neþyr Hyltons boke, ne Bridis boke, ne Stimulus Amoris, ne Incendium Amoris, no non oþer that euyr sche herd redyn þat spak so hyly of lofe of God . . . (*BkMK*, ch.17, p.39, ll.16–26)[4]

Much later in her book Margery reverts to the books that have been read aloud to her, and lists exactly the same works. In that context she mentions that the particular priest who so kindly read all these books to her had been doing so for some seven or eight years. Obviously she must have had a comprehensive knowledge of the contents of the books she lists, and a good knowledge of the lives of these mystics most likely goes with it. And Birgitta's life exposed precisely the circumstances that Margery feared would disqualify her for a religious life. They moreover seemed to have a strange point of convergence: Birgitta died in the year 1373, and that year was in all probability Margery's year of birth. Such a coincidence must have been of great significance to Margery and her spiritual development. There are passages in her book that

---

[1] *The Liber Celestis of St Bridget of Sweden (LC)*, ed. Roger Ellis, Early English Text Society 291, OUP, Oxford, New York, Toronto 1987, xii.

[2] E.g. Louise Collis, *The Apprentice Saint*, London 1964, pp.139:

> Her *Revelations* circulated widely and Margery was acquainted with them. It was her ambition to surpass this famous woman in holiness and fame. God frequently assures her that he loves her just as well as, or better than, St Bridget. Sometimes, he remarks, her visions are superior to the saint's. He never adjures his faithful Margery to emulate Bridget, but, full of envy and admiration, she cannot help doing so.

[3] Clarissa W. Atkinson, *Mystic and Pilgrim*, Ithaca and London 1983, p.35.

[4] *The Book of Margery Kempe (BkMK)*, ed. Sanford Brown Meech and Hope Emily Allen, Early English Text Society, O.S. 212, London, 1940, ch.58, p.143.

suggest she might have looked upon herself as a kind of heiress to St Bridget's spiritual heritage. This is also apparent from the way Christ addresses her and seems to link her life to that of the saint:

> For I tell þe forsoþe rygth as I spak to Seynt Bryde, ryte so I speke to þe, dowtyr, & I telle þe trewly it is trewe euery word þat is wretyn in Brides boke, & be þe it xal be knowyn for very trewth. (*BkMK*, ch.20, p.47, ll.31–35)

This statement alone justifies a further scrutiny of *The Book of Margery Kempe* and her spiritual affinity with the Swedish saint.

Personal Circumstances

In a recent review of Kenneth L. Woodward's book *Making Saints* Peter Hebblethwaite pointed out holiness was most definitely identified with virginity in the Middle Ages.[5] Neither Birgitta nor Margery were virgins. Nor did either of them have the additional advantage of being Italian, French or Spanish. For both of them, then, matrimony was a problem that had to be solved somehow and both showed anxiety in this respect.

In 1341, Birgitta and her husband decided to go to Santiago di Compostella to celebrate the silver jubilee of their wedding.[6] At least during that journey, and perhaps even earlier, Birgitta and Ulf led a life of chastity, and on the return journey they decided to take a vow of perfect chastity. The final decision on Ulf's part might have been partly due to the severe illness that befell him on their way back home, but this was certainly a wish Birgitta had repeatedly expressed. Once they reached Sweden, the matter was rapidly settled, and Ulf went to live at the Cistercian Abbey of Alvastra. When their daughter, Katherine, married, Birgitta moved to an adjacent house to be near her husband, who was then seriously ill and dying.[7]

Margery Kempe reports that she once heard such heavenly music in one of her revelations that she never again wanted to have sexual intercourse. Her love and devotion was to be set on God alone. She was not able to deny her husband his matrimonial rights, but she never wearied of repeating her wish to live chaste.[8] But Margery had to keep repeating her wish for quite some time as her husband was not yet willing to agree to this. On a journey from York, probably on their way back to Kings Lynn, he suddenly asked Margery if she would allow him to be killed, rather than to consent to making love with him, should a man come along and threaten to stab him, if she refused. It appears from the context that

---

[5] Peter Hebblethwaite, 'Tests of holiness', *Times Literary Supplement*, May 10, 1991, p.24.

[6] James Hogg, 'Sunte Birgitten openbaringe', *Spiritualität heute und gestern*, ed. James Hogg, *Analecta Cartusiana*, 35:7, Salzburg 1990, p.107.

[7] *Ibid.*, p.108.

[8] *BkMK*, ch.3, pp.11–12.

they had then been living chaste for eight weeks. It is also clear that Margery had been expressing her wish often enough for more than three years at that time. As they proceeded on their homeward journey, her husband suddenly struck a bargain: if she agreed to three things, he would give up his matrimonial right. He wanted her to share his bed as before, to give up her Friday fast, and probably most important, to pay his debts before she went to Jerusalem.[9] As Margery accepted his conditions, he declared:

> As fre mot ʒowr body ben to God as it hath ben to me. (*BkMK*, ch.11, p.25, ll.12–13)

Not satisfied with her husband's promise, Margery insisted that they should visit the Bishop of Lincoln in order to make a solemn vow of chastity in his presence.[10] On that occasion she also asked for the white clothes the Lord had commanded her to wear, another indication of her aspiration towards chastity and a kind of post-matrimonial virginity.

During her marriage Birgitta used to wear a hair shirt and spent as much time as she could possibly spare in prayer in the chapel, meditating on Christ's passion. She is also reported to have observed Lent strictly and to have abstained on all prescribed days.[11]

Roughly at the same time as Margery started her quest for chastity, she took up the habit of wearing a hair shirt which she was afraid her husband would notice. She also gave herself to fasting and keeping of vigils, getting up early in the night and betaking herself to church and remaining there till noon in prayer.[12]

Not only matters of great importance for Margery's spiritual life have precents in Birgitta's revelations. There are also rather trivial things that seem to be repeated in the life of Margery Kempe. One such episode is the pail of water that Knut Folkesson managed to throw over Birgitta in a narrow street once, and Birgitta only commented that she hoped God would spare him in the life to come.[13] Margery accounts for a similar episode in Lynn, when she calmly said she hoped God would make the trespasser a good man.[14] Birgitta received one of her revelations on horseback between Alvastra and Vadstena;[15] Margery, who usually walked, received an equally intense revelation while riding on an ass, as she and her fellow travellers were approaching Jerusalem.[16] Like Birgitta, Margery, too, was rebuked for what she said at table.[17] They both grieved because of a son who preferred a life in sexual sin to what they would have

---

[9] *BkMK*, ch.11, pp.23–25.
[10] *BkMK*, ch.15, pp.33–35.
[11] James Hogg, *op.cit.*, p.104.
[12] *BkMK*, ch.3, p.12.
[13] See Aron Andersson, *Saint Bridget of Sweden*, London 1980, p.38.
[14] *BkMK*, ch.55, p.137.
[15] Aron Andersson, *op.cit.*, p.38.
[16] *BkMK*, ch.28, p.67.
[17] Aron Andersson, *op.cit.*, p.38; *BkMK*, ch.27, p.66.

wanted.[18] As far as Margery was concerned, this was the only child she ever wrote about in her book, whereas the other thirteen are never mentioned nor are their lives accounted for.

Pilgrimages

Birgitta learnt through a prophetic vision, which she received when her husband was seriously illl on their return journey from Santiago, that she would go to Rome and Jerusalem.[19] In much the same manner Margery Kempe was told to go to the very same holy places as Birgitta had visited:

> As sche was in þese desyres, owyr Lord bad hir in hir mend ij 3er er þan sche went
> that sche schuld gon to Rome, to Iherusalem, & to Seynt Iamys, for sche wold fayn
> a gon but sche had no good to go wyth. (*BkMK*, ch.15, p.32, ll.5–9)

And in the same way as Birgitta was reassured that God would provide for her, Margery was told that she would be given all the things she needed. This assurance was repeated many times during her journey.[20]

Margery managed to join a group of pilgrims and travelled for some time in their company, but occasionally they grew irritated at her and told her to be quiet. At times they felt inclined to abandon her and occasionally they actually did. Eventually she reached the Holy Land, and visited its sacred sites.

It was when she first saw Jerusalem ahead of them that she felt such joy and grace that she nearly fell off the donkey on which she was riding.[21] She visited the Church of the Holy Sepulchre, the Mount of Calvary, the place where the apostles received the Holy Ghost, Bethlehem, Mount Quarentine where Christ fasted, the place where St John the Baptist was born, Ramleh and a good many other places. During this pilgrimage she repeatedly heard the Lord and Our Lady talk to her; Birgitta's revelations were also often communicated through the sense of hearing. But in the Holy Land Margery was also granted visions as Birgitta had been before her. Some of these revelations will be presented later on.

Margery had probably left England for Jerusalem in the autumn of 1413. The next date we know in her life is her visit to the chapel of Portiuncula in Assisi.[22] Birgitta had stayed in Jerusalem for over four months.[23] Margery's stay there

---

18 Aron Andersson, *op.cit.*, p.110; *BkMK* II, ch.1, p.221.
19 Aron Andersson, *op.cit.*, p.20.
20 Such reassurances are found e.g. in *BkMK*, ch.26, p.62 and ch.30, p.75.
21 *BkMK*, ch.28, p.67. The corresponding episode in *Liber Celestis* occurs in Book V, the prologue, p.366.
22 *BkMK*, ch.31, p.79. Margery Kempe states that she was in Assisi on 'Lammes Day', which was on August 1st. Birgitta had walked there from Rome; Birgit Klockars, *Birgitta och hennes värld*, Kungl. vitterhets, historie och antikvitets akademien, Historiska serien 16, Uppsala 1971, p.155.
23 Aron Andersson, *op.cit.*, p.118.

seems to have been much shorter. She had probably left Venice in spring or early summer, and she was back in Assisi on 1 August. Yet she had obviously managed to visit the same places as Birgitta, and some of them several times. Admittedly pilgrims in those days were taken to certain places, and not allowed to visit any holy site of their choice, but even so the places mentioned by Margery seem to suggest that she was trying to follow in Birgitta's footsteps. In the Holy Land Margery was also granted several visions, many of them remarkably close to those Birgitta had experienced in the same places. Obviously Margery's pilgrimage to Jerusalem had reminded her of Birgitta, and as Margery returned to Italy, she headed for Rome. Her stay in Rome formed an era of even more than *imitatio* of Birgitta; there are several recorded facts that amount to a near-identification with the saint. In addition to this, Margery actively tried to find out about Birgitta's life in Rome, and to visit the places where the saint had lived.

Margery gives us a brief account of how she served a poor woman, and how, at God's command, she gave away all her money.[24] Even these gestures may be identified with Birgitta, who because of her Samaritan work, experienced financial difficulties. Once she was rather curtly told by Our Lady:

> . . . If þou hafe none oþir, aske for þe lufe of God þat þe whilke is nedefull to þi
> fedinge and cleþinge, . . .   (*LC*, VI, ch.46, p.436, ll.36–37)

And so Birgitta did, and much later we find Margery involved in the same procedure to get her daily bread.[25]

Although Margery had no Latin and even less Italian, she moved about in Rome and talked to such people as could understand her. She was asked to become the godmother of a child whose mother wanted to name it after St Bridget.[26] Margery learnt that a lady who once was Birgitta's maidservant was still living at the time, and she visited her and asked her about Birgitta. Even Margery's landlord had known Birgitta, and was surprised that so kind and homely a woman had been so holy.[27] Margery also visited Piazza Farnese and the chamber where Birgitta died, and knelt on the stone where Birgitta received the revelation of her own death.[28] Then Margery gives us a detailed account of the storms and rains that occurred on one of St Bridget's days, probably on 7 October. Margery adds:

> Þorw swech tokenys þis creatur supposyd þat owr Lord wold hys holy Seyntys day
> xulde ben halwyd & þe Seynt had in mor worshep þan sche was at þat
> tyme. (*BkMK*, ch.39, p.95, ll.34–37)

This comment is rather important. It indicates that Margery Kempe must have been aware of the uncertainty that prevailed about the canonization of St Bridget

[24] *BkMK*, ch.37.
[25] *BkMK*, ch.38.
[26] *BkMK*, ch.39.
[27] *BkMK*, ch.39.
[28] *BkMK*, ch.39.

in 1414. Obviously Margery had learnt about the various setbacks that people had had to face in the canonization process. It had begun as early as 1377, but Pope Gregory XI died on 26 March 1378. His successor Urban VI was intensely engaged in settling the Great Schism in the Church, and so never managed to see this process to its completion. Pope Boniface IX had solemnly canonized Birgitta on 7 October 1391. At the Council of Constance John XXIII had wished to confirm her canonization, but in that year he was deposed from his dignity. King Eric of Sweden (1412–1439) wanted the matter clarified and finally settled, and he approached Pope Martin V (1417–1431) and asked him to confirm Birgitta's canonization, which the pope did with his Bull *Excellentium principum*, promulgated on 1 July 1419.[29] The proceedings were probably the talk of the town, and Margery would have learnt about them at Piazza Farnese, if nowhere else. Margery Kempe's remark about the saint and the storms the Lord sent in disapproval of the disregard for Birgitta also testify to the fact that to Margery St Bridget was an important saint.

Birgitta tells us about a man from the diocese of Åbo, Finland, whom she met in Rome.[30] His problem was that he could not find anyone capable of hearing his confession, as he only knew Finnish and there was no one around who could understand that language. Through Christ, Birgitta learnt what he was troubled by, and she was enabled to explain to him that his willingness to confess was sufficient. In Margery's book there is an episode that contains this confessional pattern, but in Margery's version, she herself turned to a priest who, as it happened, had no word of English.[31] God granted him the gift to understand Margery's speech, although he could not understand other people who spoke English. Priests from England had refused to listen to her, and now God helped her find a confessor in this German priest.

In Rome Margery once lost a ring that she had been wearing for a long time. It was, in her own words, 'my bone maryd ryng to Ihesu Crist'. (*BkMK*, ch.31, p.78, ll.32–33) The ring was related to the white clothes she had been wearing, and these clothes, too, seem to be a kind of bridal dress. But in addition to being a wedding ring, the ring she talks about seems to be part of the habit she originally asked the Bishop of Lincoln to give her: a white dress, a ring and a mantle.[32] The habit of a nun also included these three things, though the dress and the mantle did not always need to be white. The ring that Margery wore had, moreover, been engraved, and the words *Ihesus est amor meus* (*BkMK*, ch.31, p.78, ll.14–15) are very close to *Amor meus crucifixus est*, the motto of the Order of the Holy Saviour founded by St Bridget. Margery's habit and ring, then, seem to have had a twofold function: they were tokens of her being the

---

[29] James Hogg, *op.cit.*, pp.137–139.
[30] *LC*, Bk VI, ch.115. For this revelation see the forthcoming edition of Book VI of the *Liber Celestis*, ed. B. Bergh, SFSS, ser 2, Bd.VII:6, Uppsala.
[31] *BkMK*, ch.33.
[32] James Hogg, 'A Brigittine Legislative Collection, *Spiritualität heute und gestern*, *Analecta Cartusiana* 35:9, ed. James Hogg, Salzburg 1990, pp.80–81.

spouse of Christ, but they also formed a link to life within a religious order, and so suggest that Margery regarded herself as closely connected with those who had actually become nuns. The inscription seems to suggest that she felt a very special affiliation to St Bridget and her order. Birgitta must have been the personification of what Margery longed for and searched for: a married woman who, through a vow of chastity, restored a kind of virginity and who, at the end of her life, miraculously became a nun. Thus Birgitta could be referred to as a justification for the radical changes in Margery Kempe's life, although not the sole one.

No sooner had Margery returned to England than she started preparing for a pilgrimage to Santiago,[33] which she also managed to undertake. Admittedly, Rome, Jerusalem and Santiago di Compostella were important places for pilgrimages, but there is a strong suggestion in the choices Margery made that she was actually imitating Birgitta in these matters, too. Margery did visit Assisi and when we get to her second book it is even harder to ward off the impression that Birgitta was her ultimate model.[34] Birgitta had passed through Stralsund[35] on her way to Rome. On their pilgrimage to Santiago, Birgitta and her husband had travelled through Cologne and Aachen.[36] Margery's second book opens with a couple of chapters on the son she had such great worries about. She is happy to record that he eventually married a German lady, and the couple travelled to England to see her. There her son died, and as her daughter-in-law decided to return to Germany, Margery asked her confessor to grant her leave to accompany her daughter-in-law as far as Ipswich. To her daughter-in-law's annoyance, Margery then decided to go all the way to Germany with her. The German lady headed for Danzig, where Margery stayed for some time. But soon enough she joined a man who was going on a pilgrimage to Wilsnack, where the precious blood of Christ was venerated,[37] and this pilgrimage was undertaken in the midst of a war between the Teutonic Order and England. The journey took her to Stralsund, and from there to Aachen.[38] During this adventurous journey Margery Kempe had to pass through enemy country in the company of sundry people, penniless most of the time, and not knowing the language sufficiently to be able to manage on her own. What induced her to set out on this trip in the first place? Was there, in her mind, a lingering memory that Birgitta had been to these places, too? Or was the fame of the relics a strong enough incentive to make her go? One guess is as good as the other, with a slight slant in favour of

---

[33] *BkMK*, ch.44.
[34] Birgit Klockars, *op.cit.*, p.155.
[35] Aron Andersson, *op.cit.*, p.136.
[36] Birgit Klockars, *op.cit.*, p.166.
[37] *BkMK*, ch.4, p.232.
[38] Birgitta and Dorothea of Montau, another of the holy women whom Margery might have imitated, had undertaken pilgrimages to Aachen, famous for its relics. Cf. e.g. *The Book of Margery Kempe*, trans. by B. A. Windeatt, Harmondsworth 1985, p.329, and Birgit Klockars, *op.cit.*, p.166.

Birgitta, since there were relics to be found closer to Kings Lynn and in more peaceful places.

Revelations

Margery's constant awareness of Birgitta is repeatedly brought to the attention of any reader of her *Book*. In chapter 20, Margery seems to concentrate a number of issues that suggest her equality with, if not even superiority in relation to Birgitta. In the first instance Margery saw the sacramental elements moving in a very strange way during the consecration, and immediately afterwards she heard the Lord saying to her:

> Þow xalt no mor sen it in þis maner, þerfor thank God þat þow hast seyn. My dowtyr, Bryde, say me neuyr in þis wyse. (*BkMK*, ch.20, p.47, ll.25–27)

The Lord then warned her that this betokened vengeance in the form of an earthquake and he continued:

> . . . tel it whom þow wylt in þe name of Ihesu. For I telle þe forsoþe rygth as I spak to Seynt Bryde ryte so I speke to þe, dowtyr, & I telle þe trewly it is trewe euery word þat is wretyn in Brides boke, & be þe it xal be knowyn for very trewth. (*BkMK*, ch.20, p.47, ll.31–35)

The Lord here seems to confirm Margery's wish to take up Birgitta's mantle and heritage, by giving Margery the mission she desired. This chapter also contains one of the rare instances in Margery's *Book* where the Lord lists a number of horrors that will befall people who do not listen to His warnings:

> I may no mor, dowtyr, of my rytfulnesse do for hem þan I do. I send hem prechyng & techyng, pestylens & bataylys, hungyr and famynyng, losse of her goodys wyth gret sekenesse, & many oþer tribulacyons, & þei wyl not leuyn my wordys no þei wyl not knowe my vysitacyon. & þerfor I xal sey to hem that I made my seruawntys to prey for zow, & ze despysed her werkys & her leuyng. (*BkMK*, ch.20, p.48, ll.17–24)

As a character Margery is so different from Birgitta that she hardly ever resorts to the forceful language that Birgitta uses. But the above quotation is an exception in this respect: it echoes the style of Birgitta's revelations both in the listing of consequences to which that disobedience will lead, and in the particular choice of vocabulary. It seems very appropriate that this revelation should occur at the end of a chapter that thrice refers to St Bridget.

The two women also share concern for their married status. Margery reverts to this problem many times over, but there is one instance in particular which, though more verbose than St Bridget's passages on this matter, lists the points made by Margery's favourite saint in more or less the same order. Grieving once again because she has entered matrimony and so cannot lead a perfect religious life, Margery complains to Christ:

> Lord Ihesu, þis maner of leuyng longyth to thy holy maydens.

But Christ answers her at some length:

> ȝa, dowtyr, trow þow ryght wel þat I lofe wyfes also, and specyal þo wyfys whech woldyn levyn chast, ȝyf þei mygtyn haue her wyl, & don her besynes to plesyn me as þow dost, for, þow the state of maydenhode be more parfyte & mor holy þan the state of wedewhode, & þe state of wedewhode mor parfyte þan the state of wedlake, ȝet dowtyr I lofe þe as well as any mayden in þe world. (*BkMK*, ch.21, p.48, l.35 – p.49, l.8)

After studying *Speculum virginum*, St Bridget is reported to have written the following words:

> Virginity deserves the Crown, widowhood draws near to God and wedlock is not excluded from heaven, but obedience leads all to glory.[39]

This concern for virginity derives, of course, from the tradition to which both Birgitta and Margery belonged: that of experiencing a vocation to become the bride of Christ, or Christ's spouse, as Birgitta prefers to phrase it. St Bridget had a very strong feeling of being chosen from childhood on, and also of being under the special protection of Our Lady.[40] Like Birgitta, Margery first experienced a vocation that connected her with the Virgin. There is an instance where Margery did not know on what to meditate, and Christ answered in her mind:

> Dowtyr, thynke on my Modyr, for sche is cause of alle þe grace þat þow hast. (*BkMK*, ch.6, p.18, ll.13–15)

When the Lord's special vocation reached Birgitta after her husband's death, she was explicitly called to become the bride of Christ.[41] At an early stage Margery, too, is told that she will be regarded as Christ's spouse:

> . . . for-as-mech as þu art a mayden in þi sowle, I xal take þe be þe on hand in Hevyn & my Modyr be þe oþer hand, & so xalt þu dawnsyn in hevyn wyth oþer holy maydens & virgynes, for I may clepyn þe dere a-bowte & myn owyn derworthy derlyng. I xal sey to þe, myn owyn blyssed spowse, 'Welcome to me wyth al maner of joye & gladnes, her to dwellyn wyth me & neuyr to departyn fro me wyth-owtyn ende . . . (*BkMK*, ch.22, p.52, l.26, – p.53, l.3)

But Margery's wedding to the Godhead took place in Rome, and the second promise, granted to Birgitta that she would be told God's secrets, was then added to Margery's wedding procedures:

> Dowtyr, I wil han þe wedded to my Godhede, for I schal schewyn þe my preuyteys & my cownselys, for þu xalt wonyn wyth me wyth-owtyn ende. (*BkMK*, ch.35, p.86, ll.16–18)

Like St Bridget, who rushed off to her confessor, Margery, too, was at first shaken in her mind and found no answer to this proposal. But Christ comforted

---

[39] The English rendering is from Aron Andersson, *op.cit.*, p.15.
[40] Ingrid Ydén-Saandgren, *En krona av guld*, Stockholm 1973, p.6.
[41] *Extravagantes* 47. (*Den Heliga Birgittas Reuelaciones Extrauagantes*, Samlingar utgiuna av Svenska Fornskriftsällskapet, Ser. 11 Bd. U. Uppsala, 1956). See also Aron Andersson, *op.cit.*, pp.22–23.

her and the wedding ceremony was actually accomplished then and there in the church of the Holy Apostles in Rome, in the presence of the Son, the Holy Ghost, the mother of Jesus, the apostles and a multitude of saints, virgins and angels. The Father took Margery by her hand spiritually, saying:

> I take þe, Margery, for my weddyd wyfe, for fayrar, for fowelar, for richar, for powerar, so þat þu be buxom & bonyr to do what I byd þe do. For, dowtyr, þer was neuyr childe so buxom to þe modyr as I xal be to þe boþe in wel & in wo, – to help þe and comfort þe. And þerto I make þe suyrte. (*BkMK*, ch.35, p.87, ll.18–23)

In this one can once again perceive the competitive element in Margery's *imitatio* of St Bridget. There is the wish to inherit, in some mysterious way, graces earlier accorded to St Bridget; but there is also a longing to be even more favoured, even more loved, by the Trinity than Birgitta was.

Many of the revelations that Margery received can be found in a slightly different version in St Bridget's work. The language used in *The Book of Margery Kempe* is more 'homely', and her approach and activities very often more matter-of-fact than Birgitta's, but they follow the same lines of thought. Margery was normally not content to listen and perceive; she busied herself with all sorts of activities required by the situation, and was herself thus often involved in the actual revelation.

Both women were allowed to watch the birth of Christ. St Bridget had this revelation in Bethlehem, and she saw a maiden, the fairest she ever saw, kneeling in prayer and rapture, give birth to her firstborn, and the contemplation that Mary was involved in ended only when she felt that she had given birth.[42] It was a painless and holy event. Margery, on the other hand, acted as Mary's handmaid, and procured all the things that were necessary. St Bridget also knew what Mary would need, but as she watched the Virgin herself had brought them all along. Margery, whose vision of the Nativity followed straight after a vision of Mary's birth and a vision of a visit to Elizabeth, the mother of St John the Baptist, plunged into activity:

> And þan went þe creatur forth wyth owyr Lady to Bedlem & purchasyd hir herborwe euery nyght wyth gret reuerens, & owyr Lady was receyued wyth glad cher. Also sche beggyd owyr Lady fayr whyte clothys & kerchys for to swathyn in hir Sone whan he wer born, and, whan Ihesu was born, sche ordeyned beddyng for owyr Lady to lyg in wyth hir blyssed Sone. And sythen sche beggyd mete for owyr Lady & hir blyssyd chyld. Aftyrward sche swathyd hym wyth byttyr teerys of compassyon, hauyng mend of þe scharp deth þat he schuld suffyr for þe lofe of synful men, seying to hym, 'Lord, I schal fare fayr wyth ȝow; I schal not byndyn ȝow soor. I pray ȝow beth not dysplesyd wyth me'. (*BkMK*, ch.6, p.19, ll.10–23)

The right to be present at childbirth and to assist when necessary was clearly considered by both St Bridget and Margery as something granted them by the very fact that they were women. Their difference in social status appears in their

---

[42] *LC*, Bk VII, ch.22.

different behaviour, but they both list the necessary clothing, and they both react to the necessity of handling the newly born child.[43]

The revelation of Christ's birth is also, in both books, followed by a revelation of the adoration of the three kings. The Virgin tells St Bridget about this event, and St Bridget's revelation seems to be told to her rather than shown:

> Þe modir saide to þe spouse þat when þe kinges come to þe stabill to wirshipe hir son, þan þe childes chere was mikill gladder than it was before. And scho had a grete likinge and kepid in hir hert these wordes. (*LC*, Bk VII, ch.25, p.487, ll.21–24)

Margery, in this situation, clearly watched the event, but she was not personally involved in what she watched:

> And aftyr on þe XII Day, whan iij kyngys comyn wyth her ȝyftys & worschepyd owyr Lord Ihesu Crist being in hys Moderys lappe, þis creatur, owyr Ladys hand-mayden, beheldyng all þe processe in contemplacyon, wept wondyr sor. And, whan sche saw þat þei wold take her leue to gon hom a-ȝen in-to her cuntre, sche myght not suffyre þat they schuld go fro þe presens of owyr Lord, and for wondyr þat þei wold gon awey sche cryed wondyr sore. (*BkMK*, ch.7, p.19, ll.24–32)

Both women experienced Christ's passion very powerfully, and obviously in a series of visions that cover the whole event. These visions were given to them at the very site, Mount Calvary. This is one of the few visions where St Bridget, too, records that she was weeping,[44] a feature of medieval sanctity that Margery acquired during this revelation and to which she then remained very prone for a long period of time. It has been suggested that Christ's death on the cross at it was described by St Bridget, with its abundance of realistic detail, influenced art in the late Middle Ages and inspired artists to similar expressions in painting.[45] It seems highly probable that Margery's description of her vision at Mount Calvary comprised details she remembered from St Bridget's book. Margery's account is also given in great detail:

> Sche had so very comtemplacyon in þe syght of hir sowle as yf Crist had hangyn befor hir bodily eye in hys manhode. & whan thorw dispensacyon of þe hy mercy of owyr Souereyn Savyowr Crist Ihesu it was grawntyd þis creatur to beholdyn so verily hys precyows tendyr body, alto-rent & toryn wyth scourgys, mor ful of wowndys than euyr was duffehows of holys, hangyng vp-on the cros wyth þe corown of thorn up-on hys heuyd, hys blysful handys, hys tendyr fete nayled to þe hard tre, þe reuerys of blood flowyng owt plentevowsly of euery membre, þe gresly & grevows wownde in hys precyows syde schedyng owt blood & watyr for hir lofe & hir saluacyon, þan sche fel down & cryed wyth lowde voys,
> . . . (*BkMK*, ch.28, p.70, ll.5–18)

---

[43] *LC*, Bk VII, ch.22 and *BkMK*, ch.6, p.19.
[44] *LC*, Bk VII, ch.16.
[45] See Rune Norberg, 'Birgittinsk Konst', *Kultur historiskt lexikon för nordisk medeltid*, ed. G. Kerkkonen, A. Maliniemi and C. A. Nordman, Helsingfors 1956, Vol I, pp.578–79.

It has also been suggested that Margery's handling of the material she wanted included in her book was influenced by St Bridget's book.[46] This suggestion refers in particular to the grouping of material together, and the rather haphazard listing of events. But many of the revelations contain elements that may have been inspired by Margery's listening to St Bridget's accounts. Even revelations concerning specific members of the clergy contain such common elements, particularly if the admonitions are of a more general kind. Both Birgitta and Margery looked upon themselves as messengers, sent by God to various people whose lives and behaviour were regarded as obstacles to a true respect for the Church and its teaching.

Mission

The awareness of a special mission to which both Birgitta and Margery testify can hardly be denied. Birgitta heard the Lord speak to her and give her a special mandate in the famous passage where he called her his bride and his mouthpiece (Extravagantes 47). But this was by no means the only instance; the mandate was repeated many times over in the first book of *Liber Celestis*. in the second chapter we find the following passage:

> I haue chosen þe and taken þe to mi spouse, for it pleses me and likes me to do so, and for I will shewe to þe mi preuai secretis. For þou arte mine be manere of right, foralsmikill as þou assigned thi will into mi handes at þe time of diinge of þi husband, eftir whose bereinge þou had grete þoght and made preiere how þou might be pore for me: and þou had in will and desire to forsake all þinge for me. And þan when þou had bi right made þe þus mine, it langed to me to puruai and ordeine for þe, wharefore I take þe to me as mi spouse vnto mi awen propir delite, eftir it is acordinge and seminge þat God haue his delite with a chaste saule. As þou knawes, it langes to a spouse to be honestli and semingli araied and to be redi when þe husband will make þe weddinge. (*LC*, Bk I, ch.2, p.8, ll.14–25)

Margery's mandate was stated in the form of often repeated phrases: 'she was commanded in her mind', 'she was commanded by our Lord' or 'our Lord told her'. Both Birgitta and Margery were assured that Christ had made them pure, and so fit, for their future work. To Bridget the Lord said:

> Þan arte þou made clene when, with forþinkinge þat þou hase sinned, þou calles to minde howe, in baptime, I clensid þe fra Adam sin, and howe oft eftirwarde, fro þou was fallen in sin, I suffird þe and supported. (*LC*, Bk I, ch.2, p.8, ll.25–28)

Margery was also given a similar assurance:

> . . . of vnworthy I make worthy, & of synful I make rytful. & so haue I mad þe worthy to me, onys louyd & euyrmor lovyd wyth me. (*BkMK*, ch.21, p.49, ll.25–28)

---

[46] Roger Ellis, *LC*, xiv.

Whether Birgitta and Margery still doubted this is hard to tell, but the Virgin was sent to both of them to teach them in this matter. She approached Birgitta in the following way:

> I am Mari that broght furth verrai God and man, þe whene of aungels. Mi son lufes þe of all his herte, and þarefore lufe þou him. Þou buse be araied with clothes of grete honeste, and I shall shewe þe what þai sall be. The bose haue a shirt, a cote, a mantill, a nowche in þi breste, a crown, and shone on þi fete. (*LC*, Bk I, ch.7, p.15, ll.26–30)

As we have seen Margery, too was told to ask for a white dress, a mantle and a ring: what Birgitta was ordered to wear in a spiritual sense, Margery thought of as factual things, which she actually started wearing. Mary was also sent to Margery to teach her, and there is great similarity in the phrasing:

> A-swythe aftyr þe Qwen of Mercy, Goddys Modyr, dalyed to þe sowle of þis creatur, seying, 'My derworthy dowtyr, I bryng þe sekyr tydyngys, wytnessyng my swet Sone Ihesu wyth alle awngelys & alle seyntys in Heuyn whech louyn þe ful hily. Dowtyr, I am thy modyr, þi lady, and thy maystres for to teche þe in all wyse how þu schalt plese God best'. (*BkMK*, ch.21, p.50, ll.4–11)

'Daughter' is the term of address both Christ and Mary used in both instances; St Bridget referred to herself as the 'spouse' whereas Margery normally used 'creature', and reserved 'bride' and 'spouse' for Christ and the Godhead, when either addressed her directly. The third-person account is common to both Birgitta and Margery.

The vocation proper is followed by specific missions in both books. It is well-known that Birgitta considered bringing the pope back to Rome as her main task, but she was also busy correcting clergy and royalty who were not living a pious life.

Birgitta's social background allowed her to move with easy in circles where pastoral care of the above kind was possible. Margery, with a bourgeois background, did not have similar access to these layers of society. It is therefore rather fascinating to find that, in the proem to her book, Margery defines part of her task in the following way:

> Þan went sche be þe byddyng of þe Holy Gost to many worshepful clerkys, bothe archebysshopys & bysshoppys, doctours of dyvynyte & bachelers also. Sche spak also wyth many ankrys and schewed hem hyr maner of leuyng & swech grace as þe Holy Gost of hys goodnesse wrowt in hyr mende and in hyr sowle as her wytt wold seruen hyr to expressyn it. (*BkMK*, p.3, ll.9–16)

The first chapters in St Bridget's first book in her *Liber Celestis* are full of passages that contain phrases and expressions that are almost literally included, or sometimes only slightly re-moulded in the repeated confirmations of Margery's mission:

> Ower Lord Ihesu Crist seyd to hir mende sche schuld abyden & languren in lofe. For I haue ordeyned þe to knele befor þe Trynyte for to prey for al þe world, for many hundryd thowsand sowlys schal be sauyd be þi prayers. And þerfor, dowtyr, aske what þow wylt, & I xal grawnt þe thyn askyng. (*BkMK*, ch.7, p.20, ll.8–14)

And just as Christ promised St Bridget to see to her purity and to keep her united to himself, he also told Margery that he would chastise her, but that he would also stand by her, and she need not be afraid:

> Owyr merciful Lord Cryst Ihesu, worshepd be hys name, seyd to hir, 'Drede þe not, dowtyr, I xal take veynglory fro þe. For þei þat woshep þe þei worshep me; þei þat despysyn þe þei despysen me, & I schal chastysen hem þerfor. I am in þe, and þow in me. And þei þat heryn þe þei heryn þe voys of God. Dowtyr, þer is no so synful man in erth leuyng, yf he wyl forsake hys synne & don aftyr þi cownsel, swech grace as þu behestyst hym I wyl confermyn for þi lofe. (*BkMK*, ch.10, p.22, l.36 – p.23, l.7)

The ultimate sign to both Birgitta and Margery that they stood solely in the service of God and belonged to him only seemed to be the wedding to the Godhead.[47] Once again the difference between the two women appears in the interpretation of this wedded state. To Birgitta it was obviously an entirely spiritual event, whereas Margery was more literally minded, and inclined to interpret it in terms of her matrimonial experience.

Concluding Reflections

> Margery was well acquainted with housewives and mothers, business- and tradeswomen, nuns and anchoresses, but it is improbable that she knew anyone like herself.[48]

Obviously she learnt about many holy women, and at least one who seemed very close to her in experience, yet distanced enough to serve as an excellent model in most respects. *Imitatio* had a function in the Middle Ages that we tend to forget about too often: that of providing examples, models for devotion, set by people who were acknowledged as holy, or even as saints. Among the number of models Margery could choose from, St Bridget fulfilled even the last of these qualifications, and the life she led must have seemed most attractive. She was in every respect worthy of Margery's highest aspirations.

There seems to be enough internal evidence to prove that St Bridget was the most important model for Margery Kempe. Margery's repeated mention of St Bridget indicates her sustained interest in this particular saint. St Bridget provided her with many things to imitate: there was the matrimony – that caused Margery so much anxiety – transformed into a religious life, and there was the path to take in that transformation clearly delineated. There was also the model for a religious life that suited Margery. She had travelled much in England together with her husband, but Birgitta set the example for pilgrimages to the far away holy sites that must have had a very special appeal for Margery.

---

[47] *LC*, Bk I, ch.20 and *BkMK*, ch.35.
[48] Clarissa W. Atkinson, *op.cit.*, p.159.

Of prime importance for all this are the facts that St Bridget's book was available in English during Margery's life since she knew no Latin, and that there was a steadily growing usage of reading aloud pious books to pious women. Margery mentions a number of priests and friars who were clearly willing to do her that service. Moreover, there were linguistic qualities in St Bridget's book that made it more easily accessible to a woman who was not well versed in theology when she first felt the vocation to a different life. Barbara Obrist formulates this aspect in the following way:

> Bridget's writings are not at all marked by speculative considerations nor is her style full of mystical terminology. Rhetorical sophistication is absent, the short sentences sometimes approach spoken language, and her revelations are characterized by simplicity and directness. In both form and content, her revelations are more like the popular literature of this time. Christ and Mary address Bridget directtly and familiarly, as if to an equal, when they speak of moral problems or give directives.[49]

Not only did St Bridget's book appeal to Margery more than most things she heard people read, but when she dictated her own book, Birgitta seems once again to have been her model, so much so that the above characterization of Birgitta's style might be applied to Margery's book virtually unchanged.

Birgitta has been acclaimed as one of the Swedish writers who influenced contemporary life more than most, and gained fame far beyond the borders of her native country. She must have been a writer both by talent and temperament.[50] It is easy to register that Margery was an extremely good story-teller, and by the time she decided to have her own visions written down, she most certainly knew St Bridget's book well enough to adapt a similar linguistic approach. Throughout both books the reader feels that the author is in command: no scribe has been able to eradicate that special personal touch.

And last but not least, St Bridget was already acknowledge as a saint and so was more suitable than most as a model for a holy life, no matter how unconventional the forms of its realization were. The sad thing was that only a small section of Margery's book was printed and circulated in pious groups among her late contemporaries. Her work fell into oblivion for almost five hundred years, which deprived her of even the slightest possibility to achieve the fame and influence she might have dreamed of.

[49] 'The Swedish Visionary Saint Bridget', *Medieval Women Writers*, ed. Katharina M. Wilson, Athens Georgia, 1984, pp.236–237.
[50] Hans Aili, 'Heliga Birgitta av Vadstena', *Röster från svensk medeltid*, ed. Hans Aili, Olle Ferm and Helmer Gustavsson, Gothenburg 1991, p.120.

TRANSCENDENCE IN DEATH:
A HEIDEGGERIAN APPROACH TO
VIA NEGATIVA IN
THE CLOUD OF UNKNOWING

SONYA SIKKA

I SHOULD EXPLAIN at the outset that the way in which this paper addresses itself to *The Cloud of Unknowing* arises out of a concern with this text, not so much as a representative of a species of English literature, or of a strand in the tradition of English spirituality, but as an example of a certain way of thinking about God, the way, namely, of negation. The manner in which what is thought in a text approaches any person who thinks about that text is, of course, determined by the manner in which he or she approaches it, and my own approach involves an attempt to understand, in the manner appropriate to philosophy, the account given in *The Cloud* of the path to the transcendent God. By 'transcendent God', I mean the God that is understood as other to whatever is called 'the world', so that 'the world' must in some way, and in some sense, be negated in thought in order to think this Other.

The word 'think' may ring strangely in this context, and the notion that *The Cloud* embodies a way of thinking about the Other to the world by 'thinking away' the world might seem to miss the radicality and completeness of the kind of negation, and concentration, which this text calls for. However, the word 'thinking' is not here intended to mean the activity of one faculty, for instance the 'intellect', over and against a number of others, for instance, 'will' and 'memory', and it is certainly not being used in the sense of 'ratiocination'. Rather, what I intend to signify by this word is something similar to Heidegger's notion of *Denken* as *Gedanc*, a movement and concentration of the whole of the disposition. Thinking, understood in this way, is a kind of devotion, a constant and concentrated remaining with something; it is intention as the inclination of the innermost space and ground of the heart.[1] It is, perhaps, what the author of *The Cloud of Unknowing* means, sometimes, by 'love'.

With this in mind, the following paper will approach the 'thinking' of *The Cloud* through the thought of Martin Heidegger. The association of certain elements in Heidegger's thought with negative theology is by no means new. It is commonly recognized that there is some connection between the way in which the *via negativa* approaches the understanding and definition of God, and Heidegger's attempt to think of 'Being' through the 'ontico-ontological

---

[1] See *Was heißt Denken?* Tübingen, 1954, Section II, Lectures 3 and 4.

179

difference', the difference between Being (*das Sein*) and beings (*das Seiende*), and it is significant that, for Heidegger, when Being is thought through this difference, it also, and first, appears as 'Nothing' (*das Nichts*). In this case, Heidegger's way of thinking about Being can be seen as similar to what he describes as Nietzsche's way of thinking about the whole of the world (*das Weltganze*) a negative theology, but without the Christian God.[2]

However, this paper will, for the most part, be looking at the negative way through a different aspect of Heidegger's thought. It will examine *via negativa* in *The Cloud of Unknowing*, not primarily through Heidegger's notion of *Differenz* but mainly through his analysis, in *Being and Time*, of the structure of *Dasein* as Being-in-the-world, and through some of his observations, also in *Being and Time*, on the issue of death. I will begin by giving a brief sketch of Heidegger's discussions on these points, and will then proceed, within the terms of these discussions, to an analysis of *The Cloud* itself. In the course of this latter analysis, some further elements of Heidegger's thought, taken from *What is Called Thinking?* (the same text in which he develops the notion of thinking as *Gedanc*), will also be introduced. These are brought into the discussion as a natural development from, and extension of, some features of the analysis of *Dasein* in *Being and Time*.

1

The fundamental task of Heidegger's work, *Being and Time*, is, as he says, 'the concrete working out of the question concerning the meaning of Being'.[3] The phenomenological analysis of *Dasein* – which can be translated, simply, as 'human existence' or, more literally, as 'Being-there' – in *Being and Time* is ordered towards this end. Heidegger considers such an analysis to be a necessary preparation for the analysis of Being, in that, according to him, in order to work out the meaning of Being, it is first necessary to lay bare the nature, the *Being*, of that entity for which, and with which, Being is there.

One result of Heidegger's analysis of the Being of *Dasein* is the determination of *In-der-Welt-sein*, 'Being-in-the-world' as constitutive of that Being. For Heidegger, *Dasein* is not an isolated substance or subject which sometimes goes out of itself to 'external things', the totality which constitutes 'the world', but reveals itself as Being-in-the-world. This means that *Dasein* is not first what it is, and then sometimes also in the world; rather, Being-in-the-world is a necessary and *a priori* state of the Being of *Dasein* (SZ, 54).

[2] *Sein und Zeit*, 16th edition, Tübingen, 1986, p.1. All future references to this text will be given in brackets in the body of the essay, with the title abbreviated as SZ. The translations into English are ultimately my own, but are very much indebted to the Macquarrie/Robinson translation, Oxford, 1962.

[3] *Nietzsches metaphysische Grundstellung im abendländischen Denken: Die ewige Wiederkehr des Gleichen*, Gesamtausgabe, Band 44, Frankfurt, 1986, p.100.

Being-in-the-world is, Heidegger says, a unitary phenomenon, but one whose structure can nonetheless be divided into a number of constituent items. Out of the three items which he mentions, I will examine only two: first, 'Being-in', and, second, 'the world' (SZ, 53).

With respect to Being-in, if it is said that *Dasein* is always and essentially *in* the world, the meaning of this 'in' is not to be interpreted after the manner of Being of entities other than *Dasein*, i.e. according to the manner of Being of things within the world, like water or a glass. *Dasein* is not said to be 'in' the world as water is said to be 'in' a glass; rather, *Dasein*'s Being-in consists, in this context, of its being near and by (*bei*), its being absorbed and wrapped up in (*Aufgehen in*), the world. In other words, although *Dasein* can, of course, be regarded as a thing within the world, and can then be viewed as having the kind of spatial relationships which things within the world have to each other, when regarded with respect to its ownmost kind of Being, *Dasein*'s being in the world consists in its encountering and 'touching' entities within the world in a way in which things that are merely present-at-hand never can (SZ, 53–5). The manner of this touching is rooted in 'concern' (*Besorgen*); every way of Being-in has concern as its kind of Being (SZ, 57).

Knowledge of the world presupposes concernful Being-in. Knowing is a 'founded' mode of *Dasein*'s Being. It is founded in *Dasein*'s already being in the world, in the sense of already being by the world in concern. In the first instance, 'this Being-already-by is not merely a fixed staring at something that is purely present-at-hand. Being-in-the-world, as concern, is *taken with* (*benommen von*) the world with which it is concerned' (SZ, 61). In the form of Being-in in which *Dasein* sets its sights towards something as purely present-at-hand so as to secure it for knowledge, it steps back from the kind of everyday concernful involvement in which it manipulates and ulilizes things within the world (SZ, 61). Thus, *Dasein* does not first bring itself into the world through such knowing. Rather, the pure regarding in which *Dasein* holds itself back from a particular kind of involvement is founded in its *prior* Being-in-the-world (SZ, 62). Moreover, as a mode of Being-in, and so, of Being *towards*, things encountered within the world, even the pure regarding of this form of knowing must still be, in some sense, concernful.

To move now to the second constituent item of Being-in-the-world to be examined here, 'the world', Heidegger points out that 'world', considered as a component of Being-in-the-world, cannot signify any aggregate of entities – for instance, the totality of things within the world – but must be considered as an essential element of *Dasein*'s own Being. No consideration of 'innerworldly' entities can arrive at the Being of the world as such, since the world as such is presupposed in any such consideration. The Being of the world, that is, the 'worldliness' or 'worldhood' (*Weltlichkeit*), of the world is not a category of entities, but is an *existentiale*. This means that, with respect to its fundamental Being, ' "world" is not a determination of those entities which Dasein essentially is *not*, but a characteristic of Dasein itself' (SZ, 64). 'Worldly' then signifies a kind of Being belonging to *Dasein*, and not to the innerworldly entities towards which *Dasein*, as Being-in-the-world, comports itself (SZ, 65).

However, in order to gain some access to the phenomenon of world, Heidegger does begin by examining the Being of those entities which *Dasein* discovers as closest to it in its everyday concernful Being-in-the-world. These entities, he finds, are discovered as 'ready-to-hand' (*zuhanden*). What they essentially are is 'equipment', in that they are constituted as what they are in being assigned to a concernful project on the part of *Dasein*. Thus, the Being of such things resides in this assignation, in the networks of 'in-order-to' and 'for-the-sake-of' which constitute possibilities of *Dasein*'s own Being. Heidegger gives the simple example of a hammer, which cannot possibly be seen as a hammer, and understood as such, without reference to that for which it is employed, the task to which it is assigned or directed (SZ, 66-9).

The Being of entities encountered in everyday Being-in-the-world consists, then, in their involvement in a context of relations or assignments rooted, ultimately, in *Dasein*'s concern for its own existence. When *Dasein* understands such a context of relations, it does so in having referred or assigned itself to an 'in-order-to', in terms of a potentiality-for-Being, for the sake of which it itself is (SZ, 86). And 'the structure of that to which [*woraufhin*] Dasein assigns itself is what makes up the *worldhood* of the world' (SZ, 87). To put this differently, the things of everyday Being-in-the-world, the things of 'the world', are made present, that is, are encountered by *Dasein*, through *Dasein*'s concernful Being-in, where what *Dasein* is concerned about is its own potentiality-for-Being. The potentiality-for-Being which *Dasein* must already understand, and project, in order for things to be so presented to it, makes up the worldhood of the world. Heidegger contrasts this notion of world with Descartes' notion of world as *res extensa*, 'extended thing' (SZ, 92ff).

Because the projection of a for-the-sake-of is essentially an anticipating, and, as such, a kind of being in the future, *Dasein* in such projection, can be considered as being 'ahead' of itself. The structural whole of *Dasein*'s Being can then be defined as: 'ahead-of-itself-Being-already-in-(the-world) as Being-by (entities encountered within-the-world)' (SZ, 192). Heidegger calls this kind of Being *care* (Sorge). *Dasein*, as Being-in-the-world, is essentially care.

Care is the unity of the structure of *Dasein* as a being for which its own Being is an issue. The temporality and spatiality of *Dasein*, and so, in a derivative fashion, of innerworldly entitles, since their Being is grounded in that of *Dasein*, is determined by the structure of *Dasein*'s Being as care.

Moreover, it is because the structure of care makes *Dasein* a being that can relate itself to its own Being so as to be responsible for it that *Dasein* can be anything like 'guilty'. And Being-guilty is an essential constituent of *Dasein* as potentiality-for Being, and thus, as care. Heidegger defines Being-guilty not as any kind of 'lacking' but as 'Being-the-ground for a Being which has been determined by a "not" (*Nicht*)' (SZ, 283). *Dasein*'s Being is determined by a 'not' in that it has been 'thrown' into existence, where existence means being responsible for its own Being. This does not mean that it is responsible for its having come into Being as the entity which it is, an entity responsible for itself; on the contrary, *Dasein* can never determine its Being 'from the ground up', and in this lies the 'not', the negativity, of its past (SZ, 284). To *Dasein* also belongs a futural negativity, in that *Dasein* never 'has' achieved itself, but is always in the process of doing so, is always towards itself, is always potentiality-for-Being. Because *Dasein* is what it is only as potentiality-for-Being, such that the 'ahead-of-itself', the Being towards itself in terms of futural possibilities, is a constitutive element of its Being, and because it has not, and cannot, determine its Being from the ground up, Being-guilty belongs to the ontological constitution, and therefore to the definition, of *Dasein*. '*Dasein as such is guilty*' (SZ, 285).

Finally, on the issue of death, there are two features of Heidegger's analysis to which I would like to draw attention. The first is the fact that Heidegger's discussion of death in *Being and Time* is connected with the problem of *Dasein*'s 'wholeness' (*Gänze*). This is the problem of experiencing *Dasein* as a whole, and of getting that whole into the grasp of the understanding. One way in which wholeness can be conceived is as the ending of potentiality, a state in which there is nothing 'outstanding', nothing yet to be achieved. But if the Being of *Dasein*, as Being-in-the-world, is care, and if a constitutive element of that element of that Being is being ahead-of-itself towards possibilities of Being, then a *Dasein* with no more potentiality-for-Being is no longer *Dasein*, no longer Being-in-the-world (SZ, 236). When *Dasein* reached its wholeness in death, where its possibilities of Being come to an end, it is, of course, precisely no longer Being-in-the-world. It goes out of the world, where world is to be understood in terms of those contexts of relations rooted in *Dasein*'s potentiality-for-Being, and not as a totality of things.

This leads directly to the second point to be addressed on this issue, which is that, in its transition to no-longer-Being-there (*Nichtmehrdasein*) in death, *Dasein* necessarily loses the possibility of experiencing its own death, for *Dasein* qua *Dasein* is then no longer *there* to experience anything at all. It is true that *Dasein* experiences the death of others, but the experience of the other's transition from *Dasein* to no-longer-*Dasein*, to something which, in a way, is merely present-at-hand like other present-at-hand entities within the world, is clearly no substitute for the experience of death as a possibility of *Dasein*'s ownmost, a possibility of *my* own, existence (SZ, 237-8). For this reason, Heidegger eventually characterizes *Dasein*'s experience of its own death as a *Being towards* the end (SZ, 251). Death, as the uttermost non-relational possibility of *Dasein*'s existence, the possibility of no more Being-in-the-world, is not an event which *Dasein*, as *Dasein*, ever undergoes. It is, rather, the ever possible, never actual, extreme possibility towards which *Dasein* exists.

2

Passing now to *The Cloud of Unknowing*, an essential element of the 'work', the 'traueyle', of which this text speaks is, of course, the 'tredying down' of all 'creatures' under 'þe cloude of forʒetyng'. Indeed, at one point, the author maintains that *all* of this 'trauayle' consists 'in tredying doun of þe mynde of all þe creatures þat euer God maad, & in holdying of hem vnder þe cloude of forʒetyng named before'.[4] In saying this, he is not claiming that the whole of the process of contemplation being described consists in forgetting all 'þat euer God maad'. Rather, the claim put forward in these lines is that 'forgetting' constitutes the whole of a human being's own work within contemplation, in that it is the only part of the process which lies, to some extent, within a person's own power. Given this claim, the work of forgetting would also have to be the only part of contemplation to which a person could appropriately be exhorted.

This aspect of the contemplative process set forth in *The Cloud* can be divided, for the same of analysis, into two components: (1) the process of forgetting itself, and (2) the 'object' of forgetting, that which is to be forgotten in the process. With respect to the first of these components, the immediate response of a twentieth-century reader to the word 'forgetting' might well be the conception of an erasure within a particular faculty of the mind, namely, memory, as the faculty of recording and recalling. In this case, to forget means to delete some item of cognitive content, whether empirical, or rational, which has been impressed upon, and preserved within, this primarily passive, and primarily intellectual, faculty of reception and recall.

However, insofar as, for the author of *The Cloud*, forgetting is associated with 'tredying doun of þe mynde of', it does not signify a deletion within a retentive faculty, but is, rather, a not allowing to come to presence and a forcing out of presence, a not having present and not being in the presence of. If this negation of presence is analyzed in terms of Heidegger's conception of *Gedanc*, it means an annihilating, a negating, within thought, where thought is the inclination of the whole of the disposition towards something. In fact, in the passages from *What is Called Thinking?* referred to earlier, where Heidegger reflects upon thought as *Gedanc*, he explicitly associates it with memory as remembrance, and he considers memory, in its origin, as a keeping in mind in the sense of having present.

With respect to what is to be forgotten in the process of forgetting set forth in *The Cloud*, one point to be made is that that which is to be forgotten is that which, most of the time, is remembered, that which generally is kept in mind, and which spontaneously, and forcefully, comes to mind. This is obviously

---

[4] *The Cloud of Unknowing and Related Treatises*, ed. Phyllis Hodgson, Salzburg, 1982, p.34. All future references to this text will be given in brackets in the body of the essay, with the title abbreviated as *C*.

implicit in the simple fact that the remembrance is effortless and the forgetting is hard. What must be forgotten, then, is that of which the mind is naturally inclined to think. For the author of *The Cloud*, the things with which the mind is generally concerned and which must be forgotten are 'creatures'. A 'creature' is, in this context, any entity, whether 'goostly' or 'bodely' – spiritual or material – which can be considered as 'maad'. It is then any being which is thought of as having once not been and having been brought into existence. It is, in short, any being other than the one necessary being, God.

For Heidegger, the presence to *Dasein* of any such being, is rooted, as has been said, in the structure of its Being as care. When *Dasein* recalls an innerworldly being in its absence, what it recalls is then not something which it once simply observed and recorded, but something towards which it *is*. The forgetting of something would then be the negation of being with it and towards it in concern. It would mean the negation of its presence as a result of its detachment from any involvement in the Being of *Dasein* as care. That *Dasein* inclines towards the recollective presence, the bringing and keeping of mind, of innerworldly beings is a function of its being the kind of being which, as care, it is, a being for which its own Being is an issue.

The following two quotations from *The Cloud* are relevant in this context:

> . . . mynde or þinkyng of any creature þat euer God maad, or of any of þeire dedes ouþer, it is a maner of goostly liȝt; for þe iȝe of þi soule is openid on it & euen ficchid þerapon, as þe iȝe of a schoter is apon þe prik þat he schoteþ to. (C, ch.5, pp.13–14, ll.40–1)

> . . . ȝif þis sodein sterying or þouȝt be not smetyn sone doun, as fast for freelte þi fleschly herte is streynid þerby, wiþ sum maner of likyng ȝif it be a þing þat pleseþ þee or haþ plesid þee bifore, or elles wiþ sum maner of gruching ȝif it be a þing þat þee þink greueþ þee or haþ greued þee before. (C, ch.10, pp.19–20, ll.36–1)

The first of these quotations makes it clear that the author of *The Cloud* conceives 'mynde or þinking' as being concentrated upon something, as being fixed on something intended. In *What is Called Thinking?* Heidegger conceives of remembrance as intention in a similar way, but notes that what is remembered in the intention which recalls is what the heart holds in presence.[5] What is present, and the way in which it is present, is then still, as in *Being and Time*, a function of care. If this is applied to the first of the above statements from *The Cloud*, then it needs to be added that when the 'eye of the soul' is fixed on any 'creature', that vision is, in an *a priori* and largely implicit fashion, determined out of the structure of care. What is seen necessarily has an involvement in that structure, and the structure itself is, it must be remembered, the structure of the Being of *Dasein*.

The involvement of what is presented in the structure of care as the Being of *Dasein* is evident in an explicit, and fairly crude, way in the second quotation from *The Cloud* cited above. The fact that the thought of a thing almost

---

5 *Was heißt Denken?*, *op.cit.*, p.93.

immediately stirs the 'fleschly herte', the seat of passion, to appetition or aversion is a necessary result of the fact that the thing has been, and is, encountered from care and is not, nor has ever been, the object of 'mere' observation.

For Heidegger, it is not only things which please and displease in an obvious fashion that are involved in the structure of care, and Heidegger does not mean to reduce all that is encountered to the realm of such things. Rather, as has been indicated, he suggests that any being which is encountered in any way whatsoever is a being which *Dasein* is near or by, and as such, it is necessarily involved in one mode or another of the Being of *Dasein* as care. If, in the way of negation put forward in *The Cloud*, what is negated is all such beings, in the sense that all creatures and 'also alle þe werkes & þe condiciouns of þe same creatures' (C, ch.5, p.13, 1.33) are put out of 'mynde' (where having them in mind means, precisely, being near them and by them, having 'wetyng and felyng' of them), then what is negated is a constitutive element of the Being of *Dasein*. What is negated in that forgetting of creatures '& þe werkes of hem, so þat þi þouȝt ne þi desire be not directe ne streche to any of hem, neiþer in general ne in special' (C, ch.3, p.9, ll.16–17) is, in fact, the 'in-the-world' component of *Dasein* as Being-in-the-world. And with such a negation, the structure of care is destroyed.

The idea that what is encountered within the world, in the sense of being present to *Dasein*, is dependent for its Being upon the Being of *Dasein* can also be used to analyse the following passage from *The Cloud*:

> . . . & þerfore breek doun alle weetyng & felyng of alle maner of creatures; bot most besily of þiself. For on þe wetying & þe felyng of þiself hangiþ wetyng & felyng of alle oþer creatures; for in rewarde of it, alle oþer creatures ben liȝtly forȝetyn. For, & þou wil besily set þee to þe preof, þou schalt fynde, when þou hast forȝetyn alle oþer creatures & alle þeire werkes, ȝe, & þerto alle þin owne werkes, þat þu schal leve ȝit after, bitwix þee & þi God, a nakid weting & a felyng of þin owne beyng; þe whiche wetyng & felyng behouiþ alweis be distroied, er þe tyme be þat þou fele soþfastly þe perfeccyon of þis werk.   (C, ch.43, pp.45–6, ll.38–8)

The sense that the apprehension of all that is other to the self is contingent upon the prior apprehension of the self is certainly amenable to more than one form of philosophical analysis. Kant's notion of 'pure apperception', as the unity of consciousness demanded by the fact that, in order for there to be objects of thought, the 'I think' must be capable of accompanying all representations, naturally comes to mind here. If the above passage is analysed from a Heideggerian rather than a Kantian perspective, however, then what it articulates is rooted in the fact that the Being of everything *Dasein* encounters as within the world is grounded, ultimately, in its own Being as care, which is to say, in itself as a being for which its own Being is an issue. The negation of its own Being as care, the negation of 'þe wetyng & þe felyng of þiself', would then simultaneously constitute a negation of the Being of all other beings, of 'creatures' – but not vice versa, in that the negation of the Being of all other beings could still leave the 'wetyng and felyng' of the Being in which the Being of those beings is grounded, namely, the Being of *Dasein*.

Moreover, the Heideggerian analysis of the Being of *Dasein* also offers a possible perspective upon what *The Cloud* elsewhere suggests about the 'nakid wetyng & felyng of þin owne beyng'. For the author of *The Cloud*, the encounter with the bare self is not experienced as an encounter with any pure ego, empirical or transcendental, or, for that matter, with any thinking substance, but, primarily, as an encounter with 'synne'. A person can be left with the bare self without any remembrance of particular sins, 'but ȝit hym þink þat it is synne a lumpe, he wote neuer what, none oþer þing þan hymself' (C, ch.69, p.69, ll.5–6). It was noted that, for Heidegger, the Being of *Dasein* is essentially and ineradicably Being-guilty. Being-guilty is a necessary, and not a contingent, feature of *Dasein*, as a being for which its own Being is an issue in such a way that it is responsible for that Being. Being-guilty is rooted in *Dasein*'s selfhood as thrown potentiality-for-Being; without it, *Dasein* is not care, is not potentiality-for-Being, is not, in short, *Dasein*.

Now, 'synne', for the *Cloud*-author is what stands between the self and God: '& þou haddest God, þen schuldest þou lacke synne, & miȝtest þou lacke synne, þen schuldest þou haue God' (C, ch.40, p.44, ll.13–14). If sin is understood as being rooted, existentially, in Being-guilty (where this does not mean that the Christian notion of sin is exhausted by the existential notion of Being-guilty), then it could be said that *Dasein*'s structure as potentiality-for-Being must necessarily 'stand between' itself, that is to say, its own mode of Being, and what is conceived as the Being of God. This assumes that God is understood as 'perfect' Being, and, by consequence, as having no potentiality-for-Being because there is nothing 'more' or 'else' for such Being to be. It also assumes that the structure of potentiality-for-Being founds a variety of derivative 'guilty' existential phenomena, such as 'not yet being' and 'not having been what could, and should, have been'.

Given that the Being of *Dasein*, as care, is essentially potentiality-for-Being, and given that Being-guilty is ineradicably bound up with this kind of Being, the surpassing of Being-guilty would have to mean, for *Dasein*, the surpassing of itself. For the author of *The Cloud*, the surpassing of sin, as that which stands between the self and God is also necessarily a surpassing of a person's own 'beyng' since that being is wholly bound up with sin. Thus, he says:

> . . . no wonder þof þou loþe & hate for to þink on þiself, when þou schalt alweis fele synne a foule stynkyng lumpe, þou wost neuer what, bitwix þee & þi God: þe whiche lumpe is none oþer þing þan þiself. For þee schal þink it onyd & congelid wiþ þe substaunce of þi beyng, ȝe, as it were wiþoutyn departyng. (C, ch.43, p.45, ll.32–37)

God cannot be reached except in the surpassing of sin, but sin cannot be 'departed' from the 'beyng' of the self. Therefore, it is the very 'beyng' of the self which must be surpassed in order to reach God. The 'stronge & deep goostly sorow' which the *Cloud*-author sees as bringing about an 'abilness to resseyue' the grace which can 'distroie þis nakid wetyng & felyng of þin owen beyng' is then understandably a sorrow felt by someone 'þat wote & feliþ not onli what he is, bot þat he is' (C, ch.44, p.46, ll.15–17 & 26). Interpreted existentially, the Being of the self in both its 'what' and its 'that', and in relation to the concept of the Being of God, is now understood not as a finite substance standing in relation to an infinite substance, but as a potentiality-for-Being standing in relation to, in the sense of 'relating itself to', a mode of Being, or, rather, a modeless Being, in which there is no potentiality. That the Being of God is conceived of as not having any potentiality does not, of course, mean that it is represented as having no *potentia*, no potency or power with respect to creatures, but that, with respect to the achievement of itself, it is thought to have no potential, in that there is nothing which it either wills to be, needs to be, or should be, and yet is not.

The full accomplishment of the *via negativa* described in *The Cloud* as a path to God means, then, the complete negation of creatures and self, and this is what is longed for in the 'goostly sorow'. Such a negation is not, of course, equivalent to a literal destruction, but is a forgetting in the sense of a loss of the 'wetyng & felyng' of, a loss of the 'mynde' of. As the author says:

> . . . & ȝit in al þis sorow he [i.e. the contemplative] desireþ not to vnbe, for þat were deuelles woodnes & despite vnto God. But hym listiþ riȝt wel be; & he meniþ ful hertly þankyng to God for þe worþiness & þe ȝift of his beyng, þof al þat he desire vnsesingly for to lakke þe wetyng & þe felyng of his beyng. (C, ch.44, p.47, ll.2–6)

In Heideggerian terms, such a 'lakke' would amount to the negation of the Being, in the sense of presence, of innerworldly beings, and of the Being in which that Being is grounded, i.e. Being-there, *Da-sein*. It would mean the negation of the Being of the *Da* of *Dasein*, the 'there' of 'Being-there', which would also be the negation of the 'in-the-world' of 'Being-in-the-world'. The negation of the Being of the *Da* in *Dasein*, which is simultaneously the negation of the 'worldly' Being of *Dasein*, i.e. of the Being of *Dasein* as Being-in-the-world, is, however, the end of *Dasein* as *Dasein*. It is death. The line of reasoning carried through here can be expressed in the following way:

$$\text{Dasein (Being-there)} = \text{Being-in-the-world (} \textit{In-der-Welt-sein} \text{)}$$
$$\text{Since Being} = \text{Being, it follows that}$$
$$\text{Da (there)} = \text{in-the-world}$$

If the *via negativa* is found to be the negation of all that constitutes the 'there', the *Da* of *Dasein*, then it can be expressed as:

$$- \textit{Da}, \text{ which equals } \text{-in-the-world}$$

The 'addition' of *via negativa* to *Dasein* then means:

$$\text{Dasein} = \text{Being-in-the-world}$$
$$+ \textit{ via negativa} = - \underline{\textit{Da}} = \underline{\text{-in-the-world}}$$
$$\text{leaves sein} = \text{Being}$$

What is 'left' here is Being, but it is Being which is not *there*, which is to say, not in the world. For *Dasein*, this is death, conceived existentially. The metaphor of a 'mystical death', when applied to this instance, may then not be all that metaphoric. Only if the death of others, their passage from *Dasein* to presence-at-hand, is taken as a primary model for death does a mystical death of this sort appear as not 'real' death. To be sure, there are certain 'physical' phenomena associated with death, such as the cessation of biological processes and the fact that people do not 'return' from it. But with respect to death as a feature of *Dasein*'s existence, that existence which is always *mine*, a radical detachment of Being from world like the one which *The Cloud* aims for must yield the experience precisely of that one utterly non-relational possibility which *Dasein* as *Dasein* can never experience.

What, though, does it mean to say that what is left is not *Dasein*, but Being which is not 'there'? Given Heidegger's analysis, one thing which it would have to mean is the loss of temporality and spatiality, for these are grounded in the *Da* of *Dasein* as care. Indeed, the author of *The Cloud* says, 'tyme, steede, & body, þees þre schuld be forʒeten in alle goostly worching' (C, ch.59, pp.61–62, ll.38–1), and that forgetting is consummated in the 'noʒwhere' and nouʒt' found, initially, with the loss of creatures and self. Being which is not there, moreover, would have to be Being which is in no way modified or 'localized', Being which is in no way determinate, because it stands in no relation to any entity. It would be Being considered in itself, as wholly other to the world, but the thought of Being considered in this way yields, at least in the first instance, Nothing. And Nothing is just what the *Cloud*-author maintains is first encountered when creatures and self are forgotten. The perfection of the cloud of forgetting leads to the cloud of unknowing, which is a 'derkness' in the sense of 'a lackyng of knowyng, as alle þat þing þat þou knowest not, or elles þat þou hast forʒetyn, it is derk to þee, for þou seest it not wiþ þi goostly iʒe' (C, ch.4, p.13, ll.18–20).

It obviously cannot be said, though, that the loss of creatures and self which results in the confrontation with, or immersion in, 'nouʒt' in the form of the cloud or darkness of unknowing, is the loss of *all* potentiality-for-Being, and so the complete loss of the essence of *Dasein*. It then cannot be, at this point, a loss of all determinate, limited Being. There is, after all, still intention here, still incompleteness and striving, still *care*. The cloud of unknowing is experienced as standing between the self and God, the ultimate object of its desire and want, 'þe souerein desirable & . . . heiʒest wilnable þing' (C, ch.4, p.10, ll.20–21). If this 'þing' is found in the negation of all that would seem to make up the worldhood of the world, in that it is found in the forgetting of the 'beyng' of the self, it is nonetheless, as the ultimate object of the will, the absolute limit of *Dasein*'s own potentiality-for-Being. It is then a unique and strange sort of 'object', though, for it is unrepresentable; it is nothing in the world. The will wills, but what it wills, it knows not. And it is encouraged by the author of *The Cloud* to will precisely this that it knows not, this that it cannot 'þink', meant here in the sense of represent to itself: '& smyte apon þat þicke cloude of

vnknowyng wiþ a scharp darte of longing loue, & go not þens for þing þat
befalleþ' (C, ch.6, p.14, ll.29–30).

What the contemplative wills, and wills to 'þink' here, where 'to think' is now
meant in the sense of 'to have present and be in the presence of', is 'þe nakid
beyng' (C, ch.3, p.14, l.11), 'þe self substaunce' (C, ch.67, p.67, l.5) of God,
and the will itself is as bare and as pure as what it wills; it is 'a nakid entente
directe vnto God for himself' (C, ch.24, p.32, ll.23–24). It is an 'entente' which
has been drawn away from all 'created' things, and directed towards the Other to
all such things. That is not to say that this withdrawal and redirection is itself
supposed to be a function of the will's own power. Strictly speaking, the work
that accomplishes this unshaping and reshaping, this re-formation, of the will is
itself encountered as 'no wil, ne no desyre, bot a þing þou wost neuer what, þat
steriþ þee to wilne & desire þou wost neuer what' (C, ch.34, p.38, ll.36–37).
This work is thought to be initiated and sustained not by the will itself, but by the
Other which it seeks, and which moves it to seek nothing other than Itself.

The ultimate aim of this seeking, which can be achieved only with the aid of
that which is sought, is 'to be knit to God in spirite, & in oneheed of loue &
acordaunce of wile' (C, ch.8, p.17, ll.40–41). In the time in which such a
'oneheed' is accomplished, according to *The Cloud*, 'it may be seide in maner
þat . . . God & þou ben not two but one in spirit – insomoche þat þou or anoþer
for soche onheed þat feleþ þe perfeccion of þis werk may soþfastly, bi witnes of
Scripture, be clepid a God' (C, ch.67, p.67, ll.11–14). Presumably, what being
'one in spirit' means here is having no 'wetyng & felyng', no 'mynde', of
anything but 'þe nakid beyng' of God. That such a condition must be one in
which that 'nakid beyng' is, in some sense, comprehended, does not contradict
the statement that 'of God himself can no man þinke' (C, ch.6, p.14, l.20). In
the first place, there is, in this condition, no 'thinking', if thinking means
representing and reasoning. What is supposed to be comprehended here could
never be an object of thinking conceived in this way. In the second place, the
comprehension achieved at this point is accomplished, it is claimed, not by the
soul's own power, but by 'reformyng grace', through which the soul 'is mad
sufficient at þe fulle to comprehende al him by loue, þe which is
incomprehensible to alle create knowable miзt' (C, ch.4, p.10, ll.27–28). The
'sorow' which 'clensiþ þe soule, not onlyof synne, bot also of peyne þat he haþ
deseruid for synne', and thereby 'cleanses' it of all that separates it from God,
cannot yet bring about 'oneheed' with God. It only 'makiþ a soule abil to
resseive þat ioye, þe whiche reuip fro a man alle wetyng & felyng of his beyng'
(C, ch.44, p.46, ll.29–32), where this loss of the sense of one's own 'beyng' is a
necessary, and concommitant, condition of union with the 'beyng' of God.

Putting aside the fact that the *Cloud*-author seems at times to acknowledge the
possibility of achieving such a state, while at other times he suggests that it
cannot be accomplished 'in þis liif',[6] the achievement of *this* state would, if

---

6 'For o þing I telle þee: þat þer was neuer зit pure creature in þis liif, ne neuer зit schal

accomplished, be equivalent to the thought, in the sense of *Gedanc*, of what is 'left' of the *Da* of *Dasein* is lifted, *viz.* Being, considered in itself. If it is remembered that the worldhood of the world is grounded in the Being of *Dasein*, and that beings are there only insofar as *Dasein* is there, i.e. in-the-world, then it will also be seen that the 'thought' of Being without the *Da* of *Dasein* is at the same time the thought of Being without any relation or references, not even that of opposition, to beings, or to 'the world'. Such a thought necessarily means the end of *Dasein*, the end of potentiality-for-Being, and as such, it is the thought of death and Nothing. But, for Heidegger, 'Nothing as the Other to beings, is the veil of Being'.[7] Death is the shrine of Nothing, and Nothing is the veil of Being; the way to the thought of death and Nothing, then, is also the way to the thought of the perfect accomplishment, and absolute fullness, of Being, in which, 'every destiny of beings is already ended and perfected (*hat sich schon vollendet*) from the beginning'.[8] To quote *The Cloud* once more, 'What is he þat clepiþ it nouȝt? Sekirly it is oure vtter man, & not oure inner. Oure inner man clepiþ it Al' (C, ch.68, p.68, ll.18–20). Bracketing out the question of the ontological or existential status of what is comprehended beyond the limit of the radical negation of which *The Cloud* speaks, namely, the 'nakid beyng' of God in deifying union, such a comprehension, if accomplished, would be the 'mynde', the thought and presence, of Being in itself.

It might be objected that this claim does not take sufficiently into account the *Cloud*-author's insistence that the soul never becomes, but remains beneath, God in 'kynde' (C, ch.67, p.67, l.21), and that it only reaches God at all with the help of God, the help of grace. However, with respect to the second of these possible objections, it should be pointed out that the dynamics of the God-soul relation are, in this case, very similar to those of the *Dasein-Sein* relation, as developed in a number of Heidegger's works. I do not want to address this issue in any detail, partly because of limits of space, partly because the exposition of Heidegger's thought is not the primary purpose of this paper, and partly because this aspect of Heidegger's thought has been discussed at length in a book by John Caputo, entitled *The Mystical Element in Heidegger's Thought*.[9]

With respect to both of the points made in the above hypothetical objection, I would, however, like to say two things very briefly. The first is that the apprehension of Being which founds *Dasein* as potentiality-for-Being, and so grounds and sustains – and 'moves' – its own Being, is not determined by *Dasein* itself. The second point is that *Dasein* could never 'become' *Sein* (if such a statement even makes any sense), and nothing that I have said is meant to imply that it could. On the contrary, if the Being of *Dasein* is defined as thrown

---

be, so hiȝe rauisched in contemplacion & loue of þe Godheed, þat þer ne is euermore a hiȝe & a wonderful cloude of vnknowyng bitwix him & his God' (C, ch.17, p.26, ll.22–25).

[7] *Was ist Metaphysick?* 13th edition, Frankfurt, 1969, p.52
[8] *Idem.*
[9] New York, 1976.

potentiality-for-Being, then the 'essence' of *Dasein* is necessarily determined by a twofold negativity, and necessarily distinct from the thought of Being in itself. And this, really, is the same as saying that the Being of *Dasein*, as 'worldly' Being, is always guilty. Being, considered in itself, on the other hand, is not.

But what, it could be asked (and with perfect justification), exactly is this Being, considered in itself, this Nothing which is also Being, this 'nouȝt' which is also 'Al', (C, ch.68, p.68, ll.18–20), and which is supposed to be a definition of the Being of God? In posing to himself a similar question, the *Cloud*-author gives the only possible response:

> But now þou askest me & seiest: 'How schal I þink on himself, & what is hee?' & to þis I cannot answere þee bot þus: 'I wote neuer'.
> For þou hast brouȝt me wiþ þi question into þat same derknes, & into þat same cloude of unknowyng þat I wolde þou were in þiself.   (C, ch.6, p.14, ll.14–17)

I am not implying, of course, that I do not know in the same way in which the author of *The Cloud* does not know; there is, after all, unknowing, and unknowing. I am only saying that what might lie at the end of the path of negation is necessarily unrepresentable, and so also unspeakable and unanalysable. This paper has therefore made no attempt to analyse what might be found at the end of this path, to go into any metaphysical speculation about death, or about the Being of God. Its analysis has remained existential. Ordinarily, that is, with respect to the experience of the vast majority of people, the existential analysis of the experience of death reveals it as a Being towards, and any talk of 'undergoing' death based on this experience does then trespass into the realm of metaphysics. With respect to the experience of the *Cloud*-author, however, the case, as I have attempted to demonstrate, may be different.

As to the Being of God as the limit of potentiality-for-Being, the limit of desire, I have made no attempt to delineate what this limit might be, or to pass judgement as to its 'existence'. I have only attempted to analyse what the *Cloud*-author claims to experience, or claims is a possibility of experience. Estimating the truth-value of this experience, if this amounts to judging the truth of the proposition that there is something outside the world in which all potentiality-for-Being is fulfilled, lies wholly beyond my power. Judging the validity of the concept as arising in response to an authentic human need and 'feeling', however, does not. After all, you do not have to be a mystic to know what it means to will, 'þou wost neuer what', but nothing in the world.[10]

---

[10] Whis is not to say that such a feeling may not be, in some sense, mystical. Insofar as 'the feeling of the world as a limited whole is the mystical feeling' (Wittgenstein, *Tractatus Logico-Philosophicus*, trans. C. K. Ogden, London, 1981), any longing which seeks something outside of the world, and therefore apprehends the world as having an 'outside' which limits it, is mystical. But, in that case, to have a mystical feeling and to be a mystic are clearly two different things.

AUTHOR(S), COMPILERS, SCRIBES AND BIBLE TEXTS: DID THE *CLOUD*-AUTHOR TRANSLATE *THE TWELVE PATRIARCHS*?

ROGER ELLIS

1

THIS PAPER ORIGINATED with an unease about the ascription to the author of *The Cloud of Unknowing* of the text commonly called *Benjamin Minor*, and here called *Tretyse*, after the title Hodgson gave it from two of the manuscripts in which it appears.[1] As is well known, this text is a translation/adaptation/reworking of a text by Richard of St Victor, *The Twelve Patriarchs*.[2] In the first

---

Abbreviations: see p.220.

[1] Full title, *A Tretyse of þe Stodye of Wysdome þat Men Clepen Beniamyn*, from Kk and Har2; of the other titles offered for the work, that in F might have been preferred, *The Boke of the xii patriarkys* (though cf n.47 below for another explanation of the title). Quotation from the *Tretyse*, and from other texts by the *Cloud*-author, by page and line number alone, is from *The Cloud of Unknowing and Related Treatises*, ed. P. Hodgson, Salzburg, 1982, pp.129–145. This edition supersedes that in *Deonise Hid Diuinite and Other Treatises on Contemplative Prayer*, ed. P. Hodgson, Early English Text Society O.S. 231, London, 1955, pp.12–46 (noteworthy changes to the text of the latter are at 129/6, 129/21, 129/22, 135/25, 137/4, 137/13, 141/23, 144/15). To the twelve manuscript or early printed copies of the *Tretyse* used for the earlier edition, the later adds that in CC, without recording any variants (collation shows it to belong to Ar*, and to a subgroup of Ar*, W–Ii – for this subgroup see Early English Text Society O.S., 231 p.xxi – characterized most strikingly by the omission of the diagram on p.130). Dr. Ian Doyle also informs me of an extract corresponding to 129/1–130/21 in Peterborough Cathedral MS 8, f.123r–v. In this paper all manuscript readings other than from CC are taken from the apparatus of the edition in Early English Text Society O.S., 231. For a modern translation, see *The Pursuit of Wisdom [etc.]*, ed. and trans. J. Walsh, Classics of Western Spirituality, (abbreviated CWS), New York, Ramsay and Toronto, 1988, pp.13–47.

[2] For this title and the common alternative, see *Richard of Saint-Victor The Twelve Patriarchs [etc.]*, trans. G. A. Zinn, CWS 1979, p.7, (Zinn) used for translations in this paper (my emendations, or original translations, in square brackets). In the absence of a critical edition of the text, promised for 1992, I quote from the edition in Patrologia Latina CXCVI, cols.1–64, hereafter *BM*. I have consulted copies of *BM* in BL 1–3, Ar2, Bd1–2 and D, and record a selection of their readings, as appropriate. For information about the status of these and other readings I am grateful to Mme. Duchet-Suchaux, Paris, one of the editors of the forthcoming critical edition, whom I contacted at the suggestion of Dr. Rene Tixier, Toulouse (Dr. Tixier kindly supplied me, as well, with relevant secondary literature, and I am most grateful to him for his help). Reference will also be made to *Richard of St. Victor Selected Writings on*

edition of the *Cloud*[3] Hodgson asserted that the *Tretyse* could, 'with great probability . . . be ascribed to the . . . author' of the *Cloud*.[4] In the introduction to the second edition, she was less definite: 'the authorship of *Benjamin Minor*', she wrote, 'remains the most conjectural' of all (p.xiv). She drew particular attention to the fact that of the thirteen extant manuscript copies of the *Tretyse* – which make it, after the *Cloud*, the most popular of the works edited – nine occur in manuscript anthologies without any other works by the *Cloud*-author. Except for the *Cloud*, other works of the canon appear in this way only once (so *The Book of Priue Counseling*, preserved in ten manuscripts, and *A Pistle of Preier*, preserved in seven) or not at all (so *Deonise Hid Diuinite*, preserved in two manuscripts; *A Pistle of Discrecioun of Stirings*, in six).[5] Even the *Cloud* itself appears in this way only five times out of a total of sixteen manuscripts.[6] But that very fact should warn us against placing too much weight on the regular appearance of the *Tretyse* separately from the other texts. If, as seems likely, it was being directed at a rather less specialised audience than the other works in the canon, its semi-independent existence would provide, at best, inconclusive evidence about its authorship.

Similarly inconclusive are other pieces of evidence: two passages, for instance, where the *Cloud*-author refers to his own work by name, neither of which mentions the *Tretyse*. One, in the prologue to *Hid Diuinite* (119/2–7), explains how that work, a translation of the *Mystical Theology* of pseudo-Dionysius, is being offered as confirmation of the teaching of the *Cloud*, which had quoted from it in chapter 70; since this passage refers to no other works by the author, its silence in respect of the *Tretyse* proves nothing one way or the other. Greater significance might attach to the author's failure to refer to the *Tretyse* in a passage in his *Book of Priuy Counseling* (87/40–88/3), hereafter *Book*, which sends the reader to 'oþer diuerse places' of his own work: texts, that is, of which he expects his reader to have copies. Texts explicitly named here are the 'lityl pistle of preier', 'þe cloude of vnknowyng' and, possibly, 'Denis deuinite'. But the failure of the *Book* to name the *Tretyse* as one of the *Cloud*-author's works need not mean that he did not write the *Tretyse*. He might have done so *after* he wrote the *Book*; or he might have written the *Tretyse*

Contemplation, trans. C. Kirchberger, London, 1957. (Kirchberger)

[3] *The Cloud of Unknowing and the Book of Privy Counselling*, ed. P. Hodgson, Early English Text Society O.S. 218, London, 1944. (For a modern translation of the *Cloud*, with extensive comment, see *The Cloud of Unknowing*, ed. and trans. J. Walsh, CWS, 1981.)

[4] *Ibid.*, lxxvii (and cf pp.lxxix and lxxxv note, Early English Text Society O.S. 231, *op cit.*, pp.xxx–xxxvi).

[5] I have omitted the *Tretis of Discrescyon of Spirites* since its ascription to the *Cloud*-author may also be questionable, though in terms of manuscript distribution it broadly parallels the situation obtaining in the other texts by him, appearing only twice in this way out of a total of eight manuscripts.

[6] Admittedly, this figure is misleading to the extent that *The Cloud* also appears a further six times paired only with *Priuy Counseling*.

before the *Book* but not sent the *Book*'s first reader a copy; alternatively, if improbably, he was referring only to original works and not to translations.[7]

Interestingly, he also refers, a few pages earlier in the *Book* (85/11–23), to the climactic image of *The Twelve Patriarchs* – that is, Rachel's death in giving birth to Benjamin as an image of the death of the discursive reason when the soul is 'touchid wiþ verrey contemplacion' – and states that the allegory has featured in authoritative works on contemplation, 'not only of one or of two bot of ful many ful holy and ful worþi': probably the 'trewe Faders' referred to just before (85/2–10). These, the writer insists, are as well know to the reader as to himself.[8] This piece of evidence can be interpreted in two different ways. Either the *Tretyse* is one of the authoritative works referred to in this passage, or it is not. If it is so referred to, the *Cloud*-author's unwillingness to name himself as having produced it – a reticence which would contrast strikingly with his readiness to advertise his own writing a few pages later on – argues against his authorship of the translation. If, however, as is more likely, he is not referring to the *Tretyse* in this passage, his authorship of the work remains a possibility: which would carry the consequence either that he produced it some time after he wrote the *Book* – the second option above; or, if he had already completed the translation, that he was referring in these two passages to original works and not to translations – the third option. Here, too, the evidence proves inconclusive.

Another objection to the place of the *Tretyse* in the canon is the fact that it is so different from the acknowledged translation *Hid Diuinite*. In the latter, working from two main sources, the *Cloud*-author produced a translation extremely literal and, for the most part, intelligible and accurate (in practice this involved regular expansions of the text at points where 'þe hardnes of it' – complicated syntax and vocabulary; theological minefields – required him to offer more than 'þe nakid lettre' 119/8–9[9]): the former, according to Hodgson's notes, is more like an adaptation:

> The Middle English version is little more than a coherent synopsis of *Benj. Min.*, following the shape of the story and the main interpretations but omitting the

---

[7] The first or second of these explanations must obviously be offered to explain the absence from the list of the *Pistle of Discrecioun of Stirings*. The third would entail the consequence that the author's note about 'Denis deuinite' is a reference to the original.

[8] An interesting example of such familiarity is provided by two of the three texts in MS BL Harley 876. The first is Grosseteste's Latin translation of St John Chrysostom's version of the *testamenta* of the twelve patriarchs, preserved in many manuscripts. The second is a *libellus a magno Ricardo de Sancto Victore prosaice editus, Benjamin ab eodem intitulatus, a quodam in metrum rude redactus de studio sapientie* (f.15r).

[9] For an edition of the Latin of these two sources, and for comment on the *Cloud*-author's use of them, see Early English Text Society O.S., 231, *op. cit.*, pp.94–9; for a modern translation of one of them, see the relevant pages of the commentary by St Albert on the *Mystical Theology*, in *Albert and Thomas Selected Writings*, ed. and trans. S. Tugwell, CWS, 1988, (Tugwell) pp.134–98; and, for a translation of the original Greek, *Dionysius the Areopagite on the Divine Names and the Mystical Theology*, trans. C. E. Rolt, London, 1920.

greater part of the amplification . . . Many of the eighty-seven chapters . . . are passed over completely. Only the early short chapters . . . follow the Latin closely. The subsequent sections tend to draw from several chapters . . . close translations of selected sentences are in juxtaposition with free and greatly abridged adaptations, with an occasional personal comment or explanation not in the Latin (p.195).

Now, the one translator may easily translate different works in very different ways, witness Chaucer. In the *Boece*, Chaucer blended commentary material with the Latin original to produce a very literal translation. At the opposite end of the scale, he produced, in *The Man of Law's Tale*, a version of Trevet's story which pushed the original in directions barely suggested by it, and complicated it, in particular, by the insertion of carefully translated passages from a text of a very different colour, the *De Miseria* of Pope Innocent III.[10] We could explain this difference as the result of an understanding that different texts permit different kinds of translation: romance, if that is what we should call Trevet's story, does not have the same authoritative status, nor require a literal translation as urgently, as a profound religious or philosophical text like the *Consolation of Philosophy*. Such an argument can hardly be advanced to account for the differences between *Hid Diuinite* and the *Tretyse*, whose originals are of comparable weight and authority.

A likelier explanation involves a consideration of the presumed audiences of the two works. It must be a fair presumption, in spite of its reference to the *Cloud* in the prologue, that *Hid Diuinite* was designed for a very select readership, and never exceeded the limited circulation represented by the surviving manuscripts. By contrast, the *Tretyse* seems to have been directed at a wider, possibly lay, readership. Richard of St Victor had written *The Twelve Patriarchs*, in part, to introduce the practice of contemplation, by way of a series of ascetic and other religious practices, to 'the younger members of his community' (Kirchberger p.77, cf Zinn pp.8, 19). Consequently, Richard's allegory of Jacob's twelve children dramatizes not just an individual's growth as a contemplative – each of the children in turn representing a different stage in the progress – but also that individual's participation, with his religious brothers, in the life of a monastic community.[11] This overlap of inner and outer dramas, on one level or another, probably characterizes most writing addressed to professed

---

[10] On the *Boece*, see T. W. Machan, *Techniques of Translation: Chaucer's Boece*, Norman, Oklahoma, 1985 (Machan); on the Man of Law's Tale, R. Ellis, *Patterns of Religious Narrative in The Canterbury Tales*, London, 1986, ch.6; for another view of the latter, G. Keiser, 'The Spiritual Heroism of Chaucer's Custance', in *Chaucer's Religious Tales*, ed. C. D. Benson and E. Robertson, Chaucer Studies XV, Woodbridge, 1990, pp.121–136.

[11] Apart from the formal gender parallel between the twelve sons of Jacob and the members of a male religious community, Richard's allegory functions most clearly as an emblem of monastic life when the spiritual qualities described are also formally identified with the holders of monastic offices. This level of the allegory works least well when *BM* treats of Jacob's daughter Dina.

religious, and explains why texts produced, like the *Cloud*, for a religious readership could nevertheless be read with profit by others.[12] So when Richard writes of Zabulon, the tenth son of Jacob, that he represents hatred of sin, in oneself and in others, and laments the inability or unwillingness of the virtuous to offer correction when it is called for (ch.41), he is addressing both the individual novice and the religious superior. The latter embodies the community's religious sense in imposing correction on its wayward members:

> *habet necesse pro culpa quandoque subjectis irasci, amplius utique dolet cum cogitur eos pro culpa percutere quam cum cogitur pro eorum defensione punire* (*BM* ch.42) [he has, of necessity, to be angry at subject persons at one time or another on account of guilt, so he grieves when he is compelled to strike them for guilt more than when he is compelled to be punished on account of their defense (Zinn p.99])[13]

At the same time, the superior is not immune from the very faults of which the subject stands accused:

> *imo eos saepe per quos Deus aliorum errata corrigere disponit . . . graviter cadere permittit, ut ex propria culpa discant quam misericordes in aliorum correptione esse debeant* (*BM* ch.45) [God often allows those through whom he arranges to correct the errors of others to fall unpleasantly, so that from their own fault they may learn how merciful they ought to be in the reproach[ing] of others (Zinn p.102)][14]

That is, Zabulon marks another stage not only in the individual's relationship with God but also, since that relationship has a communal aspect for professed religious, in the individual's membership of the religious community. Such language could apply directly to seculars only if they were in positions of temporal authority; it does not appear in the *Tretyse*. Other material added to the original, notably 139/6–18, help to reinforce the simpler picture with which *The Twelve Patriarchs*, and the *Tretyse*, had started. For the most part, therefore, Zabulon appears in the translation simply as a figure of hatred of sin in oneself.[15]

---

[12] Indeed, the opening pages of *The Cloud* (prologue and ch.1) blur the distinction between the formal stages of religious life and their informing principles so as the more easily to reach a non-specialist audience. Since other features of the work can be similarly explained, I do not share the view tentatively advanced by Hodgson (pp.xii) of an original recipient ignorant of Latin. (Hodgson's view does, however, have the support of a medieval annotator of the work: see Walsh 1981 p.187 n.243.)

[13] Zinn translates *puniri* (the correct reading, according to Duchet-Suchaux: variants, BL1 *uapulare*, BL3 *punire*).

[14] In support of this point, note: (i) some of the language in this section is reminiscent of the Rule of St. Benedict on the role of the abbot; thus several Biblical quotations are common to both texts (eg the version of Ecclesiasticus 32.24 in *BM* ch. 67 *qui cum consilio cuncta agit, in aeternum non paenitebit* also occurs in *The Rule of St. Benedict*, ed. and trans. D. O. Hunter Blair, 4th ed., Fort Augustus, 1934, p.26 [ch.3, on the abbot]; (ii) other specifically religious offices or functions are also clearly implied (e.g. preaching *BM* ch.46).

[15] The text refers three times to 'synne in oureself and in oure breþren' (140/2, cf 139/

Such practices, though very different from those followed in *Hid Diuinite*, hardly prove that the *Tretyse* is the work of a different translator.

Insofar as the translator's practices in the *Tretyse* signify a writer alert to the situation of his readers and ready to adapt his text accordingly, they might provide the basis for a comparison with the original works by the *Cloud*-author, where the sense is strong of a writer responding sometimes to actual questions (*Preier* 101/1-2, *Stirings* 109/1-10, 110/1-4) and sometimes to hypothetical ones (*Stirings* 114/38, *Cloud* and *Book passim*[16]). Even *Hid Diuinite* can be accommodated to this pattern, insofar as its first-person prologue, though addressed to no particular individual, adcknowledges an ongoing process of interpretation: like the *Book*, it originates with the writer's sense of unfinished business in the *Cloud*.[17] More to the point, all the works of the *Cloud*-author, with the exception of *Hid Diuinite*, communicate a very strong sense of an actual and specific audience, one known in varying degrees to the author (in *Stirings*, not at all well, cf 110/8-11; in *Preier*, rather better, cf 107/35-37; still better in the *Cloud*, 7/36-8/17, 11/31-33). We receive no such sense of the audience of the *Tretyse*: indeed, we have to infer the audience from the translator's modifications to the original. And yet, if the *Cloud*-author were also the translator of the *Tretyse*, we might reasonably have expected him, if not to realize for us an audience which enjoys only a notional existence in his mind as he writes, at least to convey that same sense of himself, as a presence in the work, that we receive so strongly from his other works. It is, after all, possible to distinguish the 'voices' of the different unnamed preachers in the collection of sermons preserved in MS BL Royal 18 B xxiii, and to gain some sense of the different audiences whom they were trying to reach.[18] But the speaking voice we hear in the *Tretyse*, when we hear one, is generally Richard St Victor's.[19]

That last comment reminds us how difficult it is to pronounce on tone or style in a translation, and, hence, how cautious we must be in comparing the linguistic

---

25-6, 140/13), and the translator translates the passage quoted above from *BM* ch.45: but the emphasis is very much on the self.

[16] For comment on the latter, see R. Ellis, 'A Literary Approach to the Middle English Mystics', in *The Medieval Mystical Tradition in England*, ed. M. Glasscoe, Exeter, 1980, pp.109-17.

[17] Admittedly, *Hid Diuinite* is attempting to gloss a difficult idea; *Priue Counseling*, to judge by the difference between its opening paragraph and the prologue of the *Cloud*, aims rather to discourage the anticipated wider readership of the earlier work from embarking upon a work expressly geared to the understandings, if not the actual situation, of the addressee (75/2-3, cf 2/7-17).

[18] See *Middle English Sermons edited from British Museum MS Royal 18 B xxiii*, ed. W. O. Ross, Early English Text Society O.S., 209, London, 1940, and discussion pp.xix-xxvi.

[19] E.g. 'and þus it is wel prouid' (129/25, 130/9-10, Latin *quotidiano experimento docemur*), 'I prey þee' (132/20, *quaeso*, 140/22, *ut de caeteris taceam*); 'nowe haue we seyde' (133/24, *habemus*); 'ʒe' (134/20, 'saltem'); 'whatso þou be' (141/1 and following, *quisquis es*); 'for first I wolde a man lered' (143/9-10, *prius discat homo*). Emphatic address not directly occasioned by the Latin includes 'and so it is wel seyde'

features of the two translations, *Hid Diuinite* and the *Tretyse*, in order to argue
that both were, or were not, produced by the same person.[20] Conversely, faithful
translations of two texts as different stylistically as *Mystical Theology* and *The
Twelve Patriarchs* will naturally look very different, even when undertaken by
the same writer. We cannot draw very safe conclusions, for example, from the
fact that the *Tretyse* renders *invisibilis* by 'vnseable' (134/8, 143/13) or 'vnseen'
(133/33) whereas *Hid Diuinite* prefers 'inuisible' (119/20) or 'he mai not be
seen' (123/7); or that the former translates *multitudo* by 'mochilnes' (132/33)
and the latter by 'multitude' (126/24). Possibly more significant – and
significant of common authorship – is the fact that both translations use a similar
gloss 'worldly, fleschly and kyndely' (*HD* 120/21; for the phrase in the *Tretyse*,
see below p.211). This slack variant on the medieval triad of the world, the flesh
and the devil could have been generated independently by two different writers,
but is distinctive enough to suggest a single author. But if comparison of the two
translations does not yield very firm conclusions, our problems are compounded
when we compare the *Tretyse* with original works. The *Tretyse*, for example,
operates a rather less complex syntax than we find in the works of the *Cloud*-
author, but this may have as much to do with the sentence patterns of the original
Latin as with the choices of the translator.

We might be on stronger ground if we compared the uses made by the *Cloud*-
author of ideas from Richard's works with the ways in which those ideas have
been translated in the *Tretyse*. The *Cloud*-author surely included *The Twelve
Patriarchs* among the authoritative writings on contemplation which he expected
his disciple to know (see above pp.194–5). A further sign of the importance he
attaches to Richard's writings is provided by his use of material from *The Twelve
Patriarchs* and *The Mystical Ark* (or *Benjamin Major*) in chs 63-6 and 71-3 of the
Cloud. Yet his regard for their authority does not prevent him from
systematically modifying the borrowed material to bring it into conformity with
the teaching of Thomas Gallus.[21] Given the many other modifications to the
original practised by the translator of the *Tretyse*, we might have supposed, had
the *Cloud*-author translated it, that he would have found some way of modifying
Richard's teaching to bring it into line with his own. Any difference between the
teaching of the two works on the role of the affection and the imagination,

---

(136/14, 19), 'wite þou wel' (140/31), and two places where the translator provides
alternative translations of the same word or phrase ('wheþer þou wilt', 136/14, 'or
þus', 139/20: on the latter phrase, see below n.34).

[20] Anonymous translations of a single original can be fruitfully compared, though
agreement in detail need not prove common authorship. Cf., admittedly oversimple,
remarks by W. P. Cumming on the various anonymous translations of the *Liber
Celestis* of St Bridget of Sweden (*The Revelations of St. Birgitta*, ed. W. P. Cumming,
Early English Text Society O.S., 178, London, 1929, p.xx).

[21] So A. Minnis, 'The Sources of *The Cloud of Unknowing*: A Reconsideration', in *The
Medieval Mystical Tradition in England*, ed. M. Glasscoe, Exeter, 1982, (Glasscoe
1982) pp.67–70.

however, might as well point to the different audiences of the two works as to two different authors.

Nevertheless, we have an important point of reference and comparison: the *Cloud*-author's translations and original works all include translations of texts from the Vulgate, which can be readily compared with the very many quotations from the Vulgate in the *Tretyse*. *Mystical Theology* has two quotations, both blended with the author's own words, neither clearly signposted as quotations. *Hid Diuinite* translates both:

> þei wenen for to knowen hym þat *haþ maad derknes his hidyng place* (121/5–6, Lat. *ponit tenebras latibulum suum*: Psalm 17:12, for *ponit, posuit*)

> *and entren* wiþ affeccioun *into derknes, where* verely *he is*, as þe Scripture scheweþ, þe whiche is abouen all (122/15–17, Lat. *ad caliginem introeunt, ubi vere est, sicut Eloquia dicunt, qui est super omnia*, cf. Exodus 20:21, *accessit ad caliginem in qua erat deus*)[22]

Similarly the *Cloud*, though deeply marked by Biblical emphases and understandings – witness the footnotes in Hodgson or Walsh, and the marginalia of Har1[23] – has few explicit quotations, and those are usually incorporated into the author's own words, though not to the same extent as in *Mystical Theology*. The following provides a typical example of the author's practice in the work:

> to þis perfeccioun, and alle oþer, oure Lorde Iesu Criste clepiþ us himself in þe Gospel, where he biddeþ þat we schuld be parfite by grace as he hymself is by kynde (24/31–2, cf. Matthew 5/48: *estote ergo vos perfecti, sicut et pater vester caelestis perfectus est* [be therefore perfect, as your heavenly father is perfect]).

This quotation indicates its Biblical origin by the use of an introductory phrase 'in þe Gospel'; glosses the text by adding the phrases 'by grace' and 'by kynde' (for comment on these phrases, see Walsh p.153 n.132); adapts the direct speech of the original to reported speech; and makes Christ, rather than his heavenly father, the model for the contemplative. It is also noteworthy in failing to quote the Latin. This feature, which characterizes both *Hid Diuinite* and the *Cloud*, contrasts strikingly with the author's practice in the other epistles, which regularly provide accompanying Latin originals.[24] In purely formal terms the

---

[22] It is a mark of the difficulty of identifying the quotation at 122/15–17 that Hodgson's note refers us to Psalm 17.12, 96.2; Tugwell, p.153 n.51, to Exodus 20.21.

[23] The text of *The Cloud* in Har1 was prepared for extensive glossing, which, however, it received only as far as ch.2. In Hodgson's note on the glosses (Early English Text Society O.S., 218, *op. cit.*, p.178), the reference to Proverbs 7 should read 'Proverbs 5:16'.

[24] Such quotations are not always accurate, though it is unclear to what extent the errors were inadvertent, because the author was quoting from memory or from a faulty text, and to what extent they were deliberate. Thus at 78/24 *da pauperibus* (Proverbs 3:9, Vulgate *da ei*) is paralleled in copies of the Vulgate in MSS BL Royal 1Eix and 1Bv. Deliberate alterations may include 82/36 *scilicet dileccio dei et proximi* (added to Vulgate Matthew 22.40); 116/11–12 *videte vocacionem vestram, et in ea vocacione qua vocati estis, state* (conflating elements from I Corinthians 7:20 and Ephesians 4:1).

reasons for this change have to do with the fact that in the epistles the Bible quotations are less often incorporated into the text than they were in the *Cloud*, and more often mark a new stage in the development of the argument; hence, it is relatively easy to provide the corresponding Vulgate texts. (Of course, other, more important, reasons may be offered for the change: see Walsh p.11.) The contrast in practice is mostly clearly focussed by the translation, in both the *Cloud* and *Stirings*, of the same verse (Luke 10:42; *Cloud* 29/15–16, *Stirings* 116/29–30, cf 30/11–12). If we except the added gloss in *Stirings*, the two versions, both using indirect speech, are nearly identical:

> he . . . seyde þat Mary had chosen þe best partye, þe whiche schuld neuer be taken fro hir (*Cloud*)

> he seide þat Mary, in ensaumple of alle contemplatiues, had chosen þe best, þe whiche schuld neuer be take from hir (*Stirings*).

The *Cloud* does not quote the Latin; *Stirings* does.[25]

The *Tretyse* stands somewhere between the two extremes. On the one hand, taking its lead from the original, it keeps its Bible quotations generally distinct from the body of the text, and thus parallels the *Cloud*-author's practice in the *Book*, *Preier* and *Stirings*.[26] On the other hand, it resembles the *Cloud* in failing to provide the Latin for all but one of its quotations.[27] That one quotation, at the very end of the *Tretyse*, is worth lingering over: '*Ibi Beniamyn adolescentulus in mentis excessu*. þat is: þere is Beniamyn, þe ȝonge childe, in rauesching of mynde' (145/7–8, Psalm 67:28). With this verse, which Richard had given a place of honour at the head of his work (ch.1), he brought *The Twelve Patriarchs* full circle a few chapters from the end (ch.84). Readers of the *Tretyse* could hardly recognize the formal fitness of this final quotation, since it is not translated at the start of the *Tretyse*; but I imagine, as they closed the book, they could not have escaped the sense, either, that they were being pointed in the direction of a new order of religious experience, for which the whole work had been preparing them (hence, arguably, the use of Latin as a kind of *point final*).[28] This quotation is also significant because it is repeated, with the Vulgate Latin, in the *Book*: 'þere is Beniamyn a ȝong childe, in excesse of mynde' (85/21–3).

---

[25] *Maria, inquit optimus, optimam partem elegit, que non auferetur ab ea* (note the brief added gloss, *inquit optimus*, which the author translates 'þe best is Almiȝty Iesu, and he seide').

[26] The *Tretyse* has a further link with the other texts: it incorporates patristic sources into the text and translates them by indirect speech (140/21–2, cf 102/36, 40, and probably 87/4; contrast *Cloud* 70/5–6).

[27] One manuscript regularly, and another manuscript occasionally, include the Vulgate originals – F and Har2: see further below pp.207–8 – but this feature cannot have characterized the original translation.

[28] Comparable understandings may have dictated the place of the *Tretyse* in two of the three manuscript collections of the *Cloud* author's works (ie Kk, containing all of them, and Har2, wanting *Hid Diuinite*): it occurs midway through the manuscripts, after the shorter works but before *The Cloud*, *The Book* and *Hid Diuinite*.

In much the same way that the closely parallel translations from Luke 10:42 in the *Cloud* and *Stirings* provide additional evidence of their common authorship, these parallels between the *Book* and the *Tretyse* might support the inclusion of the *Tretyse* in the canon. Another Bible verse, Psalm 110:10, is translated almost identically in *Preier* and the *Tretyse*:

> *Inicium sapiencie est timor Domini*; þat is: þe biginnyng of wisdome is [þe] drede of oure Lorde God (101/27–8)
>
> þe bygynnyng of wysdom, dreed of oure Lorde God   (131/17–18):

one of several links between the two texts (EETS, O.S., 218, lxxix and lxxxv note), which led Hodgson to much the same conclusion (she speculated that 'the author wrote [*Preier*] shortly after working on the translation').

The offered evidence, however, is not straightforward. To anticipate the next section of this paper, the apparent agreement between the translations in *Preier* and in the *Tretyse* may indicate not authorial but only scribal activity. (1) Two versions exist of the Vulgate verse in *Preier*: the one printed by Hodgson has the copula *est*; another, represented by three manuscripts, wants the copula. Since the Vulgate also wants the copula, the printed version may not be authorial but merely scribal (alternatively, the scribes of the other version might have emended their exemplars to bring the text into line with the Vulgate: as we shall see, there is evidence of this practice in at least one manuscript of the *Tretyse*). There are also two versions of the translated verse: all manuscripts but the base manuscript Har1 read 'þe drede of oure lorde God'; Har1, almost certainly in error, omits the definitie article.[29] (2) A similar situation obtains in the *Tretyse*. There, the phrase 'oure Lorde God' occurs only in the base manuscript Har1 (most other manuscripts read 'oure [*or* þe] Lorde', and see further below p.206); in addition, four manuscripts add 'is' to the phrase 'drede of oure Lorde', and five add a definite article to the noun 'drede'. The evidence suggests that the original translations of this verse in *Preier* and the *Tretyse* were

> þe biginnyng of wisdome is þe drede of oure Lorde God   (*Preier*)
>
> þe bynynnyng of wysdom, dreed of oure Lorde   (*Tretyse*)

The differences between the two versions are small but significant. That in the *Tretyse* is the more literal, as we can see if we compare it with the versions produced by Rolle for his Psalter and by the translator of the Early Version (EV) of the Wycliffe Bible, and with the slightly freer rendering of the Late Version (LV) of the Wycliffe Bible:[30]

---

[29] MS H wants both Latin verse and translation (information kindly supplied by Ms. Katey Hooper, Liverpool University Library). In the first edition (Early English Text Society O.S., 231, *op. cit.*), which favoured Har1 readings whenever possible, the verse appeared (49/9) without the definite article.

[30] Quotation from Rolle is taken from *The Psalter . . . with a Translation . . . by Richard Rolle of Hampole*, ed. H. R. Bramley, Oxford, 1884; and, from Early and Late Versions of the Wycliffe Bible (EV and LV), from *The Wycliffe Bible*, ed. J. Forshall and F. Madden, 5 vols., Oxford, 1850. See also *MS Bodley 959*, ed. C.

(Rolle) bigynynge of wisdome   drede of oure lord
(EV)   the begynnyng of wisdam,   the drede of the Lord
(LV)   the bigynnyng of wisdom is the drede of the Lord

The version in the *Tretyse* is closest to that of Rolle; that in *Preier*, to the slightly less literal version in LV. (To simplify a complex situation: the more literal a resolution, the closer it keeps to the letter of the Latin; the less literal, the readier to change the letter of the Latin where necessary or helpful for the communication of the sense.) Two small features characterize the more literal translations (Rolle, *Tretyse*): they follow the Vulgate in omitting both copula and definite article before the noun 'drede' (admittedly, both versions add a copula to the noun 'bygynnyng', and a possessive adjective to the noun 'lorde', the latter a bolder resolution than we find in either EV or LV, which simply add a copula).

Other instances occur in the *Tretyse* of comparably literal practice with Bible texts. (1) One concerns the resolution of a Latin accusative and infinitive construction; (2) another, the translation of participles used adjectivally. Both are translated literally rather than with a clause:

(1) Oure Lorde haþ herd me *be had* in dispite   (132/9–10, Genesis 29.33: *audivit me dominus haberi contemptui*)

(2) (a) Hert *contrite and mekyd*, God schal not dispise   (132/16–17, Psalm 50:19: *Cor contritum et humiliatum, deus non despicies*)[31]

    (b) he was an hert *sent oute*, ʒeuyng speches [*var.* speche] of fairheed   (135/20, Genesis 49.21: *Nephthali, cervus emissus, et dans eloquia pulchritudinis*; *BM* omits 'et', and cf. n.41 below)

Once again we can demonstrate the very literal character of these translations by comparison with Rolle and the Wycliffe Bible, as also by consideration of the emendations offered by some of the scribes:

(1) EV   the Lord hath seen me ben had to dispiyt
    LV   the Lord seiʒ that Y was dispised
    (*Tretyse*) MS F   Oure Lorde haþ herd me to be had in dispite
              MSS C R   Oure Lorde haþ had me in dipsite[32]

(2) (a) Rolle   hert contrite and mekid god thou sall not despise

Lindberg, 5 vols., Acta Universitatis Stockholmiensis, Stockholm Studies in English 6, 8, 10, 13, 20, Stockholm, 1953–69, for a modern edition of EV (Genesis to Baruch). For comment on these texts, see R. Ellis, 'The Choices of the Translator in the Late Middle English Period', Glasscoe 1982 pp.29–31.

[31] The translation should read 'God, thou shalt not despise'. The BL 3 reading *despiciet* (so also D over correction, and, according to Duchet-Suchaux, MS Dijon 39), like the related Bd1 error *spernit*, shows how the error may have entered the translation.

[32] Clearly erroneous, this reading probably witnesses to unfamiliarity with the literalism and to a drive to produce a version more in line with ordinary English syntax. Just possibly the error could have originated with retranslation of the Bible verse from a faulty copy of *BM* or the Vulgate: the copy of the latter in MS BL Royal IBv, for example, reads *audiuit me dominus habere contemptui*.

> EV   a contrit herte and mekid, God, thou shalt not despise
>
> LV   God, thou schalt not dispise a contrit herte and maad meke [*var.* mekid]
>
> (*Tretyse* MS F   The hert þat ys contrite and mekyd, God schal not dispise
>
> (b) EV   Neptalym, the herte sent out, the ȝuynge the spechis of fayrnes
>
>   LV   Neptalym schal be an hert sent out, and ȝuynge spechis of fairenesse

(3) The translation of Psalm 50/19 is interesting for another reason, too: the retention of the word order of the Latin in the *Tretyse* constitutes another feature of a very literal translation. Of the three parallel versions only that of Rolle is as literal. (4) Then we have the translation of Psalm 118:128 (*omnem viam iniquam odio habui*),[33] which appears, in indirect speech, as 'he had in hateredyn alle wickyd wey' (139/29–30). The unEnglish feel of the phrase 'alle wickyd wey' can be usefully compared with Rolle ('all wickid way'). (5) Lastly, we have a verse (Psalm 4/5, '*Irascimini et nolite peccare*') translated twice, the first time very literally, the second time more idiomatically: ' "Wraþþes, and willeþ not synne." Or þus: "Beeþ wroþe, and synniþ not" ' (139/19–20).[34]

The very literal character of these translation practices contrasts strikingly with those employed in the translation of Bible texts by the *Cloud*-author. If we except the Har1 version, already noted, of Psalm 110:10 in *Preier* (101/27) – and we should, since it may be scribal – we find only one instance of comparably literal translation in the *Cloud*-author's works, in *Preier*, where the translation of Canticles 2:16 '*Dilectus meus mihi, et ego illi.* þat is: My loued vnto me and I to him' (106/19–20), requires a copula, such as it receives in other translations ('my beloved *is* mine and I *am* his') to be intelligible. Normally, however, practice is less literal, as in the following translation of James 1:12 in *Stirings*, where the author has not only added the copula and the definite and indefinite articles, as appropriate, but also translated a present participle used absolutely, as a noun, by a clause (all italicized in the quotation):

> *Beatus vir qui suffert temptacionem, quoniam cum probatus fuerit accipiet coronam vite, quam repromisit Deus diligentibus se*: he *is a* blisful man þat suffringly beriþ temptacioun, for, fro he haue ben prouid, he schal take *þe* coroun of liif, þe whiche God haþ hiȝt vnto *alle þoo þat louen* him (110/37–41).[35]

At the opposite extreme, the *Cloud*-author blurs translation and commentary, notably in the *Book*, and even mistranslates in order to make a point:

---

[33] Hodgson cites the parallel verse in Psalm 118.104; for the correct ascription, see Zinn p.96.

[34] For comment on use of the phrase 'or thus' in translation, in the *Boece*, see Machan pp.119–21. (For a parallel phrase, 'or else', see *The Mirour of Mans Saluacioun*, ed. by A. Henry, Philadelphia, 1987, p.85, l.1393.) Five manuscripts (Har5 F C R Pw) omit the alternative translation.

[35] For other examples of copula added to the text, see 81/40, 114/29; of definite and indefinite article added to the text, 81/40, 82/11. No examples occur in the quoted verses of accusative and infinitive constructions or of participles used adjectivally.

scientia inflat, karitas edificat [knowledge puffs up, charity builds up]. in knowyng is trauaile, in feling is rest (*The Book*, 98/38–9)

qui adheret [adheres] deo, vnus spiritus est cum illo. þat is to sey: Whoso draweþ nere to God, as it is bi soche a reuerent affeccioun touchid before, he is o sperit with God (*Preier*, 106/9–12).[36]

A measure of inconsistency in the translation of Bible verses thus characterizes the original works of the *Cloud*-author.[37]

Admittedly, the *Tretyse* is not characterized by uniformly literal translation either. A verse from the Beatitudes (Matthew 5:5, *beati qui lugent*) is translated with copula, 'blessed be þey' (132/12, cf. *Book* 81/40, *Stirings* 110/39). Definite and indefinite articles are regularly introduced into the translation (e.g. 138/12, for Genesis 49:14 *asinum fortis . . . inter terminos*, 'a stronge asse . . . bytwix þe teermes'). We also discover instances of free translation, though none as free as those noted in the previous paragraph. Thus the phrase 'fro þis deedly body', translating '*de corpore mortis huius*' of Romans 7:24 (138/30), has transformed a possessive noun (*mortis*) into cognate adjective ('deedly'), a change not needed for the ready communication of the sense (cf. EV, LV 'fro the body of this synne'). Moreover, most of the literal translations occur near the start of the work: which might suggest a translator concerned to indicate to his readers at the outset, by his adoption of a non-English syntax, the sacred status of the Bible texts he was translating. (Hence, I take it, the clear distinction between the kind of translation which the surrounding text receives – we might call it fluent – and that accorded to the Bible verses.) Nevertheless, the Bible translations in the *Tretyse* are on the whole more accurate, and those near the beginning of the work considerably more literal, than anything we observe in the original works of the *Cloud*-author. It is at least arguable that another writer produced them.

2

Part of the responsibility for the general acceptance of the opposite view must lie with the decision Hodgson took to edit all the works by the *Cloud*-author, as far as possible, from the one manuscript Har1. It is obviously difficult to pronounce on the status of variant readings in an original work: difficult, too, when a translator is as free with his text as ours appears to be with Richard's, to be sure exactly which parts of the original are being translated.[38] But with a translation,

---

36 On the mistranslation *adheret*/'draweþ nere to', cf *Tretyse* 133/9 (*inhaeremus*/'we drawe nere'), which might constitute further proof of linkage.
37 Hilton's Bible translations in *The Scale* are characterized by similar inconsistencies.
38 For example, consider the interpretation of Dan as 'dome' (135/6). Hodgson refers this to ch.19 (*Dan, id est judicium vocatur*), but the context argues rather for a sentence from ch.20 as source (*recte eum Dan, id est judicium, vocamus*).

we at least have the Latin as a point of ultimate appeal. And since, self-evidently, we can talk about the linguistic and translational features of the *Tretyse*, and compare them with those we find in the other texts by the *Cloud*-author, only when we know for sure that we are reading what the author(s) wrote, rather than the scribe(s), we cannot allow the status of the edited text(s) to pass without a challenge.[39]

A simple example serves to highlight the difficulty and make the point. As previously noted, the translation of the Bible verse *initium sapientiae timor domini* (Psalm 110:10) is given, in both editions, as 'þe bygynnyng of wysdom, dreed of oure Lorde God' (131/16–17). Only Har1 has the doublet 'Lorde God'; all other manuscripts read simply 'God' (so MS G from Ar*) or 'oure Lorde' (all the other Ar* manuscripts, and two of the three manuscripts from Har1*). The doublet is not used elsewhere in the *Tretyse* to translate either *dominus* or *deus*[40] and probably arose in Har1 from contamination: as earlier noted, *Preier* has the same Bible text; offers 'oure Lorde God' as the translation of *domini*; and occurs earlier in the same manuscript. In favouring the Har1 reading the editor has thus, inadvertently, manufactured a link between the two texts, and enabled the unwary to conclude that both were by the same writer.

She was more explicit about another reading, this time from Ar*, which she relegated to the apparatus in both editions. The Latin original reads

> se sentiat ab illo saepius visitari, et ex eius adventu non tantum jam consolari, imo aliquoties quodam ineffabili gaudio repleri (*BM* ch.11) [the soul often feels itself to be visited by God and from His advent not so much now to be consoled but on the contrary sometimes to be filled with a kind of ineffable joy (Zinn p.62)].

For this Hodgson offers us the reading of Har1*:

> ofttymes he feliþ hym not only be visityd of God, bot greetly coumfourtyd in his comyng (133/4–5).

So edited, the translation appears to have cut the final phrase of the Latin, and to have kept the patterning between the second and third phrases of the Latin by moving the elements *non tantum* and *imo* to the head of its own first and second phrases. In the note Hodgson defends this reading by reference to the 'characteristic balance of this author's [*sc.* the *Cloud*-author] style'; in the other manuscripts the reading 'has the syntax of an afterthought'. Yet all the Ar* manuscripts have this other reading, and, since it represents the original Latin more faithfully than that of Har1*, it can hardly be scribal:

> ofttymes he feliþ hym not only be visityd of God, and [WIi but greetly] coumfortyd in his comyng, but ofetymes also he feliþ hym fyld wiþ an vnspekeable ioye.

---

[39] Nor, to give her edition its due, did Hodgson. See Early English Text Society O.S., 231, *op. cit.*, pp.xxi–xxii for comment on a number of the manuscript readings discussed below.

[40] *Dominus* is generally translated by 'lorde' (132/8, 133/12, 135/8, 144/2, but cf 'god' 131/27, 133/23), *deus* by 'god' (138/3, but cf 135/9).

In other words, the passage as edited is almost certainly not the passage as first written, and assumptions about the style of the *Cloud*-author may need to be modified if the *Tretyse* turns out to be one of his works.

Yet more significant is a reading shared by only four Ar* manuscripts. The edited text reads:

> And þerfore whatso þou be þat coueytest to come to comtemplacioun of God, *þat is to sey, to bryng forþe soche a childe þat men clepyn in þe story Beniamyn, þat is to sey, siȝt of God*, þan schalt þou use þee in þis maner. þou schalt clepe togeders þi þouȝtes and þi desires, and make þee of hem a chirche, and lerne þee þerin for to loue only þis good worde Jesu . . . so þat þou fulfille þat is seyde in þe psalme: Lorde, I schal bles þee in chirches (144/22–30).

For the italicized phrase the four manuscripts (Har5 F C and R) offer a very different reading (I have not included the variants):

> lete hym lere for to gedire samen þe myghtes of his sawle, and lete hym study for to refreyne þe outpassyng of his mynde, and schape hym for to wone wyth hymself os a kyng in is reme to wome þat none of his sugets wore contrari.

The corresponding Latin is

> Discat ergo dispersiones Israelis congregare, studeat evagationes mentis restringere, assuescat in intimis suis immorari, exteriora omnia oblivisci . . . faciat ecclesiam non solum desideriorum, verum etiam cognitionum, ut discat verum bonum, solum amare, et ipsum solum indesinenter cogitare: In ecclesiis, inquit, benedicite Deo (*BM* ch.84) [Let [such a] one . . . learn to assemble the dispersed Israelites; let him endeavour to restrain the wanderings of the mind; let him be accustomed to remain in the innermost part of himself and to forget everything exterior. Let him make a church not only of desires but also of thoughts, in order that he may learn to love only [the] true good and to think unceasingly of it alone: 'In the churches bless God' (Zinn p.142)].

Neither version can be described as a literal translation: for Richard's *verum bonum* both – and so, we may conclude, the original translation – offer what Hodgson calls a 'Christocentric conclusion . . . characteristic of Rolle and his followers' (p.199, n. to 144/26–7). Similarly, the four Ar* manuscripts seem to have invented the metaphor, which may recall a detail in the last of Julian's showings, of the recollected mind as a king ruling over peaceful subjects. But the version edited is nothing like as close to the Latin as that found in the four Ar* manuscripts.

The interpretation of this evidence is certainly problematical: but the implied claim that the reading followed by Har1* and the other Ar* manuscripts was the original can be sustained only if we suppose that the version common to the four Ar* manuscripts was produced by retranslating that part of the text from the Latin. This could certainly have happened: the scribe of MS F, for example, probably had a copy of the Latin alongside his exemplar of the Middle English translation, since his version contains the Latin originals of the various Bible texts translated in his exemplar, and, where Richard's version diverges from that of the Vulate, he sometimes follows the former.[41] (He must also have had a Vulgate Bible to hand, since he sometimes restores the correct Vulgate reading, even when to do so produces a mismatch with the copied translation).[42] Moreover, the Middle English translation not only includes many of the Bible texts features in *BM* but also adds texts of its own for which the Latin original provided no direct warrant: these latter also appear in Latin as well as in Middle English in F.[43] On the other hand Hodgson's analysis suggests a translation sufficiently wayward to have made the use of a Latin crib time-consuming (it is so, at least, for the modern student): which leads to the conclusion that the text preserved in the four Ar* manuscripts actually reflects the original translation at that point more closely than the text as edited.[44]

To be fair, the manuscript variants do not often challenge so dramatically the claim of the edited text to represent the original translation. All the same, the balance of probability often favours the Ar* readings, particularly when they occur in passages translated from *BM*. Thus, for example, Har1* 'of his liʒt' (144/5) is manifestlyt inferior to Ar* 'of þis siʒt' (cf *BM* ch.72 *visionis hujus* and Hodgson, EETS 231, p.xx note ‡).[45]

Similar claims may be advanced even for readings from individual Ar* manuscripts. At 132/33–5, for instance, most manuscripts produce a distinctive version of a Psalm text (93:19), changing from direct to indirect speech in mid-sentence:

[41] Given the distinct possibility that the scribe of F was working from corrupt copies of both *BM* and the Vulgate – in particular, a copy of *BM* which had restored the Vulgate wording of Bible quotations – I cannot be very definite about the examples listed in this and the following notes: but at 135/20, translating Genesis 49.21, F and *BM* ch.23 both read *emissus dans* (Vulgate *emissus et dans*); at 140/19–20, translating I John 1.8, F and *BM* ch.45 read *nos ipsos* (Vulgate, *ipsi nos*).

[42] Thus at 138/11 'dwellyng' translates *habitans* (*BM* ch.38), Richard's version of Genesis 49:14 *accubans*, the latter followed by Bd1 but by no MS used by Duchet-Suchaux: here the scribe of F follows the Vulgate.

[43] Eg quotations at 135/8–9, 138/29–30. The latter were sometimes retranslated from the Middle English, as at 138/30, where 'I coueyte [F desyre] to be lesid' (cf Philippians 1.23 *desiderium habens dissolui*) appears in F *cupio dissolui*. Cf 144/29–30, where 'Lorde I schal bles þee in chirches' (cf Psalm 67:28 *in ecclesiis benedicite deo*, followed by Richard, *BM* ch.84, and so all surviving manuscripts, according to Duchet-Suchaux: Bd1 possibly reads *benedicere*) is translated in F *in ecclesiis benedicam te domine*.

[44] According to Hodgson (Early English Text Society O.S., 231, *op. cit.*, p.xxi), F C R form a small subgroup of Ar*: this appears to be confirmed by readings noted earlier n. 34) and in the following paragraph, which F C R share with Har5 and Pw. F and Pw are both late copies (Dr. Ian Doyle confirms that the former was written by the Sheen monk William Darker, 'no doubt for Syon'); the others are early fifteenth century. Some readings of F C R appear to reflect the Latin better than the corresponding readings of the other manuscripts, but the subgroup has too many errors to be considered particularly authoritative.

[45] Other examples include 136/18 'blissidheed' (Ar* 'blissid', *translating BM* ch.26 *beatus*); 142/3 'profite' (Ar* 'profe', *BM* ch.67 *experiri*); 142/15 'for' (Ar* 'for ofte',

Daiud telleþ in þe psalme þat 'after þe mochilnes of my sorowes in myn herte', he
seiþ to oure Lorde þat his coumfortes han gladid his soule

Five Ar* manuscripts, Ar F C R Pw, produce a smoother reading by rewriting
the second half of the quotation in direct speech:

Ar   þe comford of oure lorde haþ gladed my soule
F C R Pw   thy coumfortes (R Pw comforte) han gladid my soule.

Since the direct speech returns us to the actual words of the quotation
(*consolationes laetificauerunt animam meam*; the Vulgate adds *tuae*),[46] it *could*
reflect the original translation better than the edited text. (Ar's phrase 'of oure
lorde' must, of course, be scribal; so too 'comforte' of Ar R Pw.)

An obvious counterclaim suggests itself. As we have seen, F was probably
using Richard's Latin original and the Vulgate as an intermittent check on the
Middle English translation. Consequently the restoration of direct speech in the,
already-noted, manuscripts may show not the translator but merely the scribes at
work, using the Latin of the Vulgate or of *BM* to produce a more accurate
version of the Bible text than their exemplar(s) had contained.[47]

The claim is also weakened by the fact that elsewhere in the *Tretyse* the direct
speech of Bible texts is rendered by indirect (e.g. 138/11–12, 139/29–30), with
support of all manuscripts: so that the indirect speech used by most manuscripts
to translate the second half of Psalms 93:19 could well reflect their Middle
English original better than the direct speech favoured by Ar F C R Pw.
Nevertheless, we cannot discount the possibility that variants which effectively
restore the original Latin may be authoritative: notably, when the Latin provides
no direct warrant for phrases added in Har1*, and missing in Ar*; more
particularly, if the one group regularly adds, and the other as regularly omits,
such phrases. At 129/4–6, for example, the text as edited suggests that the
translator had a fondness for doublets, and an eye for scholarly distinction:

BM ch.67 *frequenter*); 144/12 man (Ar* *adds* but wiþoute doute þouȝ it be noȝt þe
deserte of man, cf *BM* ch.73 *absque dubio*). Some of the new readings accepted in the
second edition (see above n.1) are of this same order.

46 According to Duchet-Suchaux, the PL text is in error here; the critical edition of *BM*
will read *consolationes tuae*. Some MSS, eg Ar2 and Bd1, present the text in
abbreviated form (Ar2 reads *conso. t. le. a. mea.*: see further p.217 below).

47 Some of F's variants might have resulted from correction of the Middle English
against the Latin eg ch.6 *importunitate*] 129/21 'vncouenably' *or* 'vnkunningly', F
inportunably; ch.25 *prosperis . . . adversis*] 136/4 'esy . . . vnesy', F 'prosperite and
welthfulle, aduersite and . . . vnwelthfulle'; ch.40 *ordinatum*] 139/3 'parfite' (*om.*
Har5 C R), F ordred; so also its version of the title of the work (above n.1). F did not,
however, use the Latin as a regular check on the Middle English, since it miscopied 'se
God' (132/2, cf *videre . . . deum*) as 'be good'. Similarly, the scribes of C and R
appear to have had access only to their Middle English exemplar(s), since they
regularly miscopy translated Bible texts (131/27, 132/8–9, 144/3), which they could
hardly have done if they had been able to check their versions against the Latin of the
Vulgate or of *BM*: so their modifications to the text of Psalm 93.19 cannot be
interpreted simply as the result of access to a more authoritative Latin text.

Þe tone is reson, þe toþer is affeccioun or wille. Þorow reson we knowe, and þorow affeccioun we fele or loue (Ar* wants the doublets 'or wille', and 'fele or')

Richard's Latin is itself very fond of doublets and patterned phrases, but at this point it offers only

> *una est ratio, altera est affectio; ratio, qua discernamus, affectio, qua diligamus*
> (*BM* ch.3) [Reason is one thing. Affection is another thing. Reason, by which we distinguish things; affection, by which we love (Zinn p.55)]

which following our earlier rule of thumb, suggests that Ar* reading is more authoritative (so Hodgson, EETS, OS 231, p.xx, n.‡).

And even when the Latin fails to resolve cruces, because they occur in passages of original, rather than translated, writing, reference to the distinctive features of the translation will often help us to decide between variant readings in favour of Ar*. One such is repetition. There was plenty of this in the Latin: in the translation, so many examples occur of repeated phrases common to all manuscripts that we must conclude the feature characterized the original translation.[48] This in the section on the birth of 'þe double siȝt of peyne and ioy . . . in þe ymaginacioun', we have a phrase describing the 'fleschly soule . . . ȝit ruyde in goostly studies' (134/7), translating *mentem carnalem et adhuc in studiis spiritualibus rudem*: this phrase the translator reworks, on his own authority, at the start of the next sentence (134/9). Perhaps the best example, from this same section, shows the translator's response to, and development of, a pattern established in the preceding section. Richard had described a kindling of love (ch.11): now he talks of kindling the soul's desires for goodness by imaginative representations of true goods, of imagined beauty (ch.14) and of promised rewards (ch.22). This kindling of desire the translator gives us four times in a short space (134/20–21, 30–31, 135/2–3, 22–3). The drive to pattern the text in this way sometimes takes priority even over the demands of the translation. Thus, in the middle of the section describing the birth of sorrow in the soul, we are given the phrase 'a man bitterly soroweþ' (132/10). This derives not so much from the corresponding Latin phrase (*veraciter dolet*) as from the framing phrases 'þe bittirlier he soroweþ' and 'bitterly sorowen' (123/7), 132/21, translating *acerbius plangit* and *lugentibus amare*). Original material shows a similar fondness for repeated phrases.

Though such repetition occurs most obviously within a given passage, certain quasi-formulaic phrases are repeated even after a gap of some pages. Thus the triplet 'fleschly, kyndly and wordly delices', first used at 130/2 to translate *gaudium*, reappears at 136/24 to translate *superfluae delectationis*, and must have been used again at 138/6–8, though only Ar* manuscripts now have the reading:

---

[48] Sometimes these repeated phrases were not recopied but retranslated: in ch. 25 the phrase *pacem et tranquillitatem* is loosely rendered 'joie and blis' (136/11, so only Har1: all other manuscripts have the better reading 'comforth and blis') and then translated, more accurately, 'pees and rest' (136/28).

abstynence . . . fro alle maner fleschly kyndely and wordly delyte, and in fruteful suffryng of alle fleschly and wordly disese.[49]

All Har1* manuscripts omit 'kyndely'; Har1 also loses the words 'delyte . . . wordly', presumably by haplography, and the other two Har1* manuscripts abbreviate the phrase, replacing 'delyte' by 'ese' and cutting all but the words 'and disese' from the remainder of the phrase. In the editions this appears

abstynence . . . fro alle maner fleschly and wordly ese, and in fruteful suffryng of alle fleschly and wordly disese.

As edited, it looks more strongly patterned than the version I am arguing was original: but a major element in this pattern, the rhyme 'ese . . . disese' is probably scribal.[50]   Many of the Har1 and Har1* readings preferred in the two editions can be opposed on these or similar grounds. For example, at 141/39–142/4, Ar*'s patterning of the translation ('vse/vsed/vsen') is probably to be preferred to that of Har1* ('custume/custumed/usen') by virtue of the stronger link created between the three terms (they translate Latin *vsu*, *exerceri* and (?) *satagamus . . . impendere*, and provide further indication of the translator's readiness to create and extend, even at the expense of accuracy of translation, the patterns of his original).[51] And readings peculiar to Har1 provide a yet more uncertain witness to the original.[52]

3

Yet the difference between the two principal witnesses, Har1* and Ar*, is not always resolved so neatly, as we can see if we consider a passage near the end of the *Tretyse* (143/17–144/10), which we can also use to show the translator at work. This passage describes the culmination of a long process that began with the birth in the soul of fear, sorrow and hope (*BM* chs.8–10), and proceeded by way of increasing emotional and imaginative singlemindedness, allied with specific ascetic practices, to the point where the earlier imperfect observances and motives had been rendered completely virtuous ('ordeynd and mesurid', in

[49] Admittedly, the picture is complicated by the use of only two of the adjectives in the partnering phrase, and cf 137/3 'fleschly and wordly lustes', 137/26 'fleschly delites'.

[50] Thus at 137/16 several manuscripts record a clearly erroneous reading 'clereþ' or 'chereþ' (Hodgson's preferred reading 'cherischiþ' from Har1 is closer to the Latin *demulcet*), presumably because by so doing they secured a rhyme: 'Dan fereþ þe hert . . . and Neptalym chereþ/clereþ it'. Rhyme is clearly used in the *Tretyse* only at 134/25 and (the rhyme 'ese . . . diseese') 137/18–19.

[51] So too Ar*'s readings are to be preferred at 132/1 synne (Ar* 'synnes', cf 131/21 translating *mala*, 132/10,21); 135/22 'oure soules' (all MSS except Har1, 'soule': cf 134/27, 'oure wille', /35 'þeire soule' [G 'soules'], 135/2 'þeire mynde', /3 'here wille' [Ar 'wylles']; against, 134/30 'oure willes'); 136/29 'drounyd' (only Har1; Ar* 'drounken', cf 136/27 'delyten'). See also n.64.

[52] E.g. 134/17 on] of; 135/5 alle] *om.* At 135/12–13, however, the Har1 reading ('peynes to come') is probably correct (cf 134/23–4, 135/14–15).

the words of the translation), and the soul had at last learned discrimination, or the art of knowing itself. Once self-knowledge has become instinctive, the soul is ready to meet God in contemplation. The text summarizes this process, and suggests its consequences, by means of the image of a person looking into a mirror (*BM* ch.72). A dirty mirror prevents the person from seeing anything: similarly, a foul soul prevents knowledge of oneself or God. But when the soul is purified by burning desire, like a candle set before the mirror, God sends light which makes visible both the soul's unworthiness and his own great goodness. This light activates the soul's own light, and it sees 'alle maner of goostly þinges': 'be tymes' in this life, eternally in the next.

As is usual in mystical writing, the language and imagery are paradoxical. We cannot easily tell whether the imagery is functioning as a kind of summary of the narrative or whether it is describing experiences proper to the last, contemplative, stage of the process. The polar opposites of our own sinfulness and God's goodness, of which we have been given a sight immediately prior to the gift of contemplation proper, have characterized the soul's progress from its very beginnings. Similarly, the candle, with which we attempt to throw light onto the mirror, so as to see what is reflected in it, is now our desire for God, now the very illumination from God which our desire was seeking. Such paradoxes are, almost by definition, necessary features of religious writing: they remind us that religious experience engages God and the soul in a relationship where causes and effects run confusingly together, and whose every stage presupposes every other, since the same drama is being enacted throughout.

The moment of illumination is thus described by Richard:

> Exterso autem speculo et diu diligenter inspecto, incipit ei quaedam divini luminis claritas interlucere, et immensus quidam insolitae visionis radius, oculis ejus apparere (*BM* ch.72) [When the mirror has been wiped and gazed into for a long time, a kind of splendor of divine light begins to shine in it and a great beam of unexpected vision appears to his eyes (Zinn p.130)]

Though clearly translating this material (in the following quotation all words directly authorized by the original are italicized) the Middle English translation makes fairly free with it; more importantly, the manuscripts provide divergent readings at a number of points (only major variants are listed):

> And þanne, when *it is clensid* and [Ar* *add* þi candel] brennyng, and it so be þat þou wittirly *beholde þerto*: þan *byginniþ þer a maner of cleerte of þe li3t of God for to schyne in* þi soule, and *a maner of sonnebeme* þat is gostly *to apere* before [Ar* to] þi goostly *si3t*, þe whiche is [Ar* þur3 þe whoche] þe *i3e* of þi soule and [Ar* *om.* and] is openid to beholde God and godly [Ar* *and one* Harl* MS, goostli] þinges, heuen and heuenly þinges, and alle maner of goostly þinges (143/28–32).

The first half of this sentence depends very clearly on the Latin original. Even there, the translator has taken a number of minor liberties. He substitutes an intellectual for a moral emphasis when he replaces *diligenter* by 'witterly' (the two words also differ in respect of their implied time frames: *diligenter* implies a

process of time, 'witterly' the end of the process or its underlying meaning[53]).
He adds the phrase 'in þi soule' in order to specify the location of the new
experience (this added phrase repeats a point made slightly earlier, 143/117–18,
and taken from the Latin). The translator also repeats himself in respect of the
phrase 'and brennyng': a daring act of translation inspired by several phrases in
the original, but all later in the chapter. For Richard, in consequence of the
marvellous vision here described,

> . . . *mirum in modum accenditur animus, et animatur ad videndum lumen, quod est*
> *supra se. Ex hac . . . visione videndi Deum flammam desiderii conspicit . . ..*
> *Mens itaque, quae jam visionis hujus desiderio flagrat, si jam sperat, quod*
> *desiderat, jam se Benjamin concepisse cognoscat* (*BM* ch.72)   [the soul is kindled
> from above in a marvelous way and is animated to see the living light that is above
> it . . . from this vision the soul conceives the flame of longing for the sight of God
> . . . And so the mind that now burns with longing for this vision should know that
> if it already hopes for what it longs for, it has already conceived Benjamin (Zinn
> p.130)[54]

That is, spiritual fervour is one of the chief effects of visionary illumination, and
itself the guarantee of further enlightenment. This material, and this understanding, the translator transmitted faithfully when he translated the last sentence of
the quotation some lines further on (144/5–7). He had already anticipated it at
the very start of the paragraph with the, already-noted, metaphor of the burning
candle shining in the mirror, which he repeated shortly after ('and forþi clense þi
myrour, and profre þi candyl to þe fiir', 143/26–27). But this metaphor, implied
in the added phrase 'and brennyng', and clearly stated in the Ar* variant 'and þi
candel brennyng', generates a subtly different meaning from that put forward by
Richard: it makes spiritual fervour a pre-condition of visionary illumination,
almost the last stage in the ascetic process.

The disagreement between Har1* and Ar* over the last reading – is it the
mirror shining brightly or the candle? – possibly does not feel particularly
significant. Ar* makes more immediate and easy sense, though we may wonder
whether we should not apply the prinicple of the *difficilior lectio* and find the
verion in the Har1* original: at all events, the latter's burning mirror witnesses
to the same confusion of agent and instrument that I have argued characterizes
all mystical writing. It is as we reach the latter part of the quoted passage, where
few clear correspondences exist with the Latin original, that our real problems
begin. The 'maner of sonnebeme þat is ghostly' is difficult enough: a free

---

[53] According to Richard, some of the earlier processes in the spiritual life can be
achieved quite quickly, but it takes a long time for the soul to become first Joseph and
then Benjamin. The translator keeps these understandings (137/23, 142/8, 143/5–6),
but makes more of the first ('sone', added at 132/6, 132/32, 137/19, and 142/15), as if
wanting to encourage readers embarked on the laborious early stages of the spiritual
life.
[54] For P.L. *conspicit*, also found in BL 1, the correct reading is *concipit* (so
Duchet-Suchaux).

translation of the phrase *immensus quidam insolitae visionis radius*, its 'gostly' nature may have been inferred from, if not read into, the phrase *insolitae visionis*.[55] The next phrases are much more difficult to pin down. Only 'apparere' appears at all clearly in translation, as 'apere before/to'. And what of 'goostly siʒt' and 'iʒe of þi soule'? Are they possibly a kind of doublet? If so, they translate either '(*insolitae*) visionis', or, more probably, *oculis ejus* from the phrase *oculus ejus apparere* (in thus identifying an action with the instrument by which it is committed, the translation could claim the support of *BM* ch.17). Yet it is equally possible that 'goostly siʒt' and 'iʒe of þi soule' translate, respectively, *insolitae visionis* and *oculis ejus*.

What follows, however – the opening of the soul's eyes to behold God and heavenly things – has very little correspondence with the Latin, and that little must result from misreading, if not of rewriting. The statement that the soul's eyes are opened could just result from a misreading of *apparere* as *aperire*,[56] alternatively, we have to conclude that the translator has imposed upon his text a meaning derived from other spiritual writers, perhaps Rolle.[57] Similarly, the God who is seen when the soul's eyes are opened comes from later in the chapter, where he is presented as the object not of sight but only of desire: what is seen at this point in the original is simply spiritual *light*.

Lodged centrally in this largely rewritten passage is a major disagreement betwen Har1* and Ar* concerning the relation of the clause 'þe whiche is þe iʒe of þi soule' to the rest of the sentence. The Har1* version produces an ungrammatical construction and leaves unclear how the appearing of the spiritual light relates to the opening of the soul's eyes: it links the two activities only in a relationship of co-ordination ('and'), possibly of temporal sequence. The Ar* version is both grammatically more secure, and clearer about the relation to one another, as cause and effect, of the two spiritual graces. Though I prefer the greater precision of the latter version, the former might, by design or (more likely) accident, prove truer to the vagaries of mystical *experience*: we might recall Julian's inability to create any more complex links between the

---

[55] Elsewhere Richard makes a tacit equation between the rarity of an experience and its spiritual nature (e.g. ch. 1 'all long to be wise yet few are able to be wise', Zinn p.54).

[56] Parallels for this practice occur elsewhere, e.g. in the translations of Jean de Meun: 'unsure whether the Latin should be *vinis* or *venis*, he translates both words' (L. C. Brook, 'The Translator and His Reader', in *The Medieval Translator* vol.2, ed. R. Ellis, Westfield Publications in Medieval Studies, London, 1991, p.121). My analysis of the BL Claudius B I translation of St. Bridget's *Liber* will reveal comparable practices. Alternatively, the translator's copy of *BM* might have contained the doublet *apparere et aperire* (no surviving copy of the text does, according to Duchet-Suchaux): for comparable scribal practice in the *Liber*, see *Sancta Birgitta Revelaciones Book I*, ed. C.-G. Undhagen, Samlingar utgivna av Svenska Fornskriftsallskapet, Ser.2, Bd.VII:1, Uppsala, 1978, pp.79–80 and n.130, 197–8.

[57] On the opening of the soul's eye to look into heaven in Rolle, see *The Incendium Amoris of Richard Rolle of Hampole*, ed. M. Deanesley, Manchester, 1915, pp.188–9.

elements of her first showing than she could evidence by her repeated use of the phrase 'in this'.[58] Which of these readings is authorial we cannot say.

It is diffiuclt even to characterize the two main scribal traditions. The two cruces of this passage ('when it is clensid and [þi candel] brennyng', 'þe whiche is [þurȝ þe whoche] þe iȝe of þi soule') support a view of Har1* as imprecise and, to a degree, ungrammatical, and Ar* as the opposite. Elsewhere, though, it is Har1* which attempts precision, and Ar* which leaves relations hanging loose. When, for instance, the Har1* scribe writes that the soul's sorrow for sin 'bringeþ in trewe coumforte' (132/17–18), invoking a relation of cause and effect, it is the Ar* scribe who settles for the looser – and more suggestive – phrase, 'is trewe coumforte'.

4

Yet even when the manuscripts agree, problems remain. One concerns the very nature and scope of the translation. We have already noted Hodgson's view of the *Tretyse* as 'little more than a coherent synopsis' juxtaposing 'close translations of selected sentences . . . with free and greatly abridged adaptations' (p.195). The achievement of the translator may, however, have been more modest, at least in respect of cuts to the text, since at least one version of Richard's original circulated which contained only extracts – this version is found in MS BL Arundel 507 (ff.24v–28r), hereafter Ar2 – and many of the distinctive features of the *Tretyse* probably result from faithful translation of just such a version. Thus the opening words of the *Tretyse*,

> a greet clerk þat men clepyn Richard of Seinte Victore, in a book þat he makiþ of þe studie of wisdom, witnessiþ and seiþ þat two miȝtes ben in a mans soule, ȝouen of þe Fader of heuen, of whome alle good comiþ (129/1–4),

take us straight into *BM* ch.3 (*omni spiritui rationali gemina quaedam vis data est ab illo patre luminum, a quo est omne datum optimum*). It is, however, not *BM* but Ar2 to which we turn for the original of these opening words (the latter begins, f.24v, with the phrase *secundum Ricardum in libello suo de studio sapientie* and continues with the material from *BM* ch.3); as also for the phrase introducing the first son:

> þe first childe þat Lya conceyuid of Jacob was [*all MSS but Har1* is] Ruben, þat is drede (131/16–17)
>
> *primogenitus Lye ex Jacob Ruben id est timor animi* (Ar2, f.26v: *BM* ch.8 wants the phrase).

At the other end, Ar2 concludes, like the *Tretyse*, with Psalm 67:28 (discussed above pp.201–2). It also includes, f.24v, the diagrammatic representation of the

---

[58] For comment on this feature, see R. Ellis, 'Revelation and the life of faith: the vision of Julian of Norwich', *Christian* 6, 1980, 61–71, p.67.

family tree which characterizes most manuscript copies of the *Tretyse*.[59] More importantly, it regularly cuts its text, and otherwise rearranges it, at the same points as the *Tretyse* does. Thus, for example, the rearranged order of phrases in the *Tretyse* at 133/32–134/3, and accompanying minor gaps, are exactly paralleled in Ar2.[60] Similarly, larger gaps in the translation correspond exactly to gaps in Ar2's copy of the text: most of *BM* chs.40–41, and all of chs.74–83, are cut in the translation (the gaps occurring at 139/30–31 and 144/21–2); the same material is also cut at the corresponding points in Ar2. The closeness extends to individual details: whereas *BM* ch.6 describes the troublesome distractions of the imagination, when we pray, as *phantasias cogitationum vel quaslibet imagines rerum* ['phantasies of thoughts or other sorts of images of things' (Zinn p.59)], Ar2 cuts the second phrase, as does the version in the *Tretyse* ('so many diuerse fantasies of yuel þouȝtes', 129/23–4). Similarly, 'holy desires' (135/23) is closer to Ar2's *desideria sancta* than to *BM* ch.22 'desideria bona' (possibly the compiler of Ar2 was remembering the parallel phrase 'desideria sancta' in *BM* ch.3, translated 'holy desires' at 129/6).[61] Regrettably, Ar2 is not the actual source of the *Tretyse*: or, if it was, it was subjected to significant modifications which might suggest either that the translator was acting as author or that he had access to other versions of *BM*, whether full copies or digests like Ar2. Thus the latter includes material from *BM* chs.28–30 not translated in the *Tretyse* (based on Genesis 30:14–15, the passage tells how Ruben brought back mandrakes for his mother). It also interrupts the sequence it shares with the *Tretyse* – at a point corresponding to *Tretyse* 131/14 – with material from much later in *BM*, concerning Dan and Neptalym, Gad and

---

59 For a reproduction of the Har1 diagram, see the frontispiece of Early English Text Society O.S., 231, *op. cit.* The diagram does not appear to have figured in copies of the complete Latin text in this country – it appears in none of the manuscripts studied personally, nor in copies in libraries in Cambridge (Corpus Christi, Gonville and Caius, Peterhouse, St. John's, University) or Oxford (St. John's, Merton) – and it is likely that its presence in Ar2 provides strong evidence of the origins of the *Tretyse*. The accompanying allegorizations of Ruben, Judas and Dyna link Ar2 more clearly to Ar* than to Har1* (for the Ar* readings, see the apparatus to p.131) and argue, once again, for the superiority of the former's readings.

60 The order in *BM* ch.13 is *sicut ad Liam . . . intellectus purus* (translated *Tretyse* 133/ 35–134/3); *nato itaque Juda . . . incipit velle cognoscere* (*Tretyse* 133/32–4); *quanto plus crescit Judas . . . studium cognoscendi* (*Tretyse* 134/3–5). The order of the phrases in the *Tretyse* corresponds to that in Ar2, as do the cuts of material between them (*sed quid aliud per Judam . . . amorem summi boni'*, 'ubi amor, ibi oculus. . . per intelligentiam videre*).

61 The Bd2 copy of *BM* (ff.166v–176) was also examined, but without success, for links with Ar2 and the *Tretyse*. Bd2 contains most of *BM* chs.64–85. Although chs.64–6 act as a sort of summary of the earlier stages of the work, preliminary to the labours of self-knowledge and the graces of contemplation (symbolized by Joseph, Benjamin and the Transfiguration), the greater emphasis on these latter in Bd2, and corresponding reduction in the account of the lower reaches of the spiritual life, clearly distinguish it from Ar2 and the source of the *Tretyse*.

Joseph. (Why it does so is a puzzle, since the four also appear in their proper places later in the compilation, the text partially repeating itself at this later point.) In these instances the translator could, arguably, have been working from Ar2, and cutting still further the latter's cut version of *BM*. So too, when Ar2 agrees with *BM* and against the *Tretyse* in respect of the ordering of phrases, it is possible that the translator was working from Ar2 and rearranging its phrases for purposes of his own. But the *Tretyse* also includes readings which agree with *BM* and against Ar2 ('ponished', 136/10, *BM* ch.25 *affligitur*, cf Ar2 *restringitur*). And Ar2 fails to include some of the Bible verses which the *Tretyse* translates (Genesis 49:21 and Psalm 50:19, see above p.203), or it abbreviates the latter parts of Bible verses which the *Tretyse* translates fully (for a single example, see n.46 above): so it cannot have acted as sole source of the translation. Until we do find the actual source, we cannot be sure whether, and how far, the changes to the original that we observe in the translation have been introduced by the translator, on his own authority, and how far they show him operating as humble scribe of a text which had itself introduced the changes: but when and if that source is brought to light, comments on the nature and purpose of the translation, including some made earlier in this paper, may need revising.

Nevertheless, tentative conclusions are possible. Major cuts to the text of *BM* in the *Tretyse* will probably turn out to have been introduced by the compiler. Rearrangements to the order of translated material could be the responsibility of either the compiler or the translator (my guess is that they will turn out to be the work of the compiler). Similarly, additions which do not disturb the grammatical relations of the original could be the work of either compiler or translator – though, since Ar2 makes few additions to the original, and those mostly modest (that at the start of *BM* ch.8, quoted above, p.215 is typical), the larger additions will probably reveal the hand of the translator: so too, yet more clearly, additions or cuts which significantly alter the grammatical relations of the original. Thus the picture which the *Tretyse* offers of Zabulon as hatred of sin in oneself (above p.197) may bespeak not the translator but his source. On the other hand, the ways in which the *Tretyse* reinforces the patterning of *BM* by riding roughshod over its original wording (see above pp.209–10), or transforms the grammatical relations of *BM* (in the image of the candle and the mirror, see above pp.212f.), almost certainly show the translator at work, not the compiler of his Latin source.

5

This laborious and finally inconclusive search for the author of the *Tretyse* – and, it now turns out, the original of the translation – has made much of the translated Bible texts; so it is perhaps appropriate to end with a few remarks about some of those not in Richard's original but added to the translation – whether by the compiler of the source or the translator himself we cannot presently tell – as a way of focussing our sense of the translation's achievement.

Richard had organized his text around Bible quotations, derived principally from the account of the birth of Jacob's sons in Genesis 29–30, and from the blessings of their father on them in Genesis 49; then from subsequent references to the tribes of Israel descended from them (in, for example, Psalm 67).[62] The Bible verses are used in part to organize the argument; but since they are regularly repeated within and across chapters, and as regularly interwoven with other texts on the same theme or using similar language, they also function as aids to meditation.[63] The translation retains most of them, occasionally, as we saw, adapting them, and also adding texts of its own, mostly from Richard's main source. Arguably, these added texts not only reinforce the meaning of the original: they improve upon it.

For example, the latter part of the section on the birth of love in the soul under the figure of the birth of Lya's fourth son Judas (133/1–29: the relevant portion is 133/12–23), bears only a loose relation to the corresponding material in *BM* (chs.11–12: the translation makes many cuts to this material). In *BM* Judas is interpreted as *confitens* (meaning not merely acknowledgement of sin but also grateful thanksgiving to God). This etymology, which Richard inherited from patristic sources (Kirchberger p.77, Zinn pp.10–12), derives ultimately from the prophetic words of Lya at the birth of the child in Genesis 29:35 (*modo confitebor domino'*, *et ob hoc vocavit eum Iudam* ['now I shall confess to the Lord', and therefore she called the child Judas]). Richard does not quote this verse, but the translation does, twice, applying it the second time to the faithful soul, and uses it to order the section (133/12–15). Similarly, the section concludes, on its own authority, with a Bible verse on the same theme: 'of þis schrift spekiþ Dauid ful ofttymes in þe psalme whan he seiþ: 'Makiþ it knowe to God for he is good' (133/22–3).[64] Virtually the same effect has resulted from these changes as would have happened had the whole passage been translated literally. If the letter of the original has changed, its spirit has not. The cuts may even have brought the meaning into clearer focus.

Yet more interesting is the development of the allegory relating to the sons of Rachel's maid Bala, namely Dan and Neptalym (in particular, 135/5–24). Once again there is little, apart from the etymologies (135/5–7, 14, 16, 19–20), that directly translates Richard's words in chs.21–3. The allegorisation of Dan as 'dome' fairly obviously derives from Rachel's words after his birth ('Oure lorde haþ demed me', in the translator's version of Genesis 30:6), and from the prophetic account of him by his aged father in Genesis 49:16 ('Dan schal deme

---

[62] Richard also quotes extensively from the Psalms and the Wisdom literature of the Old Testament; devotes several chapters (75ff) to the account of the Transfiguration (Matthew 17; as earlier noted, pp.215–16, none of this section was translated in the *Tretyse*); and uses the Beatitudes in Matthew 5 (cf 132/12) as a subsidiary principle of organization.

[63] Thus his account of Isacchar in chapters 38–9 can be seen as an extended meditation on the text of Genesis 49:14: the words of the verse are quoted at least six times in ch.39.

[64] The Har1* reading 'psalme' is almost certainly in error; Ar* reads 'sauter'.

his folk': Richard included this, but not the former, verse). So interpreted, Dan can then be applied to our necessary condemnation of 'alle vnleueful þouȝtes [*illecebrosa[s] cogitationes*]'; but his real function is to show the imagination in action, suppressing all such thoughts by representing to itself the pains promised in the next world for sin:

> *ad officium Dan spectat per repraesentationem poenae reprimere exsurgentia vitia* (*BM* ch. 22)
>
> it falliþ to Dan to put doune yuel sogestyons of synne by siȝt of peynes to come (134/28–9).

To this material, the translation adds Rachel's speech, already quoted, on the birth of Dan: and this prepares for another, much more daring, addition to the original:

> when Bala brouȝt forþ Dan, Rachel seide þus: Oure Lorde haþ demed me. þat is to sey: Oure Lorde haþ euenyd me vnto my sister, Lya (135/8–10).

Here we have a kind of gloss on the added speech, itself added to Richard's text, and interpreting Rachel's words on the birth of Dan in the light of her speech on the birth of Neptalym (*comparavit me Deus cum sorore mea*, Genesis 30:8). This speech is retranslated later in the passage, again on its own authority ('I am maad liche to myn sistre, Lya', 135/15–16), to explain the interpretation of Neptalym's name as 'lyknes [*comparatio vel conversio*]': but also to show the imagination in action creating images of the joys of heaven so as to encourage the practice of virtue (hence Neptalym is also interpreted by the translator 'þe siȝt of ioies to come'). Used twice in this way, the one speech binds together the two sons and creates with the utmost economy a link between the two functions of the imagination which Richard takes several chapters to explore.

This link partners a yet more imaginative one, between the two sons of Bala and the previously-born sons of Lya. The latter were interpreted as, respectively, dread and sorrow for sin; hope of forgiveness; and love of God. Rachel is now 'maad liche' her sister in that her maid's two children, as it were, recapitulate imaginatively what her sister's four children expressed emotionally. Thus the dread of pain to come associated with Dan is the imaginative equivalent of the 'drede and sorow in . . . felyng' (135/13) associated with Ruben and Symeon, and the logical consequence of them: a felt dread and sorrow for sin, that is, is logically completed by an imaginative projection of its consequences. And so it is with Neptalym, whose imaginative creation of the joys of heaven complements and completes the 'hope and loue of ioye to come in . . . felyng' (135/18) which issued in the earlier births of hope and love in the soul. Such a link is implicit at best in the original. Whoever made it had a finely developed sense of the necessary unity of the spiritual life.

The achievement of the translator of the *Tretyse*, whoever he was, needs to be seen, then, in relation to the activities of the scribes of his own text and the scribe who compiled the Latin version from which he translated. In their different ways these different figures all attest to the necessary unity of – or at least commerce between – scribal, editorial, translational and authorial roles in the production of the work.[65] We may regret that the text as edited has needlessly complicated the question of its own authorship. In the end, of course, it cannot greatly matter whether or not the *Cloud* author produced the *Tretyse*: but I cannot help feeling that we might look at the text with different eyes, and more respectful attention, if we were able to prove he did not.[66]

ABBREVIATIONS

Sigla of manuscripts of the *Tretyse*, taken from Hodgson's 1982 edition of *The Cloud of Unknowing* (full reference n.1), are:

Ar*   (Hodgson 1982 Ar dagger, corresponding to EETS OS 231 (fuller reference n.2) Group B) = the agreement of Ar Har5 F C R Pw G W Ii CC

Har1*(corresponding to EETS OS 231 Group A) = the agreement of Har1 Kk Har2

Ar   British Library MS Arundel 286
C   California H. E. Huntington Library MS 127
CC   Cambridge Corpus Christi College MS 385
F   Cambridge University Library MS Ff. vi. 33
G   Glasgow University Hunterian Library MS 258
H   Liverpool University, Cohen Library, MS Ryl. F.4. 10
Ii   Cambridge University Library MS Ii. vi. 39
Har1   British Library MS Harleian 674
Har2   British Library MS Harleian 2373
Har5   British Library MS Harleian 1022
Kk   Cambridge University Library MS Kk. vi. 26
Pw   printed text, Henry Pepwell, London 1521
R   Boston Mass. W. K. Richardson's Library MS 22
W   Westminster School MS

Sigla of manuscripts of the Latin original consulted:
Ar2   British Library MS Arundel 507
Bd1   Oxford Bodleian Library MS Bodley 36
Bd2   Oxford Bodleian Library MS Lat. th. e 5
BL1   British Library Add. 10433
BL2   British Library Add. 16167

---

[65] Cf. remarks by C. W. Marx, 'Problems of Editing a Translation: Anglo-Norman to Middle English,' in *The Medieval Translator* vol.2, *op. cit.*, pp.266–7.
[66] For a careful analysis of the *Tretyse* which assumes both that the *Cloud*-author wrote it and that he translated it directly from *BM*, see D. Holladay, 'A Study of the Tradition of the Concepts of Measure and Discretion and its Interpretation in Some Middle English Texts', Exeter MPhil thesis, 1989, pp.124–66. The modern translation in Walsh 1988 also takes Hodgson's edition at face value.

BL3   British Library Royal 8Fi
D   Oxford Bodleian Library MS Digby 200

Other abbreviations not in common use are explained in the notes: *BM* (n.2), CWS (n.1), EV (n.30), Glasscoe 1982 (n.21), LV (n.30), Kirchberger (n.2), Machan (n.10), Tugwell (n.9), Walsh 1981 (n.3), Walsh 1988 (n.1), Zinn (n.2).